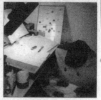

樋口大輔

Even if I could redo my life all over again, I probably wouldn't. I have meandered about and taken a very winding path, until finally reaching where I am today. But I don't think it was a waste. Of course, a shorter path is better than a longer one. It's much easier. But because I took the longer path, I gained valuable experience and met important people in my life. That's why I can say today, with a smile, that the path I took was good. But, what about you? The above is just some nonsense that came to my mind as we all approached the end of the 20th century.

– Daisuke Higuchi

Daisuke Higuchi's manga career began in 1992 when the artist was honored with third prize in the 43rd Osamu Tezuka Award. In that same year, Higuchi debuted as creator of a romantic action story titled **Itaru**. In 1998, **Weekly Shonen Jump** began serializing **Whistle!** Higuchi's realistic soccer manga became an instant hit with readers and eventually inspired an anime series, debuting on Japanese TV in May of 2002. The artist is currently working on a yet-to-be-published new series.

WHISTLE!
VOL. 3: VOR

The SHONEN JUMP Graphic Novel Edition

STORY AND ART BY
DAISUKE HIGUCHI

English Adaptation/Marv Wolfman
Translation/Naomi Kokubo
Touch-Up Art & Lettering/Jim Keefe
Cover, Graphics & Layout/Sean Lee
Editor/Eric Searleman

Managing Editor/Elizabeth Kawasaki
Director of Production/Noboru Watanabe
Editorial Director/Alvin Lu
Executive Vice President & Editor in Chief/Hyoe Narita
Sr. Director of Licensing & Acquisitions/Rika Inouye
Vice President of Sales & Marketing/Liza Coppola
Vice President of Strategic Development/Yumi Hoashi
Publisher/Seiji Horibuchi

Printed in the U.S.A.

Published by VIZ, LLC
P.O. Box 77010 • San Francisco, CA 94107

SHONEN JUMP Graphic Novel Edition
10 9 8 7 6 5 4 3 2 1
First printing, December 2004

THE WORLD'S
MOST POPULAR MANGA

SHONEN JUMP
GRAPHIC NOVEL

www.viz.com

www.shonenjump.com

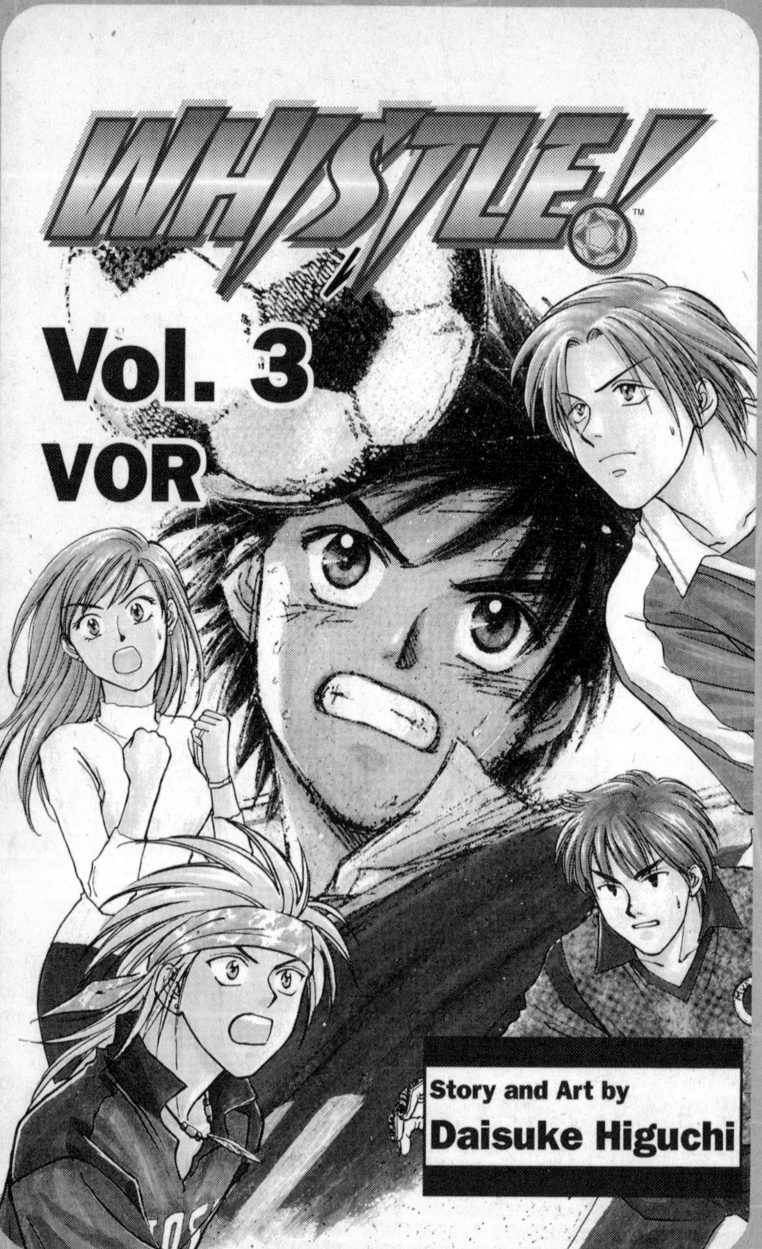
WHISTLE!™
Vol. 3
VOR
Story and Art by
Daisuke Higuchi

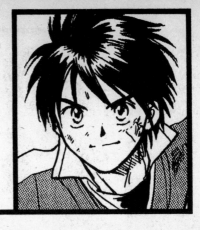

SHŌ KAZAMATSURI

● JOSUI JUNIOR HIGH
SOCCER TEAM
FORWARD

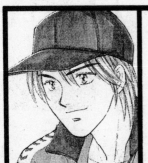

KŌ KAZAMATSURI

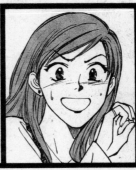

YŪKO KATORI

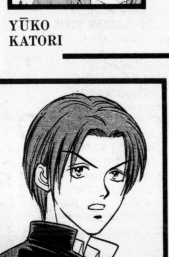

TATSUYA MIZUNO

● JOSUI JUNIOR HIGH
SOCCER TEAM
MIDDLE FIELDER

C H A R A C T E R S

KATSURŌ SHIBUSAWA

MUSASHINOMORI SOCCER TEAM

FAMOUS GOAL KEEPER

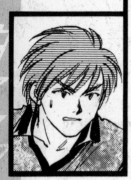

SEIJI FUJISHIRO

MUSASHINOMORI SOCCER TEAM

ACE STRIKER

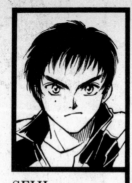

SHIGEKI SATŌ

JOSUI JUNIOR HIGH SOCCER TEAM

TEMPORARY GOAL KEEPER

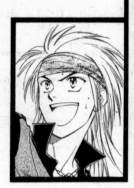

STORY

NOT WANTING TO GIVE UP HIS DREAM OF PLAYING SOCCER, SHŌ KAZAMATSURI, WHO WAS THE SUBSTITUTE PLAYER AT MUSASHINOMORI, A SCHOOL KNOWN FOR ITS EXCELLENT SOCCER TEAM, TRANSFERS SCHOOLS TO JOSUI JUNIOR HIGH.

WITH THE ADDITION OF NEW MEMBERS, INCLUDING SHIGEKI, THE JOSUI JUNIOR HIGH SOCCER TEAM WORKS HARD TO PREPARE FOR THE SPRING TOURNAMENT. HOWEVER, IT TURNS OUT THAT THEIR FIRST OPPONENT IS MUSASHINOMORI. THE HUGE DISPARITY IN POWER BETWEEN JOSUI AND MUSASHINOMORI IS PROVEN WHEN MUSASHINOMORI SCORES TWO POINTS THE MOMENT THE GAME BEGINS. BUT WHEN THEY START DEFENDING TOGETHER, JOSUI FENDS OFF THE OPPOSING TEAM, UNTIL THEY FINALLY GET AN OPPORTUNITY FOR A FREE-KICK. BUT TATSUYA'S KICK IS BLOCKED BY THE GOALKEEPER, SHIBUSAWA, WHO IS KNOWN AS THE GUARDIAN DEITY OF MUSASHINOMORI...

WHISTLE!

**Vol. 3
VOR**

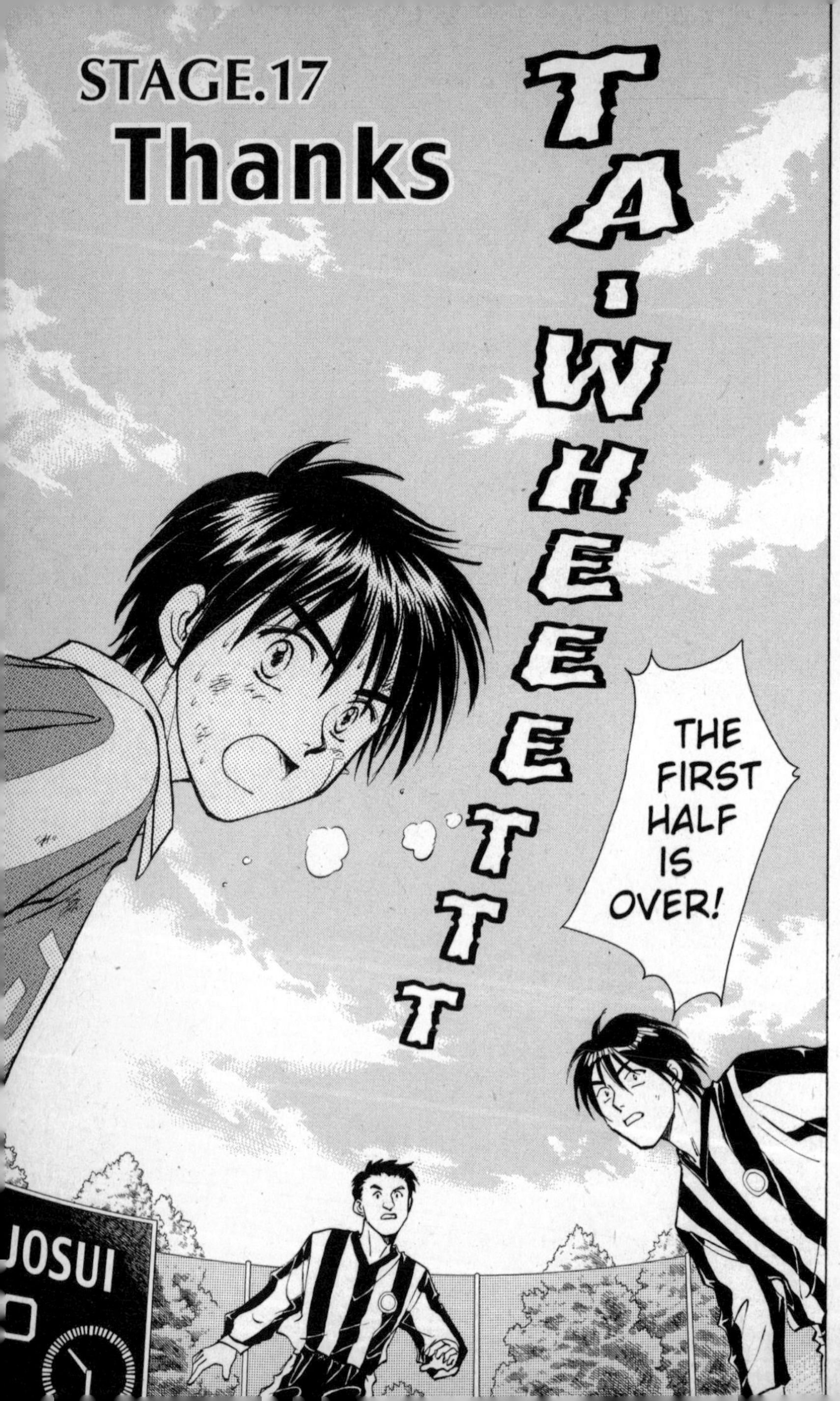
STAGE.17
Thanks
TA-WHEEETTT
THE FIRST HALF IS OVER!
JOSUI

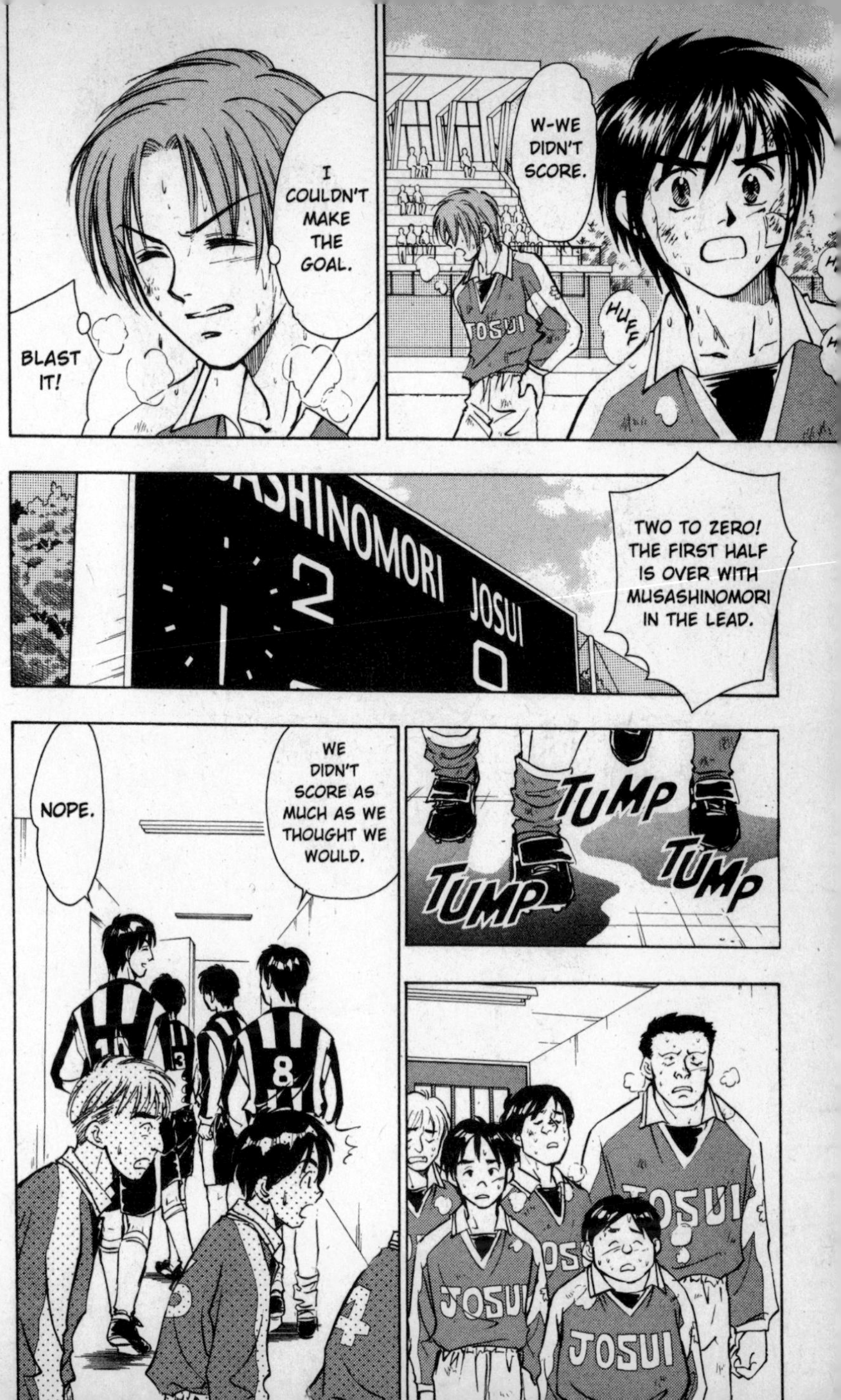
W-WE DIDN'T SCORE.
HUFF
I COULDN'T MAKE THE GOAL.
BLAST IT!
TWO TO ZERO! THE FIRST HALF IS OVER WITH MUSASHINOMORI IN THE LEAD.
JOSUI
2
0
TUMP
TUMP
TUMP
WE DIDN'T SCORE AS MUCH AS WE THOUGHT WE WOULD.
NOPE.

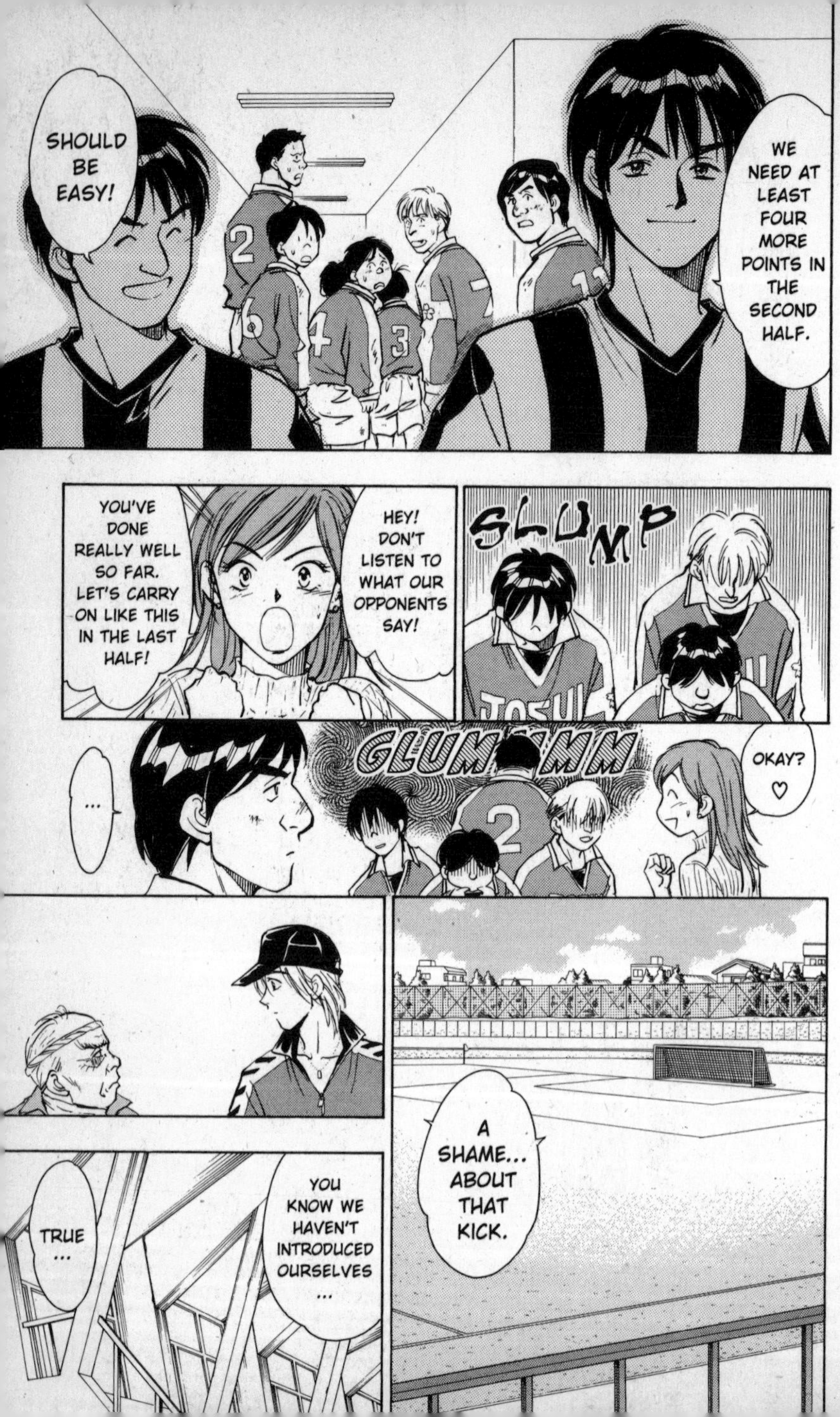
WE NEED AT LEAST FOUR MORE POINTS IN THE SECOND HALF.
SHOULD BE EASY!
SLUMP
HEY! DON'T LISTEN TO WHAT OUR OPPONENTS SAY!
YOU'VE DONE REALLY WELL SO FAR. LET'S CARRY ON LIKE THIS IN THE LAST HALF!
OKAY? ♡
GLUMMMM
...
A SHAME... ABOUT THAT KICK.
YOU KNOW WE HAVEN'T INTRODUCED OURSELVES...
TRUE...

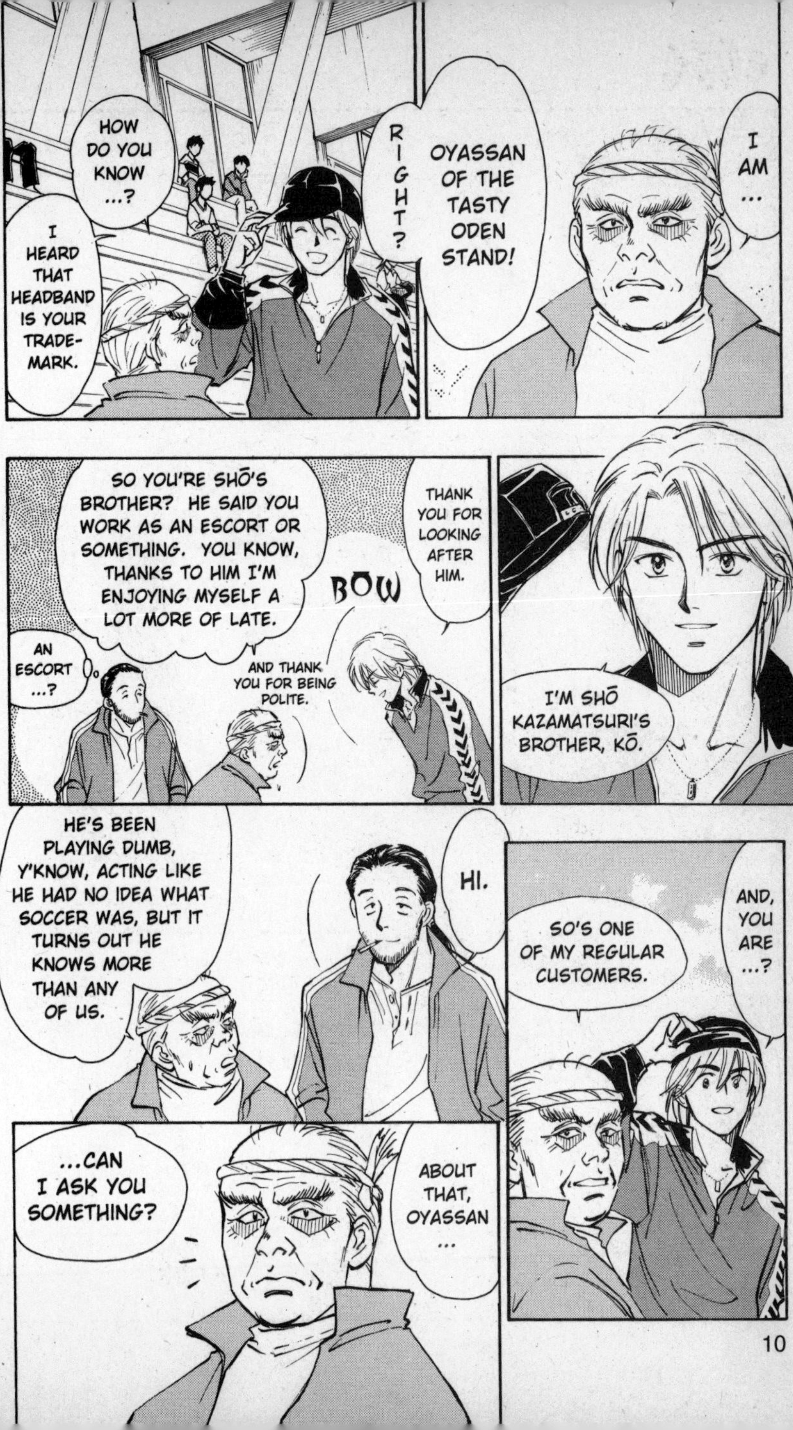
I AM ...
OYASSAN OF THE TASTY ODEN STAND!
RIGHT?
HOW DO YOU KNOW ...?
I HEARD THAT HEADBAND IS YOUR TRADEMARK.
I'M SHŌ KAZAMATSURI'S BROTHER, KŌ.
THANK YOU FOR LOOKING AFTER HIM.
BOW
AND THANK YOU FOR BEING POLITE.
SO YOU'RE SHŌ'S BROTHER? HE SAID YOU WORK AS AN ESCORT OR SOMETHING. YOU KNOW, THANKS TO HIM I'M ENJOYING MYSELF A LOT MORE OF LATE.
AN ESCORT ...?
AND, YOU ARE ...?
SO'S ONE OF MY REGULAR CUSTOMERS.
HI.
HE'S BEEN PLAYING DUMB, Y'KNOW, ACTING LIKE HE HAD NO IDEA WHAT SOCCER WAS, BUT IT TURNS OUT HE KNOWS MORE THAN ANY OF US.
ABOUT THAT, OYASSAN ...
...CAN I ASK YOU SOMETHING?

READ THIS WAY

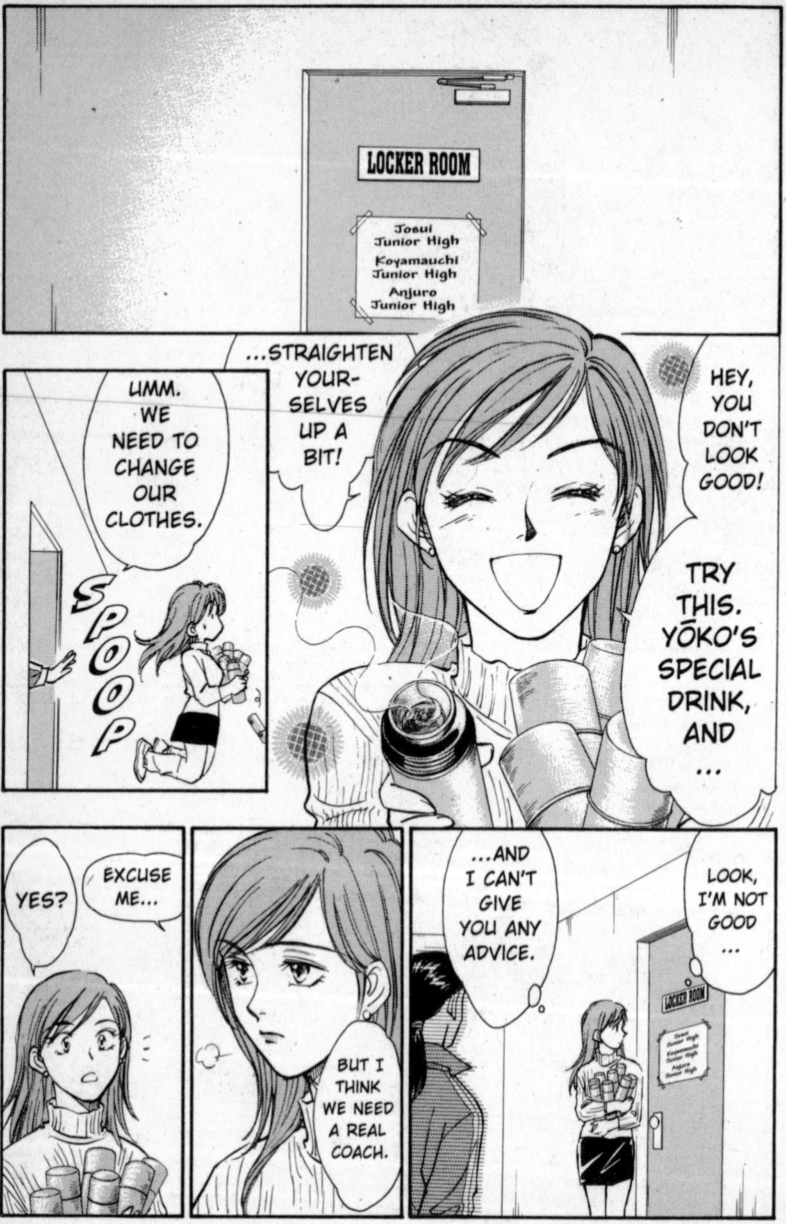
LOCKER ROOM
Josui Junior High
Koyamauchi Junior High
Anjuro Junior High
HEY, YOU DON'T LOOK GOOD!
TRY THIS. YŌKO'S SPECIAL DRINK, AND ...
...STRAIGHTEN YOURSELVES UP A BIT!
UMM. WE NEED TO CHANGE OUR CLOTHES.
SPOOP
LOOK, I'M NOT GOOD ...
...AND I CAN'T GIVE YOU ANY ADVICE.
LOCKER ROOM
BUT I THINK WE NEED A REAL COACH.
EXCUSE ME...
YES?

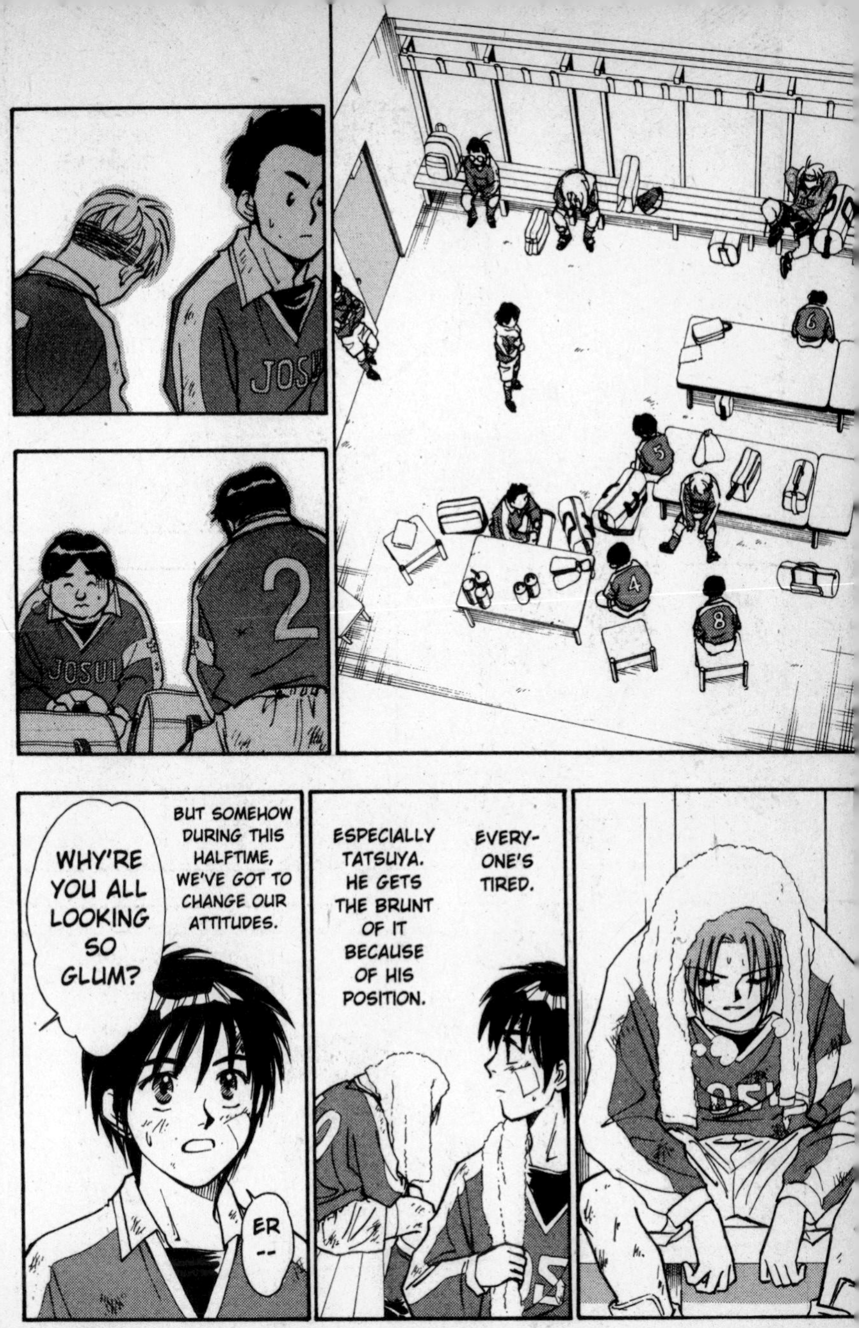
EVERY-ONE'S TIRED.
ESPECIALLY TATSUYA. HE GETS THE BRUNT OF IT BECAUSE OF HIS POSITION.
BUT SOMEHOW DURING THIS HALFTIME, WE'VE GOT TO CHANGE OUR ATTITUDES.
WHY'RE YOU ALL LOOKING SO GLUM?
ER --

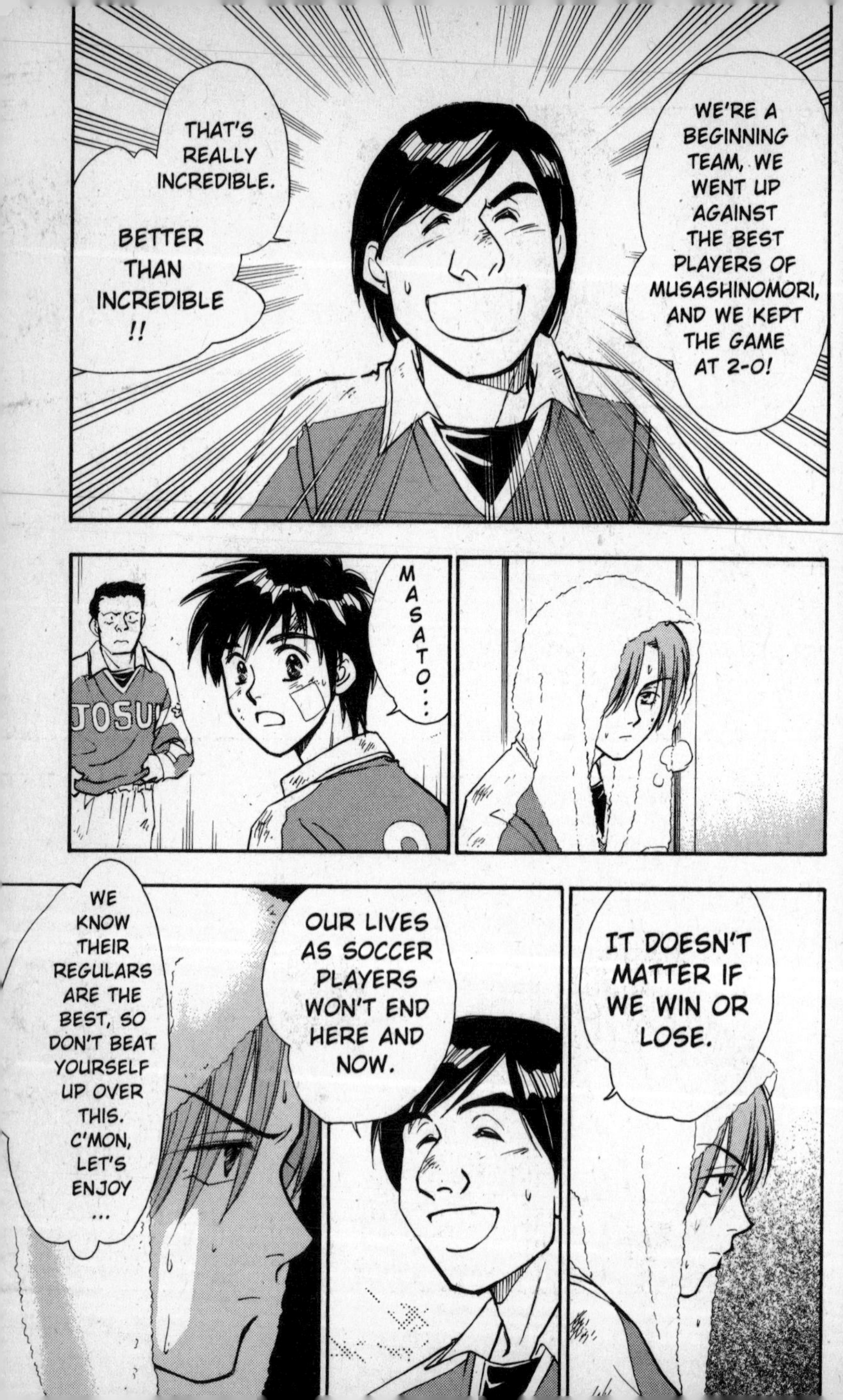
WE'RE A BEGINNING TEAM, WE WENT UP AGAINST THE BEST PLAYERS OF MUSASHINOMORI, AND WE KEPT THE GAME AT 2-0!
THAT'S REALLY INCREDIBLE.
BETTER THAN INCREDIBLE!!
MASATO...
JOSU
IT DOESN'T MATTER IF WE WIN OR LOSE.
OUR LIVES AS SOCCER PLAYERS WON'T END HERE AND NOW.
WE KNOW THEIR REGULARS ARE THE BEST, SO DON'T BEAT YOURSELF UP OVER THIS. C'MON, LET'S ENJOY...

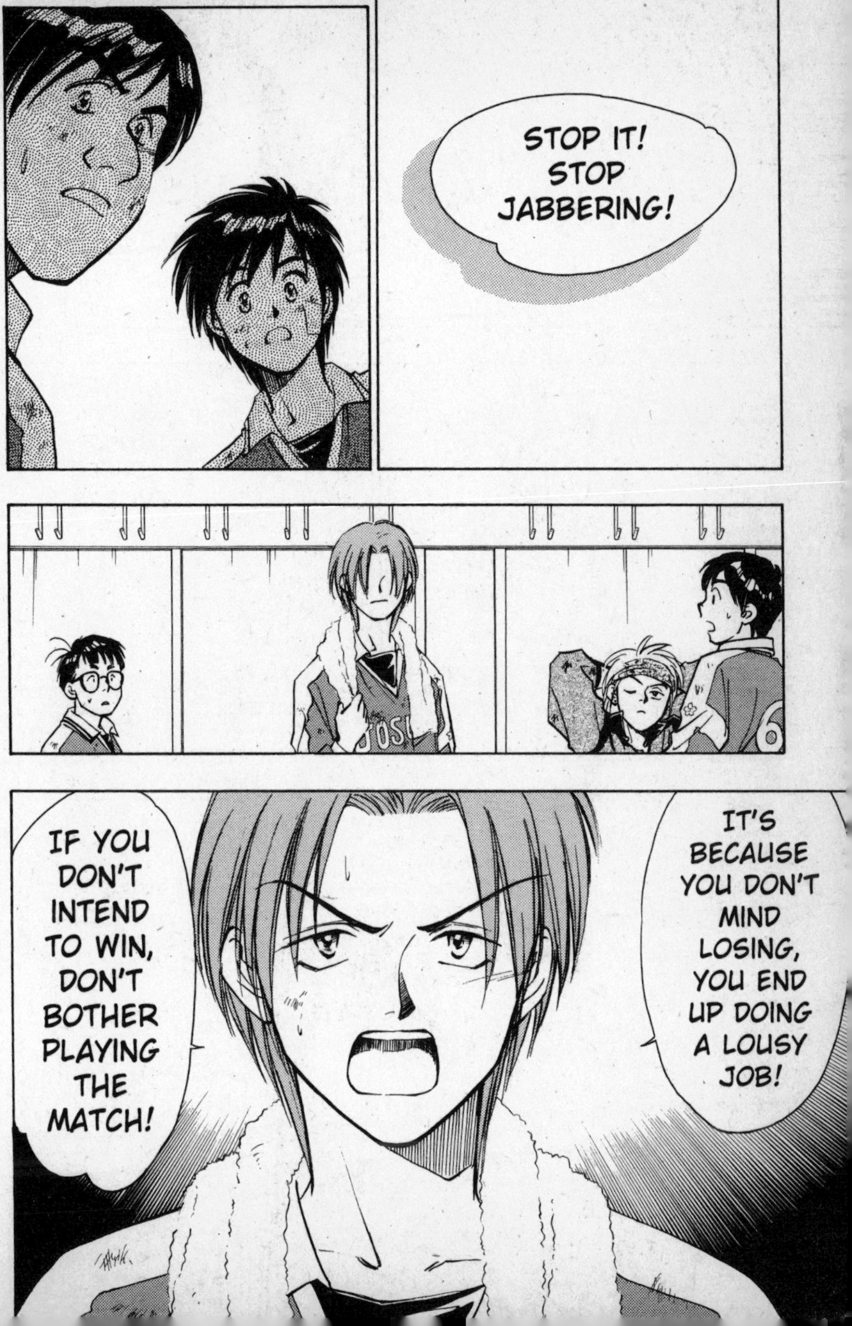
STOP IT! STOP JABBERING!
IT'S BECAUSE YOU DON'T MIND LOSING, YOU END UP DOING A LOUSY JOB!
IF YOU DON'T INTEND TO WIN, DON'T BOTHER PLAYING THE MATCH!

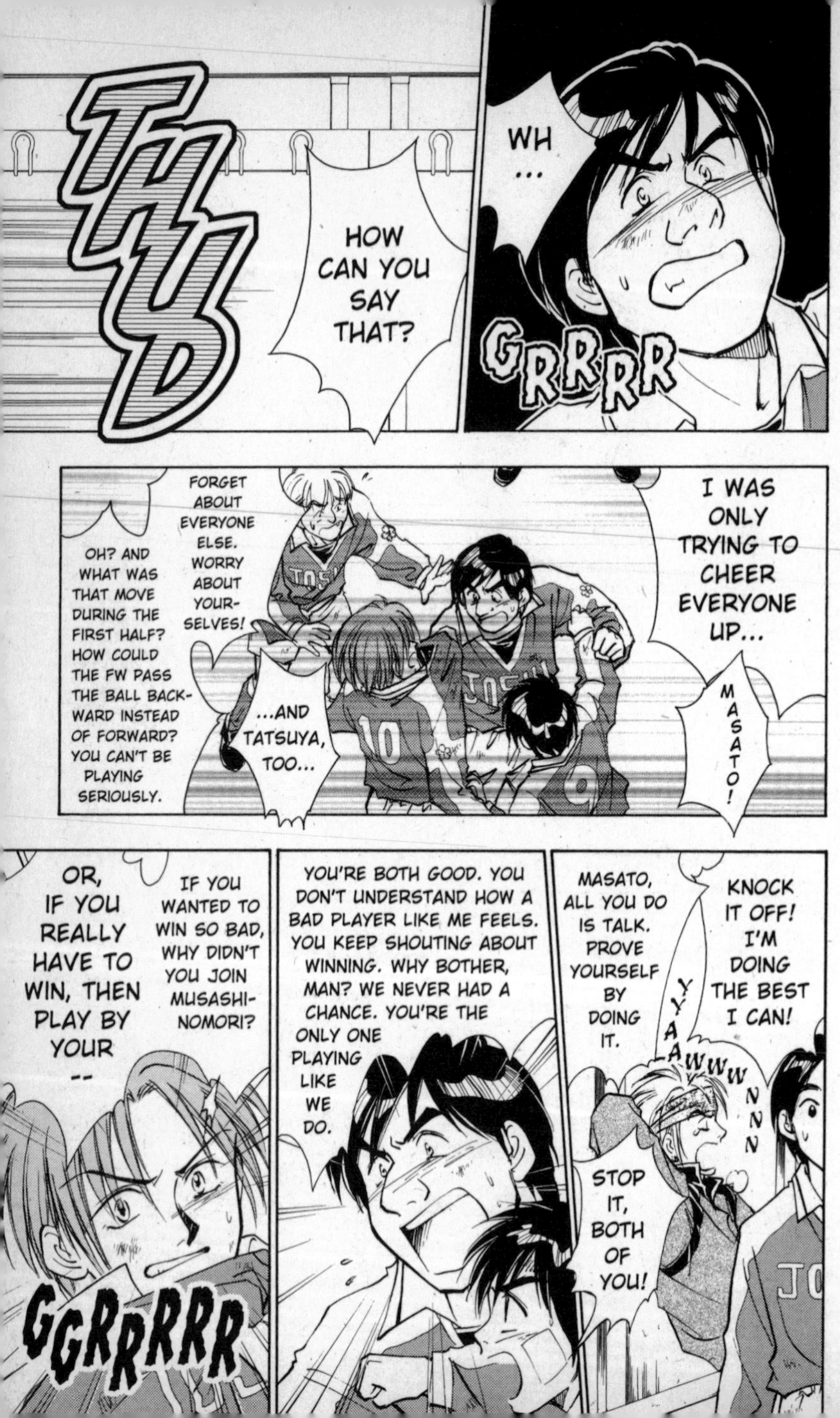
WH ...
GRRRR
HOW CAN YOU SAY THAT?
THUD
I WAS ONLY TRYING TO CHEER EVERYONE UP...
MASATO!
FORGET ABOUT EVERYONE ELSE. WORRY ABOUT YOURSELVES!
...AND TATSUYA, TOO...
OH? AND WHAT WAS THAT MOVE DURING THE FIRST HALF? HOW COULD THE FW PASS THE BALL BACKWARD INSTEAD OF FORWARD? YOU CAN'T BE PLAYING SERIOUSLY.
KNOCK IT OFF! I'M DOING THE BEST I CAN!
MASATO, ALL YOU DO IS TALK. PROVE YOURSELF BY DOING IT.
YYAAAWWWNNN
STOP IT, BOTH OF YOU!
YOU'RE BOTH GOOD. YOU DON'T UNDERSTAND HOW A BAD PLAYER LIKE ME FEELS. YOU KEEP SHOUTING ABOUT WINNING. WHY BOTHER, MAN? WE NEVER HAD A CHANCE. YOU'RE THE ONLY ONE PLAYING LIKE WE DO.
IF YOU WANTED TO WIN SO BAD, WHY DIDN'T YOU JOIN MUSASHI-NOMORI?
OR, IF YOU REALLY HAVE TO WIN, THEN PLAY BY YOUR --
GGRRRRR

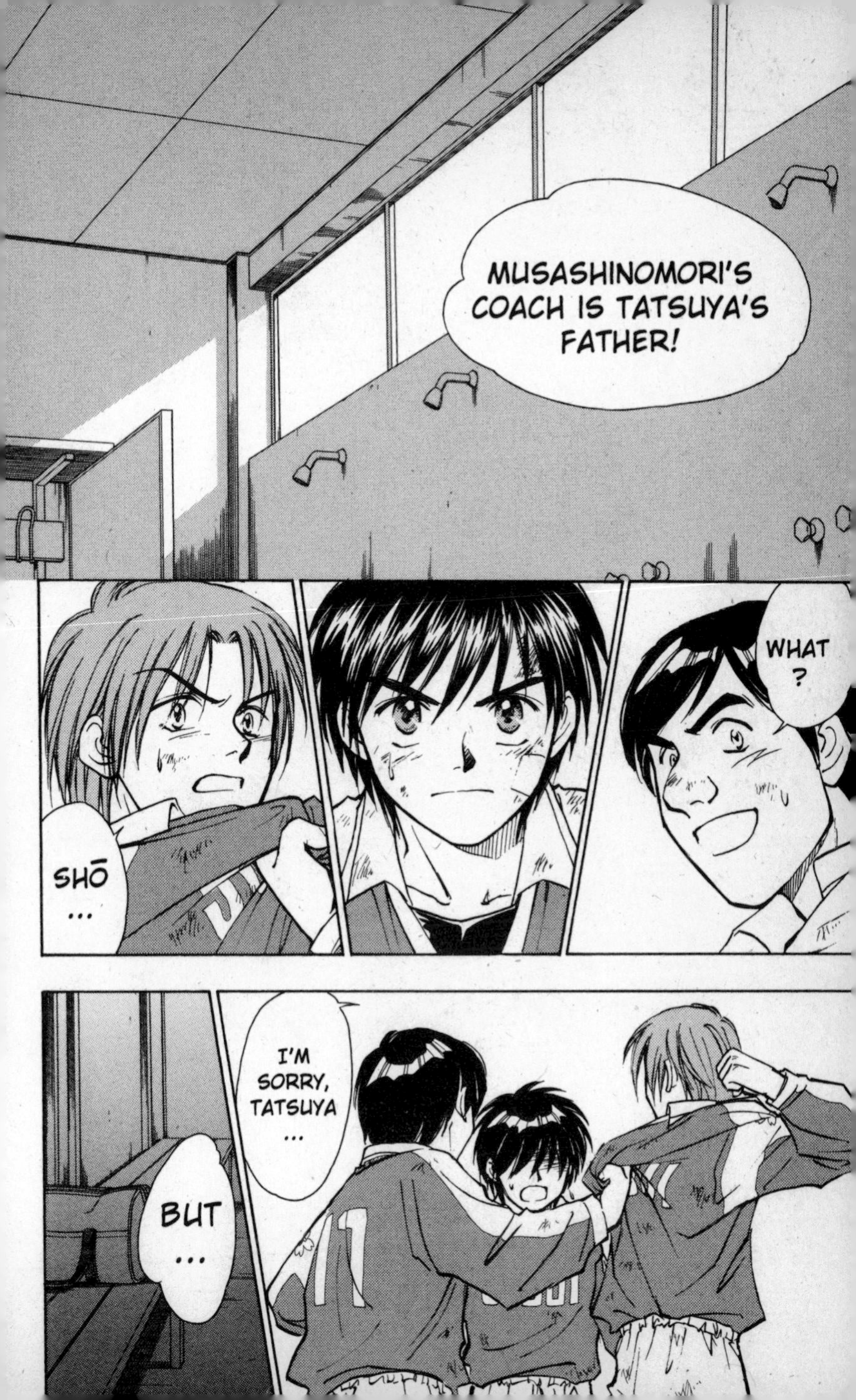
MUSASHINOMORI'S COACH IS TATSUYA'S FATHER!
WHAT ?
SHŌ ...
I'M SORRY, TATSUYA ...
BUT ...

READ THIS WAY

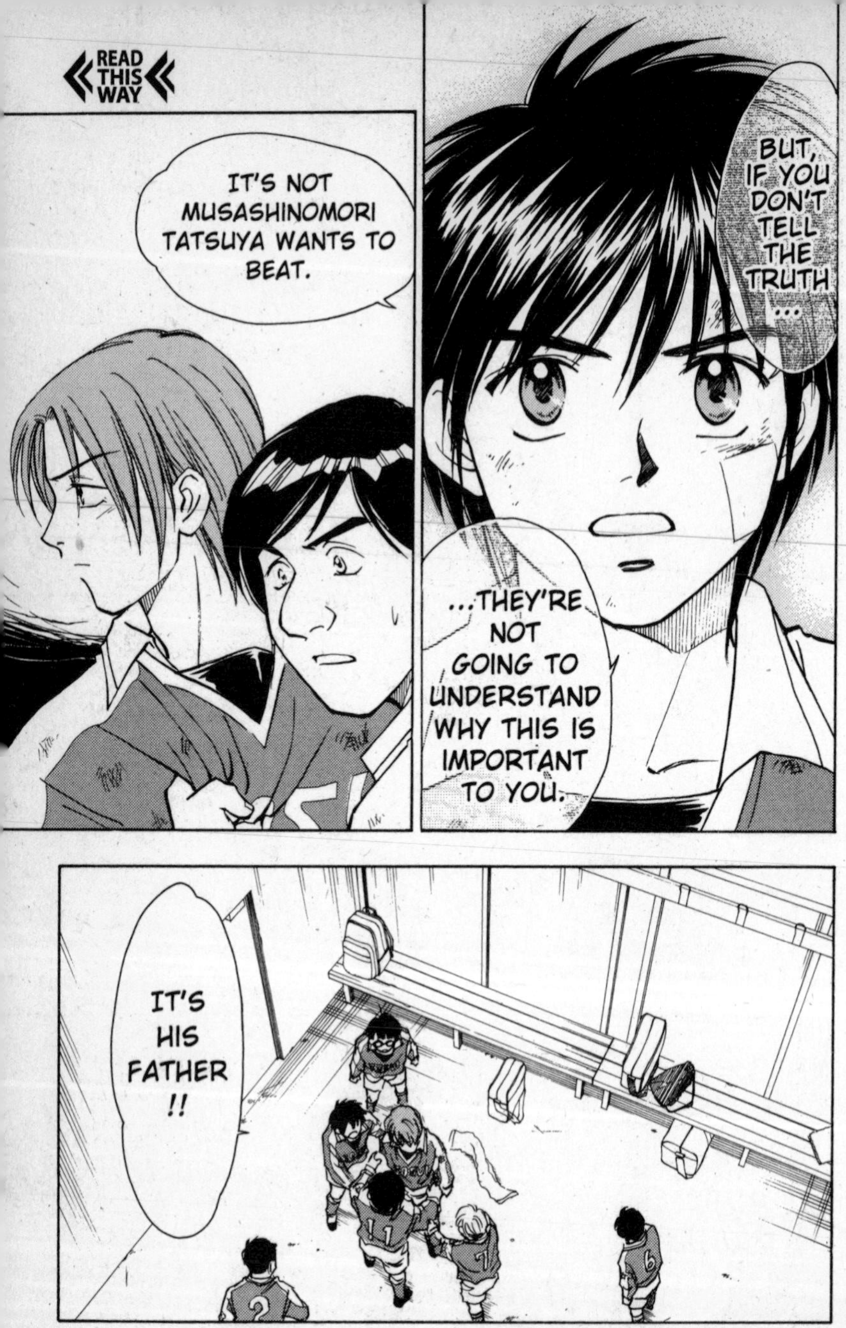
BUT, IF YOU DON'T TELL THE TRUTH...
...THEY'RE NOT GOING TO UNDERSTAND WHY THIS IS IMPORTANT TO YOU.
IT'S NOT MUSASHINOMORI TATSUYA WANTS TO BEAT.
IT'S HIS FATHER!!

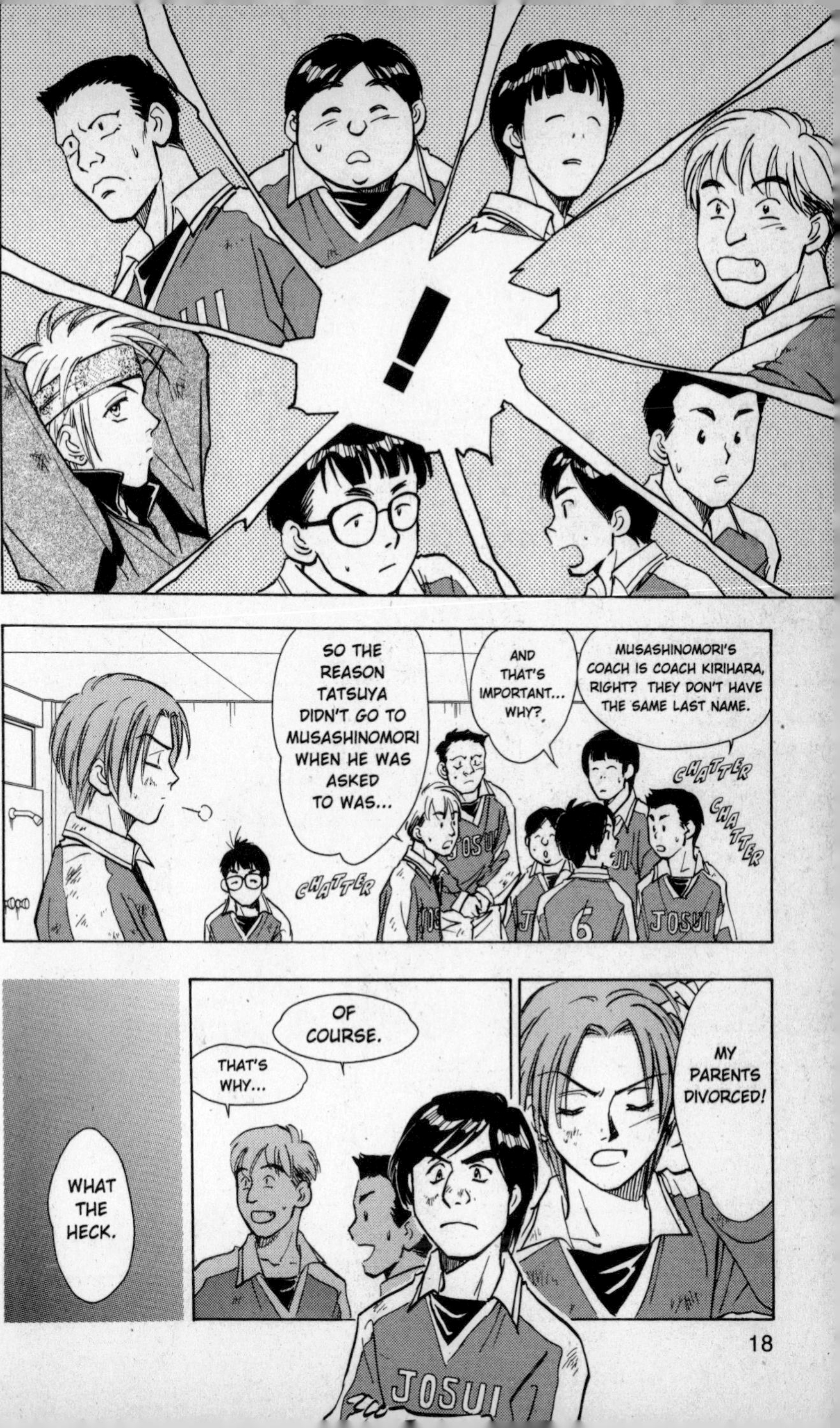
!
MUSASHINOMORI'S COACH IS COACH KIRIHARA, RIGHT? THEY DON'T HAVE THE SAME LAST NAME.
AND THAT'S IMPORTANT... WHY?
SO THE REASON TATSUYA DIDN'T GO TO MUSASHINOMORI WHEN HE WAS ASKED TO WAS...
CHATTER
CHATTER
CHATTER
MY PARENTS DIVORCED!
OF COURSE.
THAT'S WHY...
WHAT THE HECK.

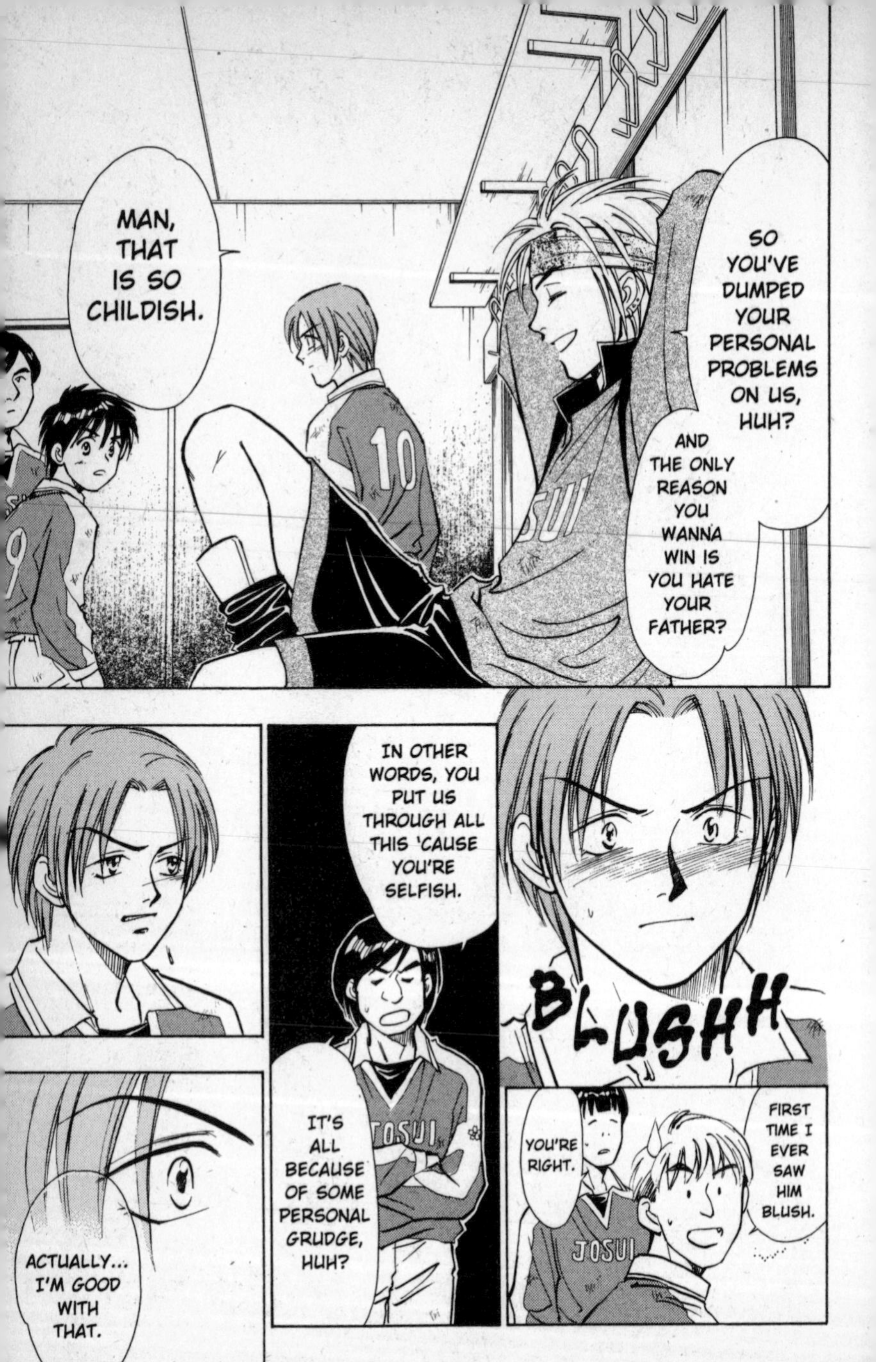
SO YOU'VE DUMPED YOUR PERSONAL PROBLEMS ON US, HUH?
AND THE ONLY REASON YOU WANNA WIN IS YOU HATE YOUR FATHER?
MAN, THAT IS SO CHILDISH.
BLUSHH
FIRST TIME I EVER SAW HIM BLUSH.
YOU'RE RIGHT.
IN OTHER WORDS, YOU PUT US THROUGH ALL THIS 'CAUSE YOU'RE SELFISH.
IT'S ALL BECAUSE OF SOME PERSONAL GRUDGE, HUH?
ACTUALLY... I'M GOOD WITH THAT.

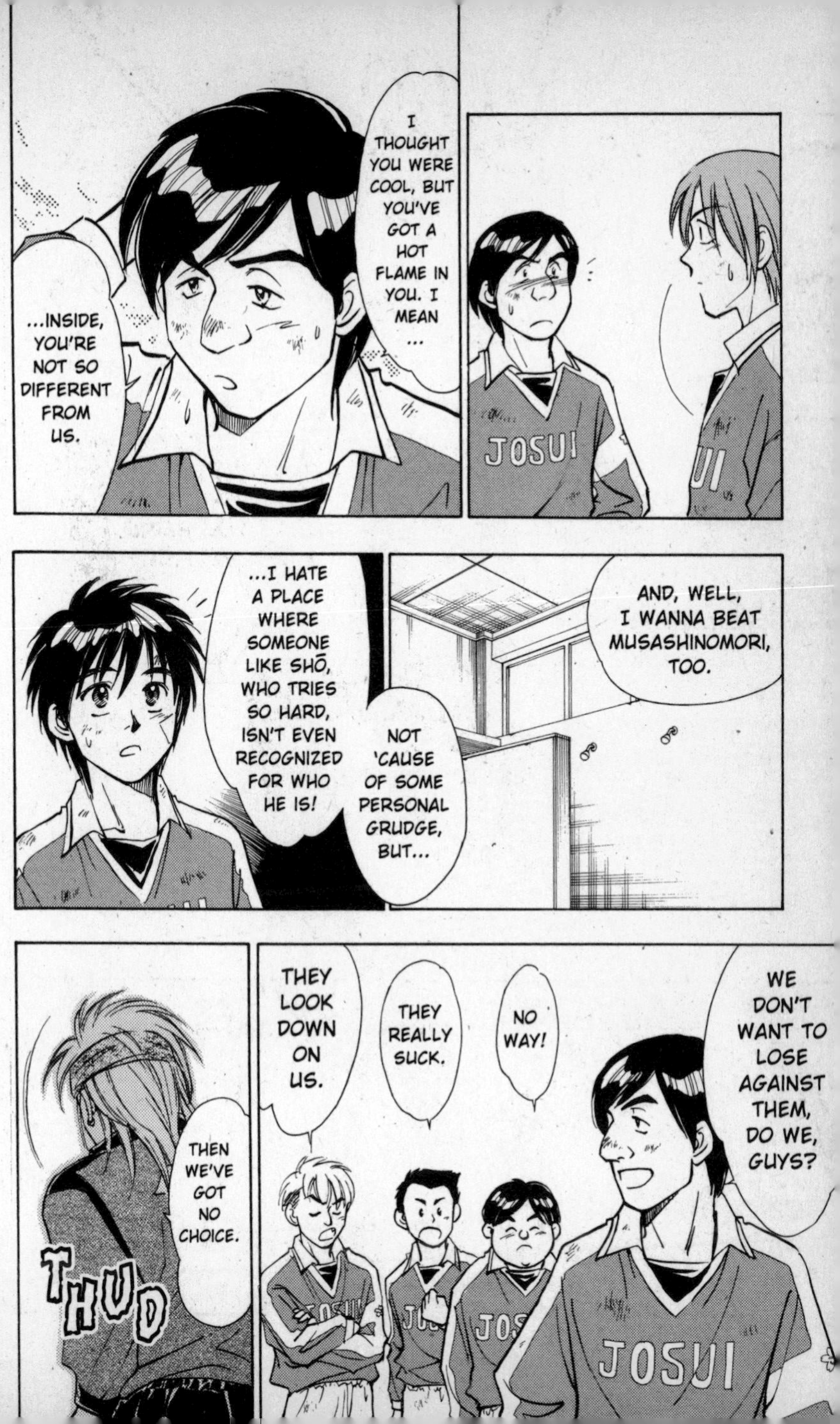
I THOUGHT YOU WERE COOL, BUT YOU'VE GOT A HOT FLAME IN YOU. I MEAN ...
...INSIDE, YOU'RE NOT SO DIFFERENT FROM US.
JOSUI
AND, WELL, I WANNA BEAT MUSASHINOMORI, TOO.
NOT 'CAUSE OF SOME PERSONAL GRUDGE, BUT...
...I HATE A PLACE WHERE SOMEONE LIKE SHŌ, WHO TRIES SO HARD, ISN'T EVEN RECOGNIZED FOR WHO HE IS!
WE DON'T WANT TO LOSE AGAINST THEM, DO WE, GUYS?
NO WAY!
THEY REALLY SUCK.
THEY LOOK DOWN ON US.
JOSUI
THEN WE'VE GOT NO CHOICE.
THUD

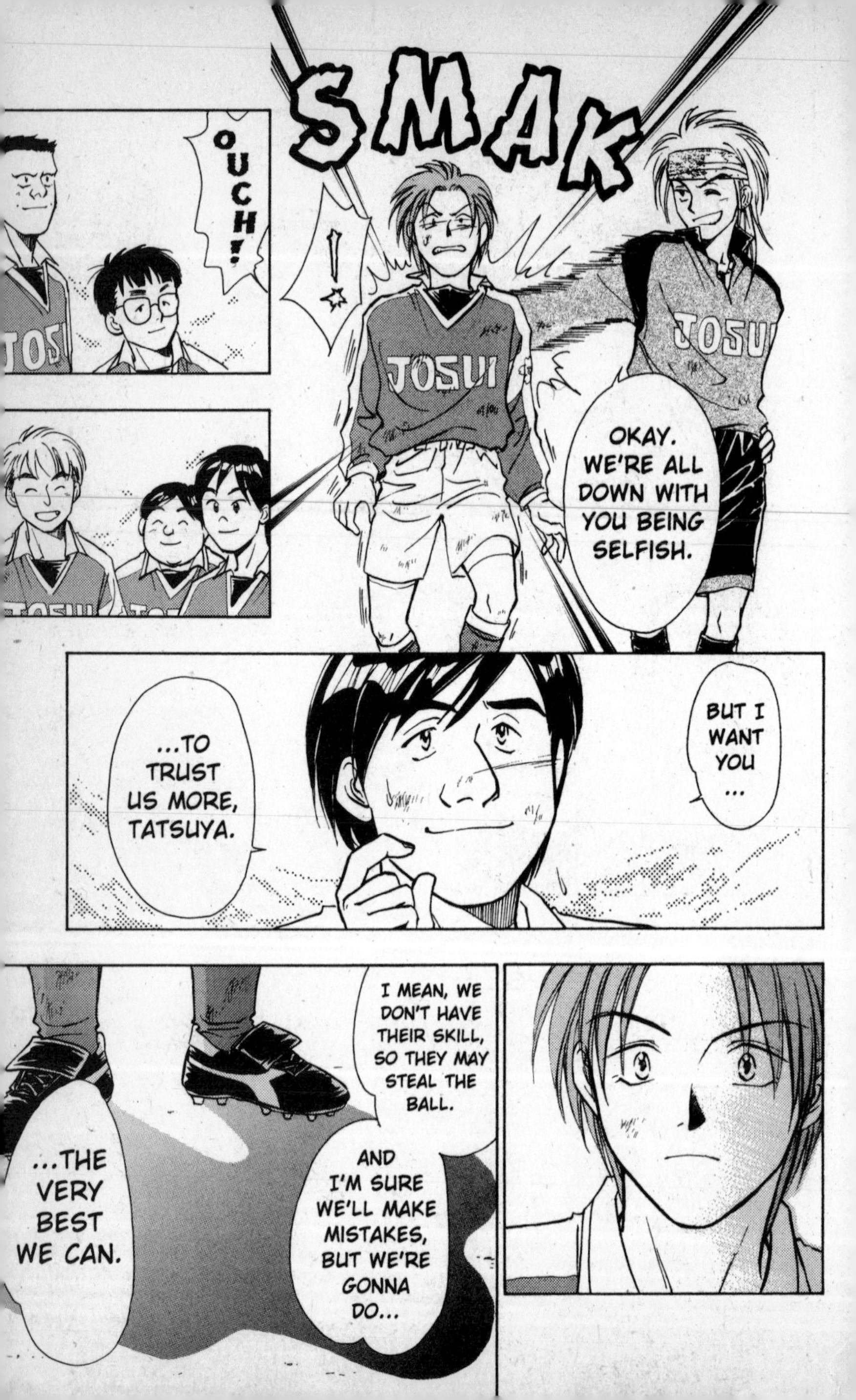
SMAK
!
OKAY. WE'RE ALL DOWN WITH YOU BEING SELFISH.
OUCH!!
BUT I WANT YOU...
...TO TRUST US MORE, TATSUYA.
I MEAN, WE DON'T HAVE THEIR SKILL, SO THEY MAY STEAL THE BALL.
AND I'M SURE WE'LL MAKE MISTAKES, BUT WE'RE GONNA DO...
...THE VERY BEST WE CAN.

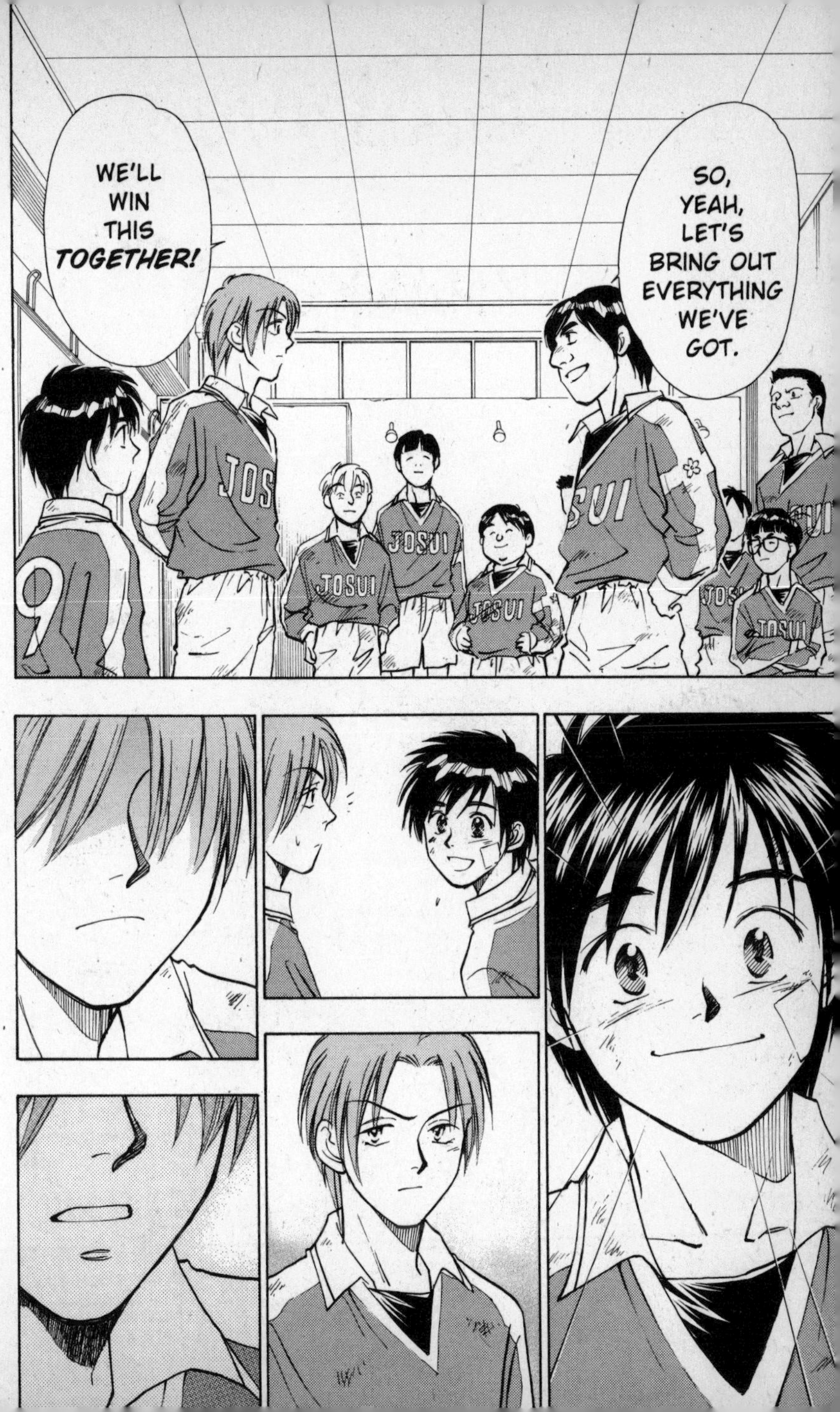
SO, YEAH, LET'S BRING OUT EVERYTHING WE'VE GOT.
WE'LL WIN THIS *TOGETHER!*

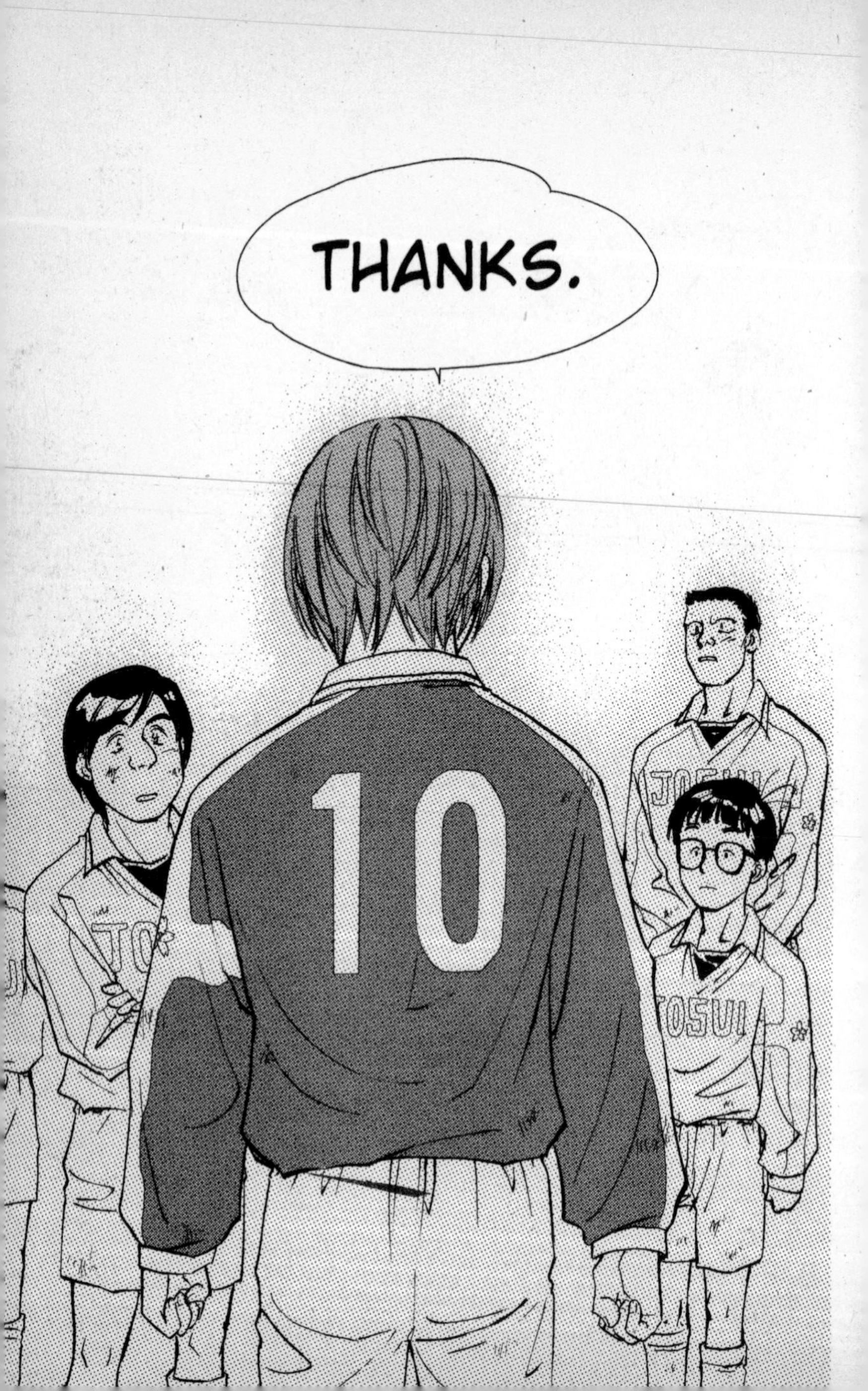
THANKS.

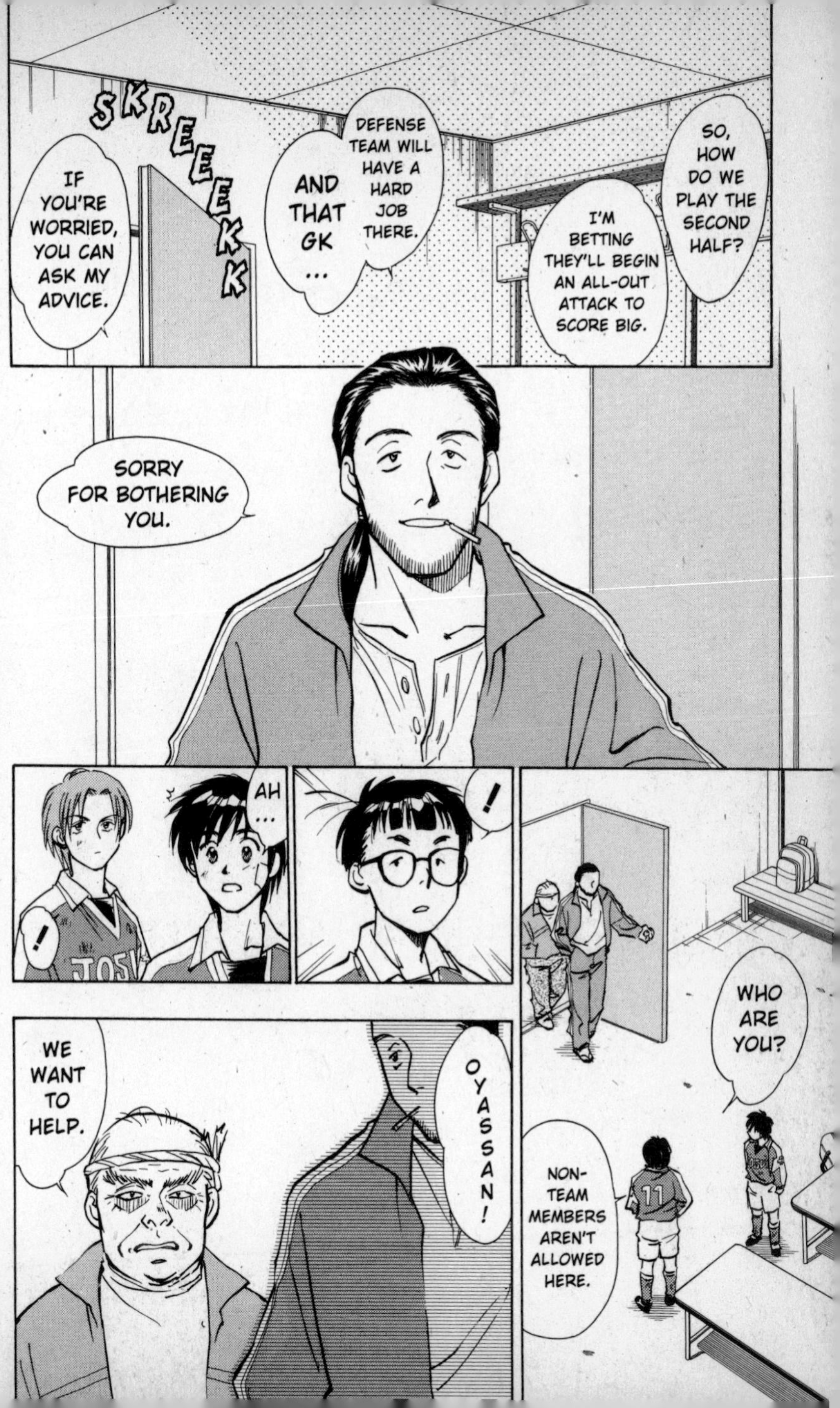
SO, HOW DO WE PLAY THE SECOND HALF?
I'M BETTING THEY'LL BEGIN AN ALL-OUT ATTACK TO SCORE BIG.
DEFENSE TEAM WILL HAVE A HARD JOB THERE.
AND THAT GK ...
SKREEEEK
IF YOU'RE WORRIED, YOU CAN ASK MY ADVICE.
SORRY FOR BOTHERING YOU.
WHO ARE YOU?
NON-TEAM MEMBERS AREN'T ALLOWED HERE.
!
AH ...
!
OYASSAN!
WE WANT TO HELP.

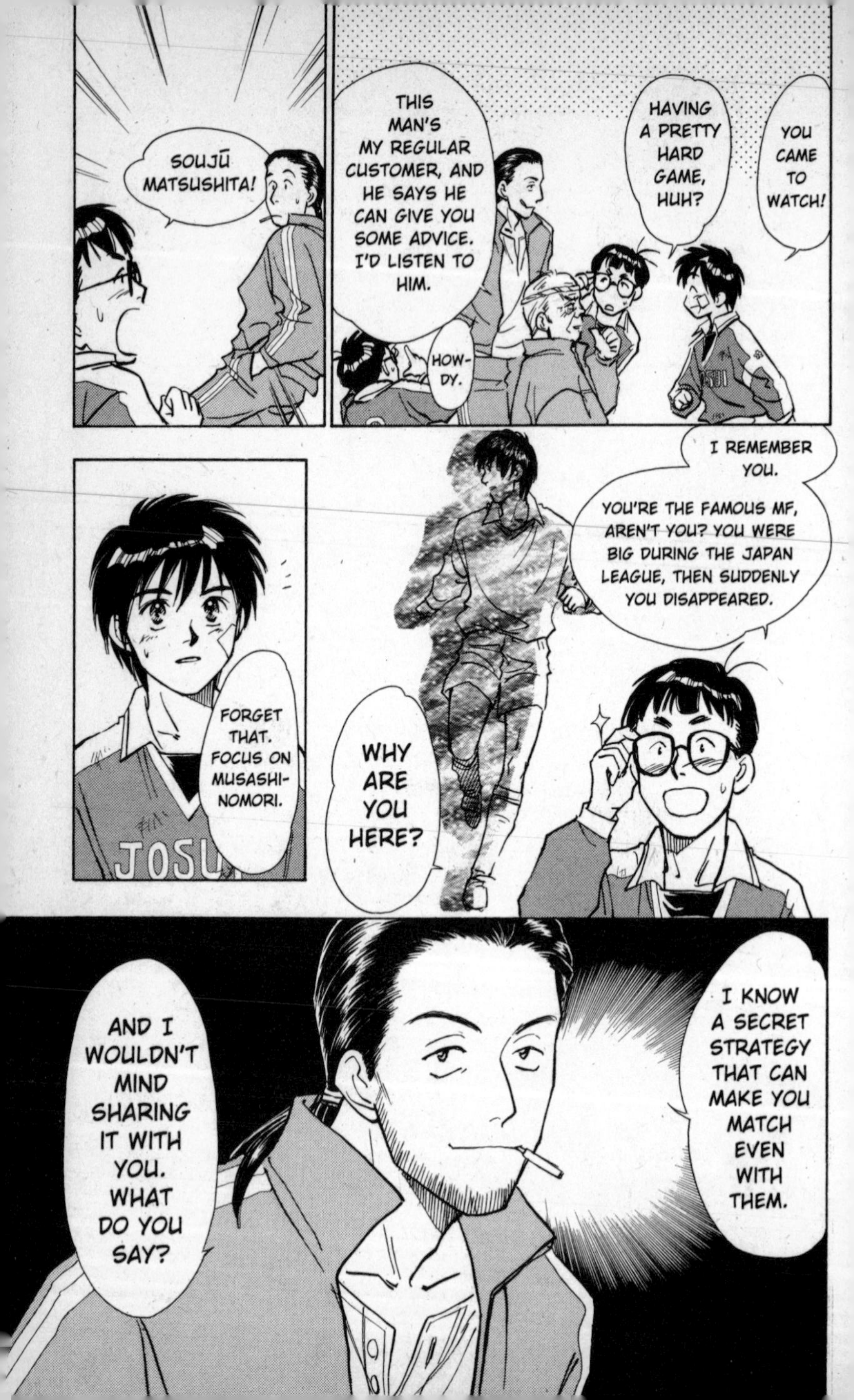
YOU CAME TO WATCH!
HAVING A PRETTY HARD GAME, HUH?
THIS MAN'S MY REGULAR CUSTOMER, AND HE SAYS HE CAN GIVE YOU SOME ADVICE. I'D LISTEN TO HIM.
HOW-DY.
SOUJŪ MATSUSHITA!
I REMEMBER YOU.
YOU'RE THE FAMOUS MF, AREN'T YOU? YOU WERE BIG DURING THE JAPAN LEAGUE, THEN SUDDENLY YOU DISAPPEARED.
WHY ARE YOU HERE?
FORGET THAT. FOCUS ON MUSASHI-NOMORI.
I KNOW A SECRET STRATEGY THAT CAN MAKE YOU MATCH EVEN WITH THEM.
AND I WOULDN'T MIND SHARING IT WITH YOU. WHAT DO YOU SAY?

● OLD STORY ABOUT THE EXCITING J LEAGUE MEMBERS.

THE COUNTRY MAN, OKANO, JOINED NICHIDAI FROM MATSUE NICHIDAI HIGH SCHOOL. OF COURSE HE WENT ON TO JOIN THE SOCCER TEAM. HOWEVER, THE TEAMMATES HIS AGE WERE ALL FROM FAMOUS SCHOOLS, WHO WERE ACCEPTED INTO THE SCHOOL BECAUSE OF SPECIAL RECOMMENDATIONS THEY RECEIVED BASED ON THEIR SKILLS. OKANO, WHO ENTERED THE SCHOOL BY PASSING THE GENERAL ENTRANCE EXAM, WASN'T EVEN NOTICED BY THE COACH. AT THE END OF THE FIRST YEAR, THEY HAD THE ANNUAL FRESHMEN MATCH. ON THE PAMPHLET FOR THE MATCH, THE NAMES OF ALL THE FRESHMEN WERE SUPPOSED TO BE LISTED. OKANO'S NAME WAS MISSING DESPITE THE FACT THAT HE WAS THERE THE ENTIRE YEAR PREPARING JUICE FOR THE REGULARS GAME AFTER GAME AND KEEPING THE SCORE AT EVERY MATCH. HOWEVER, DURING HIS SECOND YEAR, A NEW COACH WAS ASSIGNED TO WORK WITH THE FIRST AND THE SECOND YEAR PLAYERS, AND HE TOOK NOTICE OF OKANO'S SPEED. THUS, OKANO EVENTUALLY SUCCEEDED IN BECOMING A REGULAR PLAYER.

WHAT ABOUT THE PLAYER HONDA OF THE YOKOHAMA ANTLERS? I'VE HEARD THAT SINCE HE WAS A GRADE-SCHOOL KID HE WAS NOT ALLOWED TO PLAY LIKE OTHER NORMAL KIDS, BUT INSTEAD HE PLAYED SOCCER ALL DAY LONG. AFTER THE PRACTICE SESSION AT SCHOOL, HE RECEIVED SPECIAL TRAINING FROM HIS FATHER AT A PARK NEARBY, AND EVERY NOW AND THEN HE WAS SEEN RUNNING ALONG WITH HIS FAVORITE DOBERMAN DOG FOLLOWING HIS FATHER'S CAR. AND BEFORE HE WENT TO SLEEP, HE HAD TO PRACTICE HEAD-KICKS, VOLLEY-KICKS AND SUCH ON HIS FUTON. TO TOP IT OFF, BECAUSE HONDA WAS SMALL, HE WAS FORCED TO DRINK MILK AND RAW EGGS EVERY MORNING, BECAUSE THEY THOUGHT THIS DRINK WOULD HELP HIM GROW BIGGER. HIS LIFE WAS TOTALLY A SOCCER VERSION OF "STAR OF GIANT." WHAT HONDA LEARNED WHILE AT THE GRADE SCHOOL IS THAT DRINKING MILK AND EGGS WON'T MAKE A KID GROW ANY BIGGER.

--TATSUYA WATANABE (WINNING RUN)

STAGE.18
If You Can Dream, You Can Do It!

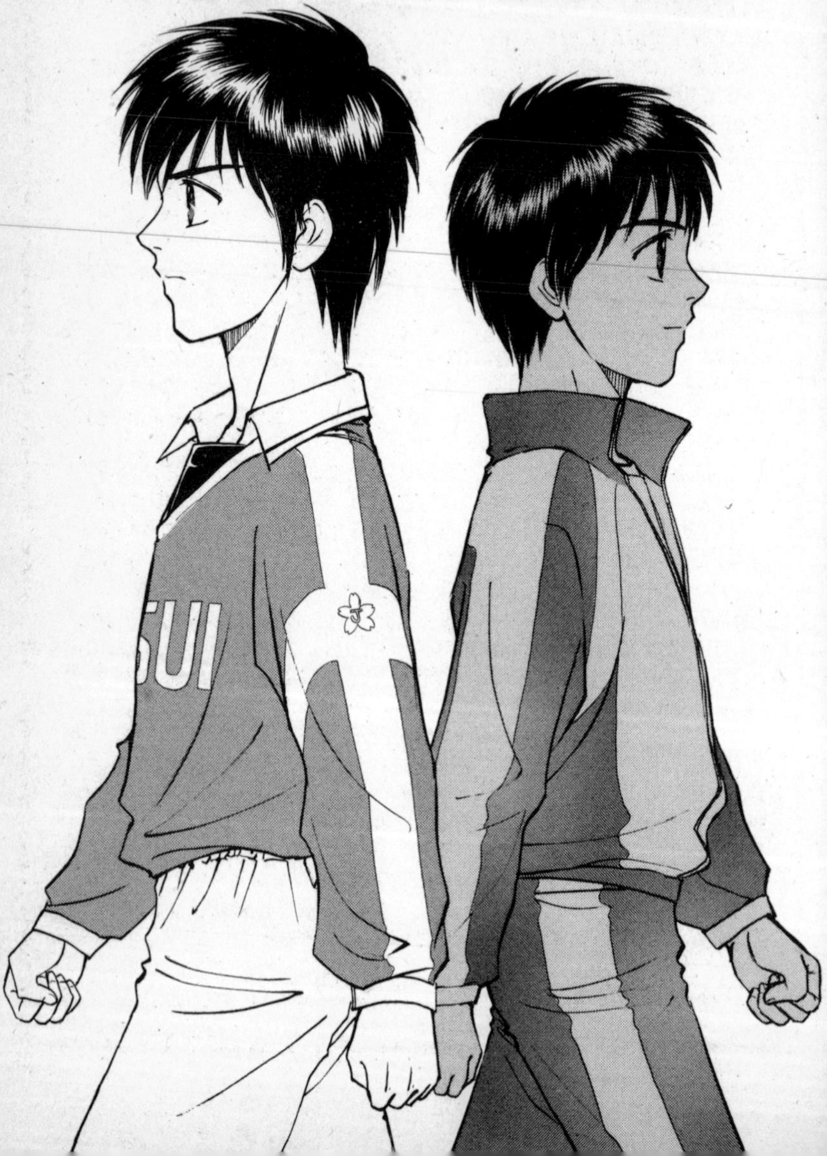
SUI

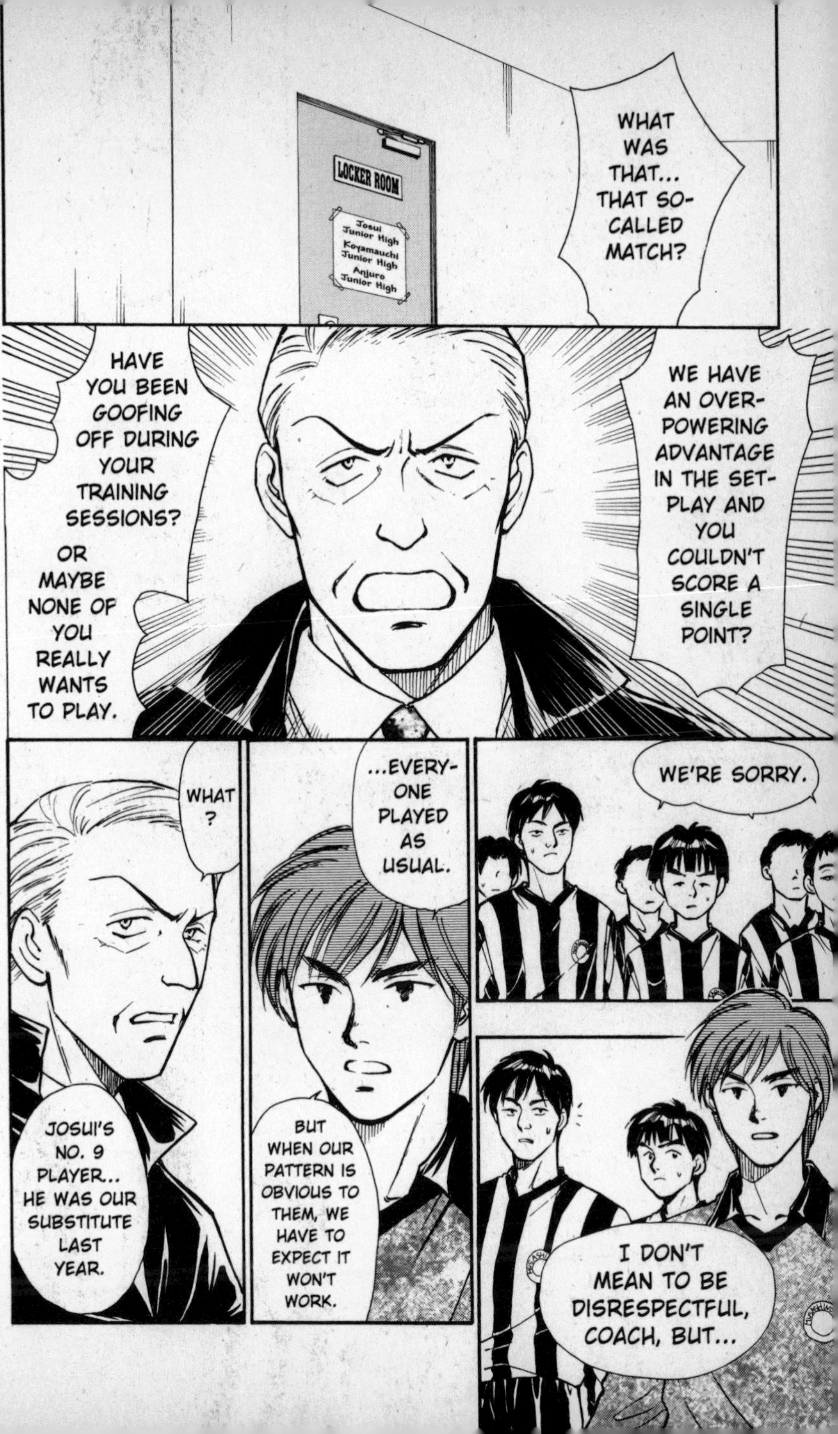
LOCKER ROOM
Josui Junior High
Koyamauchi Junior High
Anjuro Junior High
WHAT WAS THAT... THAT SO-CALLED MATCH?
WE HAVE AN OVER-POWERING ADVANTAGE IN THE SET-PLAY AND YOU COULDN'T SCORE A SINGLE POINT?
HAVE YOU BEEN GOOFING OFF DURING YOUR TRAINING SESSIONS?
OR MAYBE NONE OF YOU REALLY WANTS TO PLAY.
WE'RE SORRY.
I DON'T MEAN TO BE DISRESPECTFUL, COACH, BUT...
...EVERY-ONE PLAYED AS USUAL.
BUT WHEN OUR PATTERN IS OBVIOUS TO THEM, WE HAVE TO EXPECT IT WON'T WORK.
WHAT?
JOSUI'S NO. 9 PLAYER... HE WAS OUR SUBSTITUTE LAST YEAR.

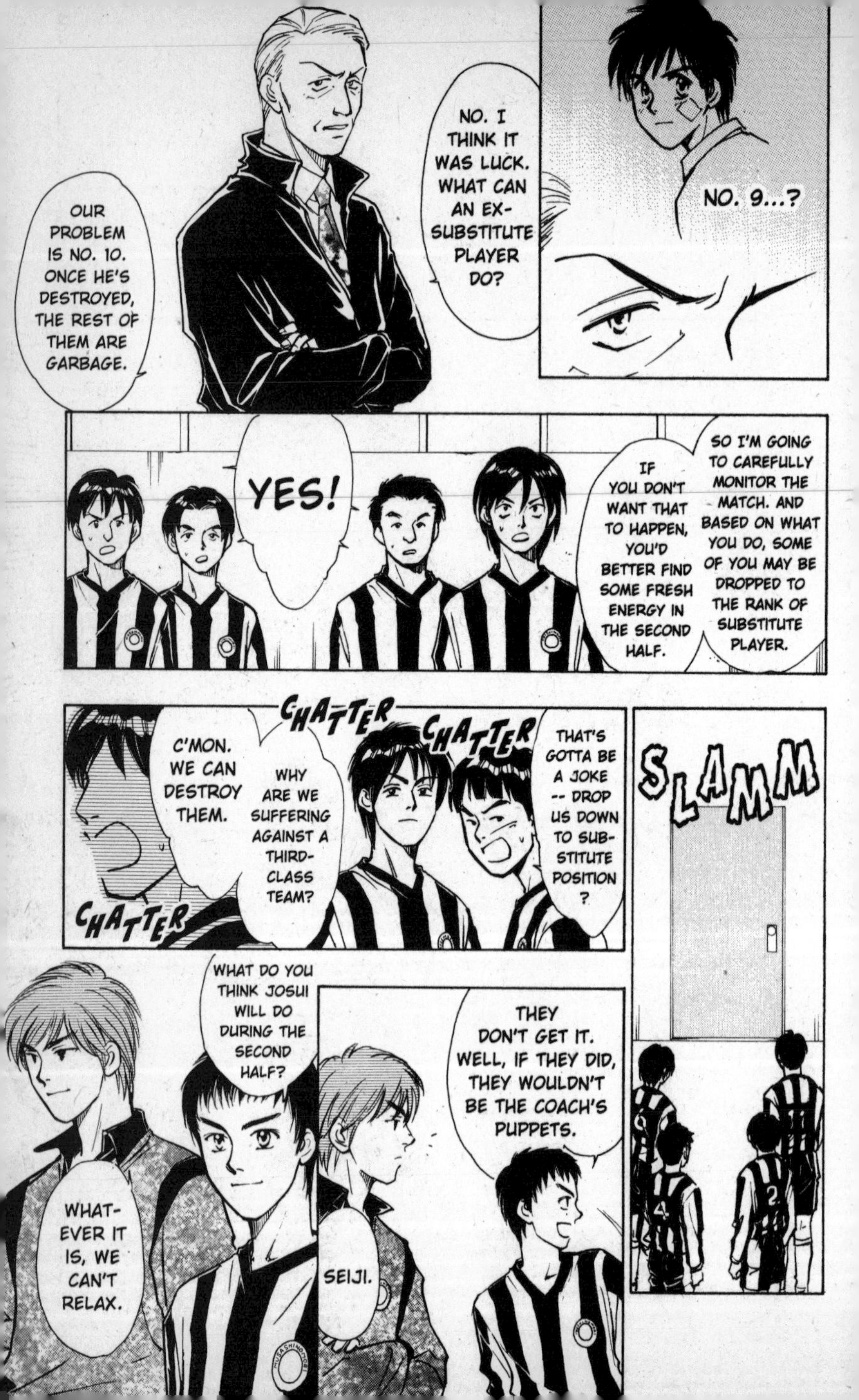
NO. 9...?
NO. I THINK IT WAS LUCK. WHAT CAN AN EX-SUBSTITUTE PLAYER DO?
OUR PROBLEM IS NO. 10. ONCE HE'S DESTROYED, THE REST OF THEM ARE GARBAGE.
SO I'M GOING TO CAREFULLY MONITOR THE MATCH. AND BASED ON WHAT YOU DO, SOME OF YOU MAY BE DROPPED TO THE RANK OF SUBSTITUTE PLAYER.
IF YOU DON'T WANT THAT TO HAPPEN, YOU'D BETTER FIND SOME FRESH ENERGY IN THE SECOND HALF.
YES!
SLAMM
THAT'S GOTTA BE A JOKE -- DROP US DOWN TO SUB-STITUTE POSITION?
CHATTER
CHATTER
WHY ARE WE SUFFERING AGAINST A THIRD-CLASS TEAM?
C'MON. WE CAN DESTROY THEM.
CHATTER
THEY DON'T GET IT. WELL, IF THEY DID, THEY WOULDN'T BE THE COACH'S PUPPETS.
WHAT DO YOU THINK JOSUI WILL DO DURING THE SECOND HALF?
SEIJI.
WHAT-EVER IT IS, WE CAN'T RELAX.

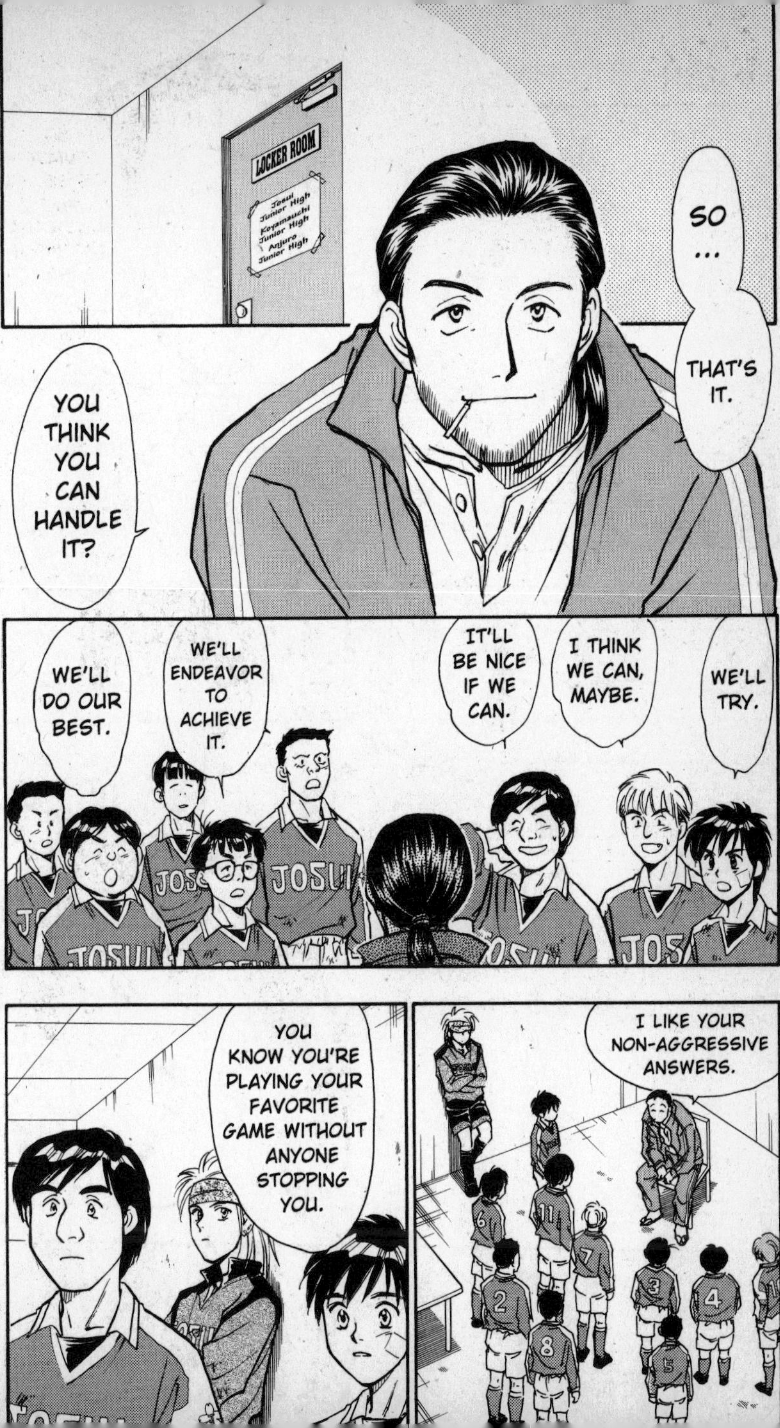
SO ...
THAT'S IT.
YOU THINK YOU CAN HANDLE IT?
LOCKER ROOM
Josui Junior High Koyamauchi Junior High Anjuro Junior High
WE'LL TRY.
I THINK WE CAN, MAYBE.
IT'LL BE NICE IF WE CAN.
WE'LL ENDEAVOR TO ACHIEVE IT.
WE'LL DO OUR BEST.
I LIKE YOUR NON-AGGRESSIVE ANSWERS.
YOU KNOW YOU'RE PLAYING YOUR FAVORITE GAME WITHOUT ANYONE STOPPING YOU.

READ THIS WAY

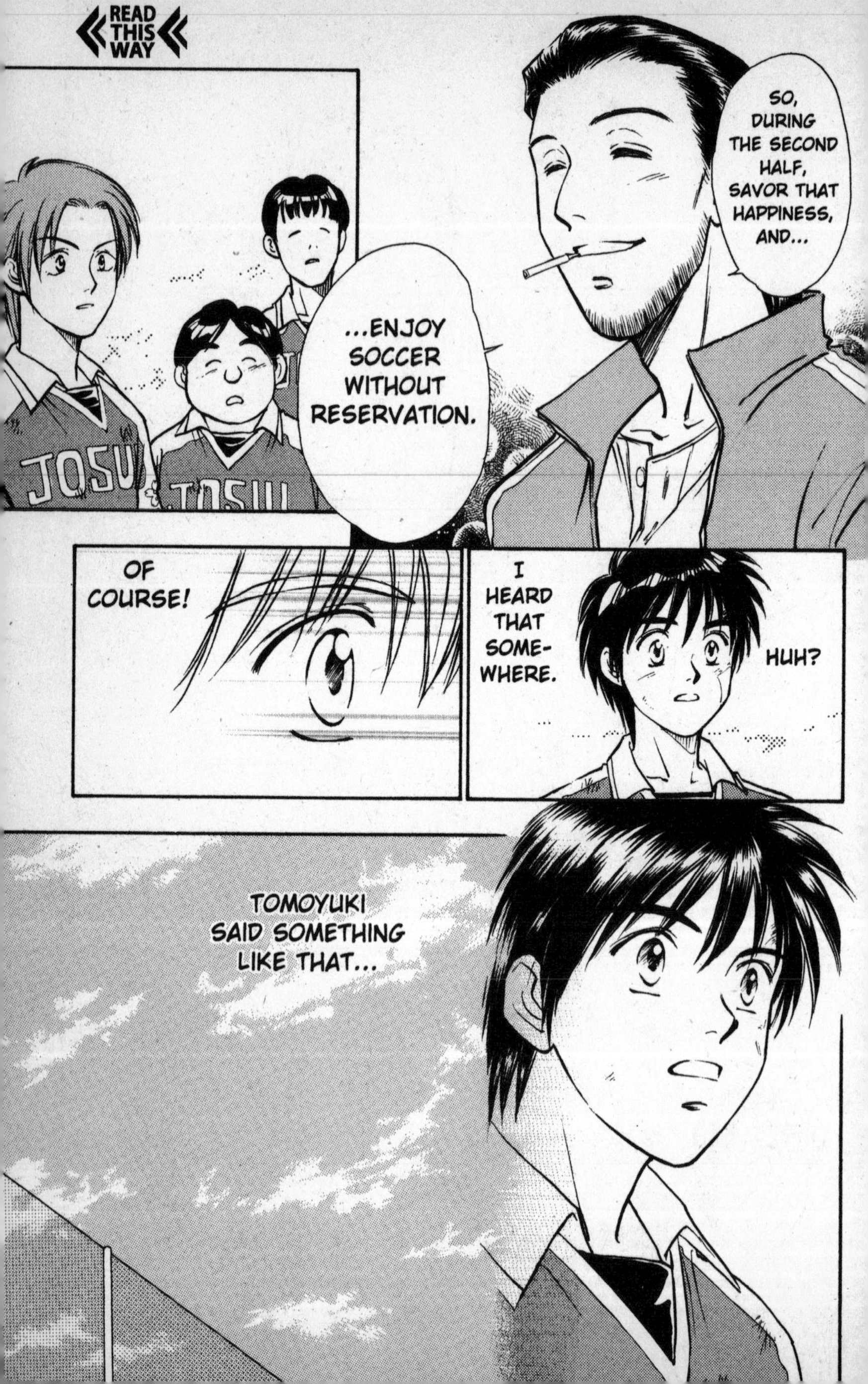
SO, DURING THE SECOND HALF, SAVOR THAT HAPPINESS, AND...
...ENJOY SOCCER WITHOUT RESERVATION.
HUH?
I HEARD THAT SOME-WHERE.
OF COURSE!
TOMOYUKI SAID SOMETHING LIKE THAT...

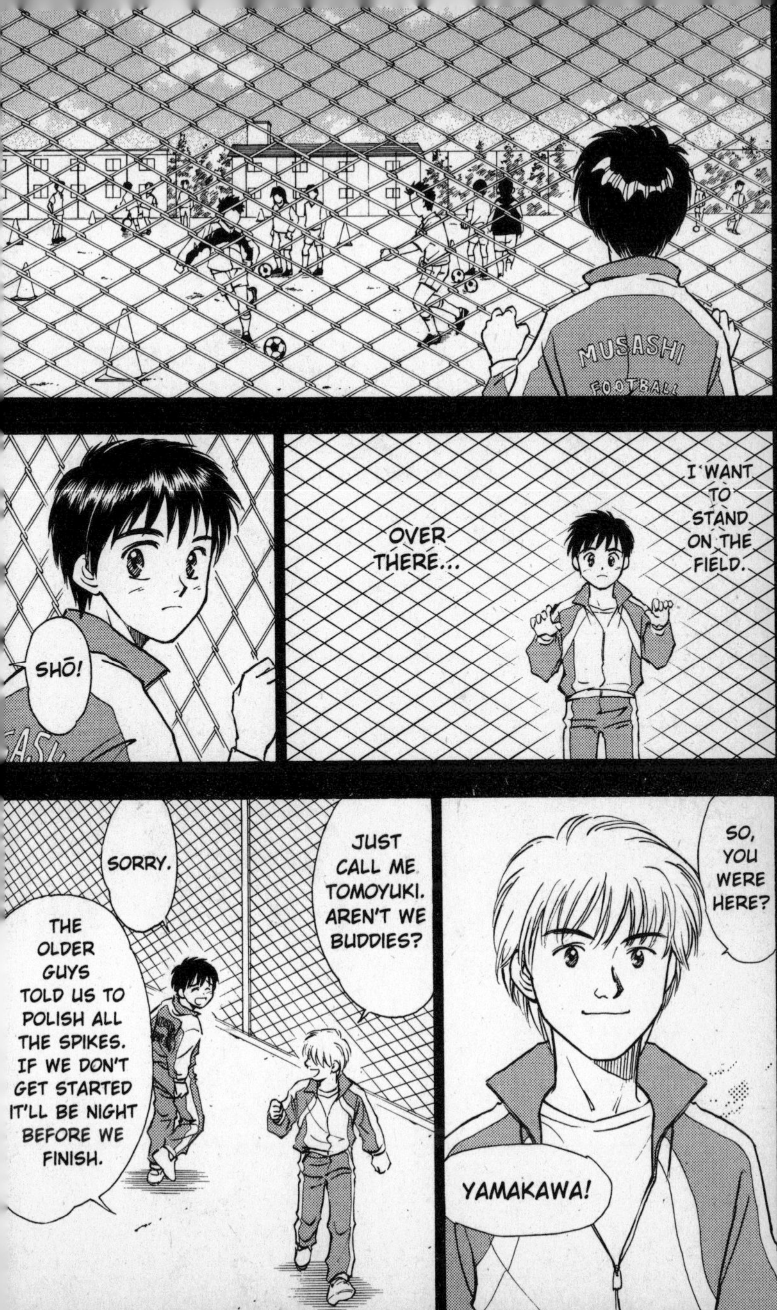
MUSASHI
FOOTBALL
I WANT TO STAND ON THE FIELD.
OVER THERE...
SHŌ!
SO, YOU WERE HERE?
YAMAKAWA!
JUST CALL ME TOMOYUKI. AREN'T WE BUDDIES?
SORRY.
THE OLDER GUYS TOLD US TO POLISH ALL THE SPIKES. IF WE DON'T GET STARTED IT'LL BE NIGHT BEFORE WE FINISH.

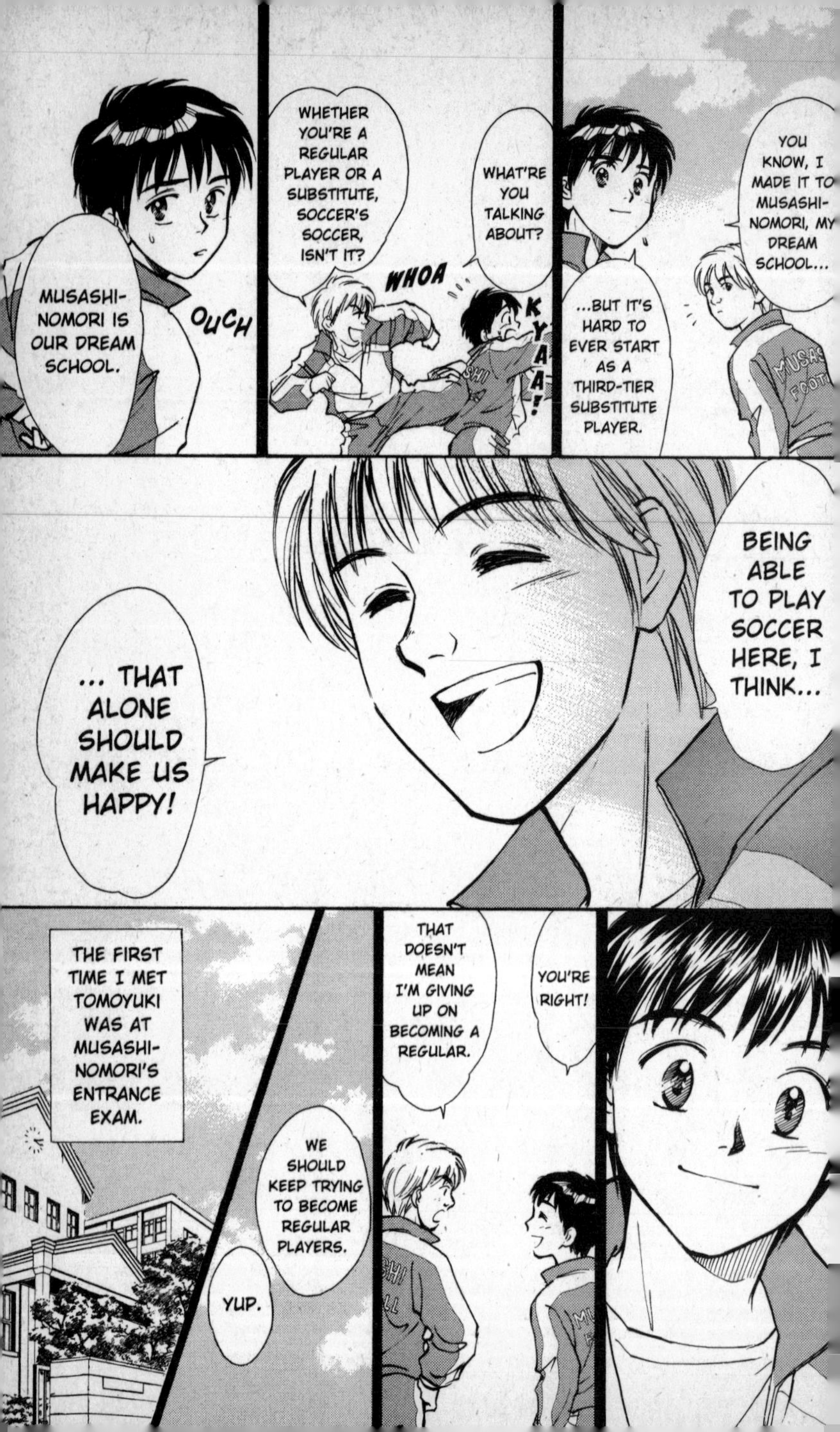
YOU KNOW, I MADE IT TO MUSASHI-NOMORI, MY DREAM SCHOOL...
...BUT IT'S HARD TO EVER START AS A THIRD-TIER SUBSTITUTE PLAYER.
WHAT'RE YOU TALKING ABOUT?
WHETHER YOU'RE A REGULAR PLAYER OR A SUBSTITUTE, SOCCER'S SOCCER, ISN'T IT?
WHOA
KYAA!
MUSASHI-NOMORI IS OUR DREAM SCHOOL.
OUCH
BEING ABLE TO PLAY SOCCER HERE, I THINK...
... THAT ALONE SHOULD MAKE US HAPPY!
YOU'RE RIGHT!
THAT DOESN'T MEAN I'M GIVING UP ON BECOMING A REGULAR.
WE SHOULD KEEP TRYING TO BECOME REGULAR PLAYERS.
YUP.
THE FIRST TIME I MET TOMOYUKI WAS AT MUSASHI-NOMORI'S ENTRANCE EXAM.

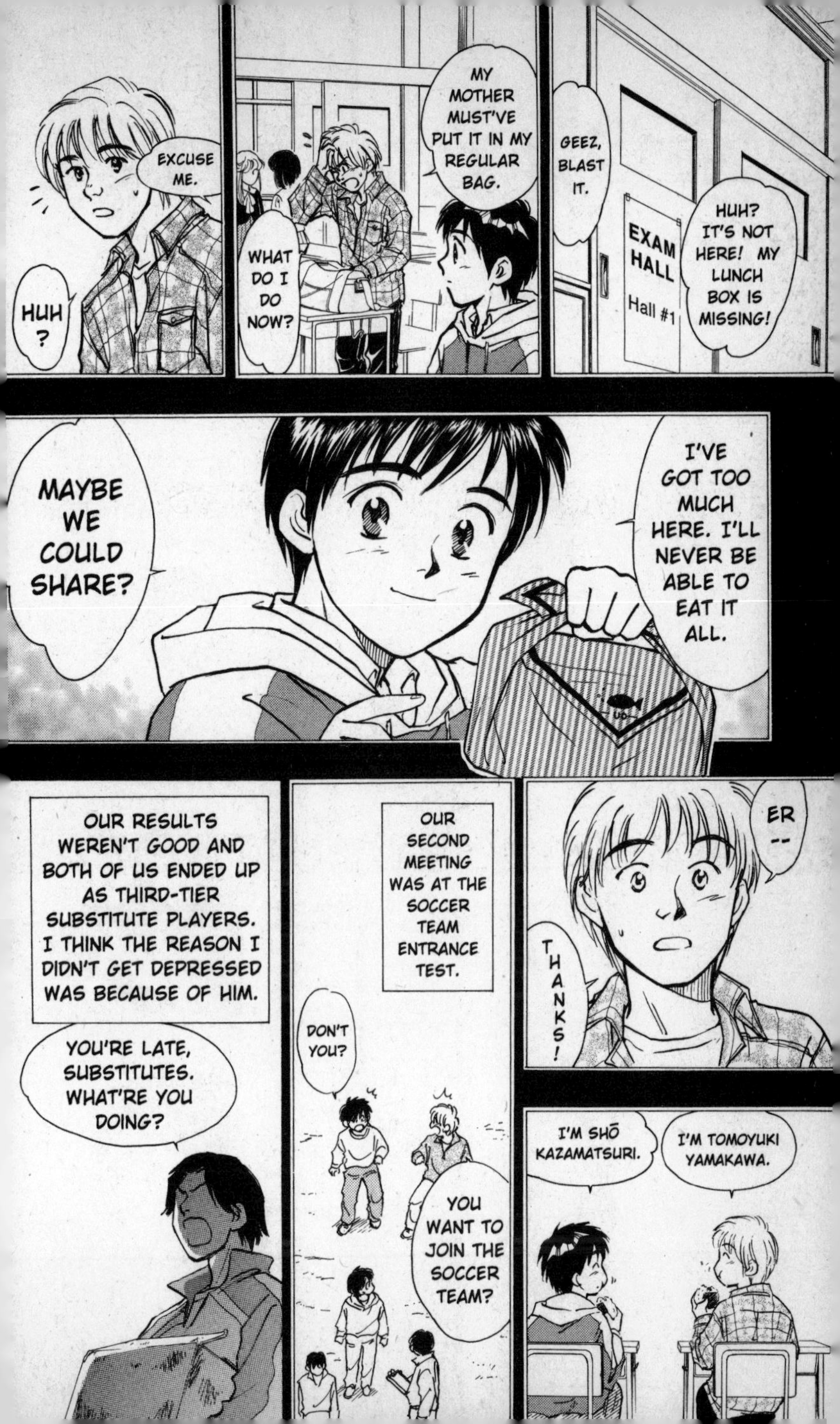
HUH? IT'S NOT HERE! MY LUNCH BOX IS MISSING!
EXAM HALL
Hall #1
GEEZ, BLAST IT.
MY MOTHER MUST'VE PUT IT IN MY REGULAR BAG.
WHAT DO I DO NOW?
EXCUSE ME.
HUH?
I'VE GOT TOO MUCH HERE. I'LL NEVER BE ABLE TO EAT IT ALL.
MAYBE WE COULD SHARE?
ER --
THANKS!
I'M TOMOYUKI YAMAKAWA.
I'M SHŌ KAZAMATSURI.
OUR SECOND MEETING WAS AT THE SOCCER TEAM ENTRANCE TEST.
YOU WANT TO JOIN THE SOCCER TEAM?
DON'T YOU?
OUR RESULTS WEREN'T GOOD AND BOTH OF US ENDED UP AS THIRD-TIER SUBSTITUTE PLAYERS. I THINK THE REASON I DIDN'T GET DEPRESSED WAS BECAUSE OF HIM.
YOU'RE LATE, SUBSTITUTES. WHAT'RE YOU DOING?

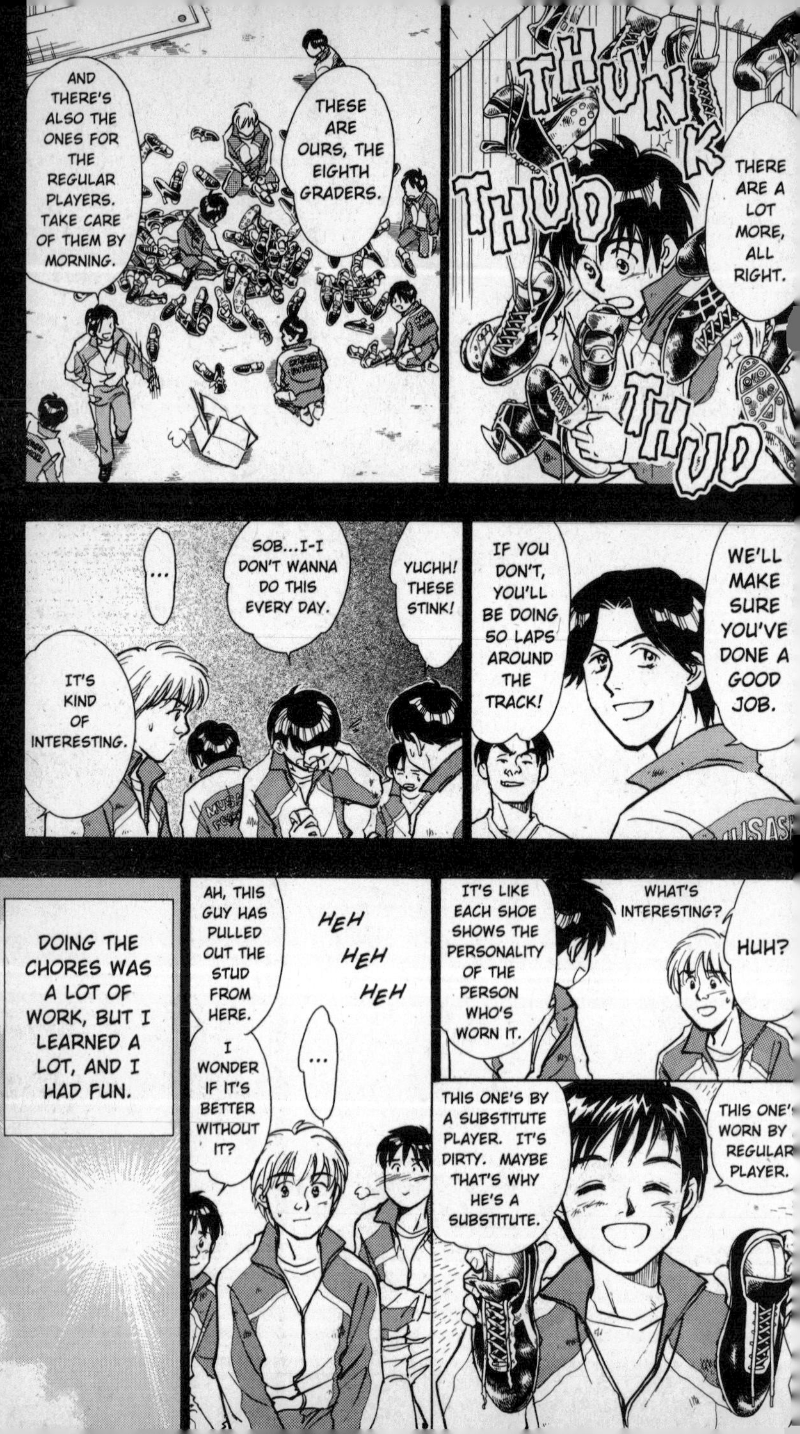
THUNK
THERE ARE A LOT MORE, ALL RIGHT.
THUD
THUD
THESE ARE OURS, THE EIGHTH GRADERS.
AND THERE'S ALSO THE ONES FOR THE REGULAR PLAYERS. TAKE CARE OF THEM BY MORNING.
WE'LL MAKE SURE YOU'VE DONE A GOOD JOB.
IF YOU DON'T, YOU'LL BE DOING 50 LAPS AROUND THE TRACK!
YUCHH! THESE STINK!
SOB...I-I DON'T WANNA DO THIS EVERY DAY.
...
IT'S KIND OF INTERESTING.
WHAT'S INTERESTING?
HUH?
IT'S LIKE EACH SHOE SHOWS THE PERSONALITY OF THE PERSON WHO'S WORN IT.
THIS ONE' WORN BY REGULAR PLAYER.
THIS ONE'S BY A SUBSTITUTE PLAYER. IT'S DIRTY. MAYBE THAT'S WHY HE'S A SUBSTITUTE.
AH, THIS GUY HAS PULLED OUT THE STUD FROM HERE.
HEH HEH HEH
I WONDER IF IT'S BETTER WITHOUT IT?
...
DOING THE CHORES WAS A LOT OF WORK, BUT I LEARNED A LOT, AND I HAD FUN.

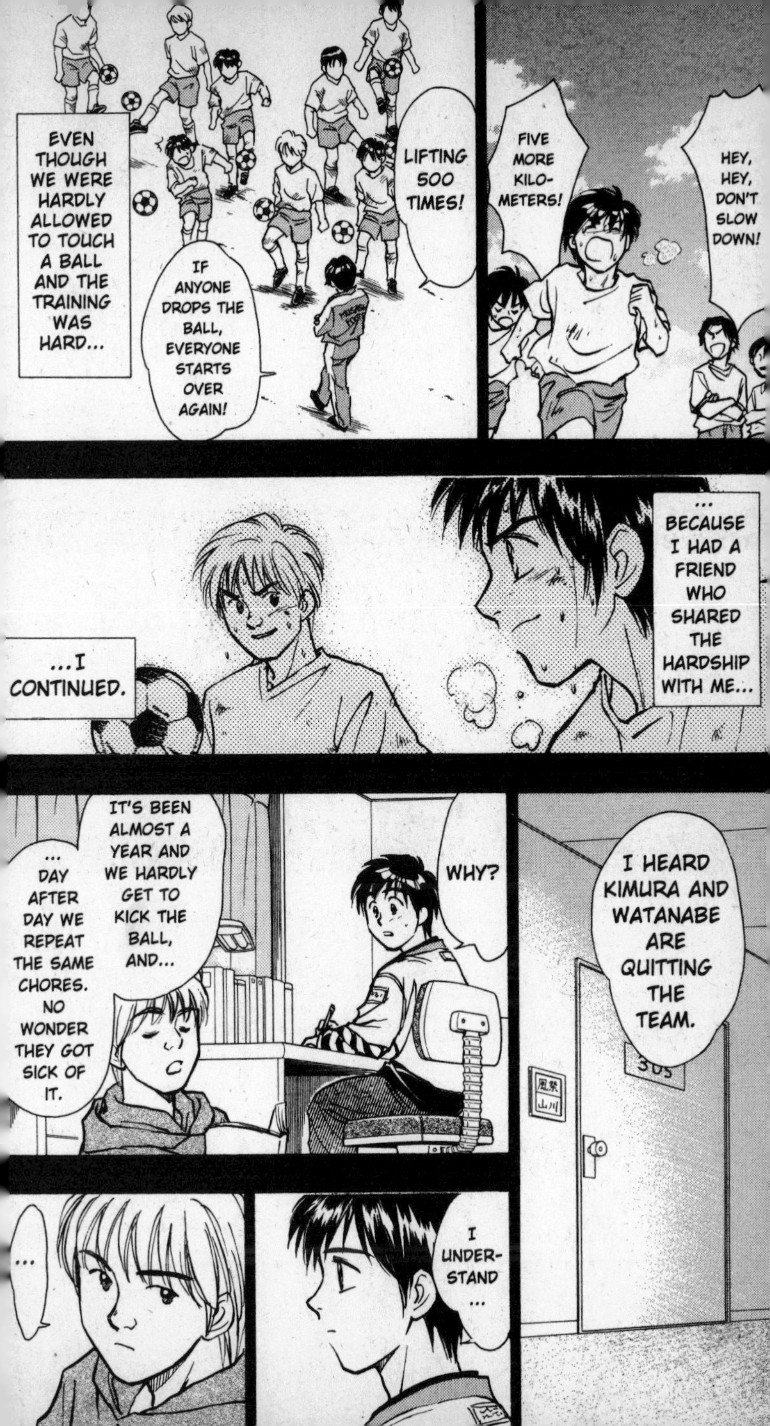
HEY, HEY, DON'T SLOW DOWN!
FIVE MORE KILO-METERS!
LIFTING 500 TIMES!
IF ANYONE DROPS THE BALL, EVERYONE STARTS OVER AGAIN!
EVEN THOUGH WE WERE HARDLY ALLOWED TO TOUCH A BALL AND THE TRAINING WAS HARD...
...BECAUSE I HAD A FRIEND WHO SHARED THE HARDSHIP WITH ME...
...I CONTINUED.
I HEARD KIMURA AND WATANABE ARE QUITTING THE TEAM.
WHY?
IT'S BEEN ALMOST A YEAR AND WE HARDLY GET TO KICK THE BALL, AND...
...DAY AFTER DAY WE REPEAT THE SAME CHORES. NO WONDER THEY GOT SICK OF IT.
I UNDER-STAND...
...

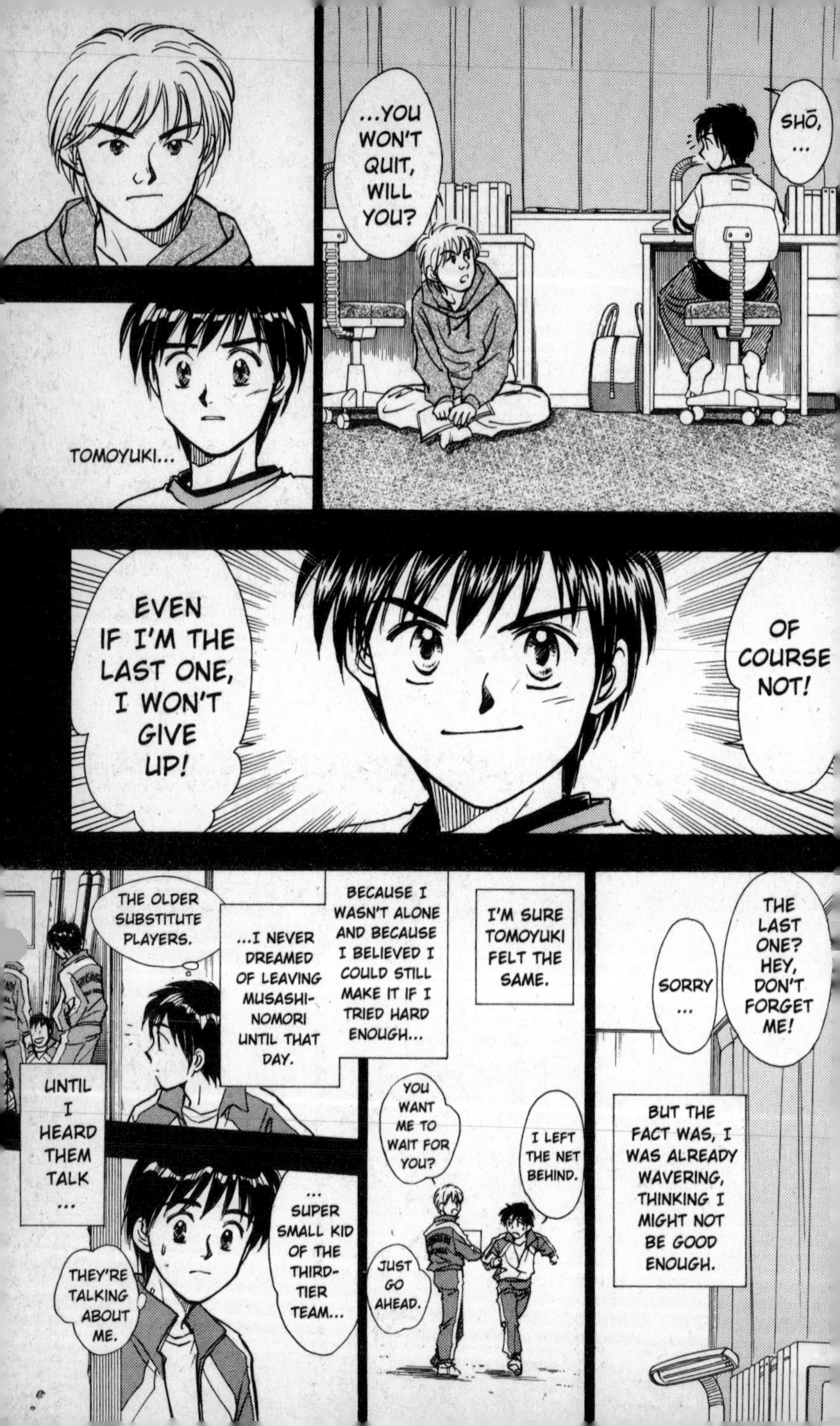
SHŌ, ...
...YOU WON'T QUIT, WILL YOU?
TOMOYUKI...
OF COURSE NOT!
EVEN IF I'M THE LAST ONE, I WON'T GIVE UP!
THE LAST ONE? HEY, DON'T FORGET ME!
SORRY...
BUT THE FACT WAS, I WAS ALREADY WAVERING, THINKING I MIGHT NOT BE GOOD ENOUGH.
I'M SURE TOMOYUKI FELT THE SAME.
I LEFT THE NET BEHIND.
YOU WANT ME TO WAIT FOR YOU?
JUST GO AHEAD.
BECAUSE I WASN'T ALONE AND BECAUSE I BELIEVED I COULD STILL MAKE IT IF I TRIED HARD ENOUGH...
...I NEVER DREAMED OF LEAVING MUSASHI-NOMORI UNTIL THAT DAY.
THE OLDER SUBSTITUTE PLAYERS.
...SUPER SMALL KID OF THE THIRD-TIER TEAM...
UNTIL I HEARD THEM TALK...
THEY'RE TALKING ABOUT ME.

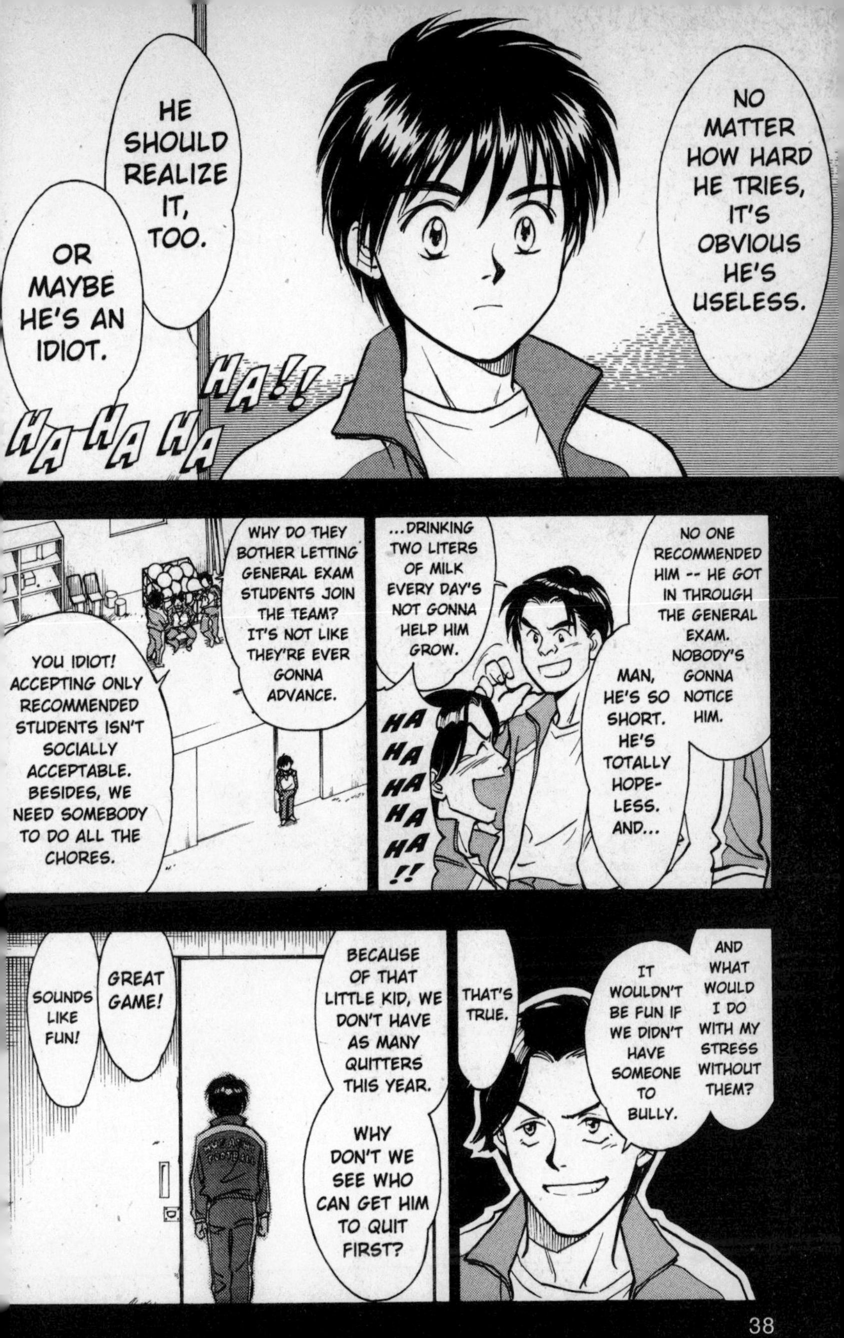
NO MATTER HOW HARD HE TRIES, IT'S OBVIOUS HE'S USELESS.
HE SHOULD REALIZE IT, TOO.
OR MAYBE HE'S AN IDIOT.
HA HA HA HA!!
NO ONE RECOMMENDED HIM -- HE GOT IN THROUGH THE GENERAL EXAM. NOBODY'S GONNA NOTICE HIM.
MAN, HE'S SO SHORT. HE'S TOTALLY HOPE-LESS. AND...
...DRINKING TWO LITERS OF MILK EVERY DAY'S NOT GONNA HELP HIM GROW.
HA HA HA HA HA HA!!
WHY DO THEY BOTHER LETTING GENERAL EXAM STUDENTS JOIN THE TEAM? IT'S NOT LIKE THEY'RE EVER GONNA ADVANCE.
YOU IDIOT! ACCEPTING ONLY RECOMMENDED STUDENTS ISN'T SOCIALLY ACCEPTABLE. BESIDES, WE NEED SOMEBODY TO DO ALL THE CHORES.
AND WHAT WOULD I DO WITH MY STRESS WITHOUT THEM?
IT WOULDN'T BE FUN IF WE DIDN'T HAVE SOMEONE TO BULLY.
THAT'S TRUE.
BECAUSE OF THAT LITTLE KID, WE DON'T HAVE AS MANY QUITTERS THIS YEAR.
WHY DON'T WE SEE WHO CAN GET HIM TO QUIT FIRST?
GREAT GAME!
SOUNDS LIKE FUN!

READ THIS WAY

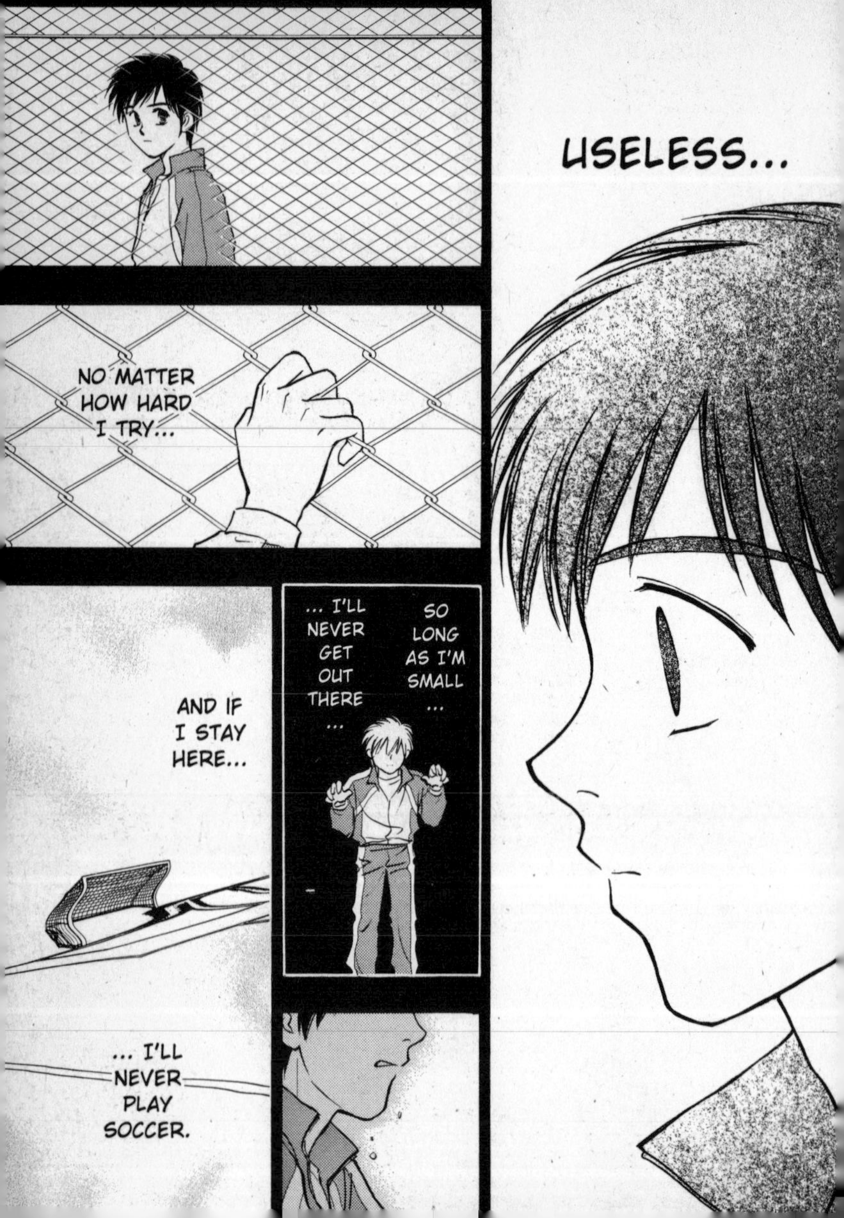
USELESS...
NO MATTER HOW HARD I TRY...
SO LONG AS I'M SMALL...
... I'LL NEVER GET OUT THERE ...
AND IF I STAY HERE...
... I'LL NEVER PLAY SOCCER.

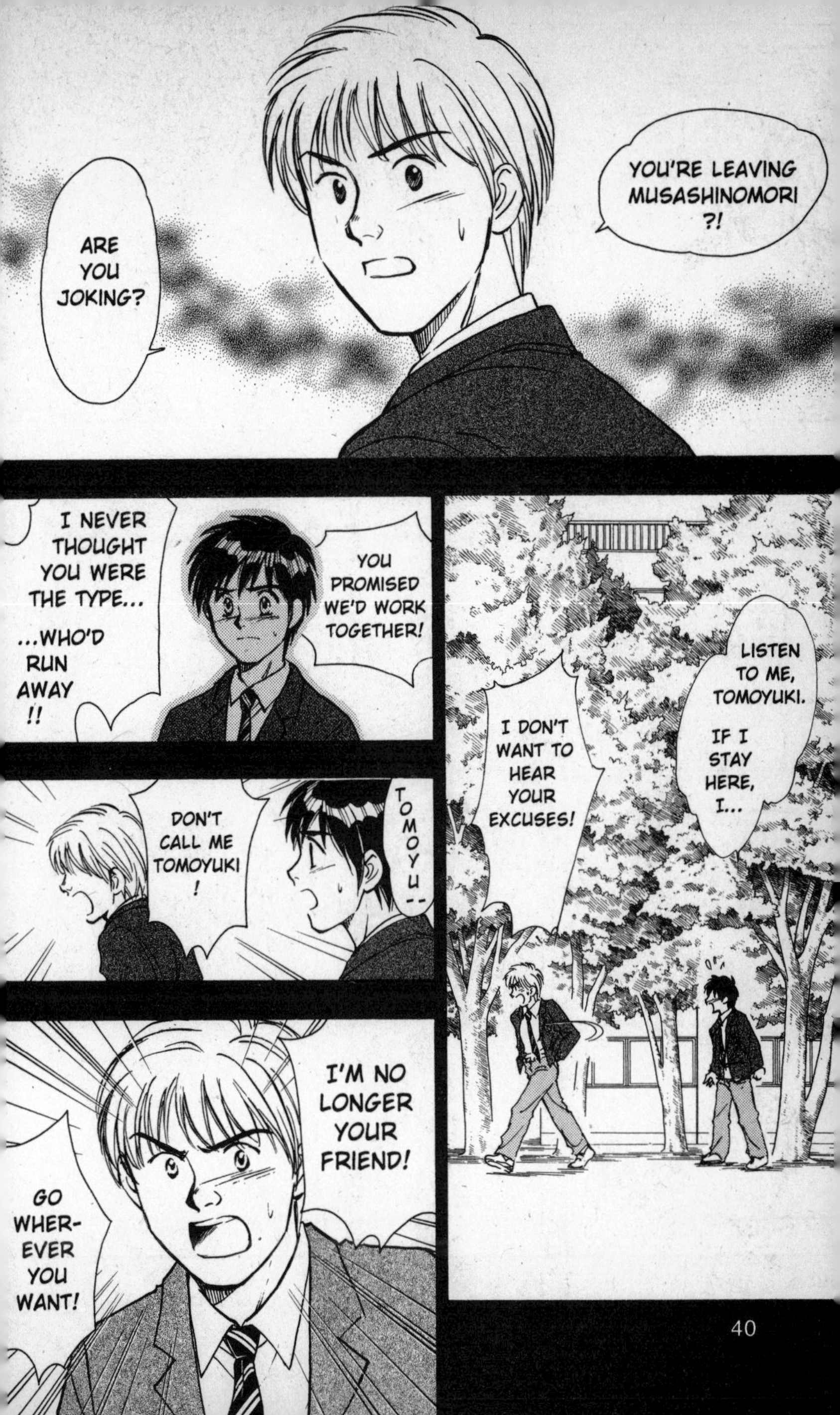
YOU'RE LEAVING MUSASHINOMORI ?!
ARE YOU JOKING?
LISTEN TO ME, TOMOYUKI.
IF I STAY HERE, I...
I DON'T WANT TO HEAR YOUR EXCUSES!
YOU PROMISED WE'D WORK TOGETHER!
I NEVER THOUGHT YOU WERE THE TYPE...
...WHO'D RUN AWAY !!
TOMOYU--
DON'T CALL ME TOMOYUKI !
I'M NO LONGER YOUR FRIEND!
GO WHER-EVER YOU WANT!

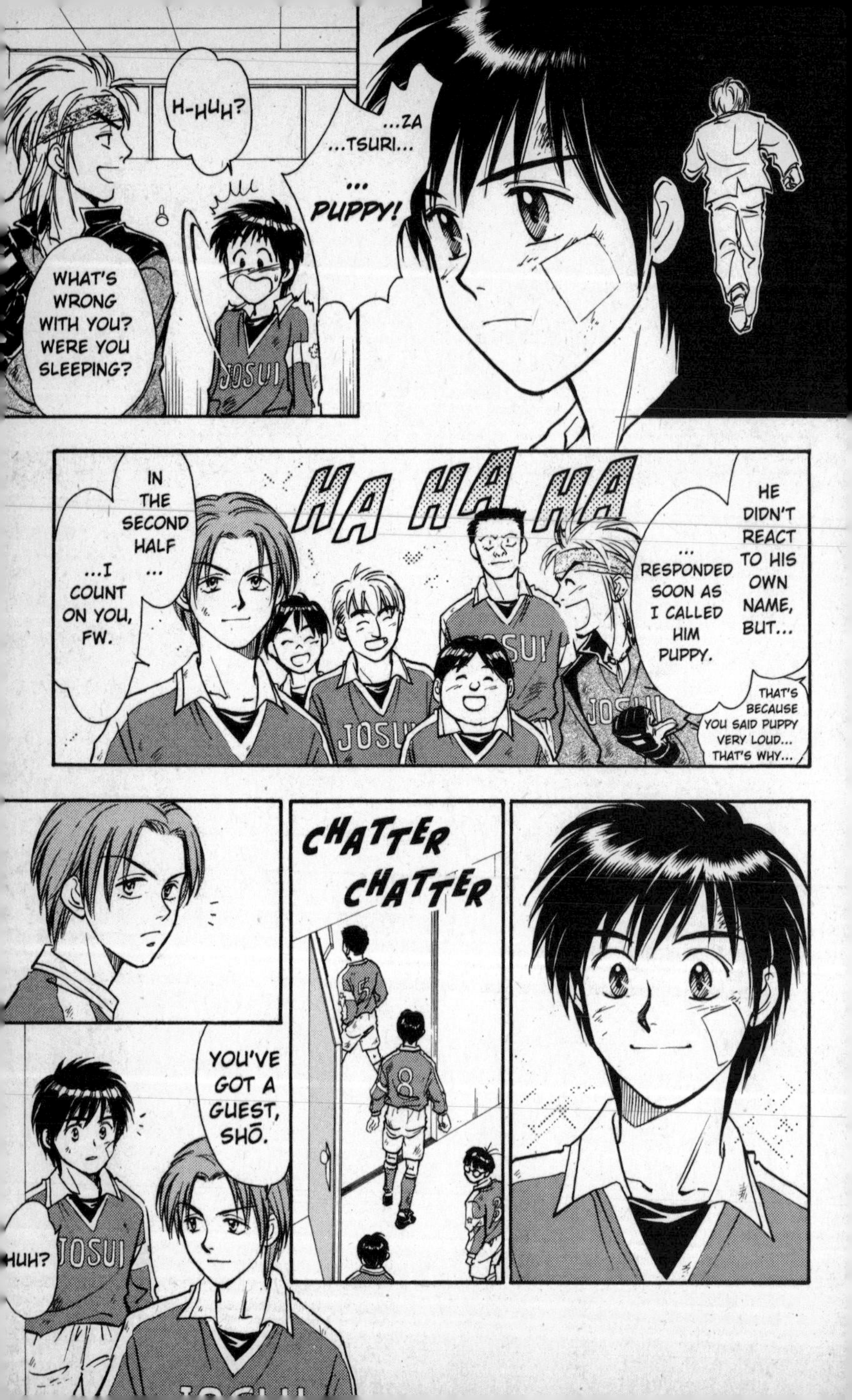
...ZA ...TSURI... ... PUPPY!
H-HUH?
WHAT'S WRONG WITH YOU? WERE YOU SLEEPING?
HA HA HA HA
HE DIDN'T REACT TO HIS OWN NAME, BUT...
...RESPONDED SOON AS I CALLED HIM PUPPY.
THAT'S BECAUSE YOU SAID PUPPY VERY LOUD... THAT'S WHY...
IN THE SECOND HALF ...
...I COUNT ON YOU, FW.
CHATTER CHATTER
YOU'VE GOT A GUEST, SHŌ.
HUH?

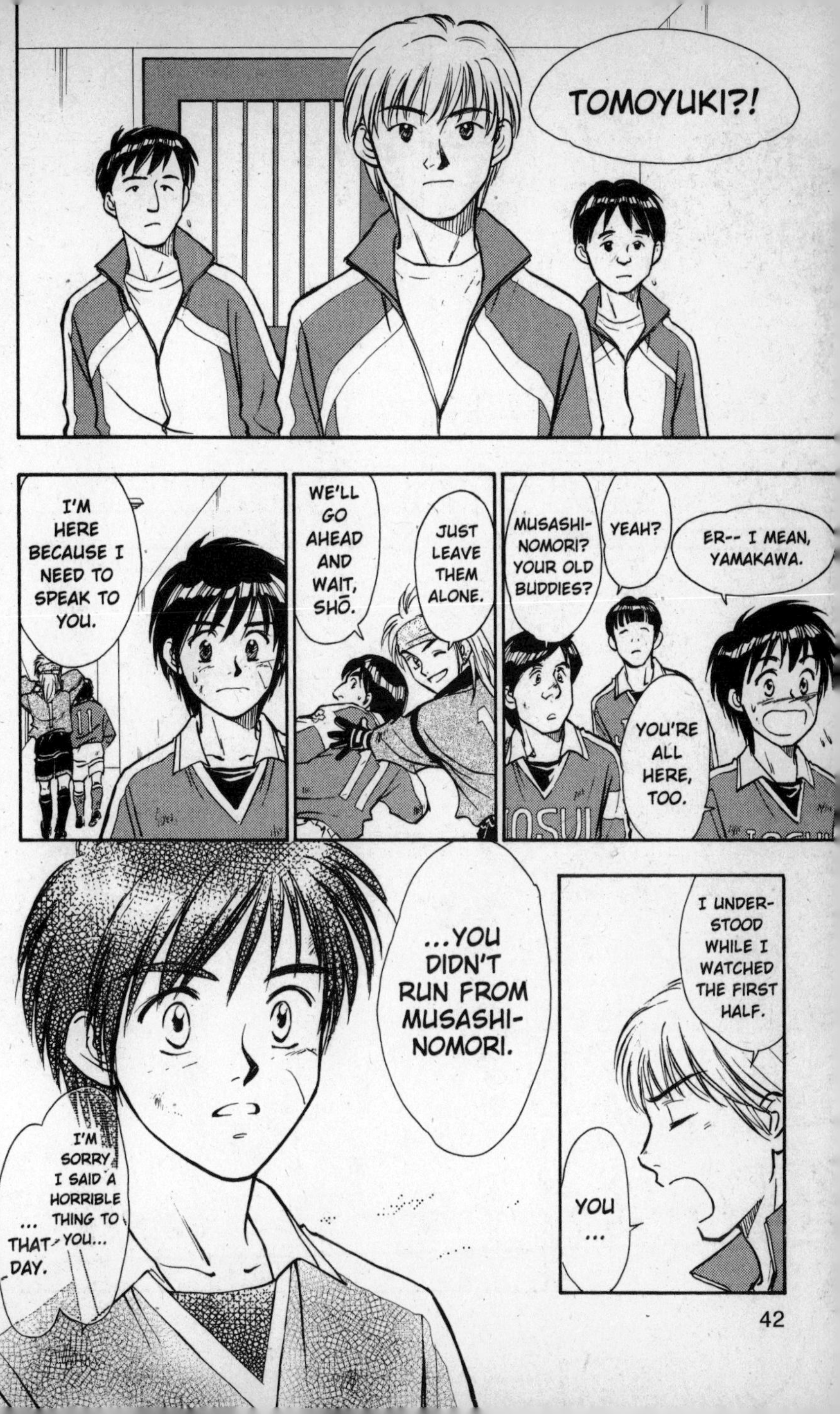
TOMOYUKI?!
ER-- I MEAN, YAMAKAWA.
YEAH?
MUSASHI-NOMORI? YOUR OLD BUDDIES?
YOU'RE ALL HERE, TOO.
JUST LEAVE THEM ALONE.
WE'LL GO AHEAD AND WAIT, SHŌ.
I'M HERE BECAUSE I NEED TO SPEAK TO YOU.
I UNDER-STOOD WHILE I WATCHED THE FIRST HALF.
YOU ...
...YOU DIDN'T RUN FROM MUSASHI-NOMORI.
I'M SORRY I SAID A HORRIBLE THING TO YOU... ...THAT DAY.

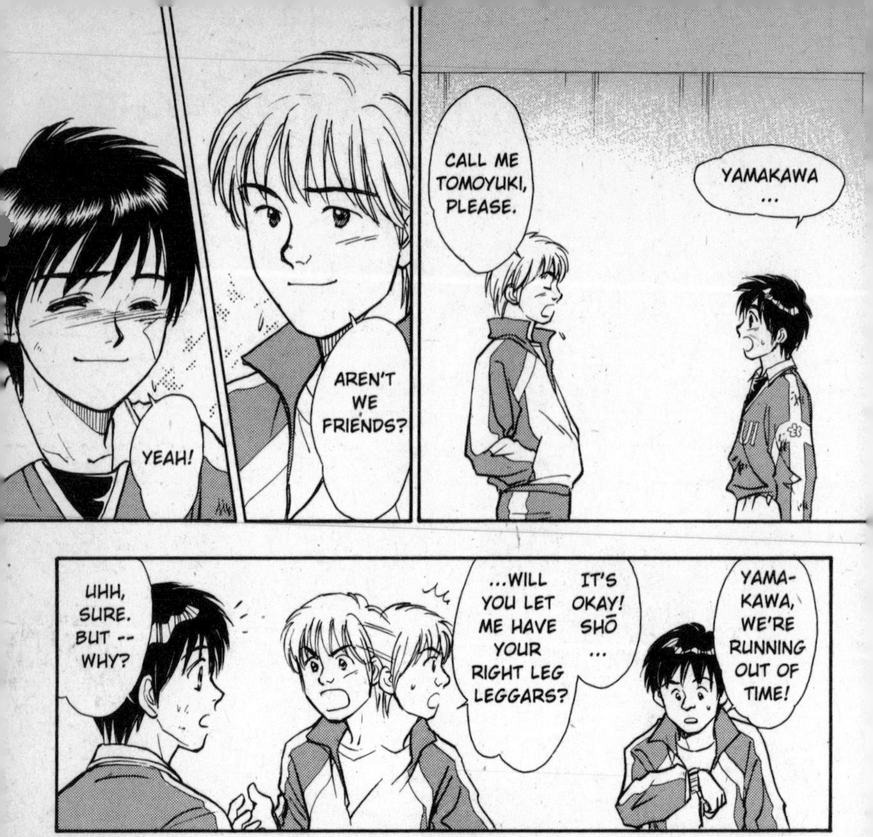
YAMAKAWA ...
CALL ME TOMOYUKI, PLEASE.
AREN'T WE FRIENDS?
YEAH!
YAMAKAWA, WE'RE RUNNING OUT OF TIME!
IT'S OKAY! SHŌ ...
...WILL YOU LET ME HAVE YOUR RIGHT LEG LEGGARS?
UHH, SURE. BUT -- WHY?

***NOTE:** LEGGARS IS A PROTECTIVE GEAR WORN UNDER THE STOCKING TO PROTECT THE LEG/SHIN.*

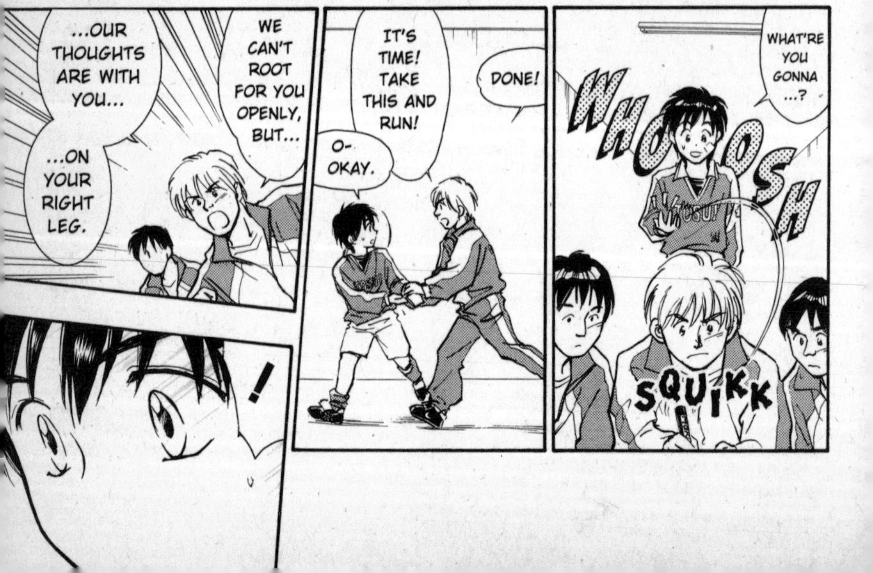
WHAT'RE YOU GONNA ...?
WHOOOSH
SQUIKK
DONE!
IT'S TIME! TAKE THIS AND RUN!
O-OKAY.
WE CAN'T ROOT FOR YOU OPENLY, BUT...
...OUR THOUGHTS ARE WITH YOU...
...ON YOUR RIGHT LEG.
!

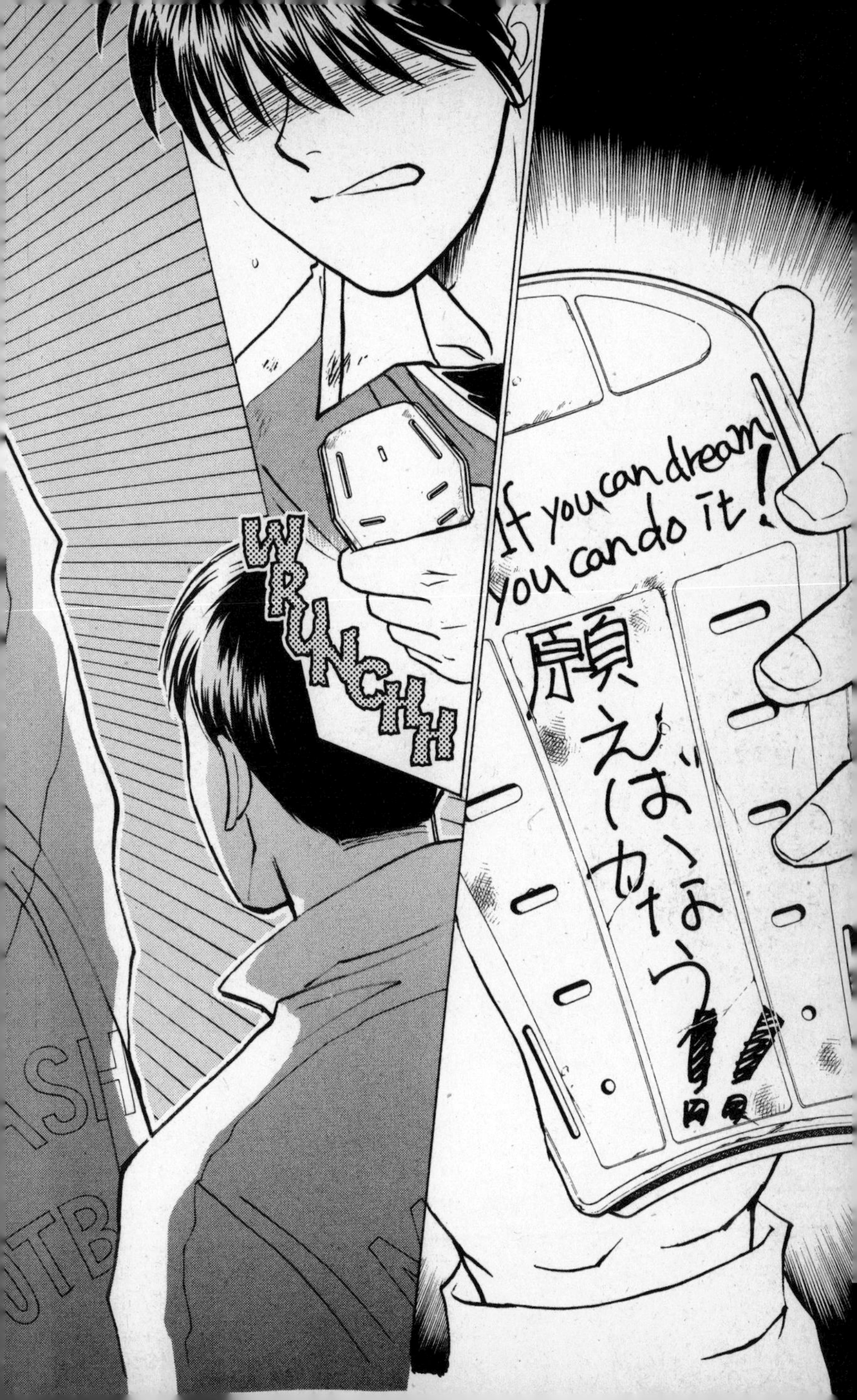
If you can dream you can do it!
願えばかなう!!
WRUNCHH

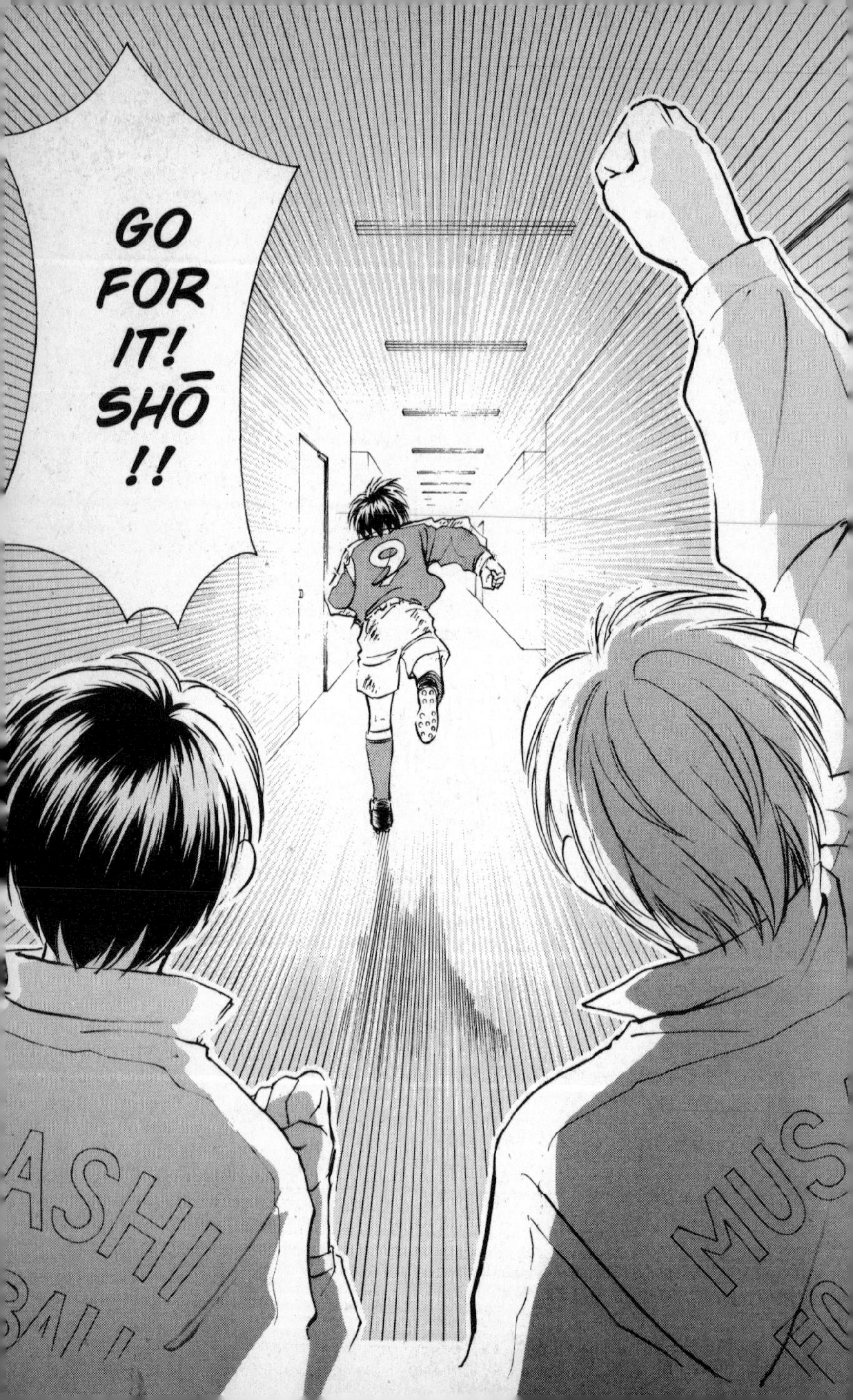
GO FOR IT! SHŌ!!

● MISCELLANEOUS FAMOUS PLAYS THAT I REMEMBER

NOVEMBER 3, 1992, AT THE HIROSHIMA BIG ARCH, THE JAPAN TEAM WAS PLAYING THE LAST MATCH AGAINST THE IRAQ TEAM. IT WAS DURING THE 10TH ASIAN SOCCER HIROSHIMA TOURNAMENT (ASIAN CUP), GROUP LEAGUE. PREPARING FOR THE OPENING OF J-LEAGUE, AND HOPING TO MAKE IT TO THE AMERICAN WORLD CUP, JAPAN INVITED HANS OFUTO TO COACH THE TEAM AT THE DYNASTY CUP, WHICH WAS HELD IN BEIJING (WHERE JAPAN, CHINA, SOUTH KOREA AND NORTH KOREA ATTENDED). THE JAPAN TEAM WON. THAT'S WHY THIS ASIAN CUP WAS AN IMPORTANT EVENT FOR THE JAPAN TEAM TO DEMONSTRATE TO THE JAPANESE FANS HOW STRONG THEY'D BECOME.

THE JAPAN TEAM'S OPPONENT AT THE GROUP LEAGUE WAS UAE (UNITED ARAB EMIRATE), NORTH KOREA AND IRAQ. TOP TWO TEAMS WILL BE ABLE TO MOVE ON TO THE SEMI-FINALS. THE JAPAN TEAM TIED WITH THE UAE TEAM AT THE FIRST MATCH, AND THE FOLLOWING MATCH WAS AGAINST THE NORTH KOREA TEAM. NORTH KOREA'S TEAM WAS CONSIDERED A LOWER LEVEL TEAM, AND YET THE JAPAN TEAM STRUGGLED AND ENDED UP WITH ANOTHER TIE. ALSO THAT DAY, THE JAPAN TEAM WAS TO MATCH AGAINST THE IRAQ TEAM. BECAUSE OF THE TWO PREVIOUS TIES, UNLESS THE JAPAN TEAM WON THIS MATCH, THEY WOULD NOT BE ABLE TO MOVE ON TO THE SEMI-FINALS, WHILE THE IRAQ TEAM, WHICH HAD A WIN AND A LOSS SO FAR, COULD MOVE ON TO THE SEMI-FINALS EVEN IF THEY TIED. TO TOP IT OFF, THE IRAQ TEAM WAS THE CHAMPION OF THE BEIJING ASIAN CUP IN 1990.

EVERYONE THOUGHT THAT "THE JAPAN TEAM MUST AT LEAST WIN ONCE AT AN EVENT HELD IN JAPAN. THEY MUST DEMONSTRATE HOW STRONG THE TEAM HAD BECOME."

HOWEVER, THE GAME MAKER MORAS WAS NOT IN GOOD CONDITION AND WAS EXCLUDED FROM THEIR STANDARD MEMBERS OF THE JAPAN TEAM. THE IRAQ TEAM SET UP HEAVY DEFENSES FROM THE GET-GO -- THE COUNTERING WAS THEIR STRATEGY. ALTHOUGH THE JAPAN TEAM HAD AN ABSOLUTE LEAD, THEY FAILED IN BREAKING THROUGH THE IRAQ DEFENSE. DURING THE SECOND HALF, AFTER ABOUT EIGHT MINUTES INTO THE GAME, ONE OF THE IRAQ PLAYERS WAS KICKED OUT OF THE GAME, LEAVING THE IRAQ TEAM WITH 10 PLAYERS. TWENTY-THREE MINUTES INTO THE GAME, COACH OFUTO MADE AN AGGRESSIVE MOVE. IN ADDITION TO YOSHIDA AND KITAZAWA, HE LET RAMOS AND NAKAYAMA PLAY. HOWEVER, THE IRAQ TEAM'S INTENTION WAS TO END THE GAME AS A TIE, AND THEY DEFENDED THEIR GOAL TIGHTLY. THE CLOCK SHOWED IT WAS PAST 40 MINUTES INTO THE SECOND HALF. AT THAT POINT, THE JAPAN TEAM KEPT ONLY TWO PLAYERS ON THEIR SIDE OF THE FIELD AND SENT HASHIRATANI AND IHARA, WHO WERE THE CENTER-BACKS, TO JOIN THEIR OFFENSES.

IT HAPPENED WHEN IT HIT 42 MINUTES MARK. IHARA, WHO RECEIVED THE PASS FROM RAMOS, MADE A THROUGH PASS TO KAZU. KAZU, WHO PULLED OUT FROM THE EDGE OF THE OFF-SIDE, KICKED THE BALL HARD USING HIS RIGHT LEG DESPITE THE DIFFICULT ANGLE. THAT KICK LED THE TEAM TO VICTORY. AT THE INTERVIEW AFTER THE GAME, KAZU SAID, "I PLACED MY SOUL IN THAT BALL." THEREAFTER, JAPAN DEFEATED CHINA AND UAE, SEIZING THE SHINING POSITION AS THE NO. 1 ASIAN TEAM.

--TATSUYA WATANABE (WINNING RUN)

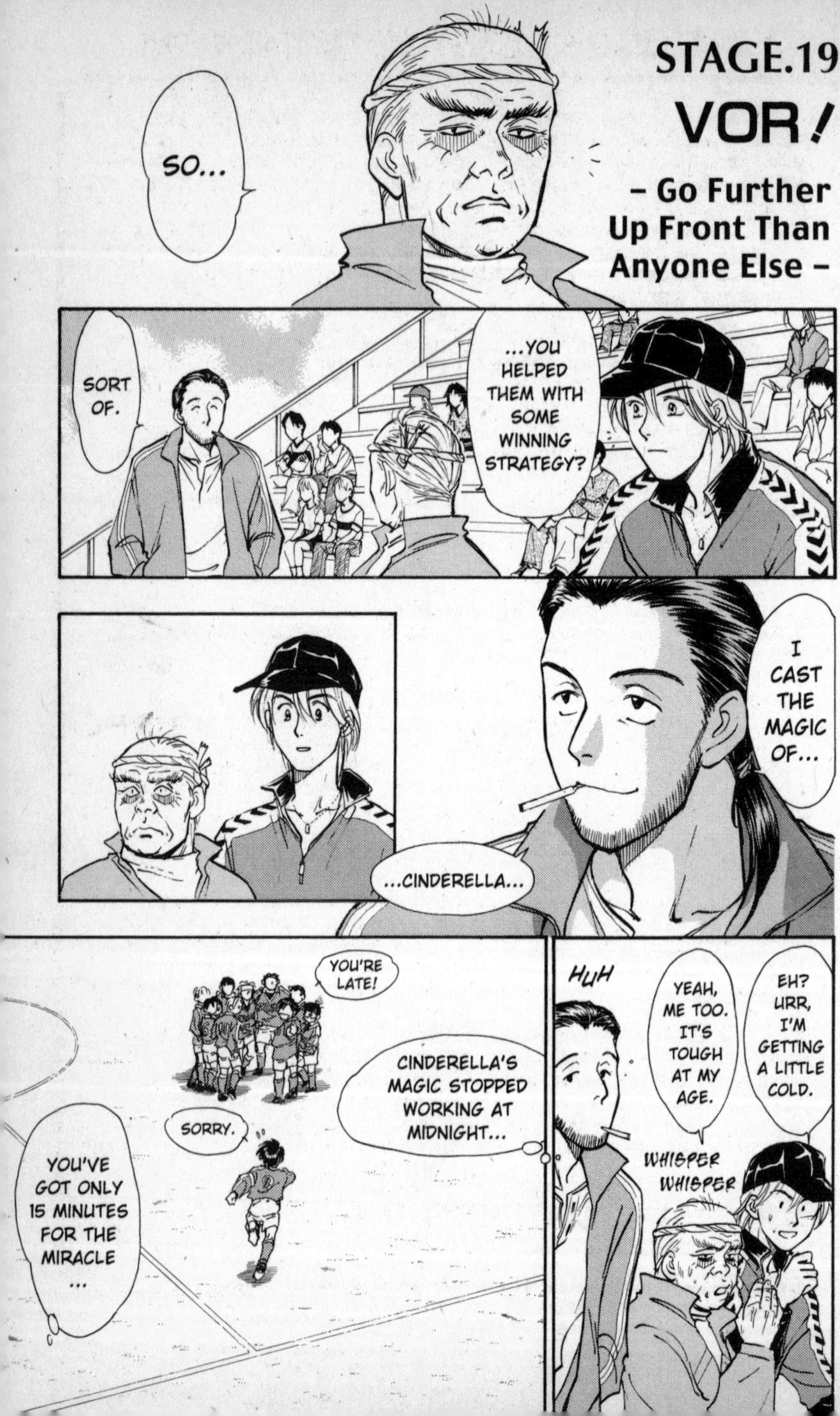
STAGE.19
VOR!
- Go Further Up Front Than Anyone Else -
SO...
...YOU HELPED THEM WITH SOME WINNING STRATEGY?
SORT OF.
I CAST THE MAGIC OF...
...CINDERELLA...
EH? URR, I'M GETTING A LITTLE COLD.
YEAH, ME TOO. IT'S TOUGH AT MY AGE.
HUH
WHISPER WHISPER
YOU'RE LATE!
CINDERELLA'S MAGIC STOPPED WORKING AT MIDNIGHT...
SORRY.
YOU'VE GOT ONLY 15 MINUTES FOR THE MIRACLE ...

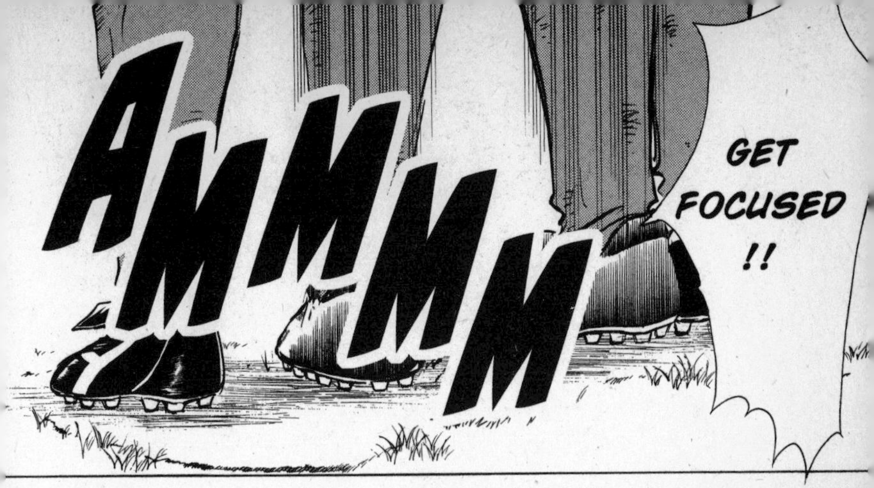
GET FOCUSED !!
AMMMM

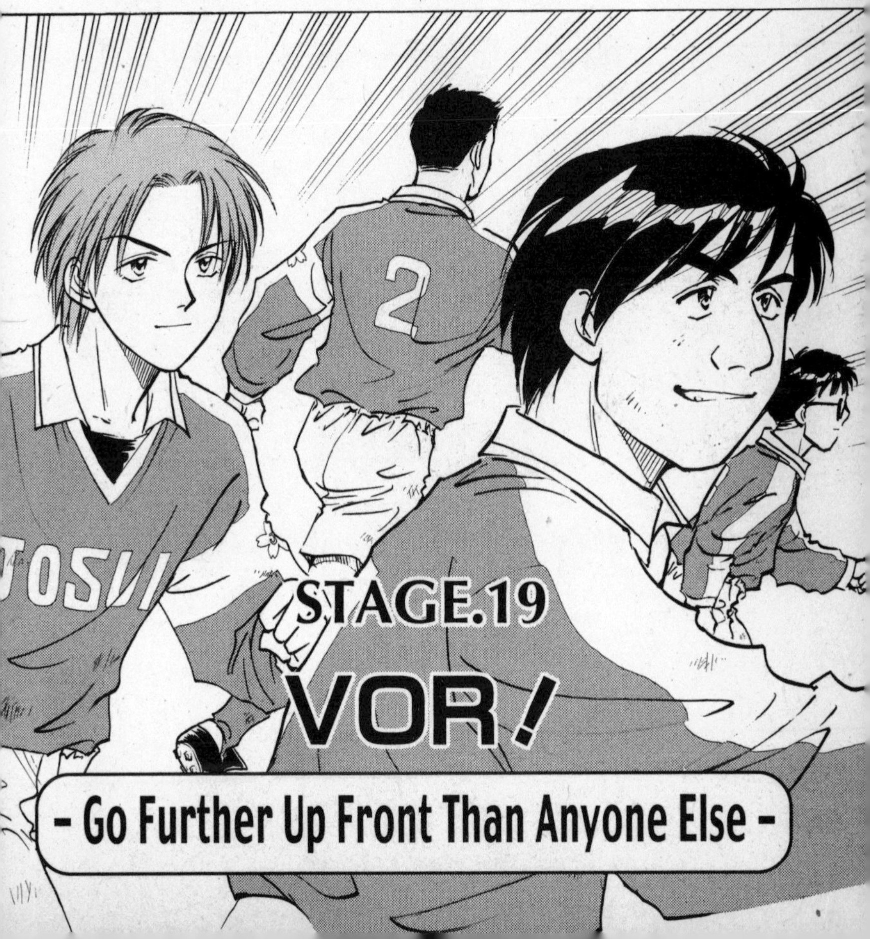

STAGE.19

VOR!

- Go Further Up Front Than Anyone Else -

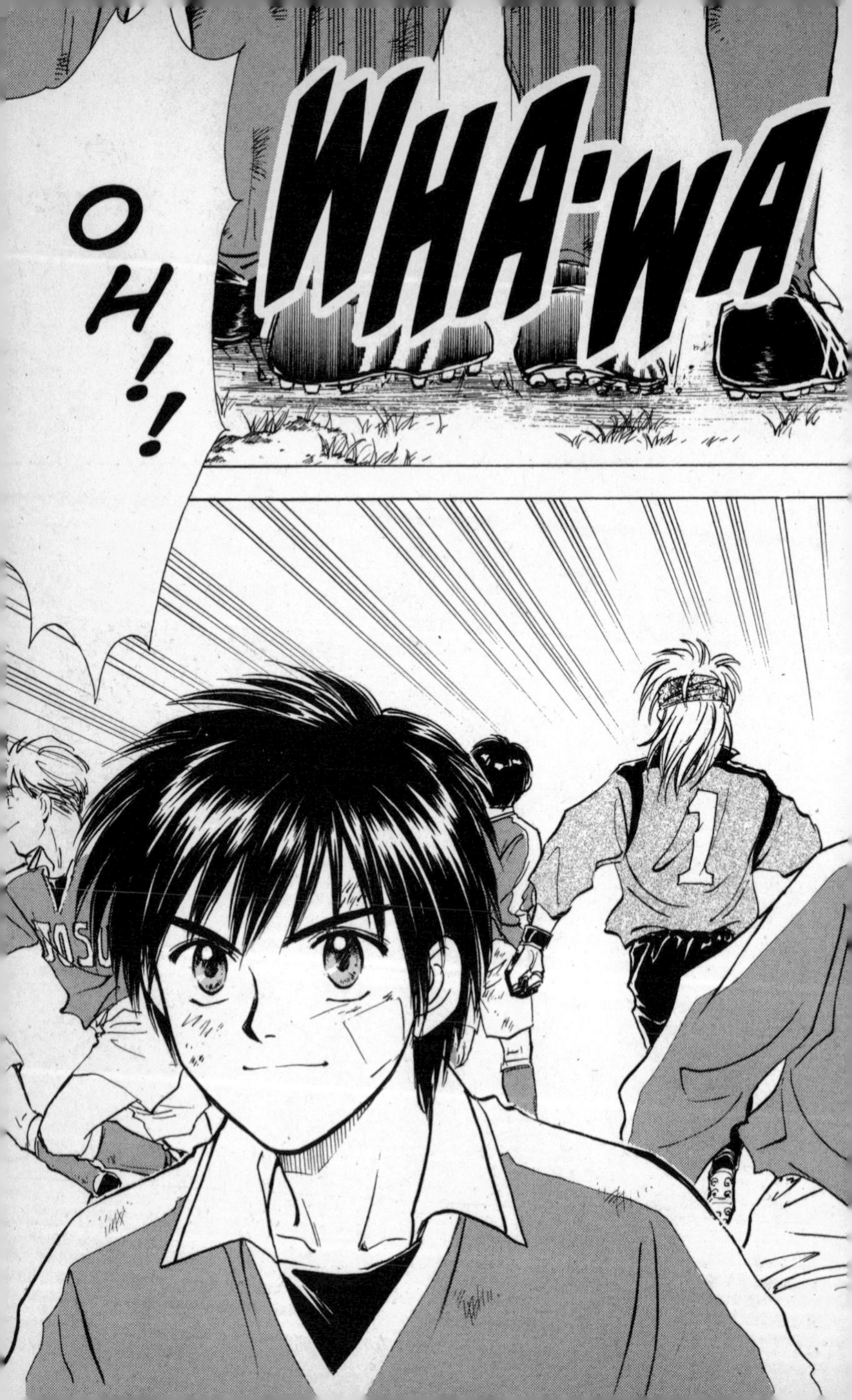
WHA-WA
OH!!

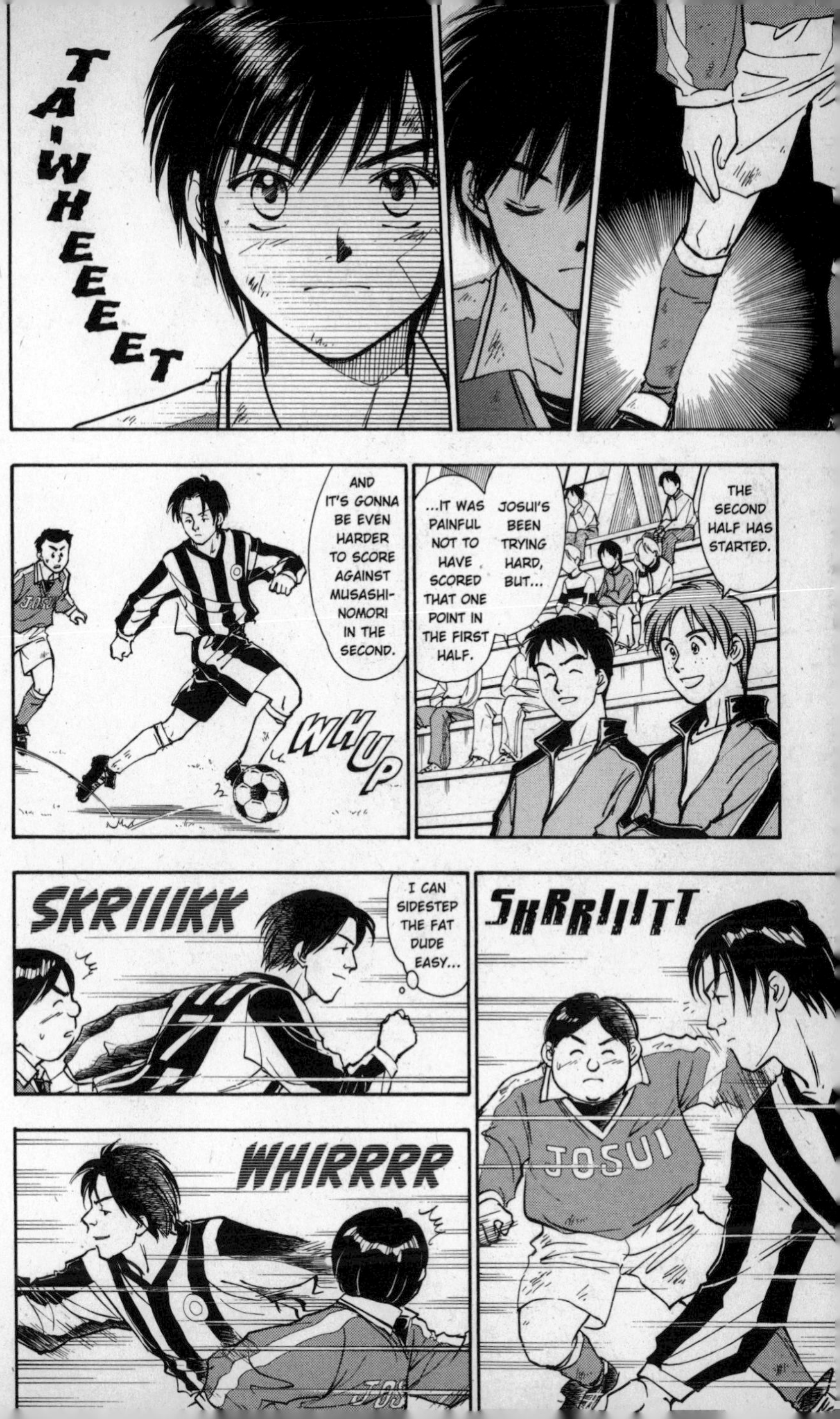

TAIWHEEEET
THE SECOND HALF HAS STARTED.
JOSUI'S BEEN TRYING HARD, BUT...
...IT WAS PAINFUL NOT TO HAVE SCORED THAT ONE POINT IN THE FIRST HALF.
AND IT'S GONNA BE EVEN HARDER TO SCORE AGAINST MUSASHI-NOMORI IN THE SECOND.
WHUP
SKRRIIITT
JOSUI
SKRIIIKK
I CAN SIDESTEP THE FAT DUDE EASY...
WHIRRRR

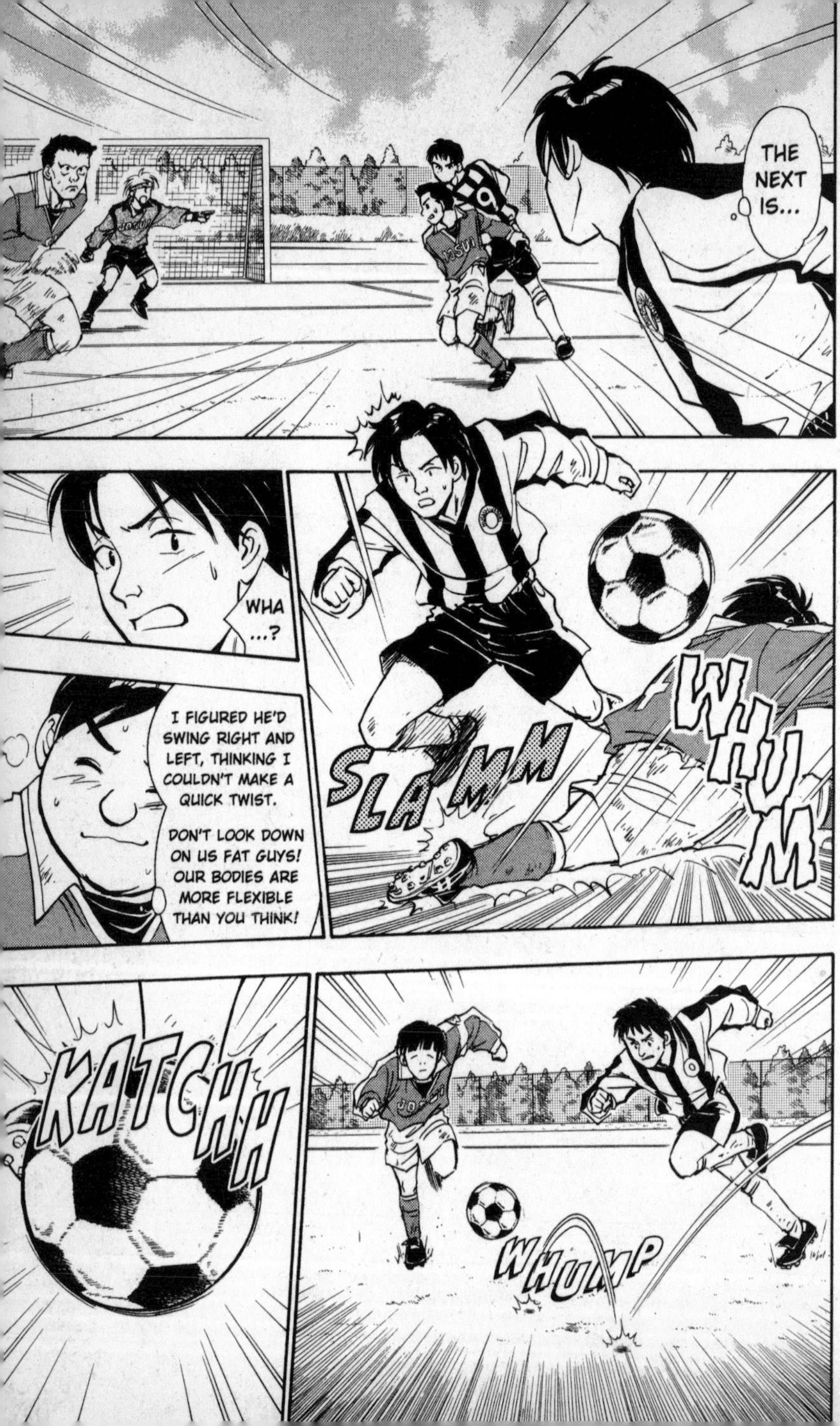
THE NEXT IS...
WHUMM
SLAMM
WHA ...?
I FIGURED HE'D SWING RIGHT AND LEFT, THINKING I COULDN'T MAKE A QUICK TWIST.
DON'T LOOK DOWN ON US FAT GUYS! OUR BODIES ARE MORE FLEXIBLE THAN YOU THINK!
WHUMP
KATCHH

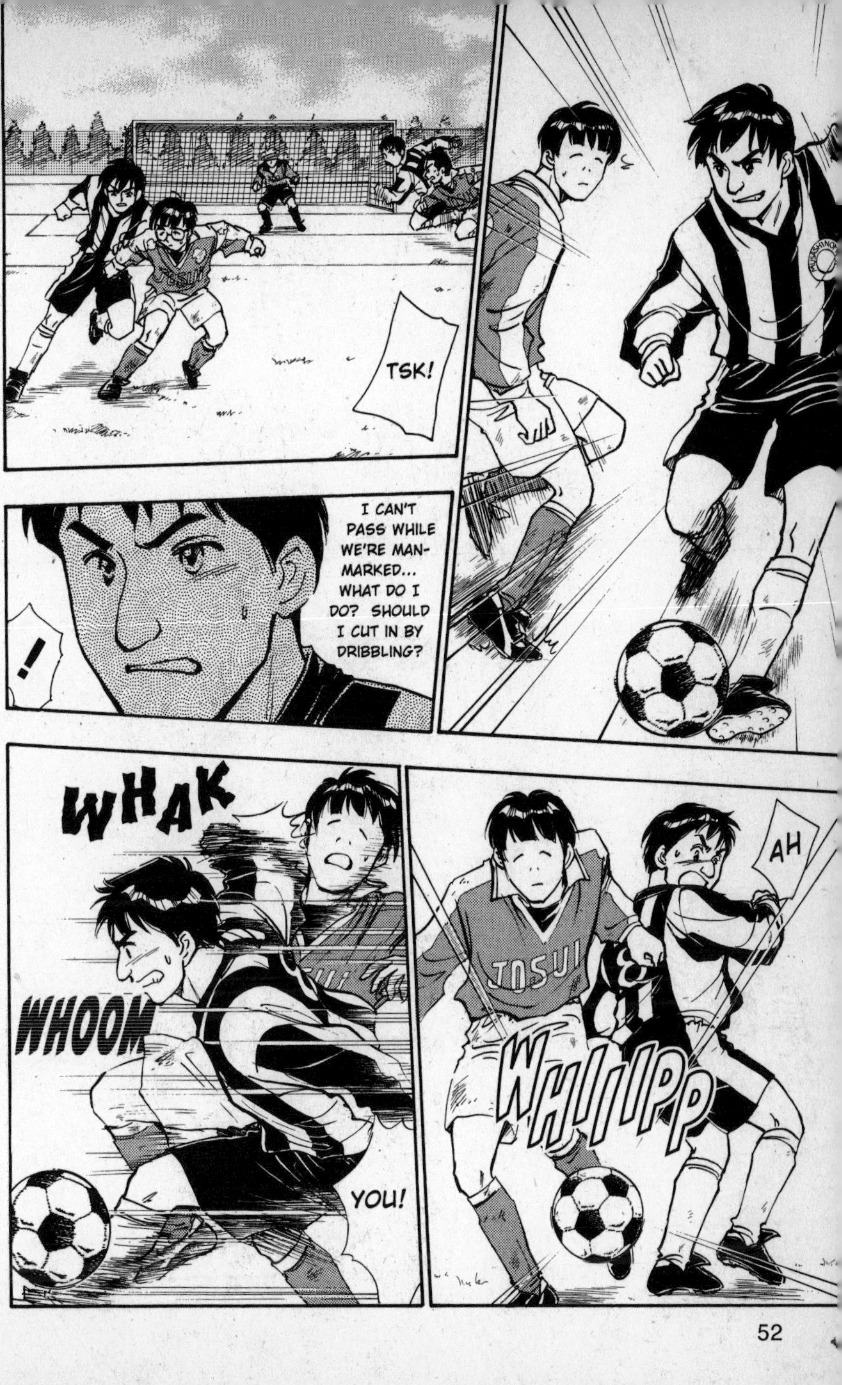
TSK!
I CAN'T PASS WHILE WE'RE MAN-MARKED... WHAT DO I DO? SHOULD I CUT IN BY DRIBBLING?
!
AH
WHIIIPP
WHAK
WHOOM
YOU!

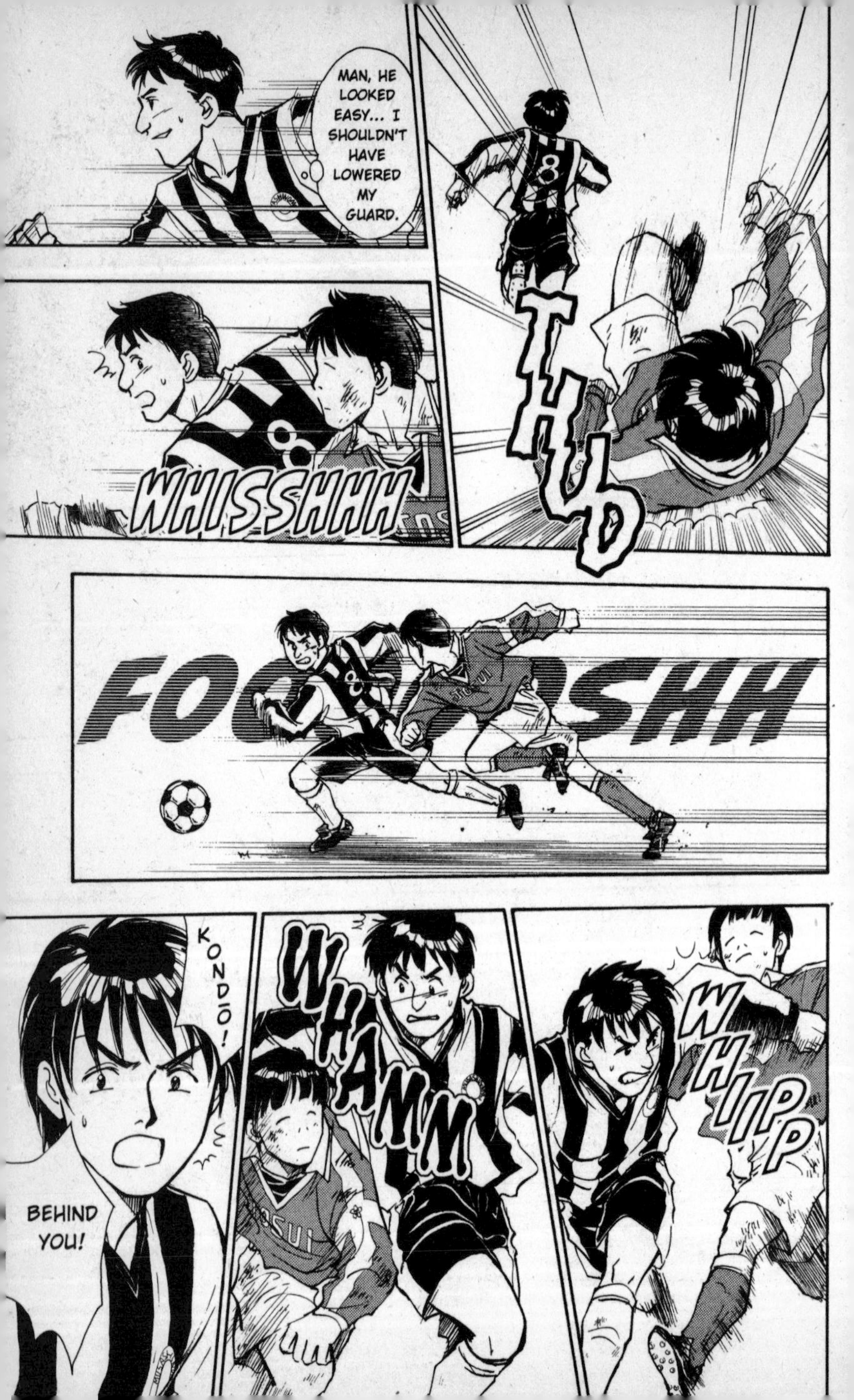
THUD
MAN, HE LOOKED EASY... I SHOULDN'T HAVE LOWERED MY GUARD.
WHISSHHH
WHIPP
WHAMM
KONDŌ!
BEHIND YOU!

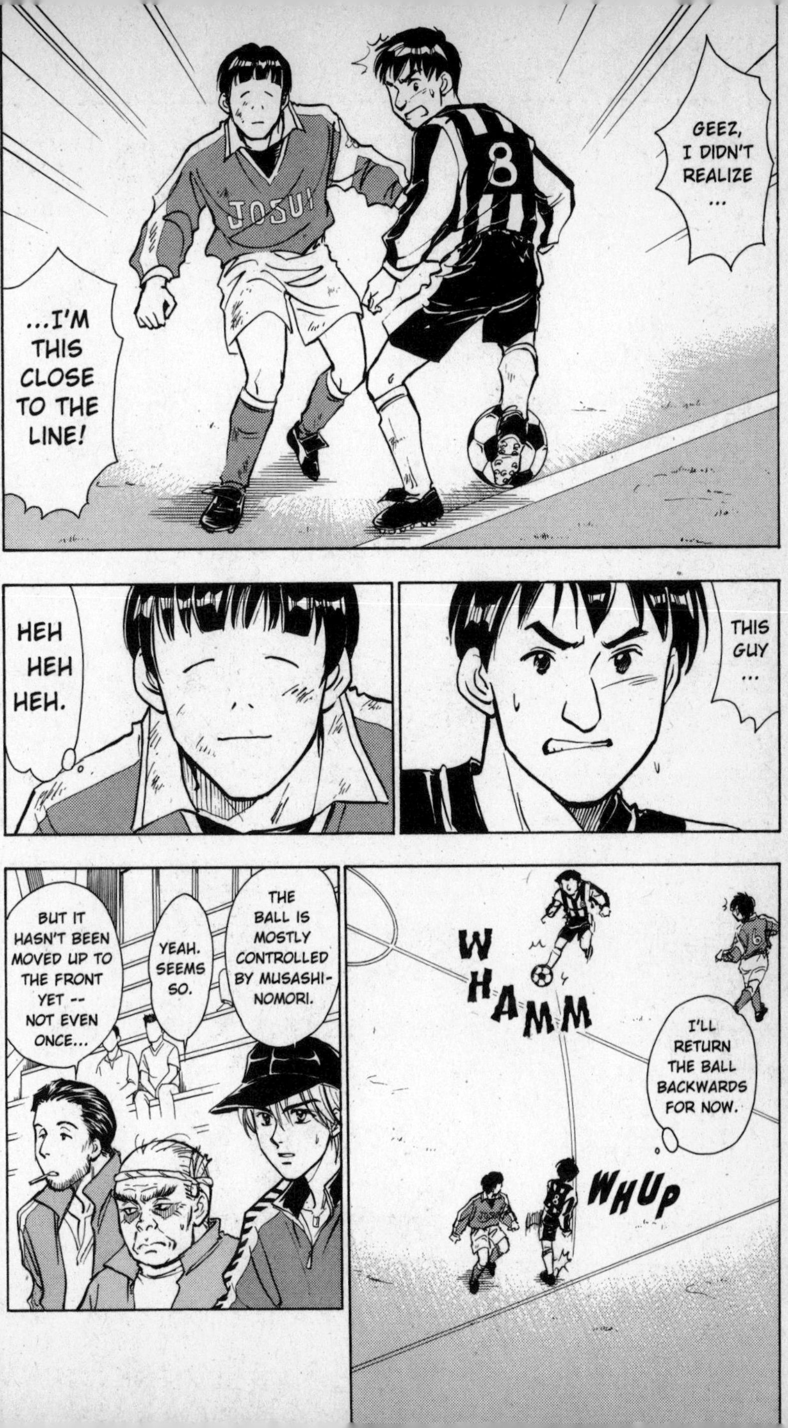
GEEZ, I DIDN'T REALIZE ...
...I'M THIS CLOSE TO THE LINE!
THIS GUY ...
HEH HEH HEH.
WHAMM
I'LL RETURN THE BALL BACKWARDS FOR NOW.
WHUP
THE BALL IS MOSTLY CONTROLLED BY MUSASHI-NOMORI.
YEAH. SEEMS SO.
BUT IT HASN'T BEEN MOVED UP TO THE FRONT YET -- NOT EVEN ONCE...

READ THIS WAY

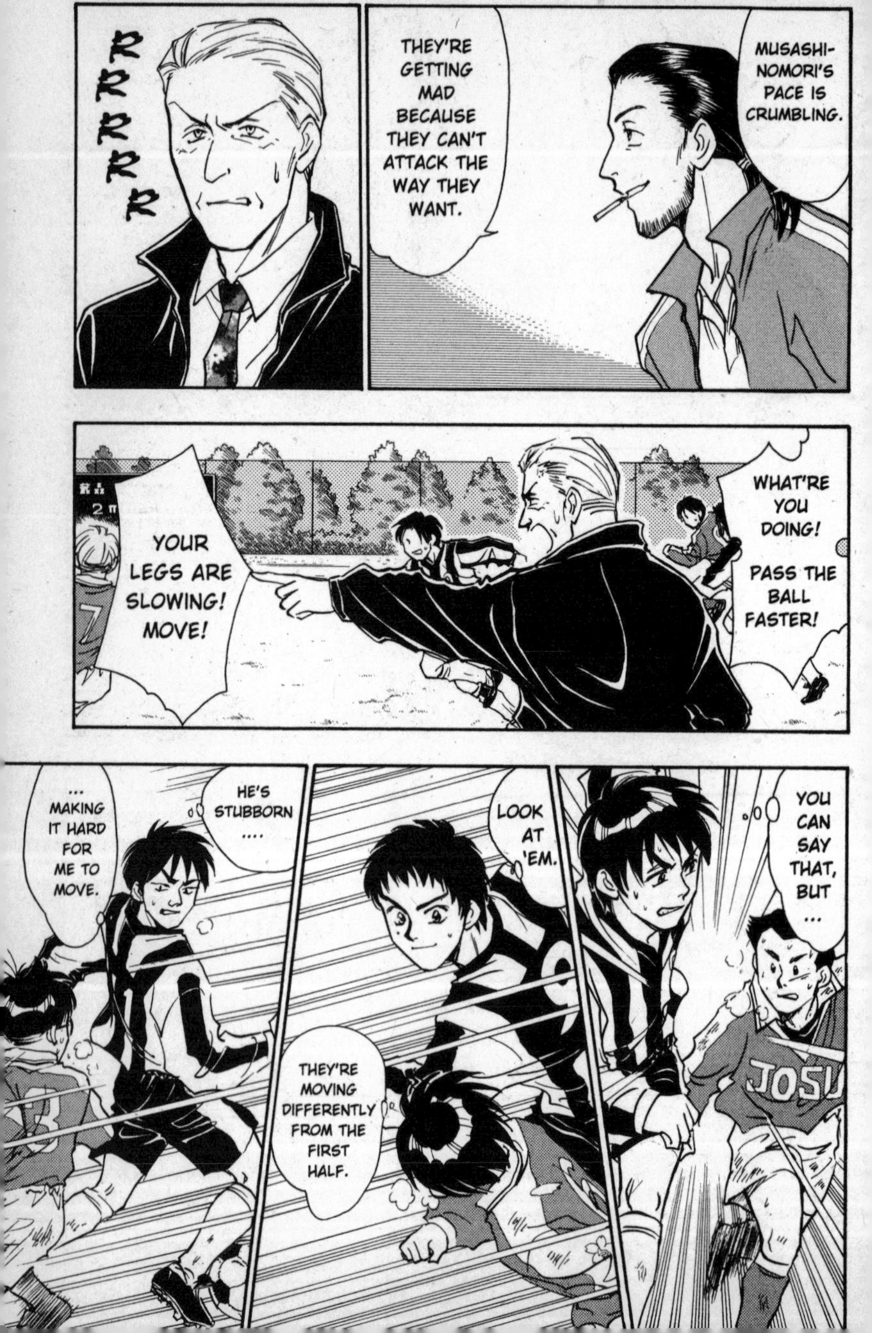
MUSASHI-NOMORI'S PACE IS CRUMBLING.
THEY'RE GETTING MAD BECAUSE THEY CAN'T ATTACK THE WAY THEY WANT.
RRRRR
WHAT'RE YOU DOING! PASS THE BALL FASTER!
YOUR LEGS ARE SLOWING! MOVE!
YOU CAN SAY THAT, BUT ...
LOOK AT 'EM.
THEY'RE MOVING DIFFERENTLY FROM THE FIRST HALF.
HE'S STUBBORN ....
... MAKING IT HARD FOR ME TO MOVE.
JOSU

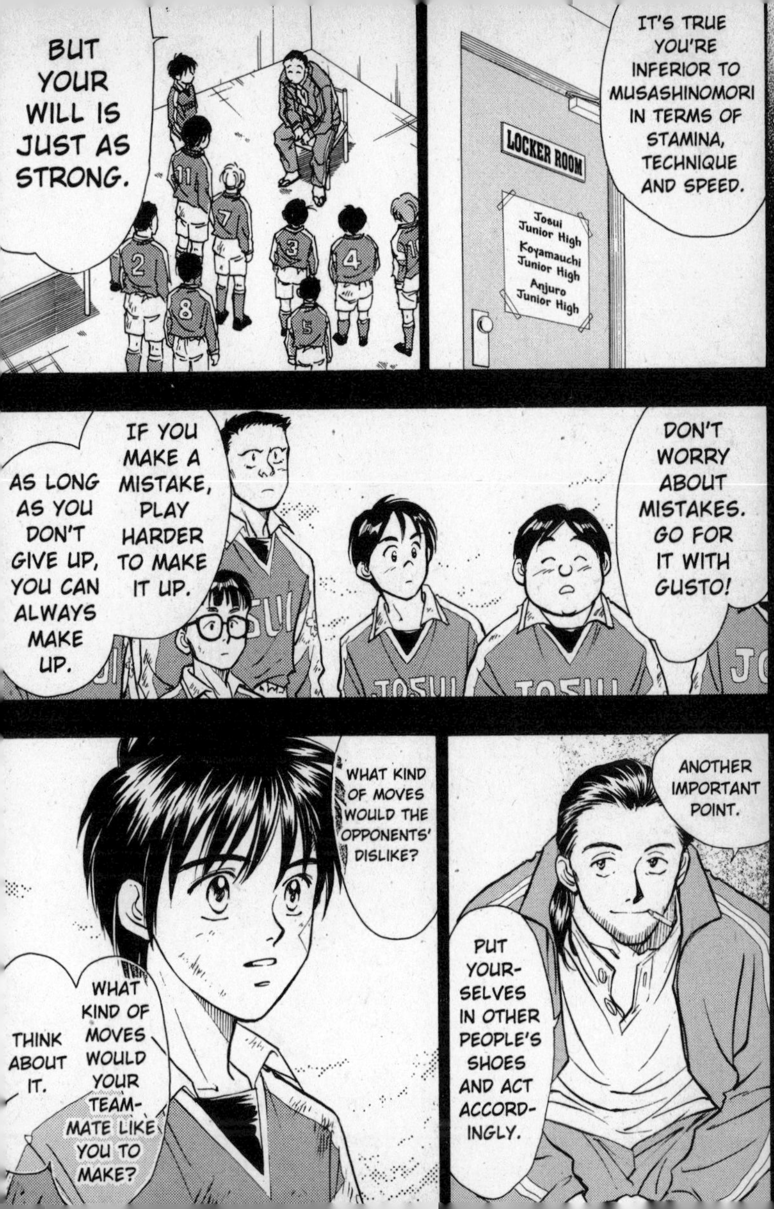
IT'S TRUE YOU'RE INFERIOR TO MUSASHINOMORI IN TERMS OF STAMINA, TECHNIQUE AND SPEED.
LOCKER ROOM
Josui Junior High
Koyamauchi Junior High
Anjuro Junior High
BUT YOUR WILL IS JUST AS STRONG.
DON'T WORRY ABOUT MISTAKES. GO FOR IT WITH GUSTO!
IF YOU MAKE A MISTAKE, PLAY HARDER TO MAKE IT UP.
AS LONG AS YOU DON'T GIVE UP, YOU CAN ALWAYS MAKE UP.
ANOTHER IMPORTANT POINT.
PUT YOURSELVES IN OTHER PEOPLE'S SHOES AND ACT ACCORDINGLY.
WHAT KIND OF MOVES WOULD THE OPPONENTS' DISLIKE?
WHAT KIND OF MOVES WOULD YOUR TEAMMATE LIKE YOU TO MAKE?
THINK ABOUT IT.

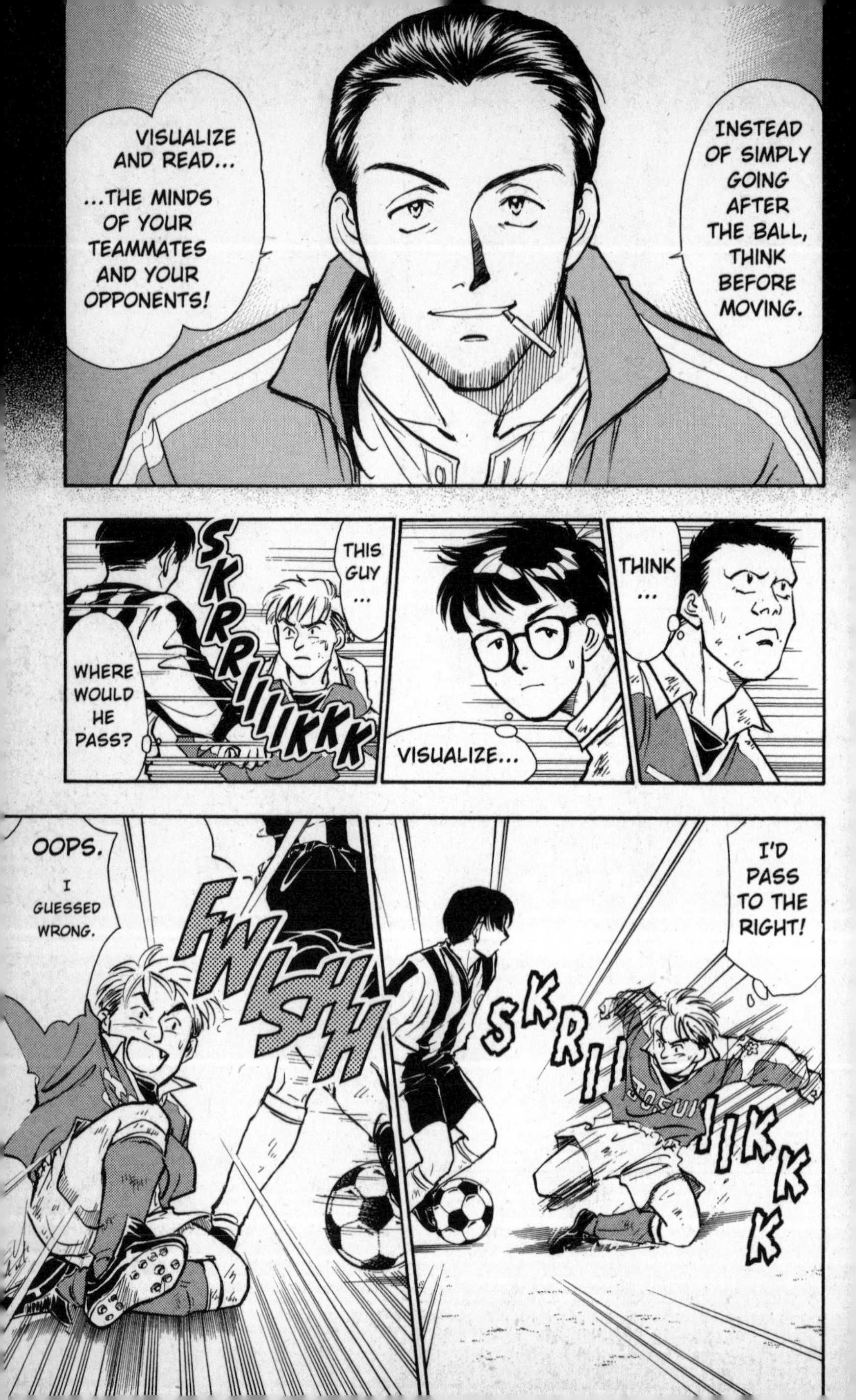
INSTEAD OF SIMPLY GOING AFTER THE BALL, THINK BEFORE MOVING.
VISUALIZE AND READ...
...THE MINDS OF YOUR TEAMMATES AND YOUR OPPONENTS!
THINK ...
VISUALIZE...
THIS GUY ...
SKRRIIIIIKKK
WHERE WOULD HE PASS?
I'D PASS TO THE RIGHT!
SKRIIIKKK
OOPS.
I GUESSED WRONG.
FWISH

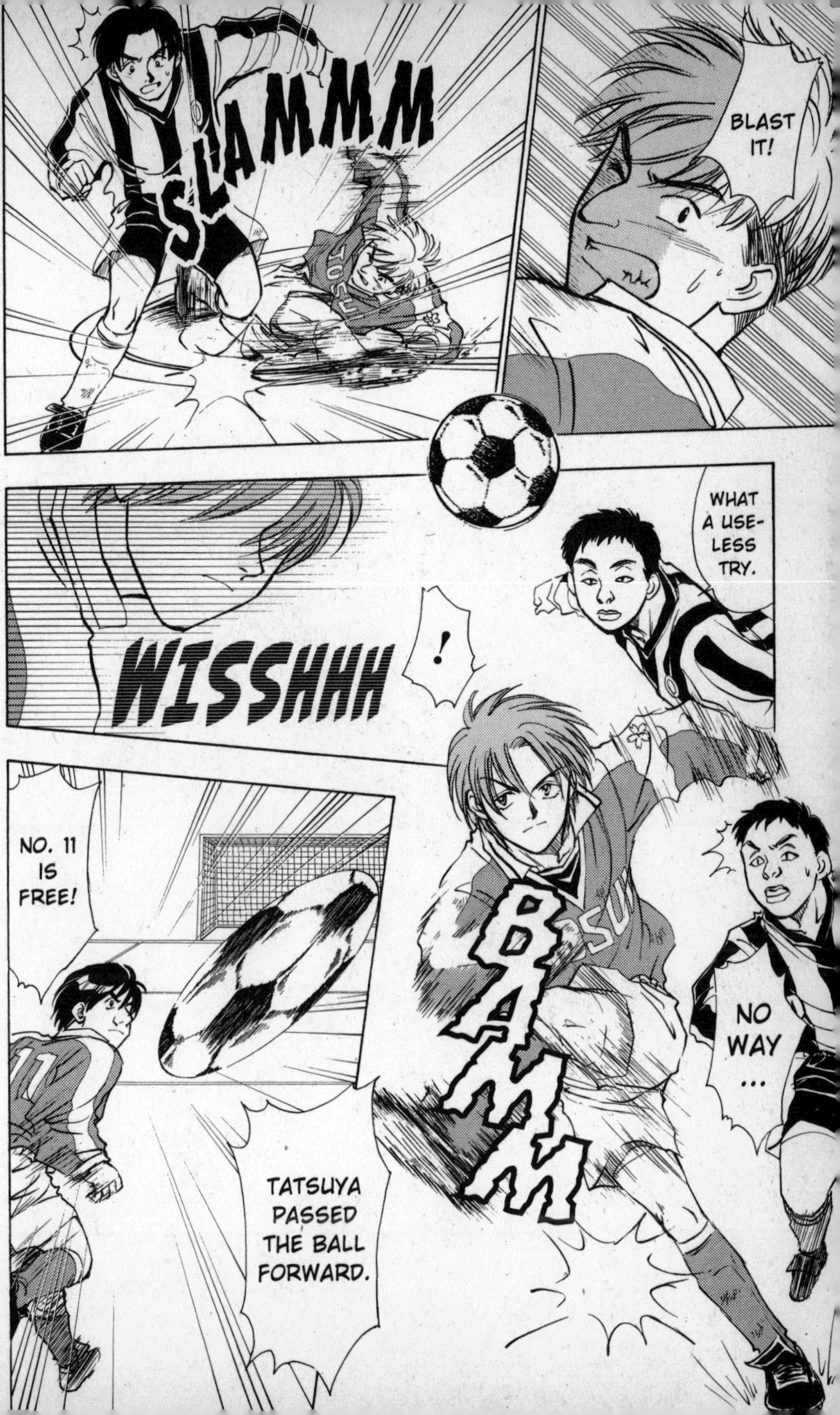
BLAST IT!
SLAMMM
WHAT A USE-LESS TRY.
!
NO WAY ...
BAMM
WISSHHH
NO. 11 IS FREE!
TATSUYA PASSED THE BALL FORWARD.

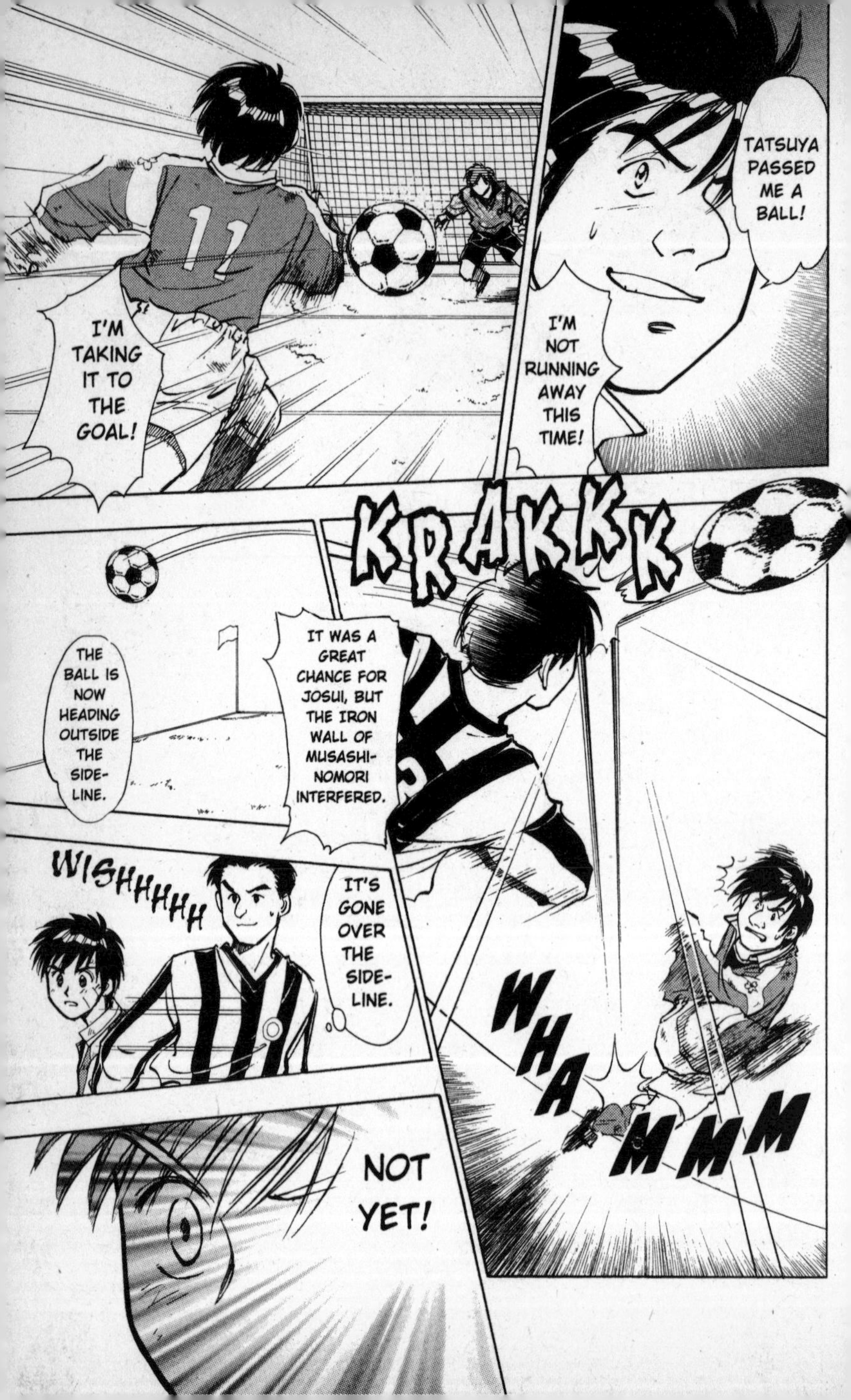
TATSUYA PASSED ME A BALL!
I'M NOT RUNNING AWAY THIS TIME!
I'M TAKING IT TO THE GOAL!
KRAKKK
WHAMMM
IT WAS A GREAT CHANCE FOR JOSUI, BUT THE IRON WALL OF MUSASHI-NOMORI INTERFERED.
THE BALL IS NOW HEADING OUTSIDE THE SIDE-LINE.
WISHHHHHH
IT'S GONE OVER THE SIDE-LINE.
NOT YET!

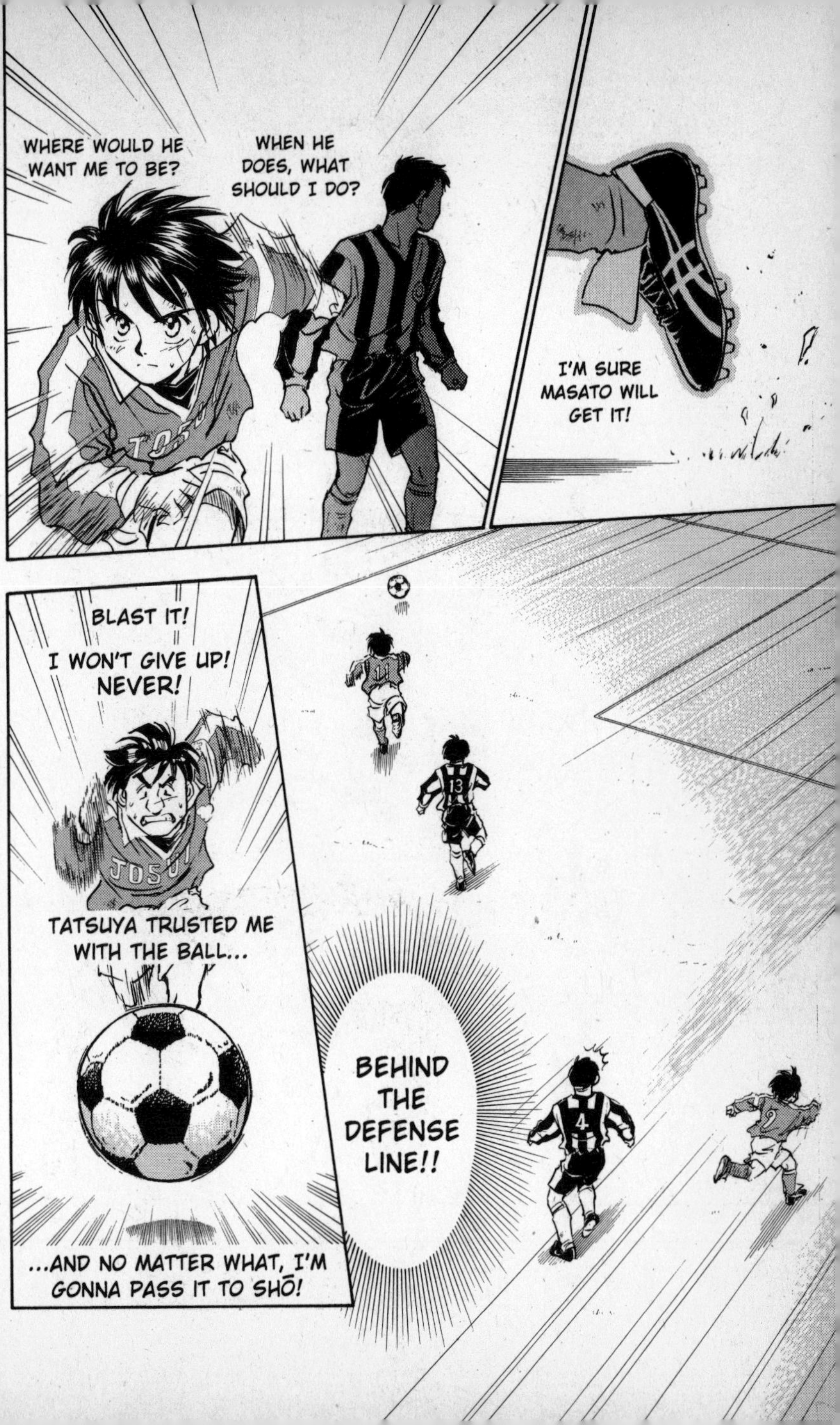
I'M SURE MASATO WILL GET IT!
WHEN HE DOES, WHAT SHOULD I DO?
WHERE WOULD HE WANT ME TO BE?
JOSUI
BEHIND THE DEFENSE LINE!!
BLAST IT!
I WON'T GIVE UP! NEVER!
JOSUI
TATSUYA TRUSTED ME WITH THE BALL...
...AND NO MATTER WHAT, I'M GONNA PASS IT TO SHŌ!

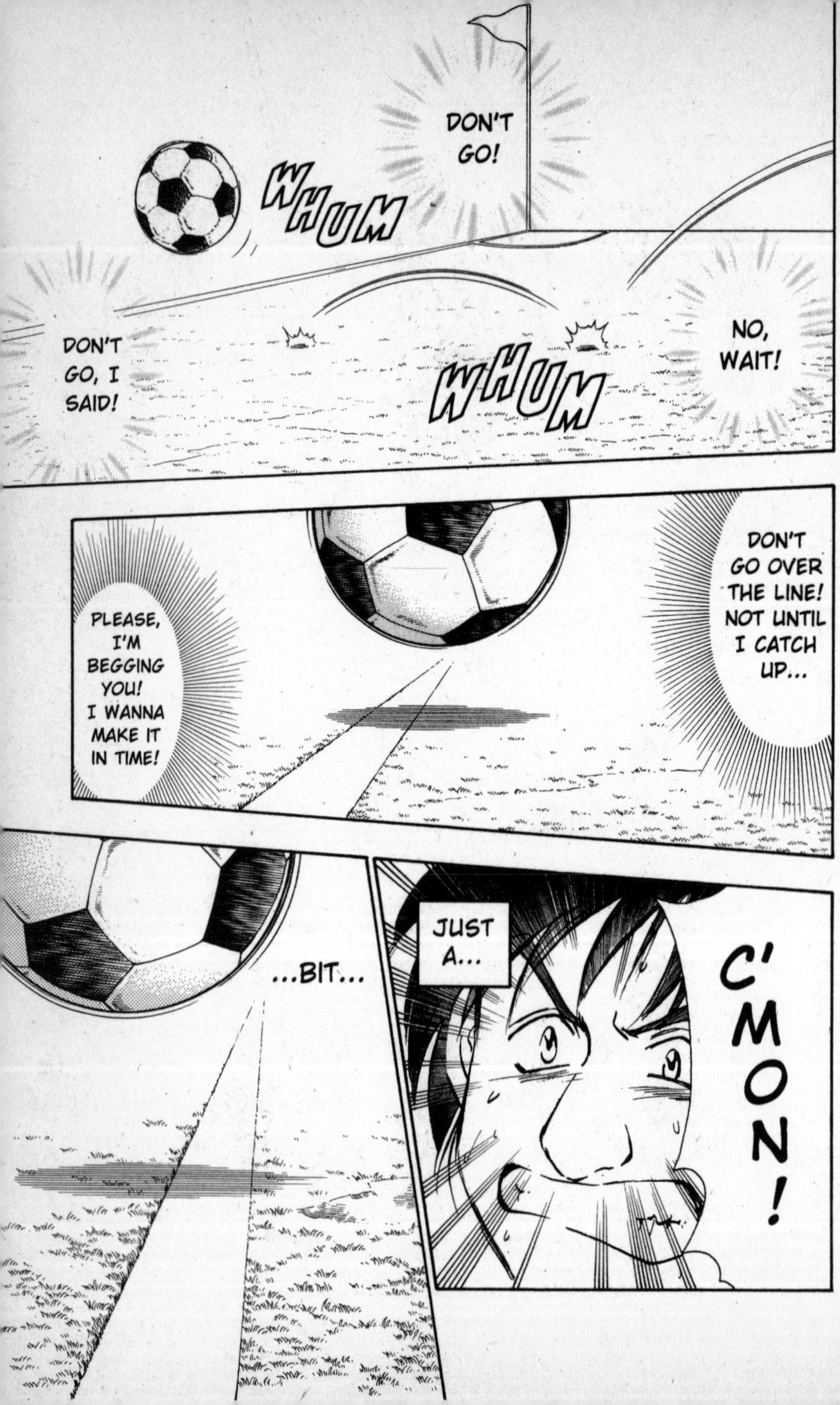
DON'T GO!
WHUM
NO, WAIT!
WHUM
DON'T GO, I SAID!
DON'T GO OVER THE LINE! NOT UNTIL I CATCH UP...
PLEASE, I'M BEGGING YOU! I WANNA MAKE IT IN TIME!
JUST A...
C'MON!
...BIT...

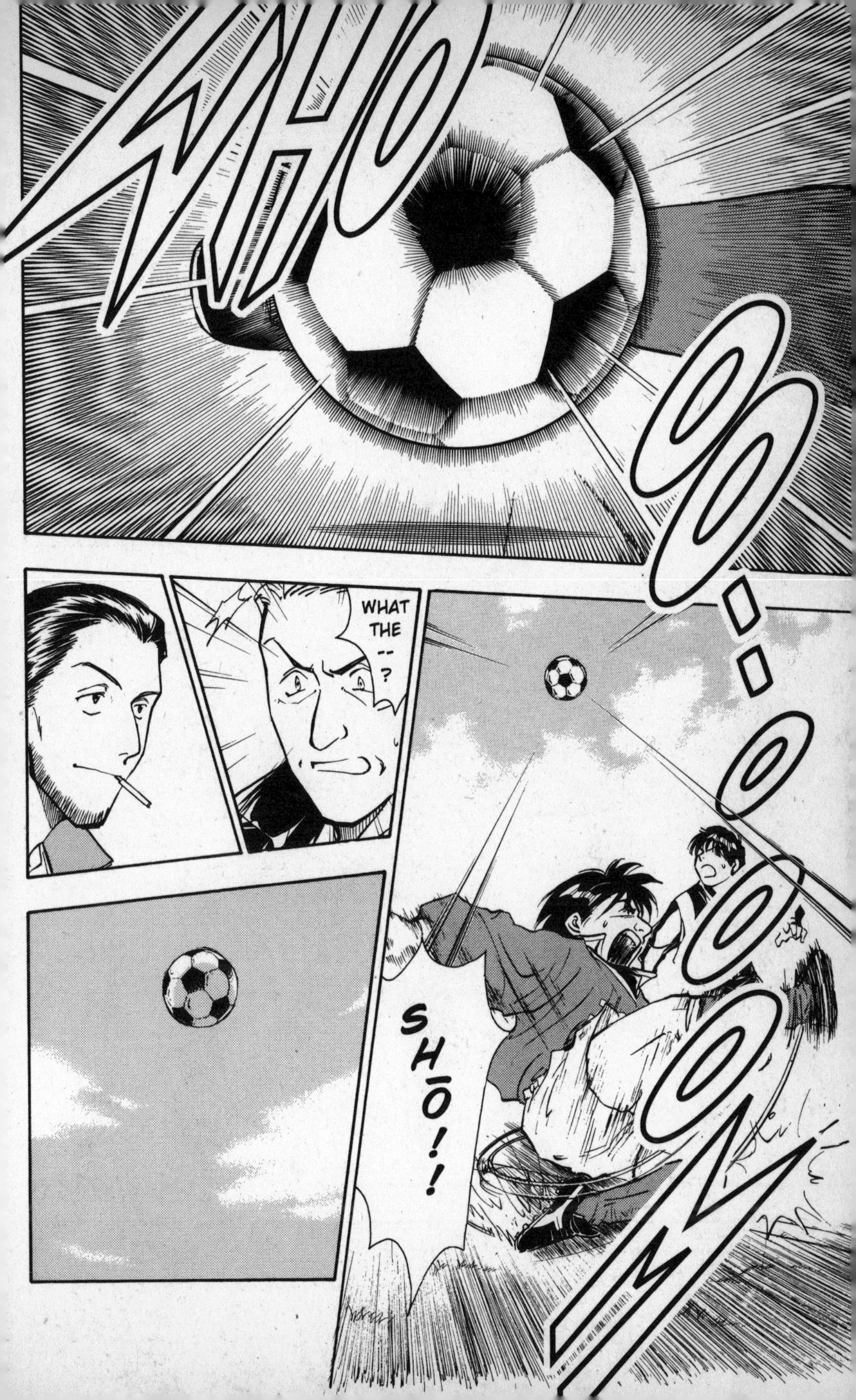
WHOOOOOOOOOOM
WHAT THE --?
SHŌ!!

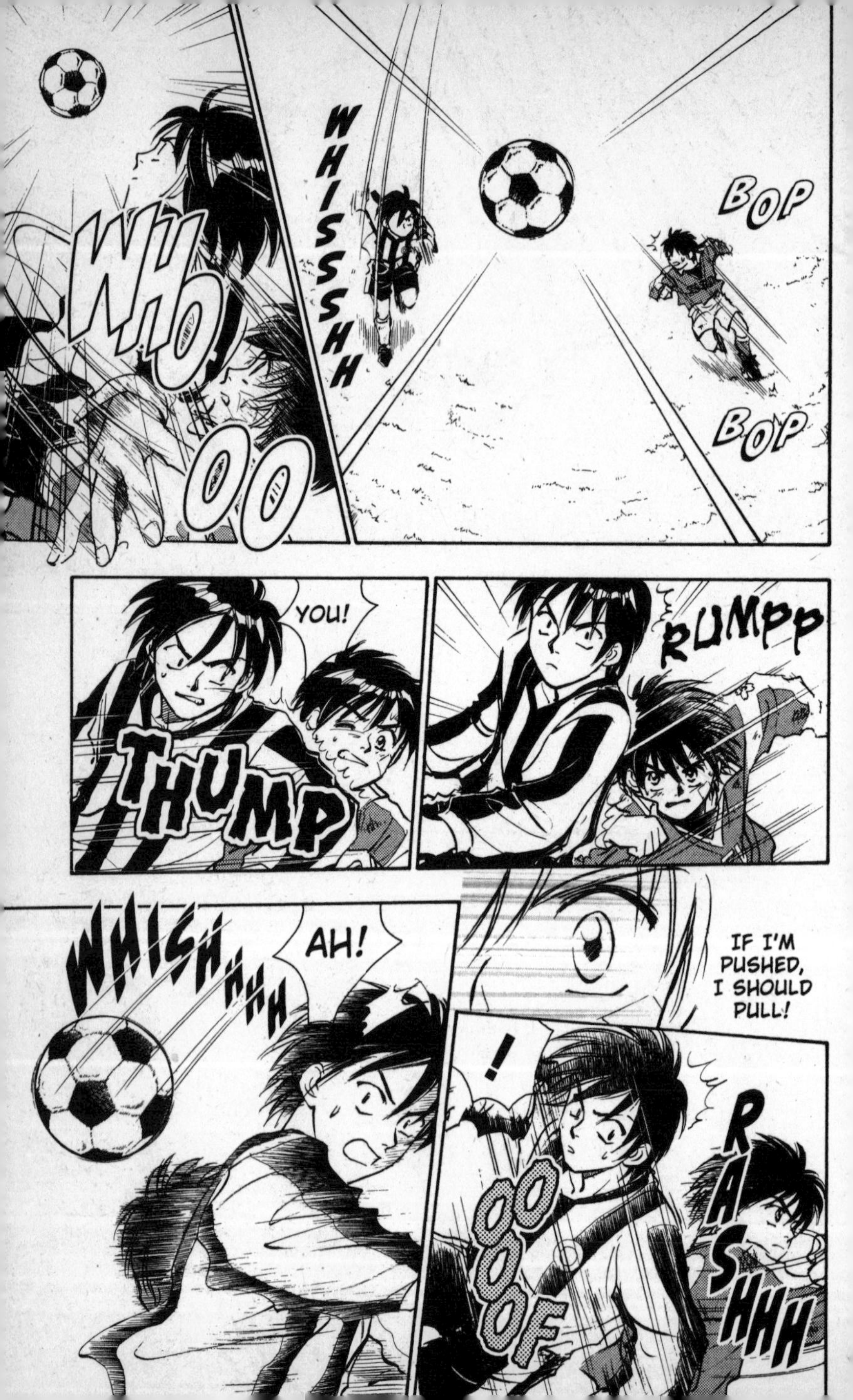
BOP
WHISSSHH
BOP
WHOOOO
RUMPP
YOU!
THUMP
IF I'M PUSHED, I SHOULD PULL!
!
OOOOF
RASHHH
WHISHHHH
AH!

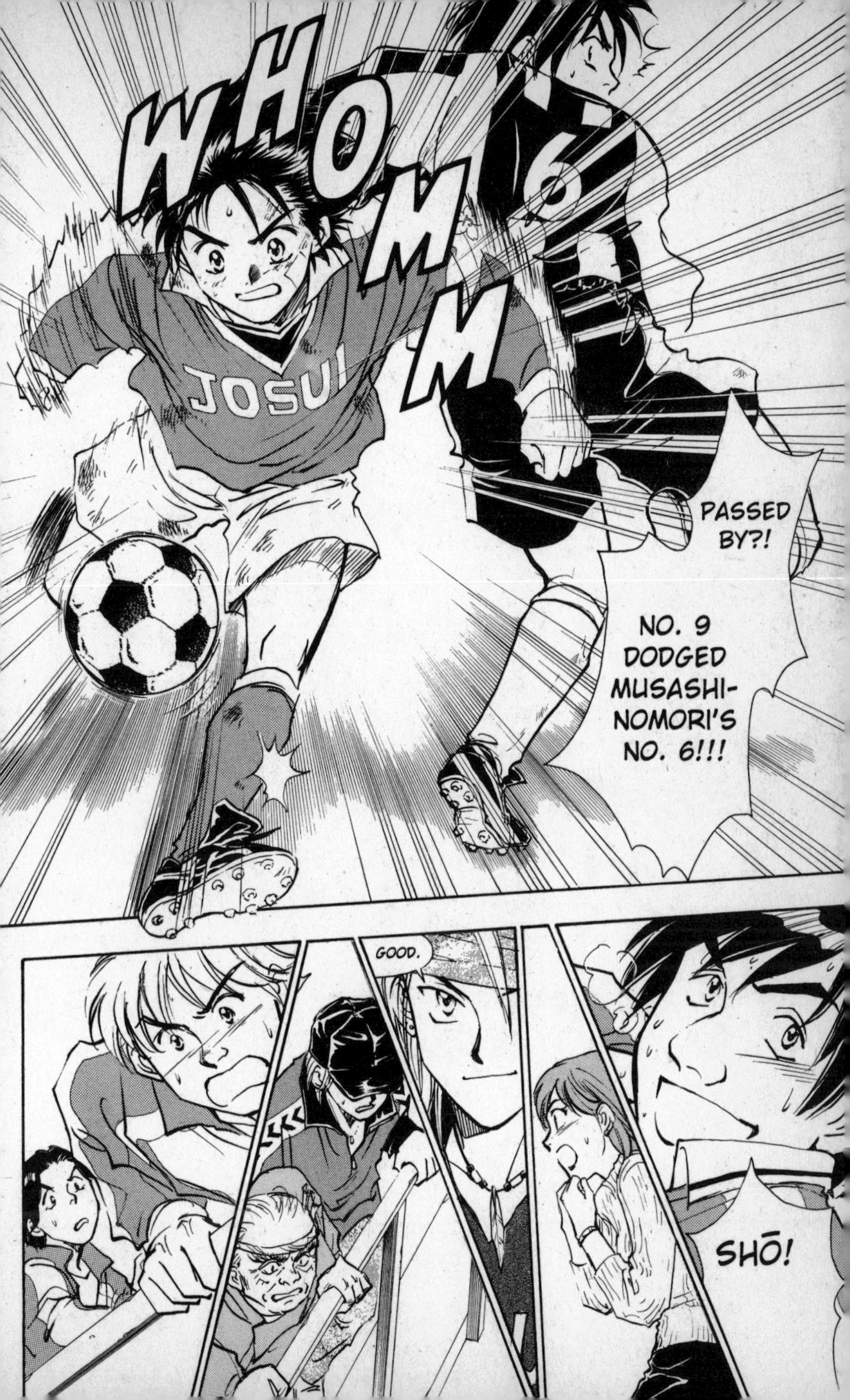
WHOMM
PASSED BY?!
NO. 9 DODGED MUSASHI-NOMORI'S NO. 6!!!
SHŌ!
GOOD.

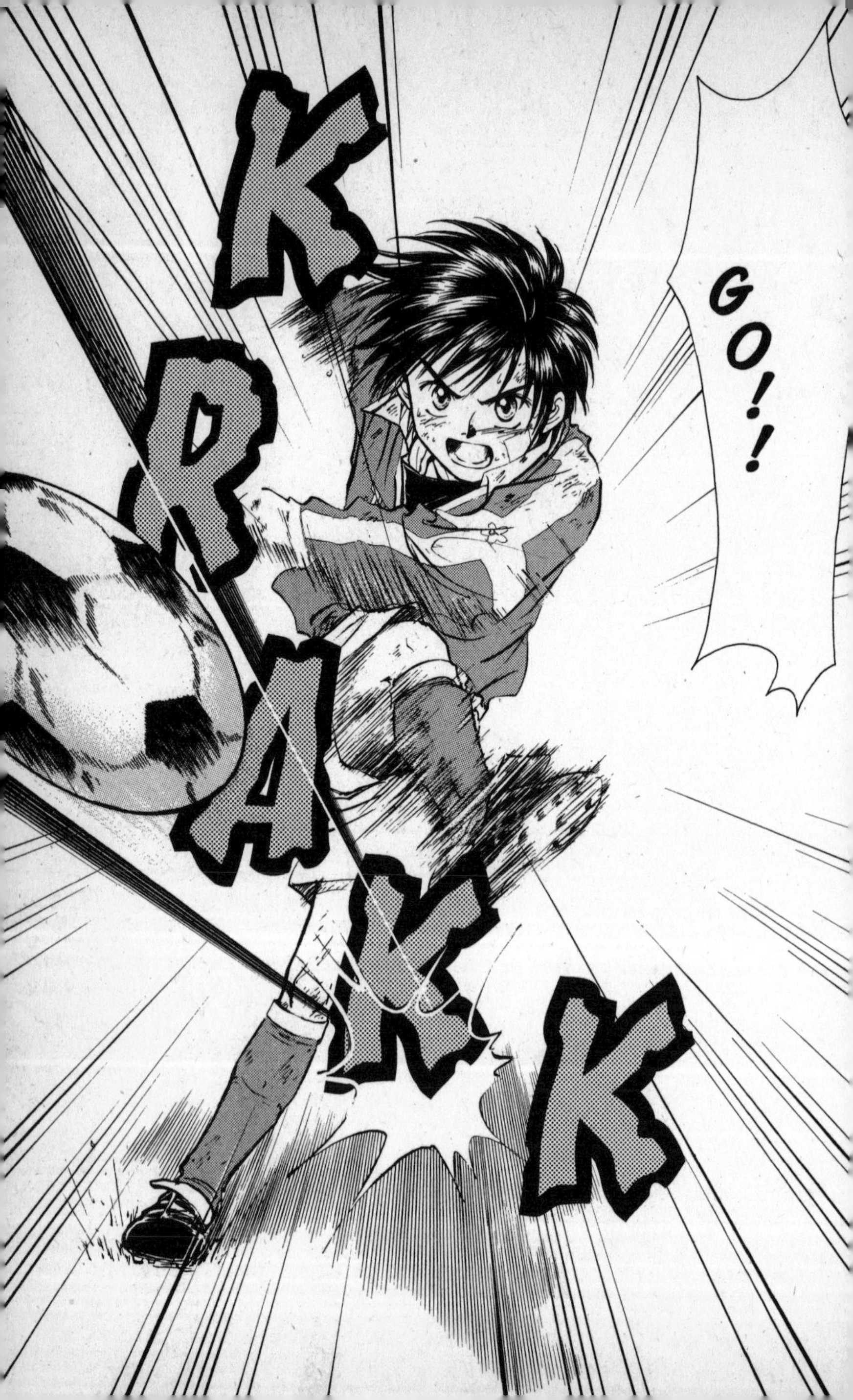
GO!!
KRAKK

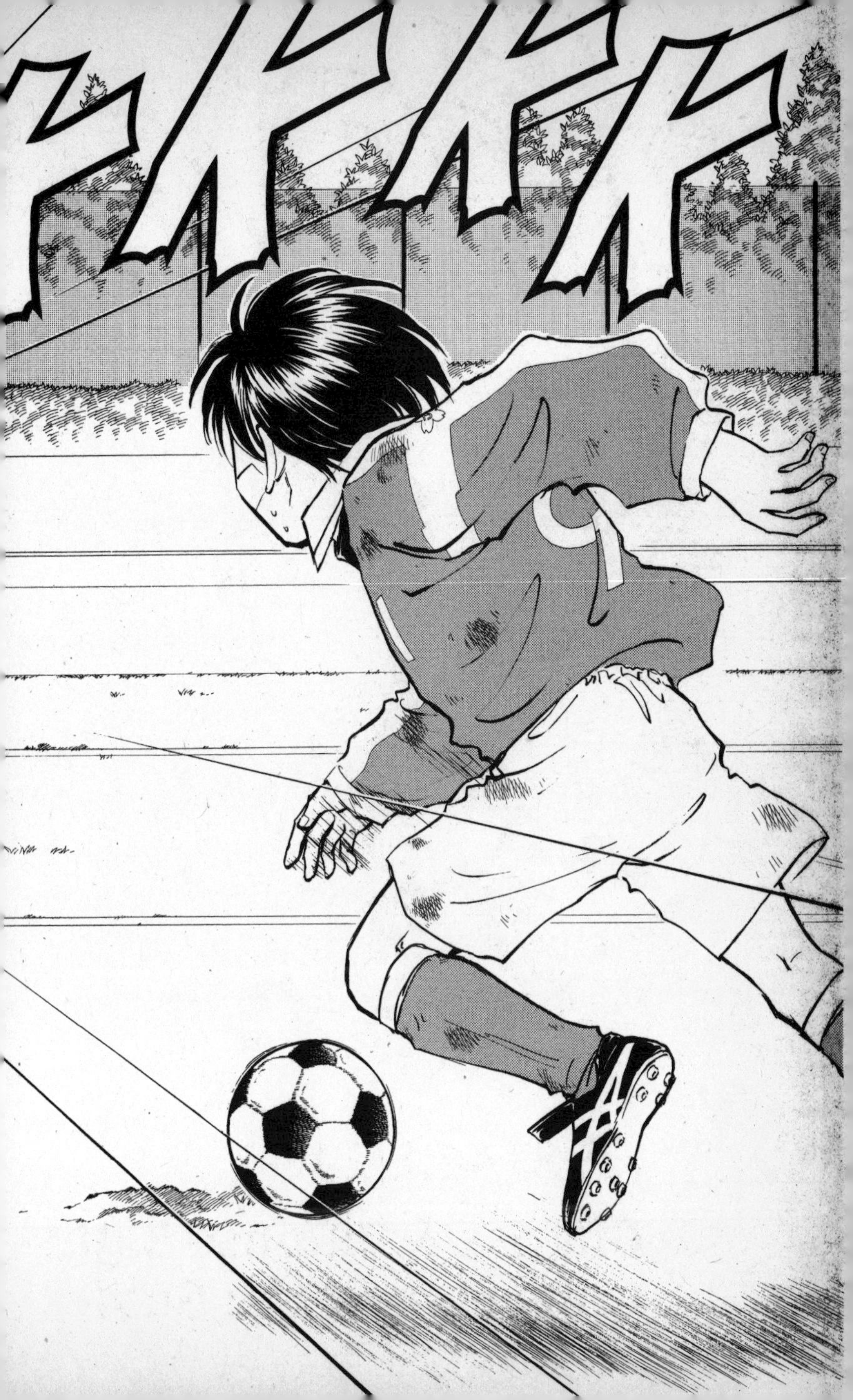

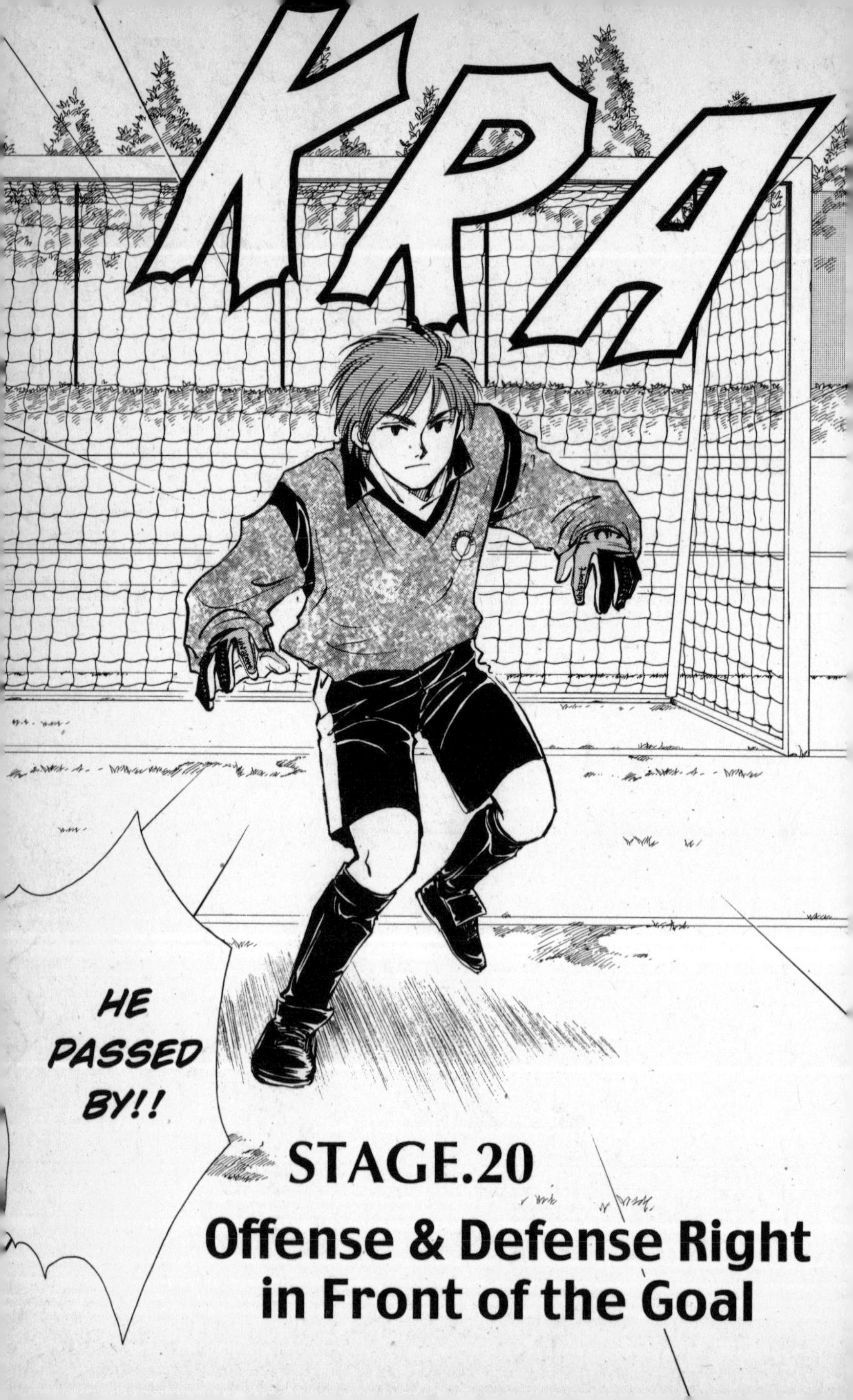
KPA
HE PASSED BY!!

STAGE.20
Offense & Defense Right in Front of the Goal

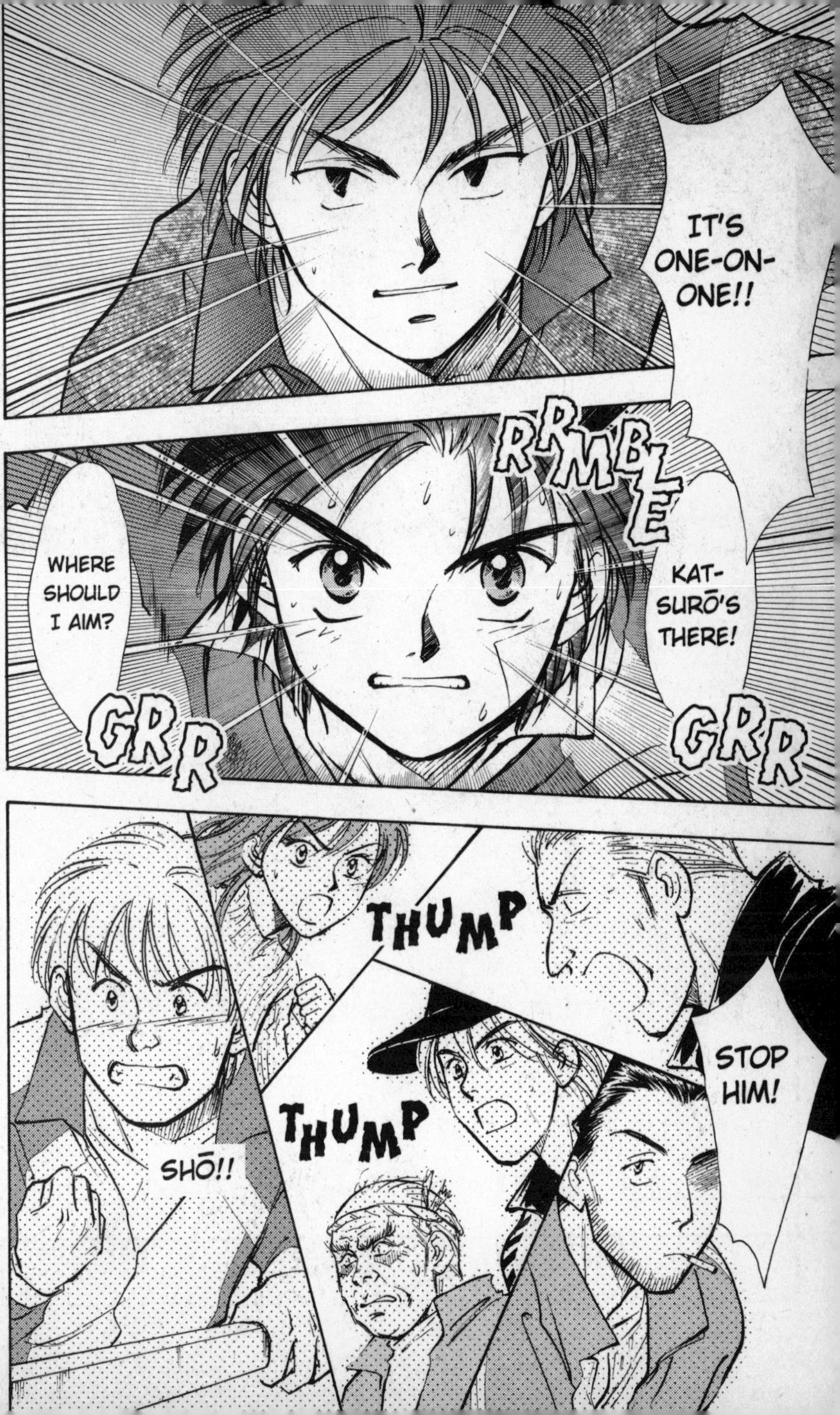
IT'S ONE-ON-ONE!!
RRMBLE
KAT-SURŌ'S THERE!
GRR
WHERE SHOULD I AIM?
GRR
STOP HIM!
THUMP
THUMP
SHŌ!!

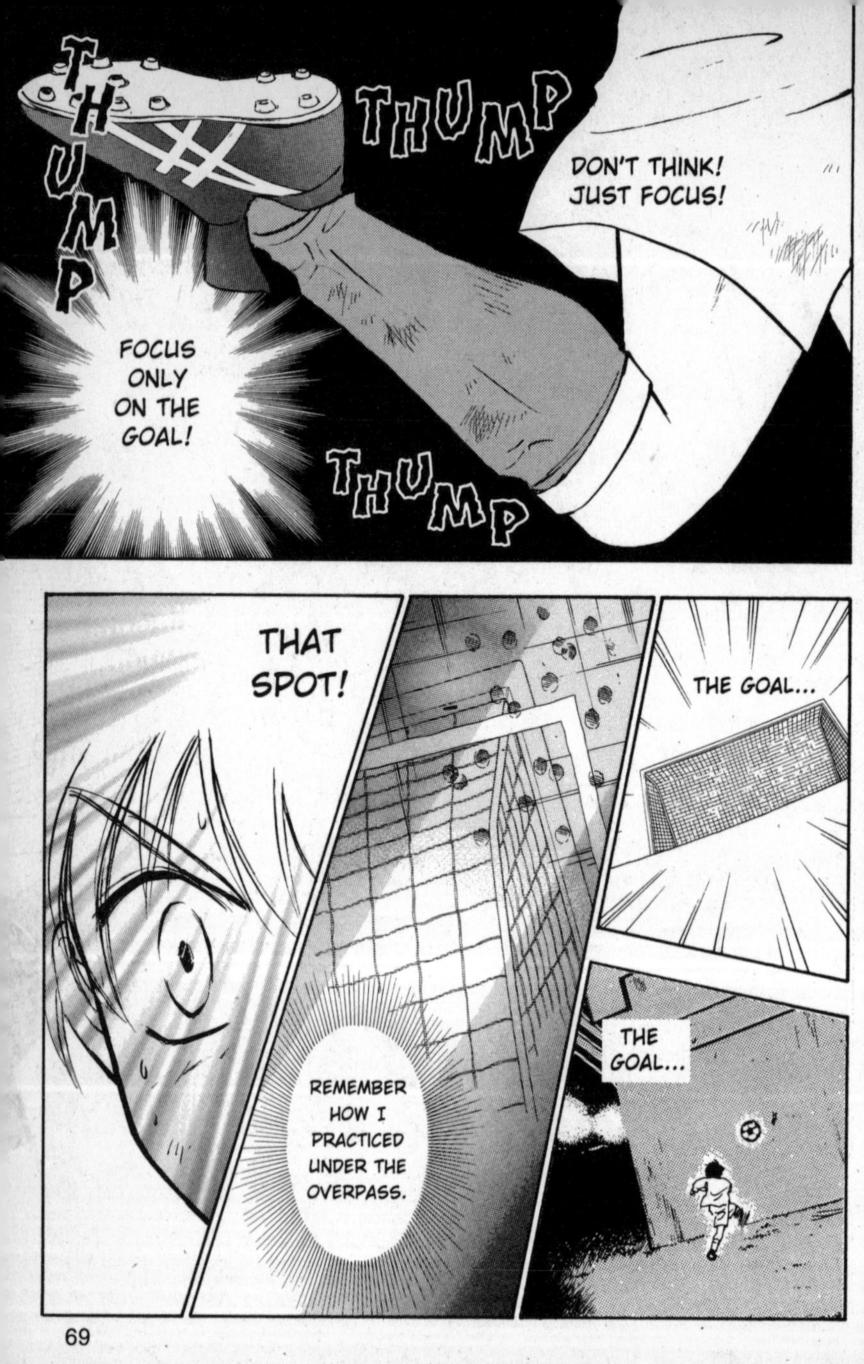
THUMP
DON'T THINK! JUST FOCUS!
THUMP
FOCUS ONLY ON THE GOAL!
THUMP
THE GOAL...
THE GOAL...
REMEMBER HOW I PRACTICED UNDER THE OVERPASS.
THAT SPOT!

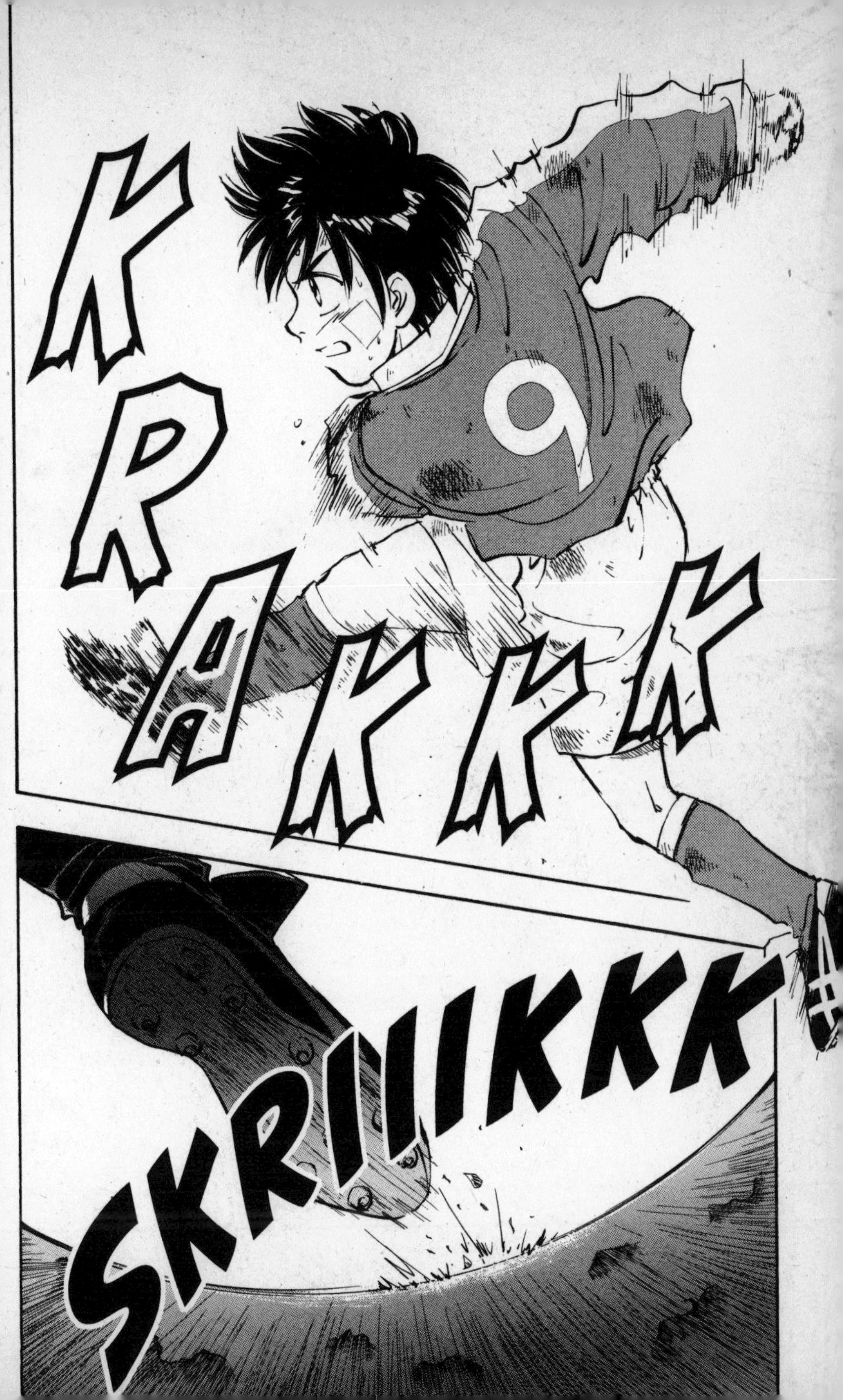
KRAKKK
SKRIIIKKK

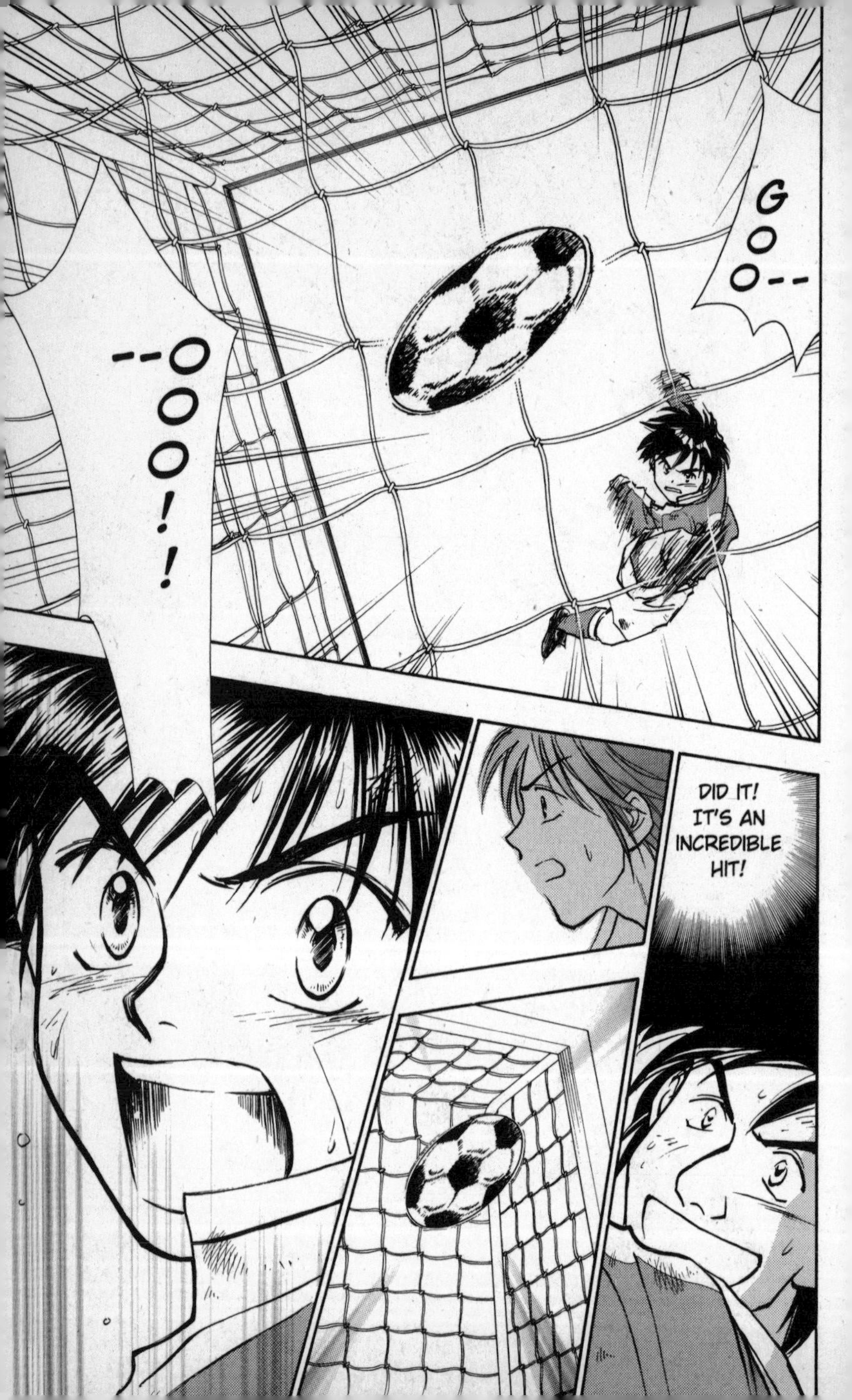
GOO--
--OOOO!!
DID IT! IT'S AN INCREDIBLE HIT!

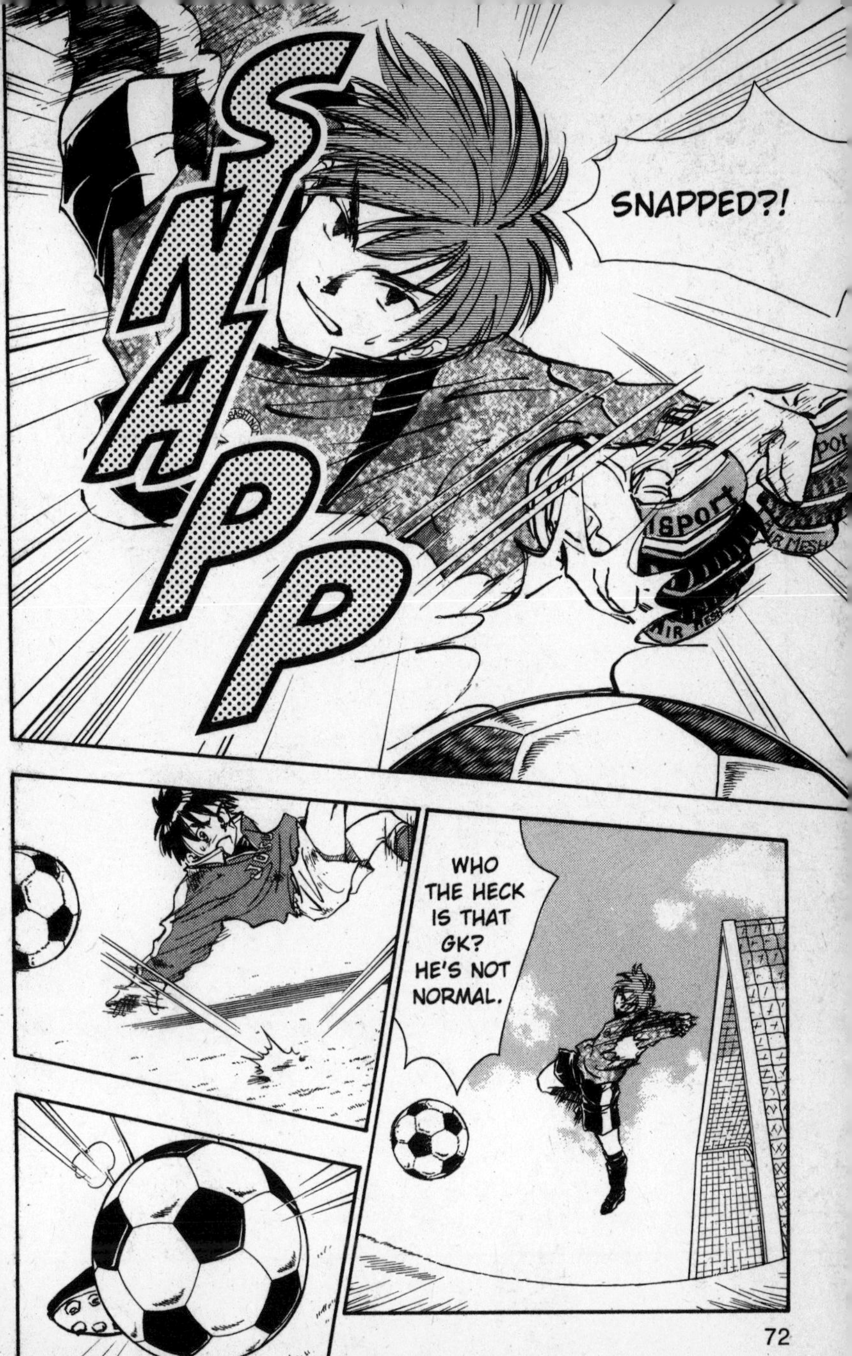
SNAPP
SNAPPED?!
WHO THE HECK IS THAT GK? HE'S NOT NORMAL.

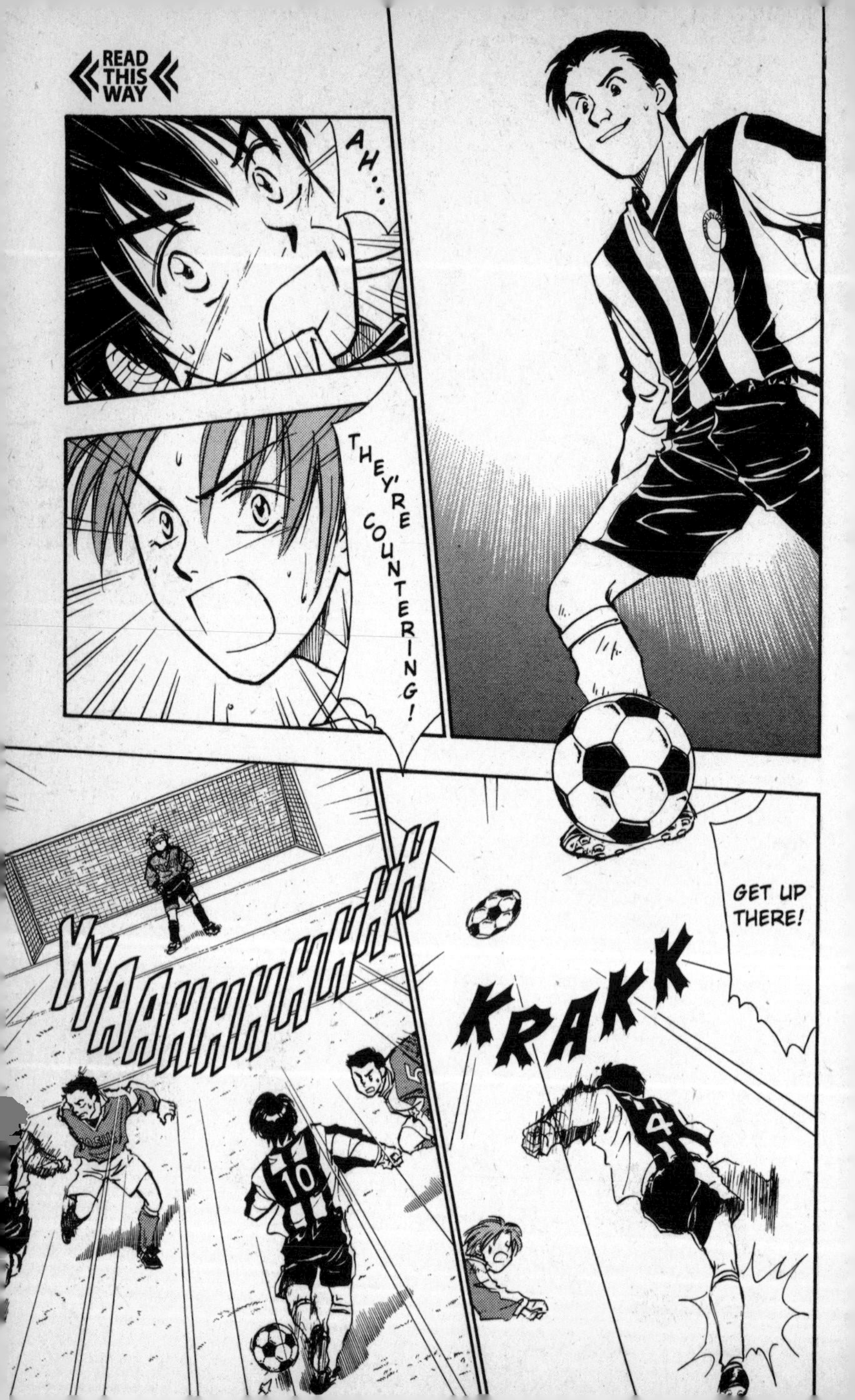
READ THIS WAY
AH...
THEY'RE COUNTERING!
GET UP THERE!
KRAKK
YAAAHHHHHHHH

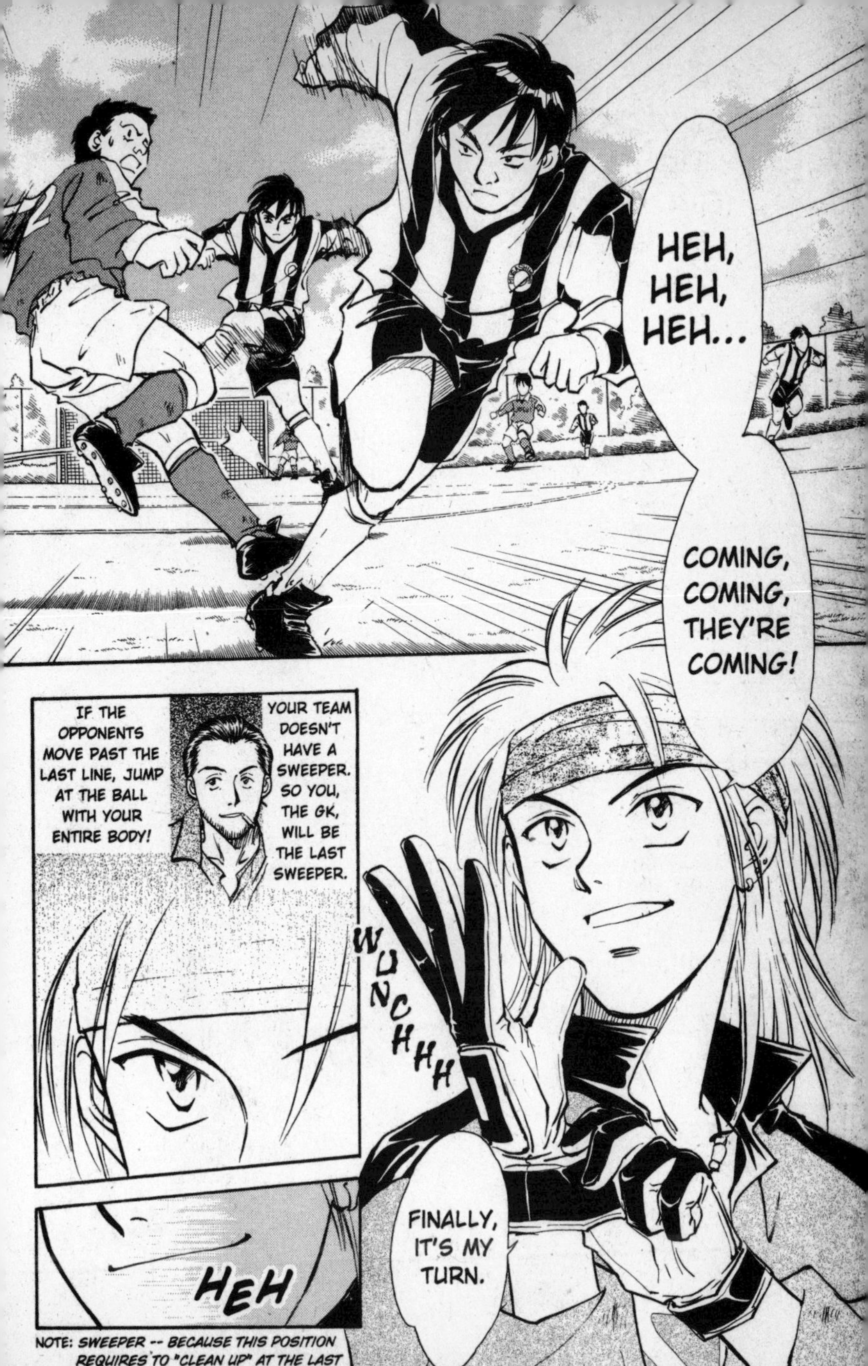
HEH, HEH, HEH...
COMING, COMING, THEY'RE COMING!
WUNCHHH
FINALLY, IT'S MY TURN.
YOUR TEAM DOESN'T HAVE A SWEEPER. SO YOU, THE GK, WILL BE THE LAST SWEEPER.
IF THE OPPONENTS MOVE PAST THE LAST LINE, JUMP AT THE BALL WITH YOUR ENTIRE BODY!
HEH

NOTE: SWEEPER -- BECAUSE THIS POSITION REQUIRES TO "CLEAN UP" AT THE LAST DEFENSE LINE, IT'S CALLED SWEEPER.

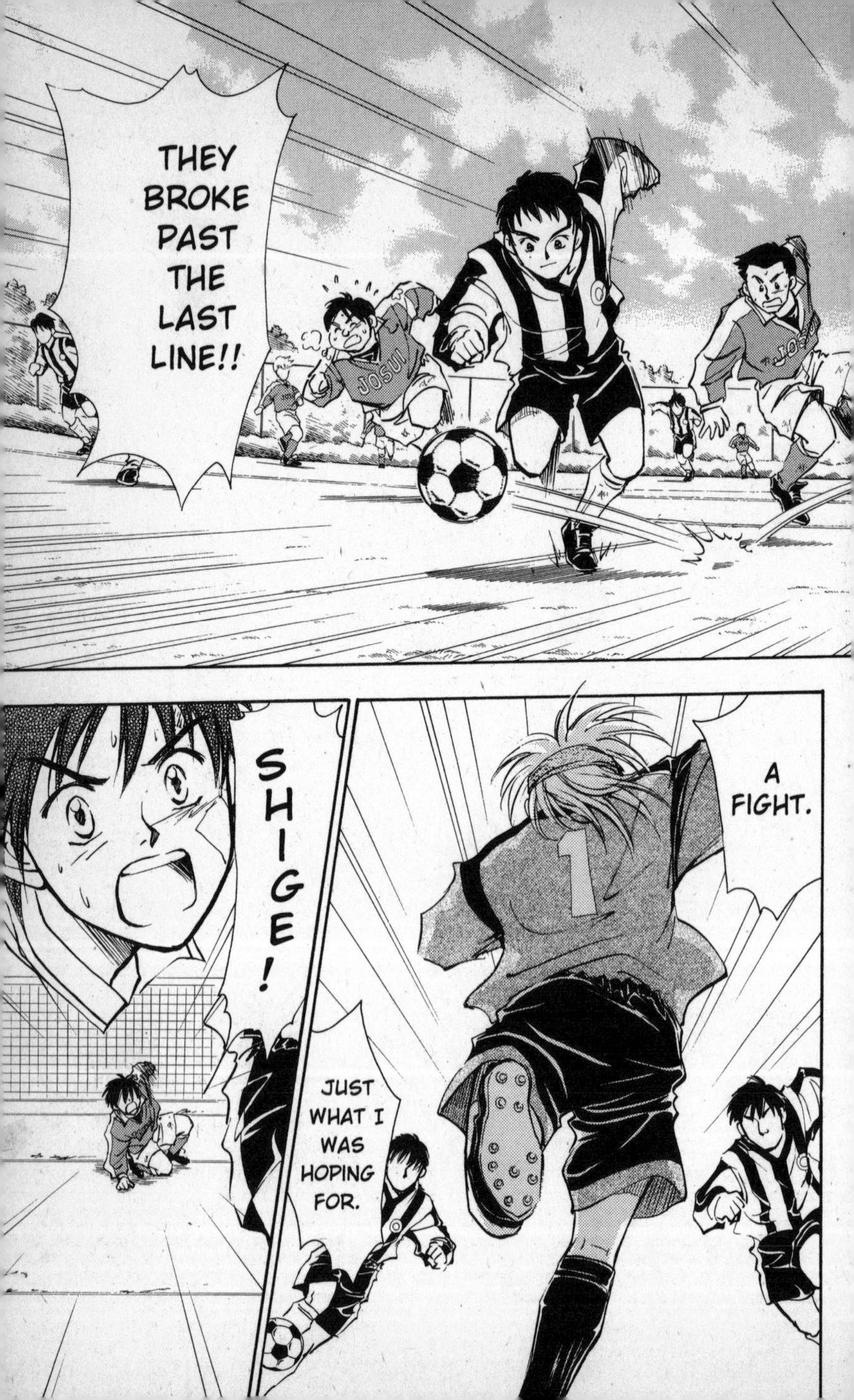
THEY BROKE PAST THE LAST LINE!!
JOSUI
A FIGHT.
JUST WHAT I WAS HOPING FOR.
SHIGE!

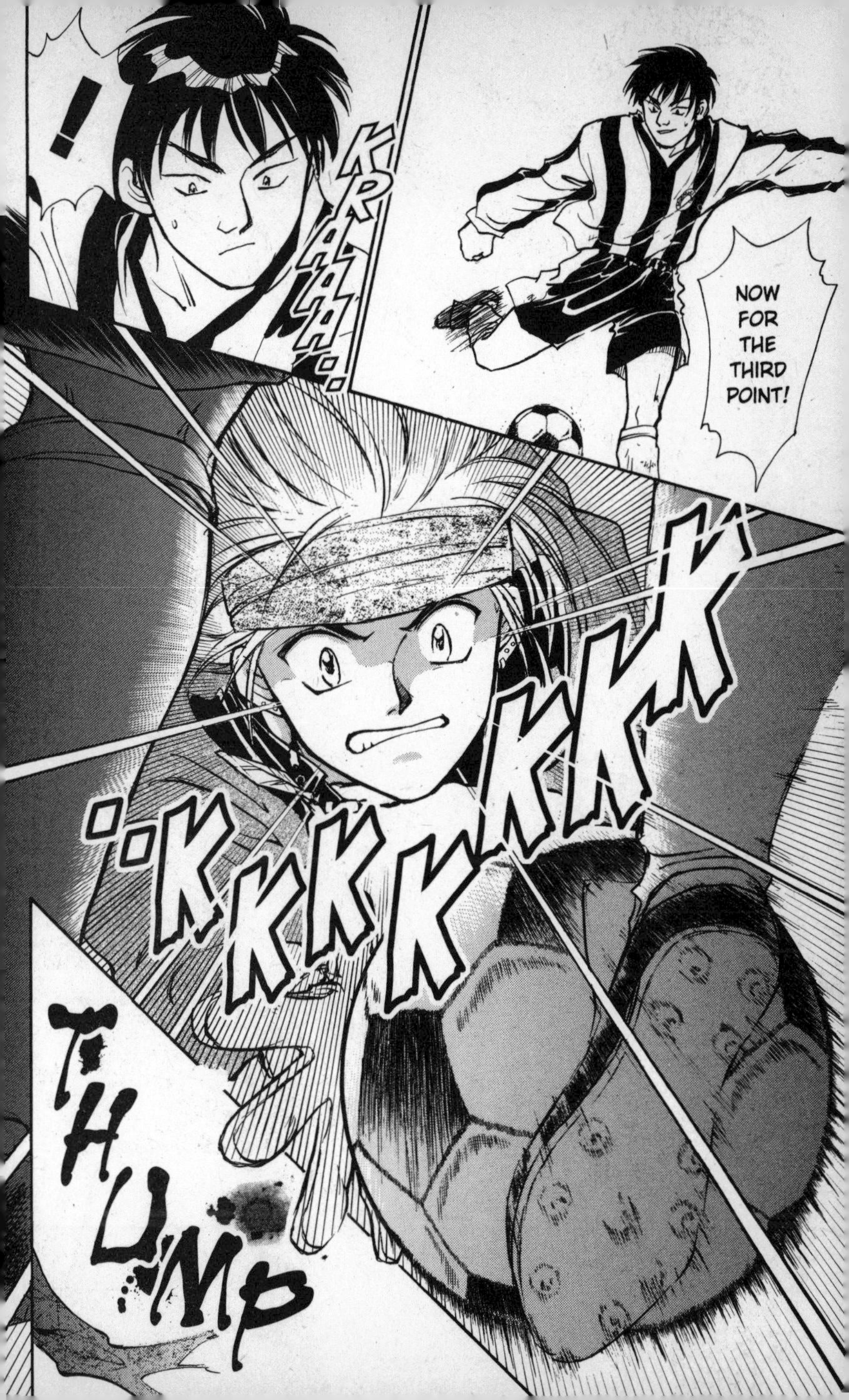
NOW FOR THE THIRD POINT!
!
KRAAAH..
..KKKKKKKKK
THUMP

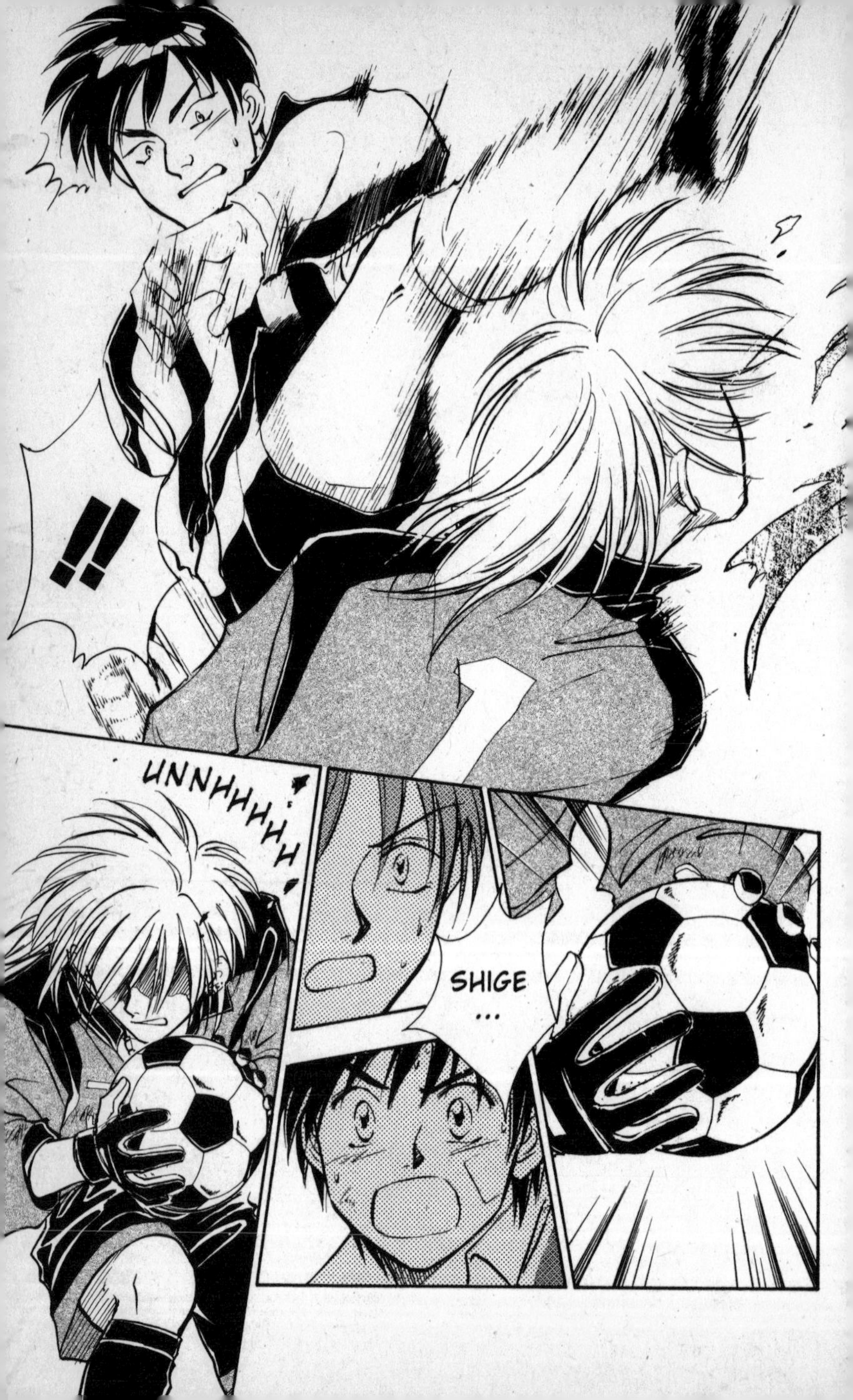
!!
SHIGE ...
UNNHHHHH!

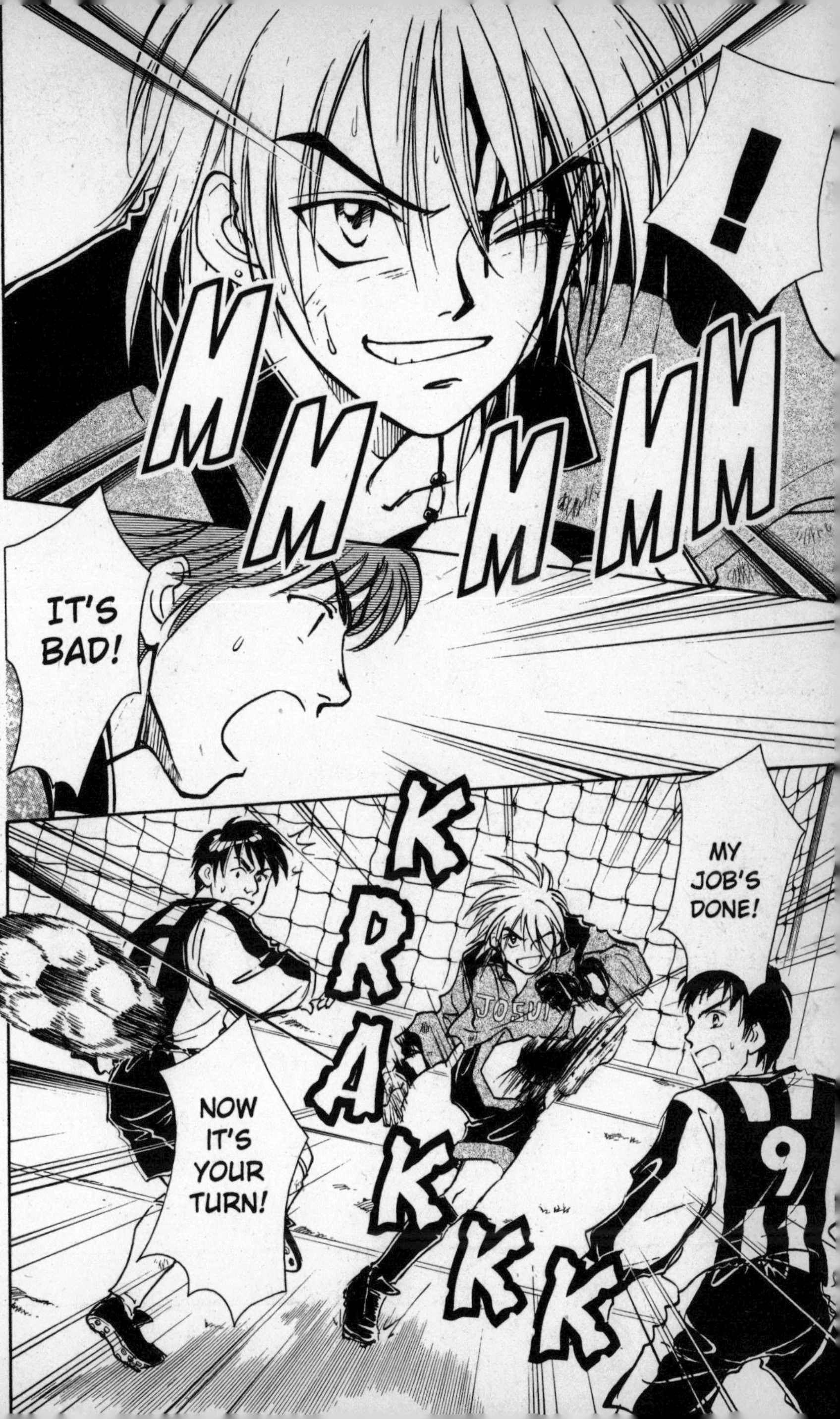
!
MMMMM
IT'S BAD!
MY JOB'S DONE!
KRAKKK
JOSUI
NOW IT'S YOUR TURN!
9

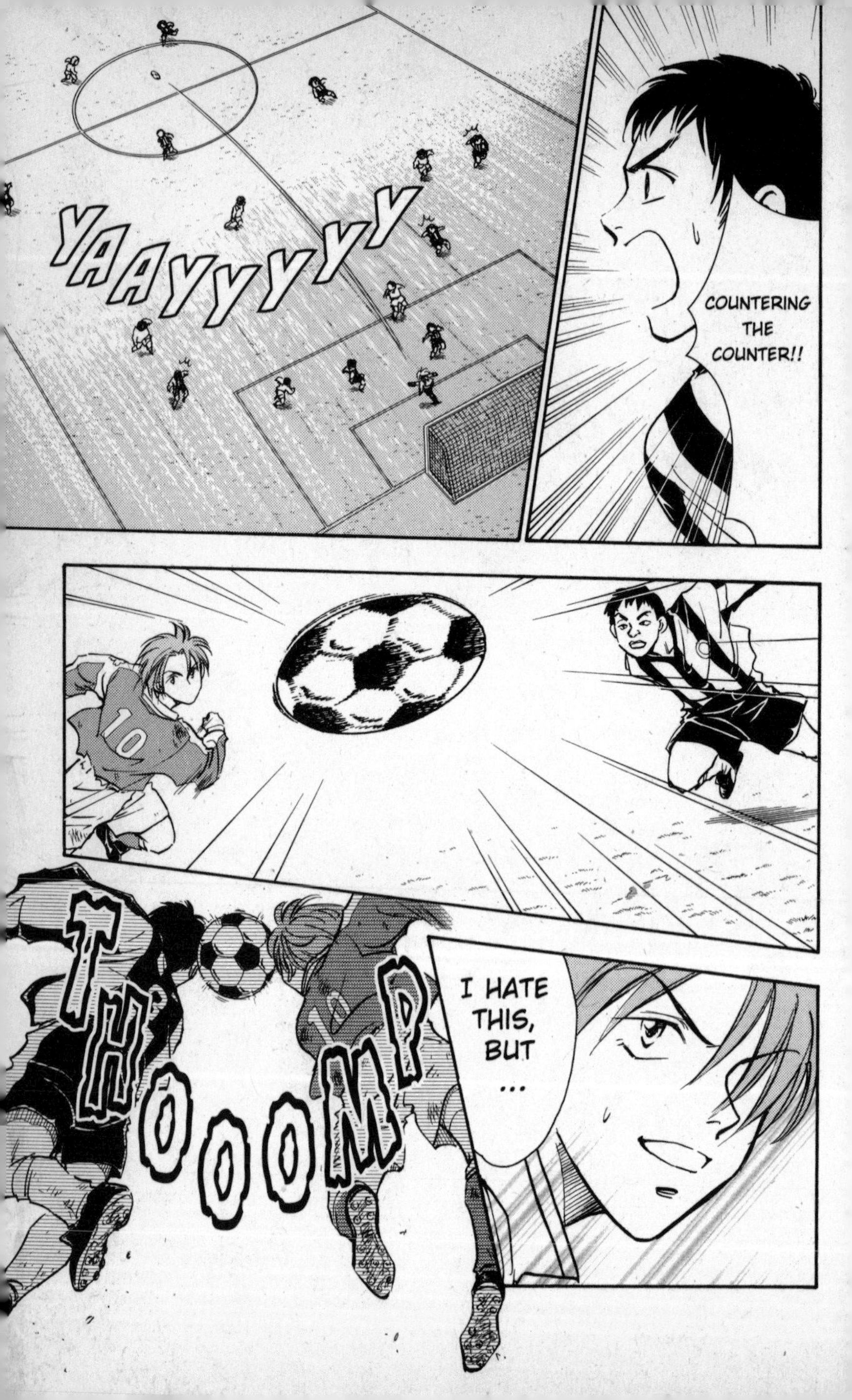
COUNTERING THE COUNTER!!
YAAYYYYY
I HATE THIS, BUT ...
THOOOMP

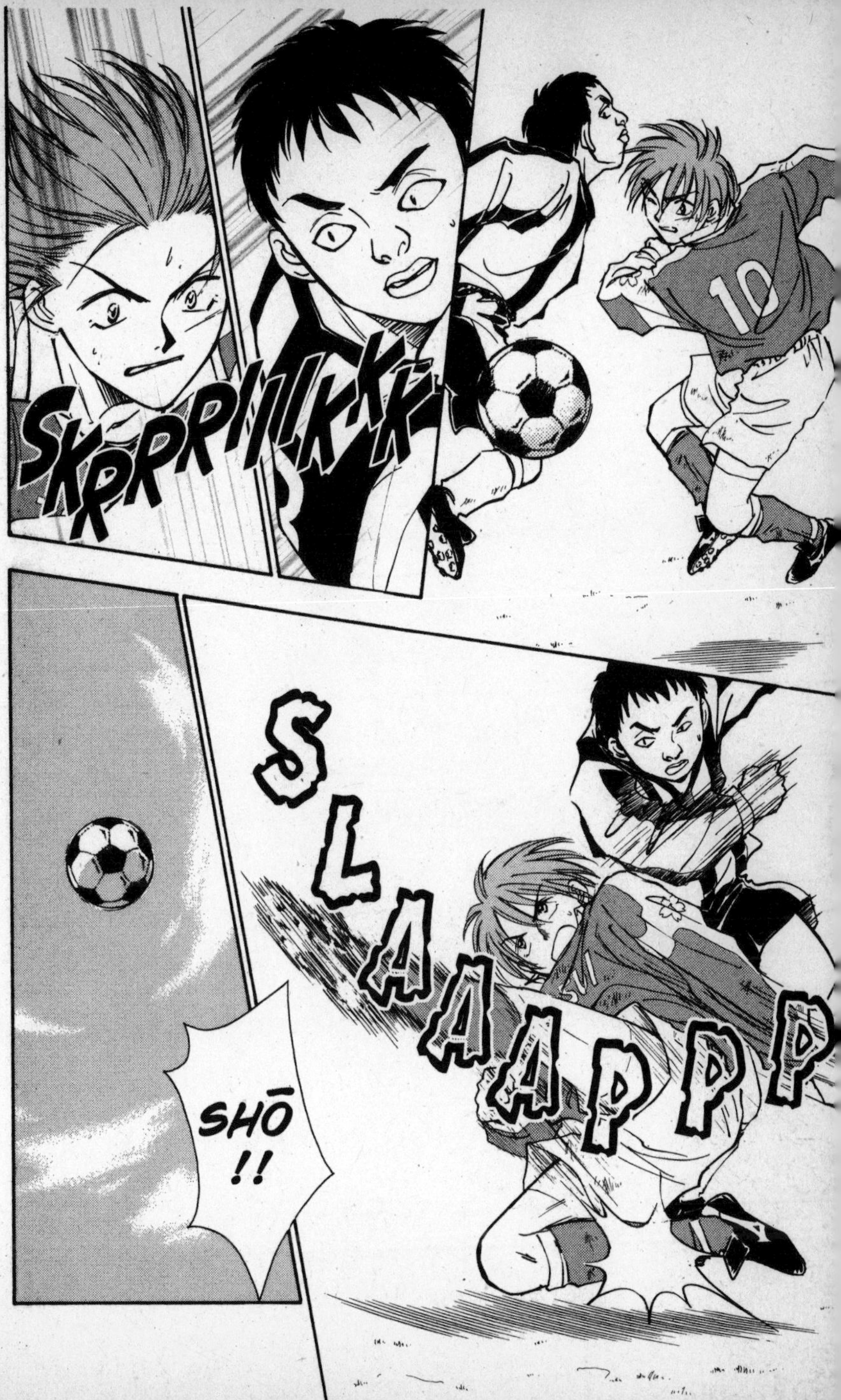
SKRPRIIIIRKKK
SLAAAAPPP
SHŌ!!

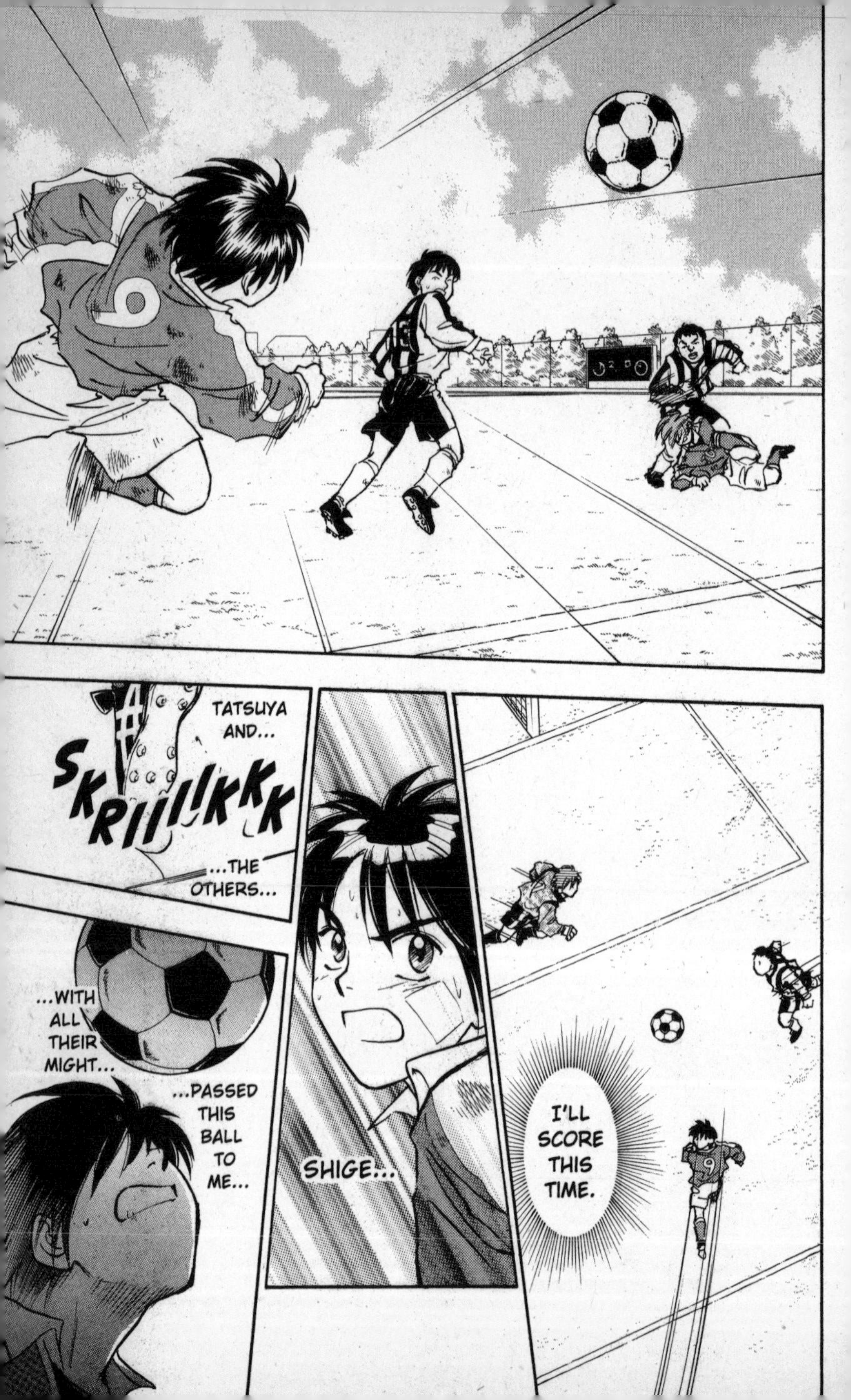
I'LL SCORE THIS TIME.
SHIGE...
TATSUYA AND...
SKRIIIIKKK
...THE OTHERS...
...WITH ALL THEIR MIGHT...
...PASSED THIS BALL TO ME...

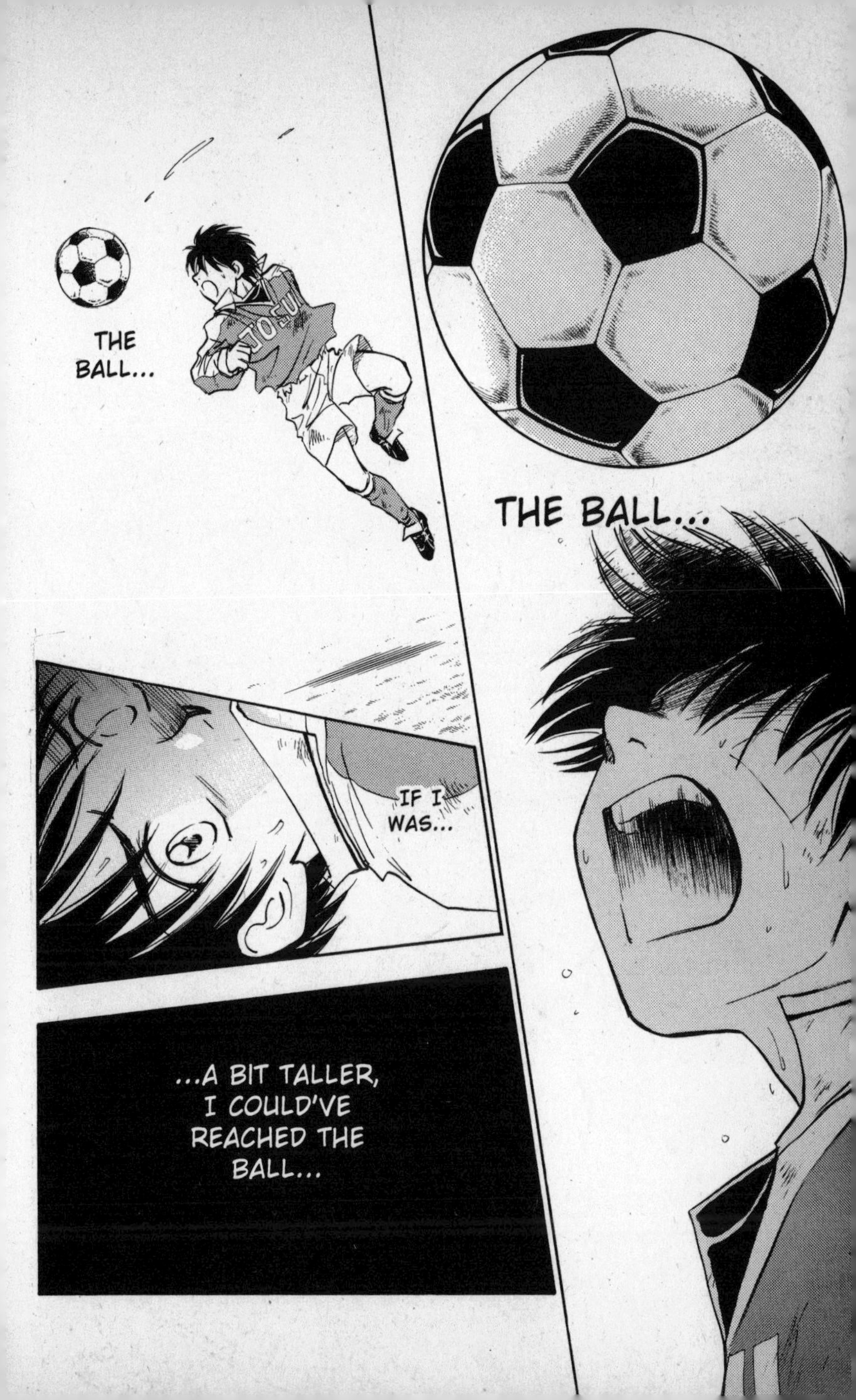
THE BALL...
THE BALL...
IF I WAS...
...A BIT TALLER, I COULD'VE REACHED THE BALL...

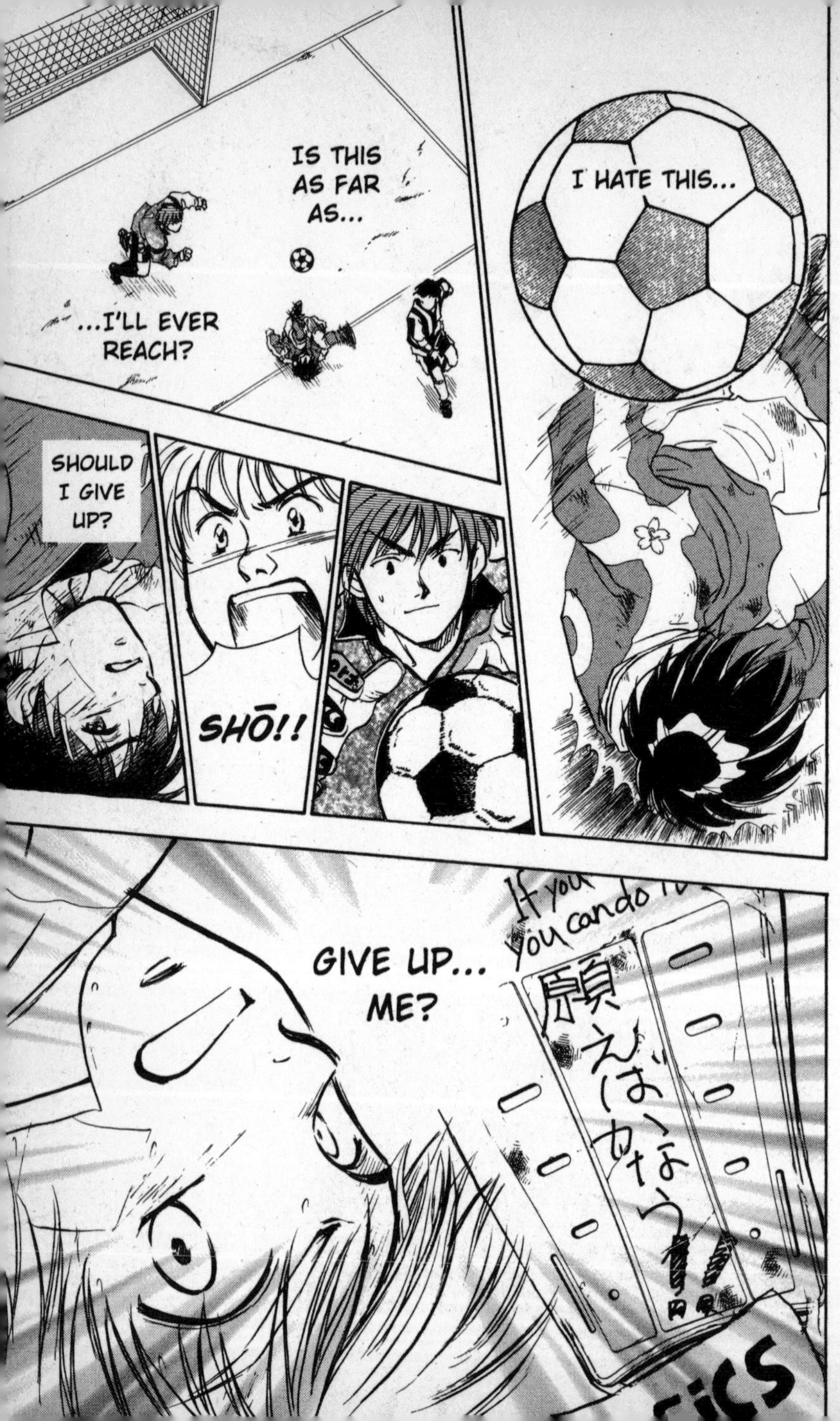
I HATE THIS...
IS THIS AS FAR AS...
...I'LL EVER REACH?
SHŌ!!
SHOULD I GIVE UP?
GIVE UP... ME?
If you
you can do it
願えばかなう。

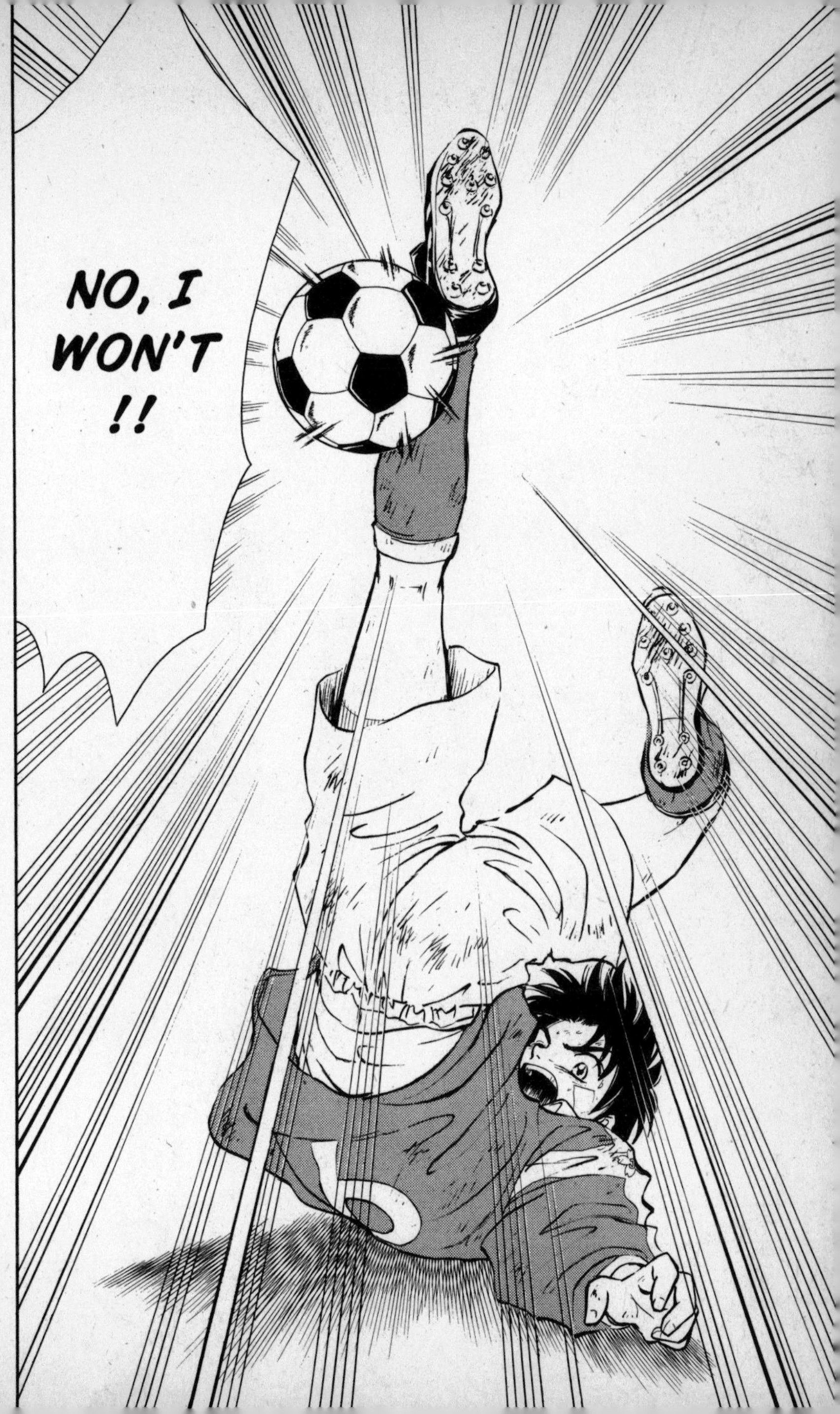
NO, I WON'T !!

STAGE.21 Go Forward

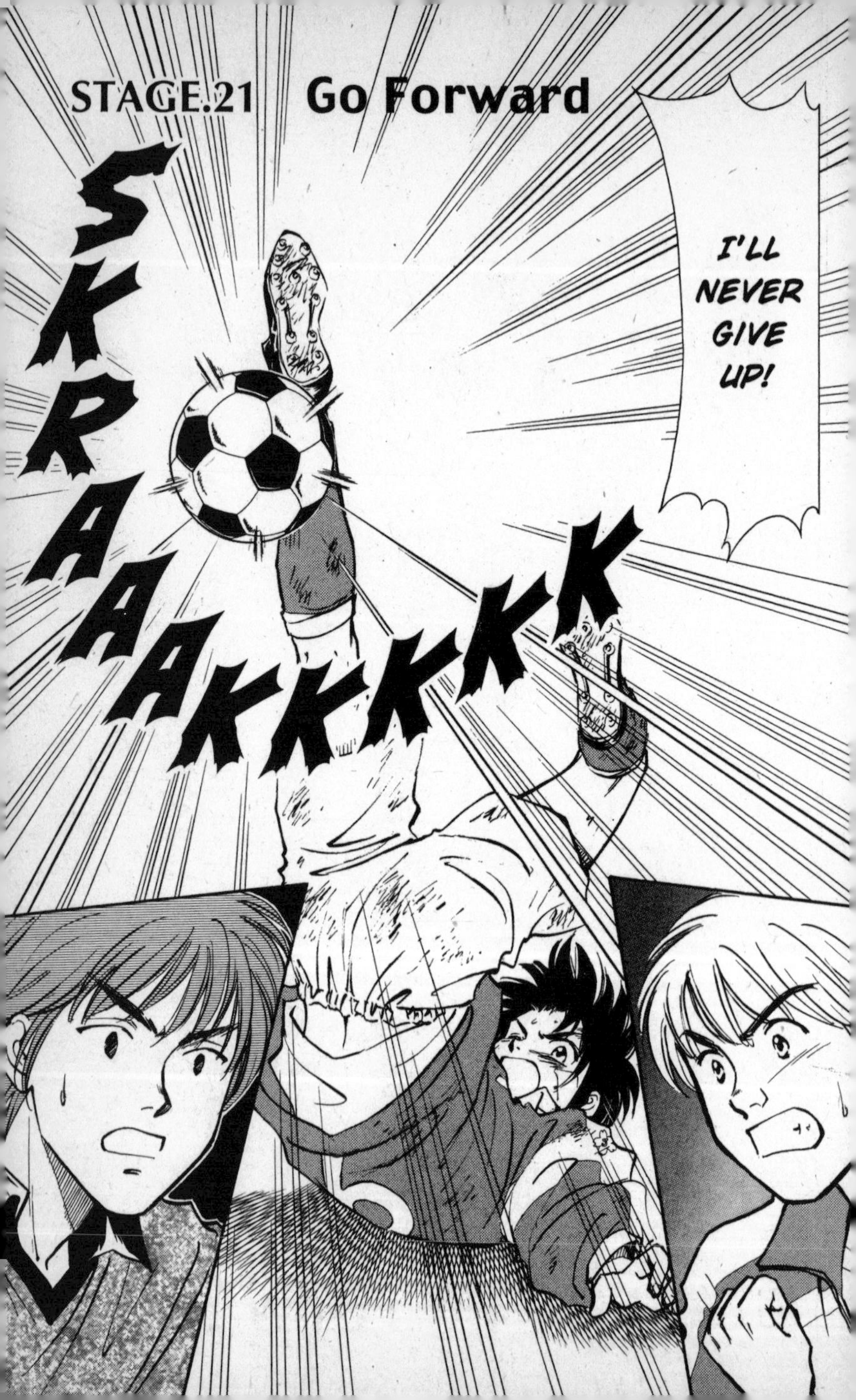
I'LL NEVER GIVE UP!
SKRAAAAKKKKKK

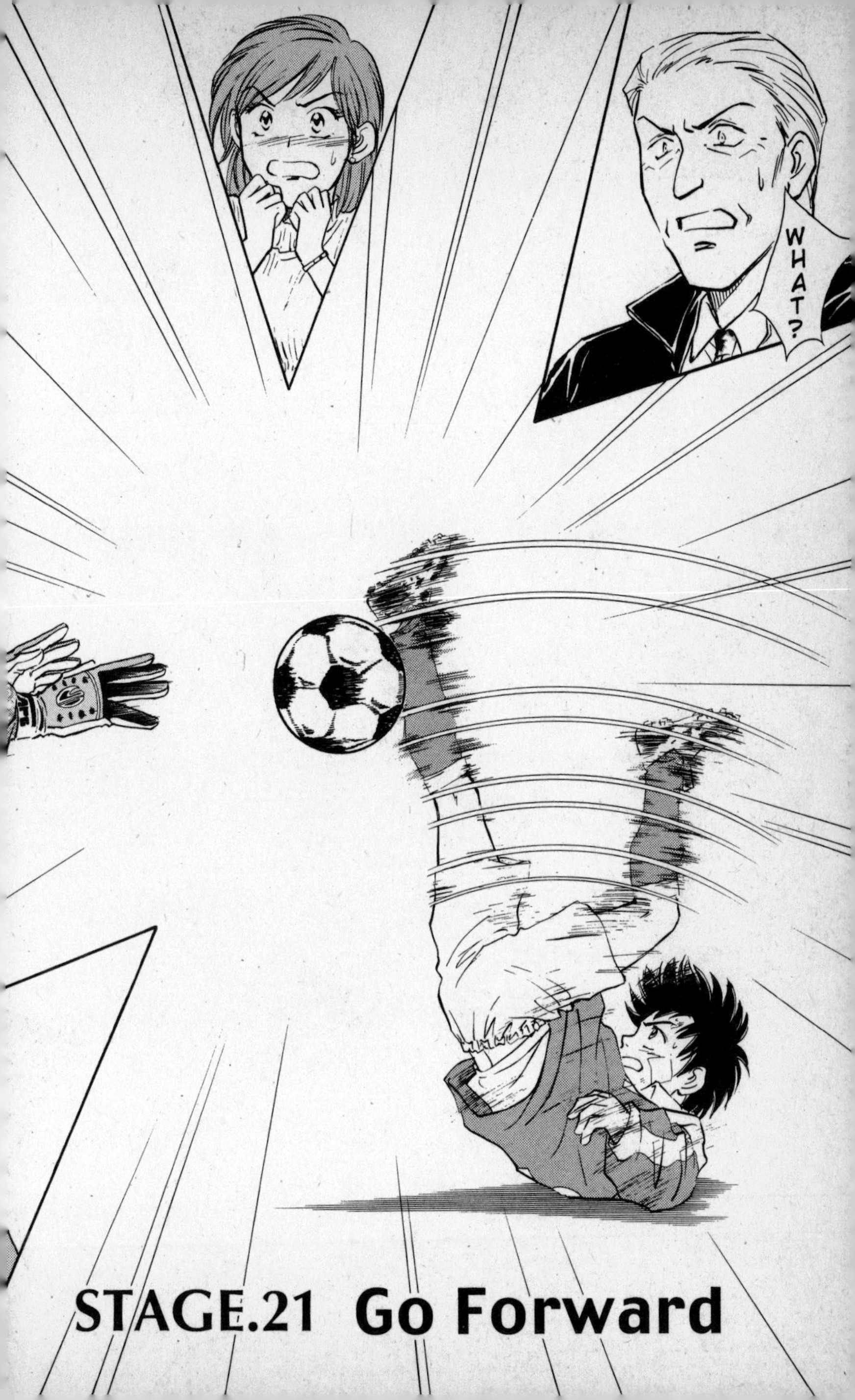
WHAT?

STAGE.21 Go Forward

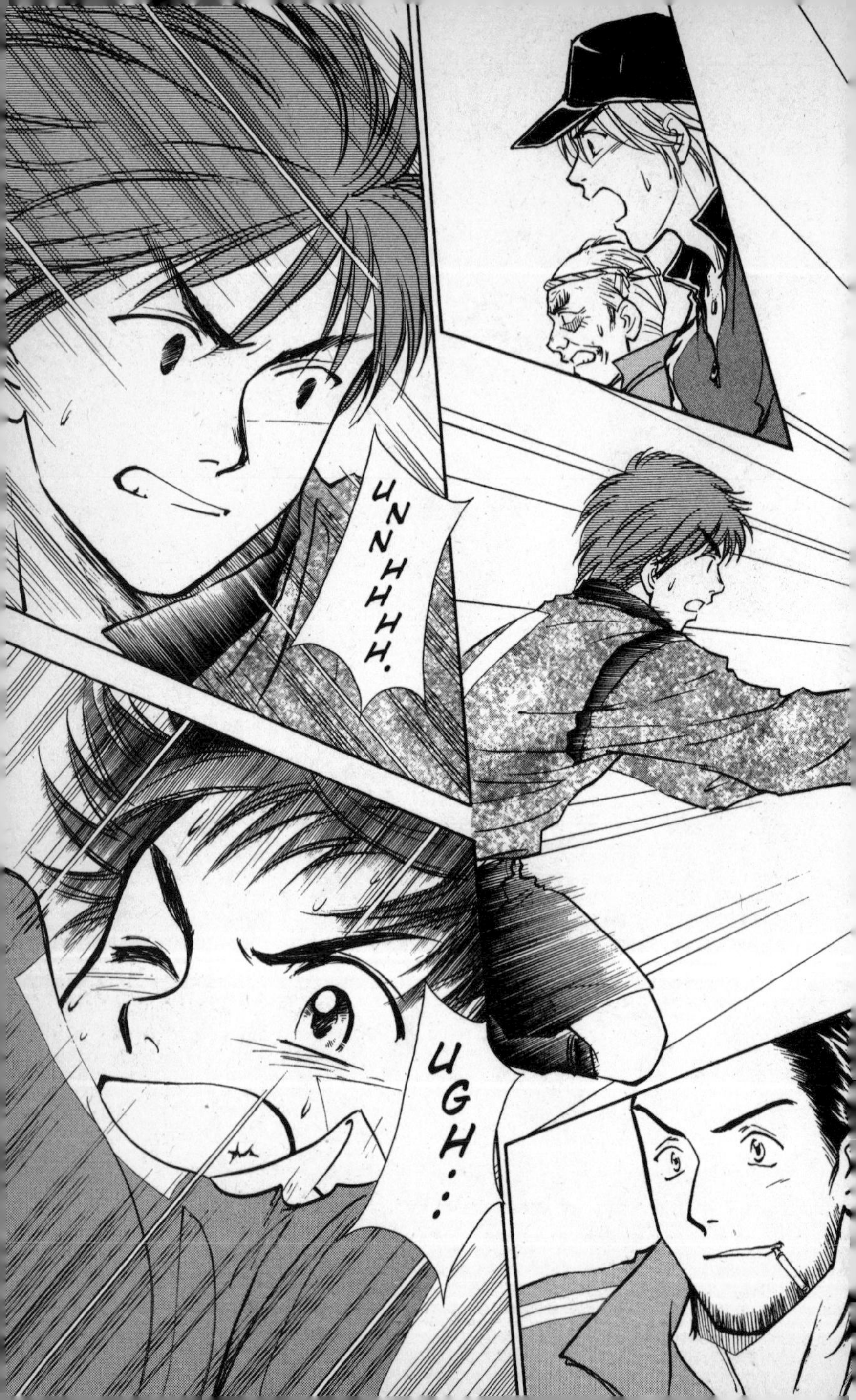
UNNHHHH.
UGH...

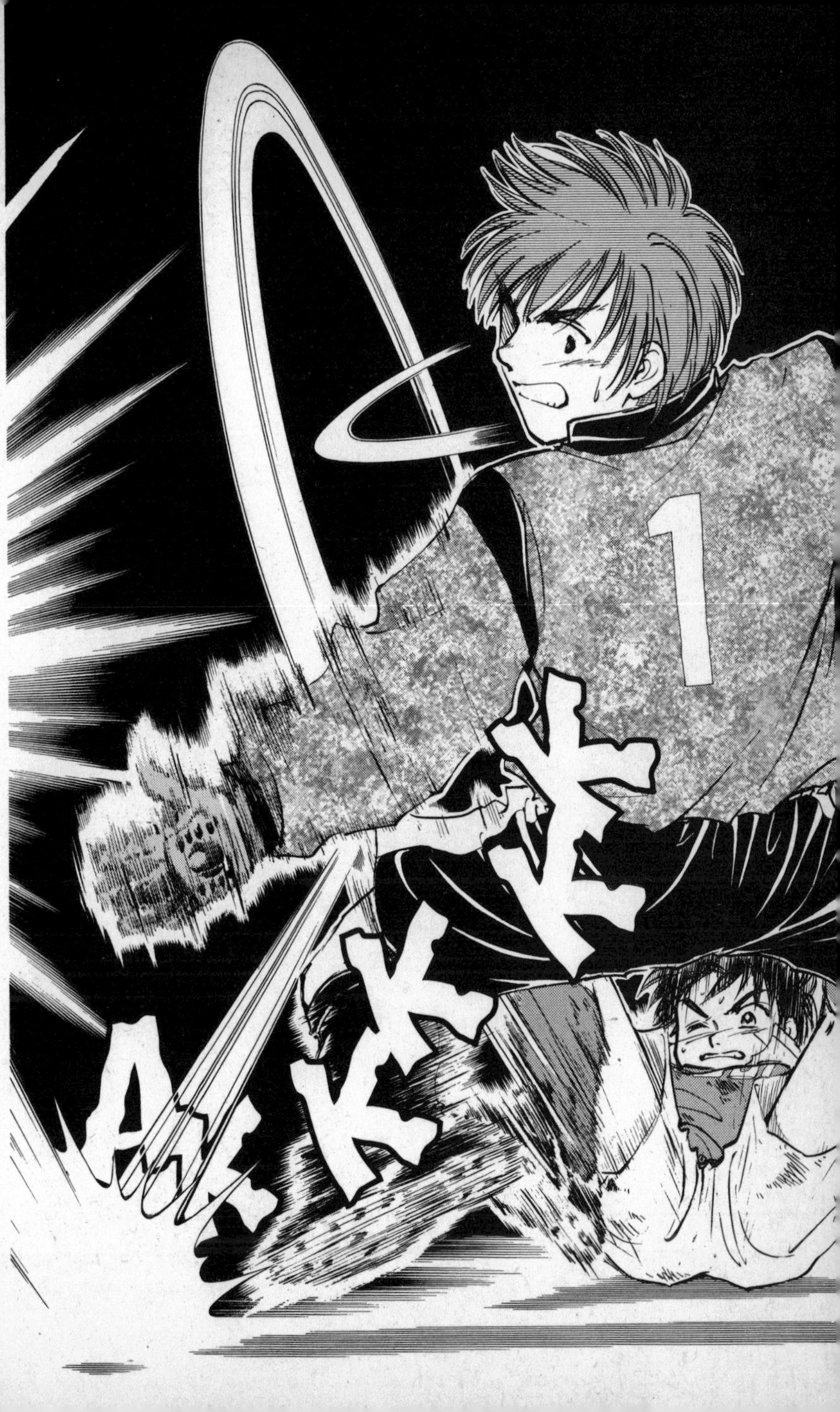
ACKK

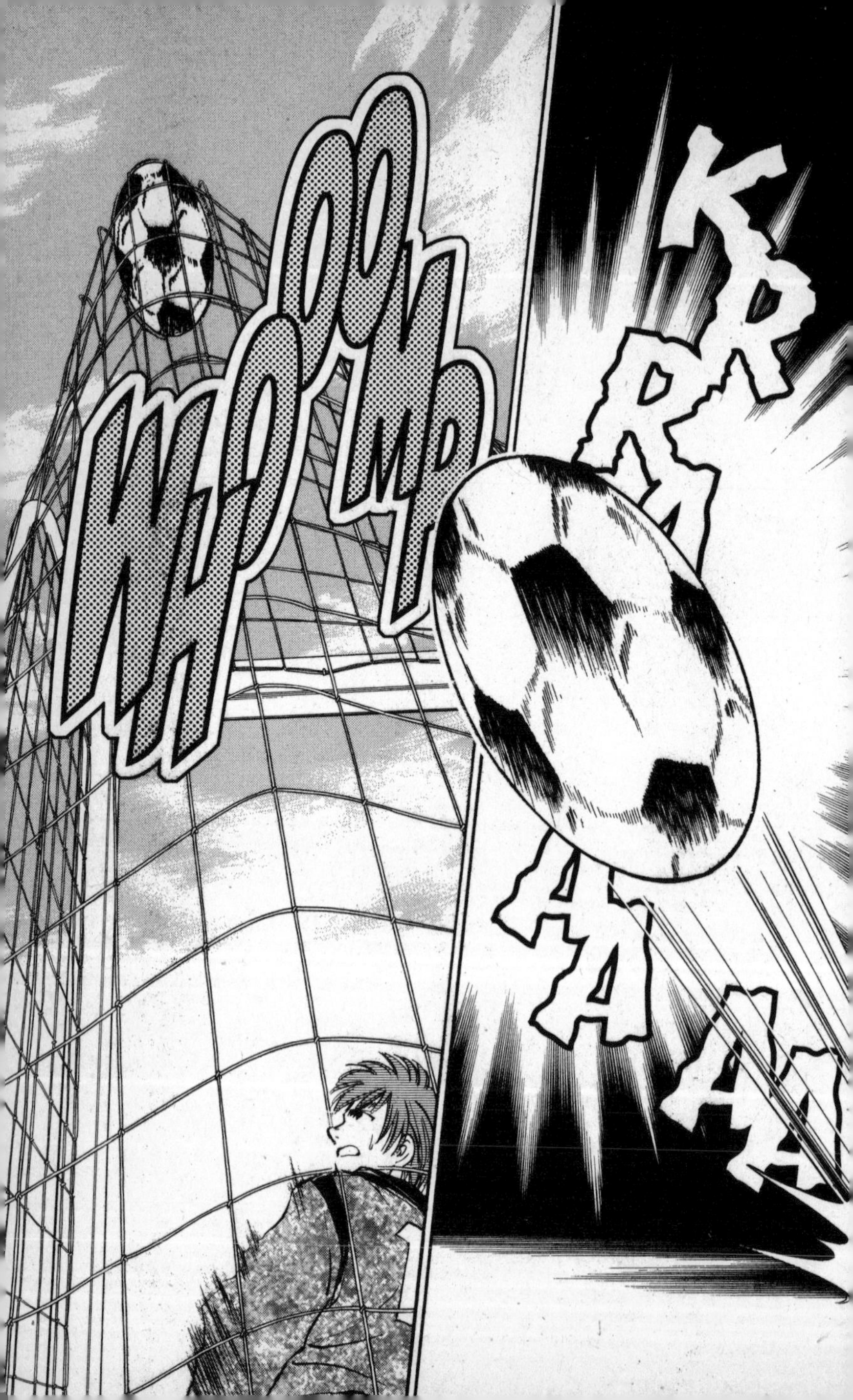
KRRAAAAA
WHOOOMP

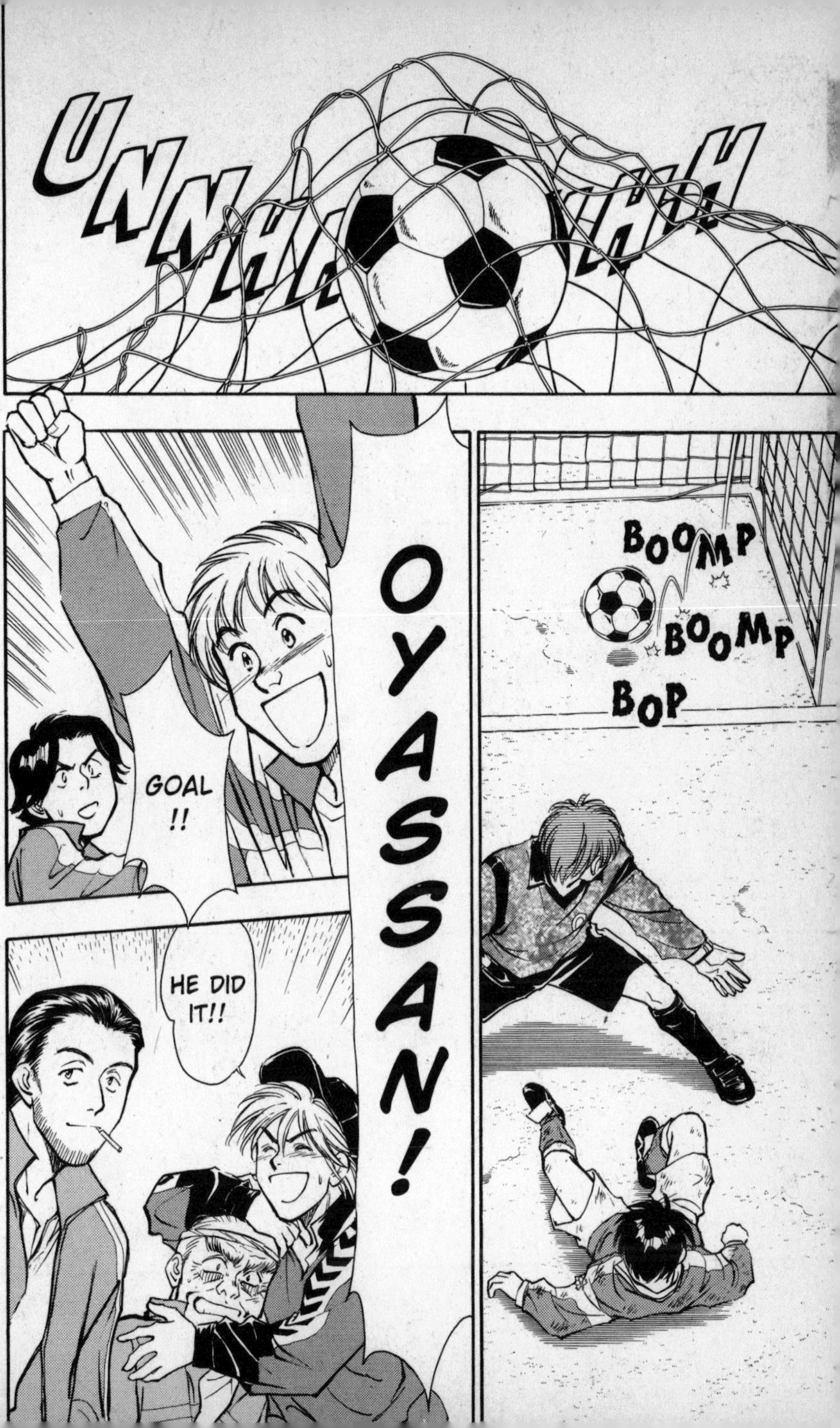
UNNHAAAH
BOOMP
BOOMP
BOP
OYASSAN!
GOAL!!
HE DID IT!!

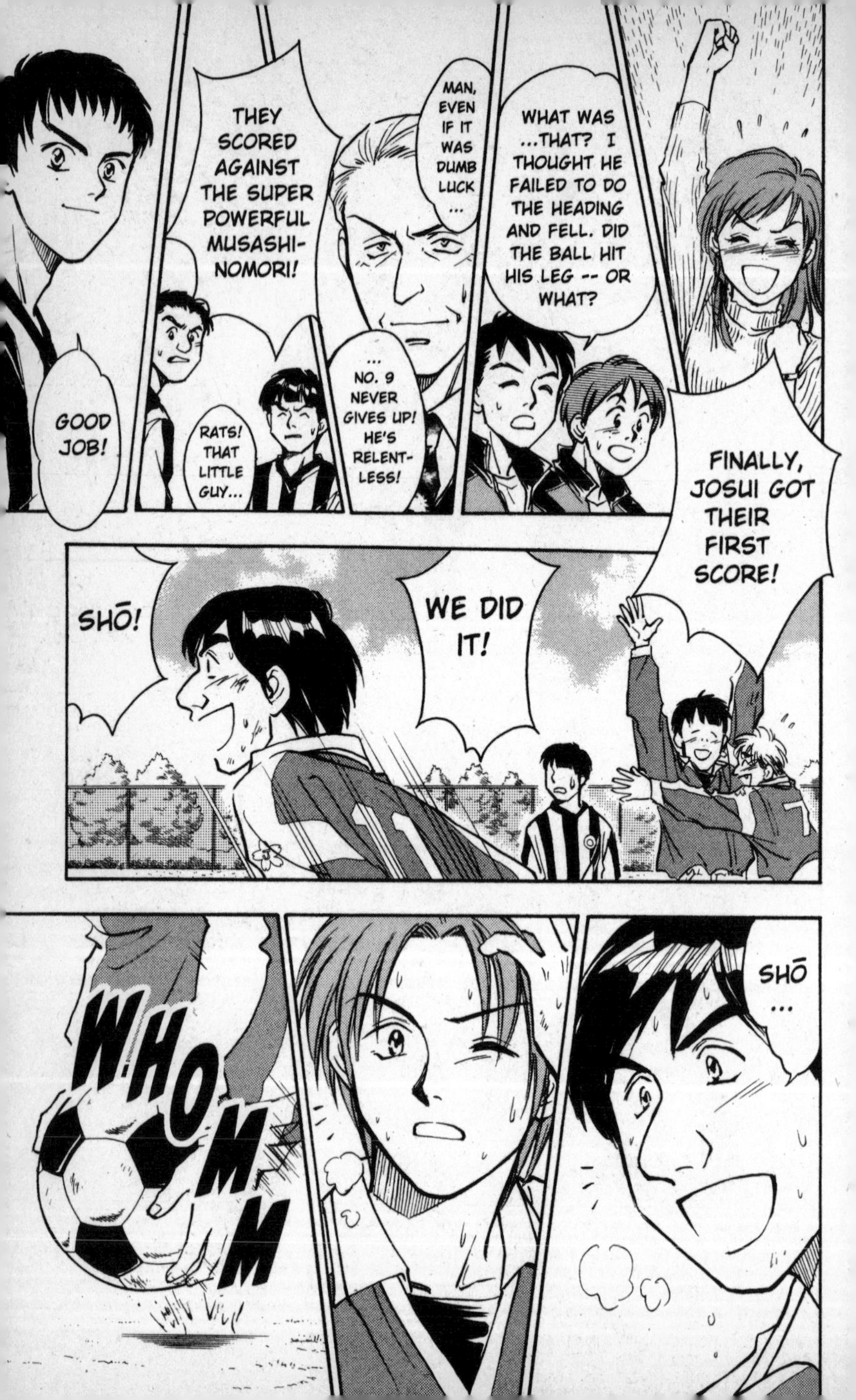
FINALLY, JOSUI GOT THEIR FIRST SCORE!
WHAT WAS ...THAT? I THOUGHT HE FAILED TO DO THE HEADING AND FELL. DID THE BALL HIT HIS LEG -- OR WHAT?
MAN, EVEN IF IT WAS DUMB LUCK ...
... NO. 9 NEVER GIVES UP! HE'S RELENT-LESS!
THEY SCORED AGAINST THE SUPER POWERFUL MUSASHI-NOMORI!
RATS! THAT LITTLE GUY...
GOOD JOB!
WE DID IT!
SHŌ!
SHŌ ...
WHOMMM

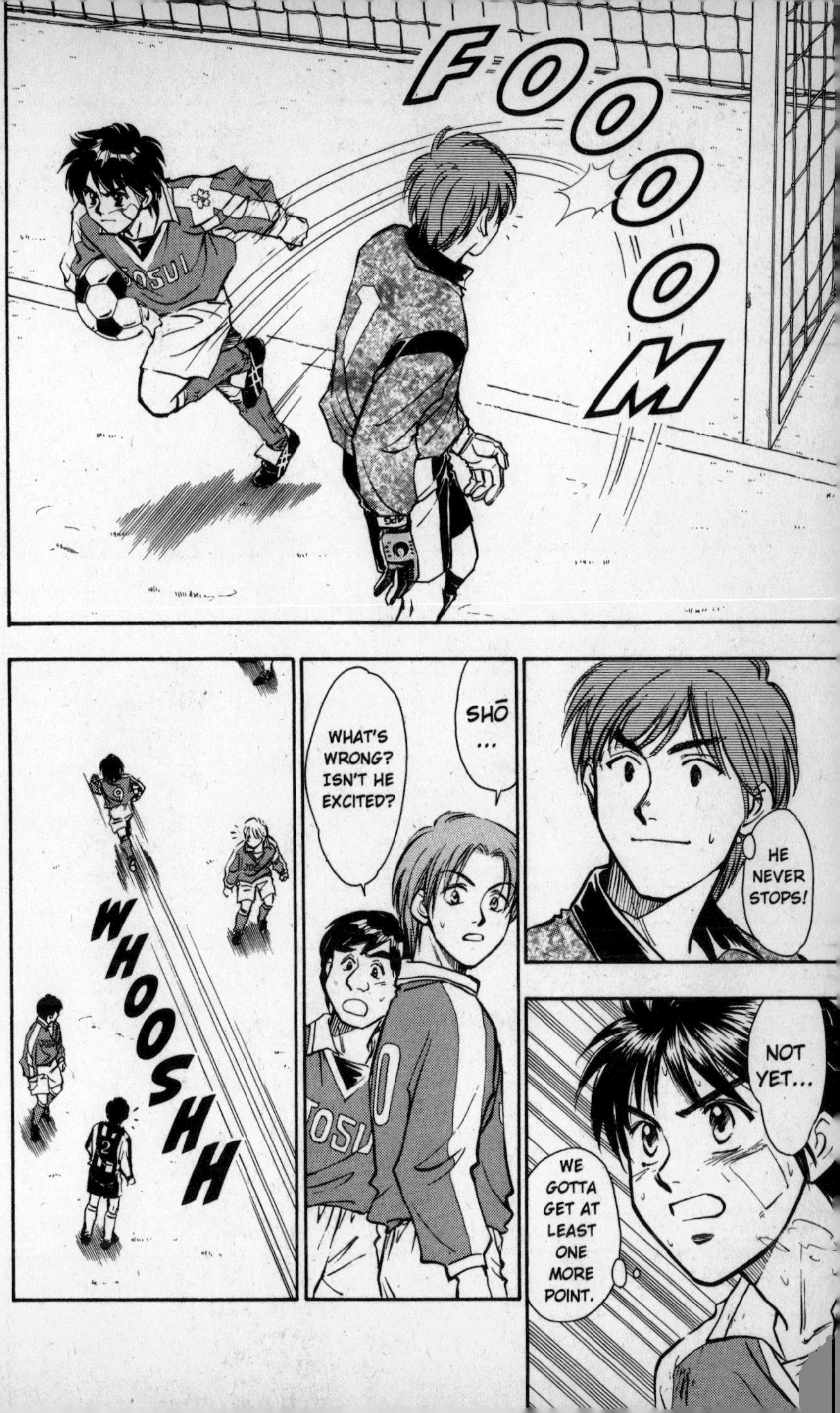
FOOOOOM
HE NEVER STOPS!
NOT YET...
WE GOTTA GET AT LEAST ONE MORE POINT.
SHŌ ...
WHAT'S WRONG? ISN'T HE EXCITED?
WHOOSHH

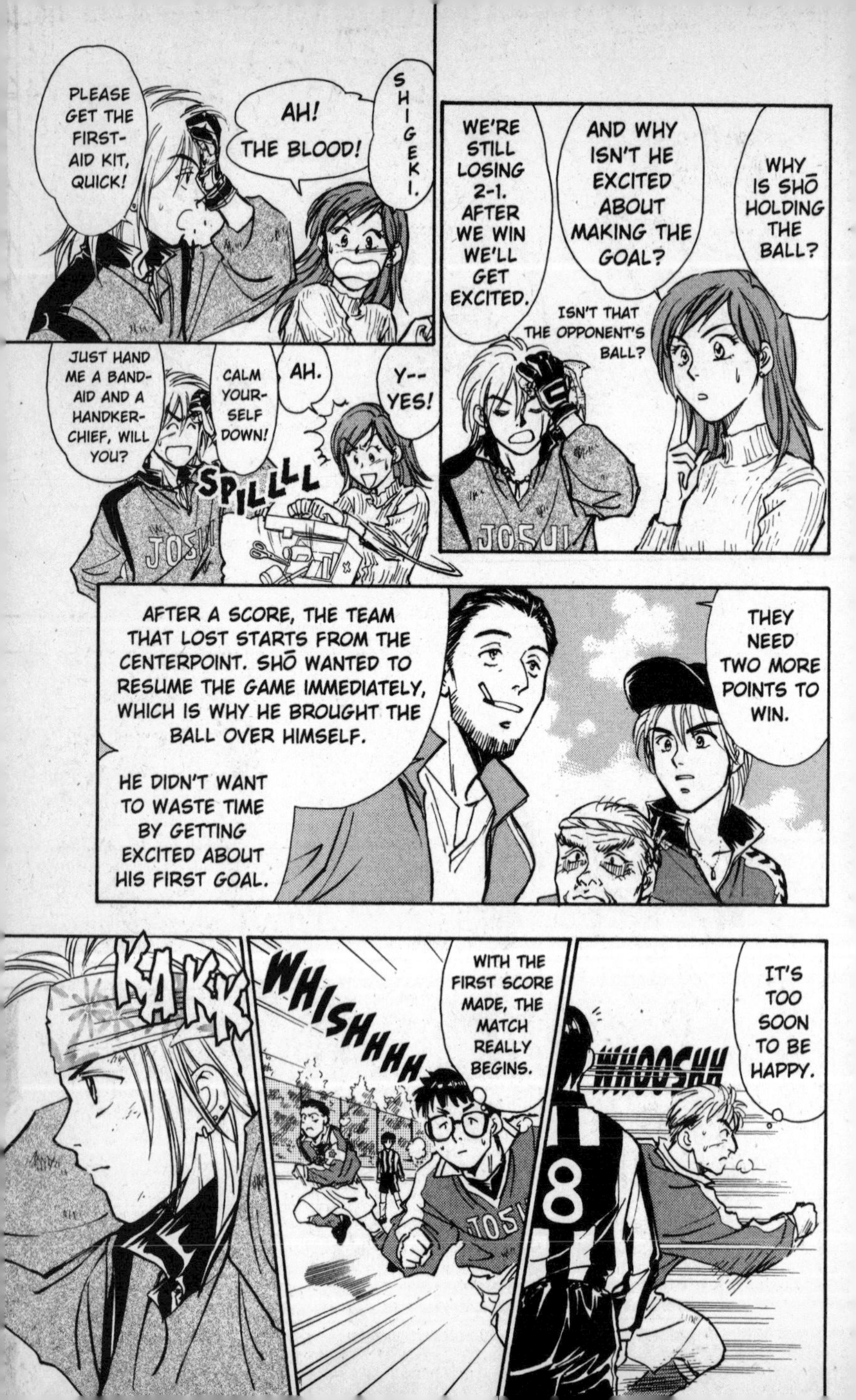
WHY IS SHŌ HOLDING THE BALL?
AND WHY ISN'T HE EXCITED ABOUT MAKING THE GOAL?
WE'RE STILL LOSING 2-1. AFTER WE WIN WE'LL GET EXCITED.
ISN'T THAT THE OPPONENT'S BALL?
SHIGEKI.
AH! THE BLOOD!
PLEASE GET THE FIRST-AID KIT, QUICK!
Y-- YES!
AH.
CALM YOURSELF DOWN!
JUST HAND ME A BAND-AID AND A HANDKERCHIEF, WILL YOU?
SPILLLL
THEY NEED TWO MORE POINTS TO WIN.
AFTER A SCORE, THE TEAM THAT LOST STARTS FROM THE CENTERPOINT. SHŌ WANTED TO RESUME THE GAME IMMEDIATELY, WHICH IS WHY HE BROUGHT THE BALL OVER HIMSELF.
HE DIDN'T WANT TO WASTE TIME BY GETTING EXCITED ABOUT HIS FIRST GOAL.
IT'S TOO SOON TO BE HAPPY.
WHOOSHH
WITH THE FIRST SCORE MADE, THE MATCH REALLY BEGINS.
WHISHHHHH
KAKK

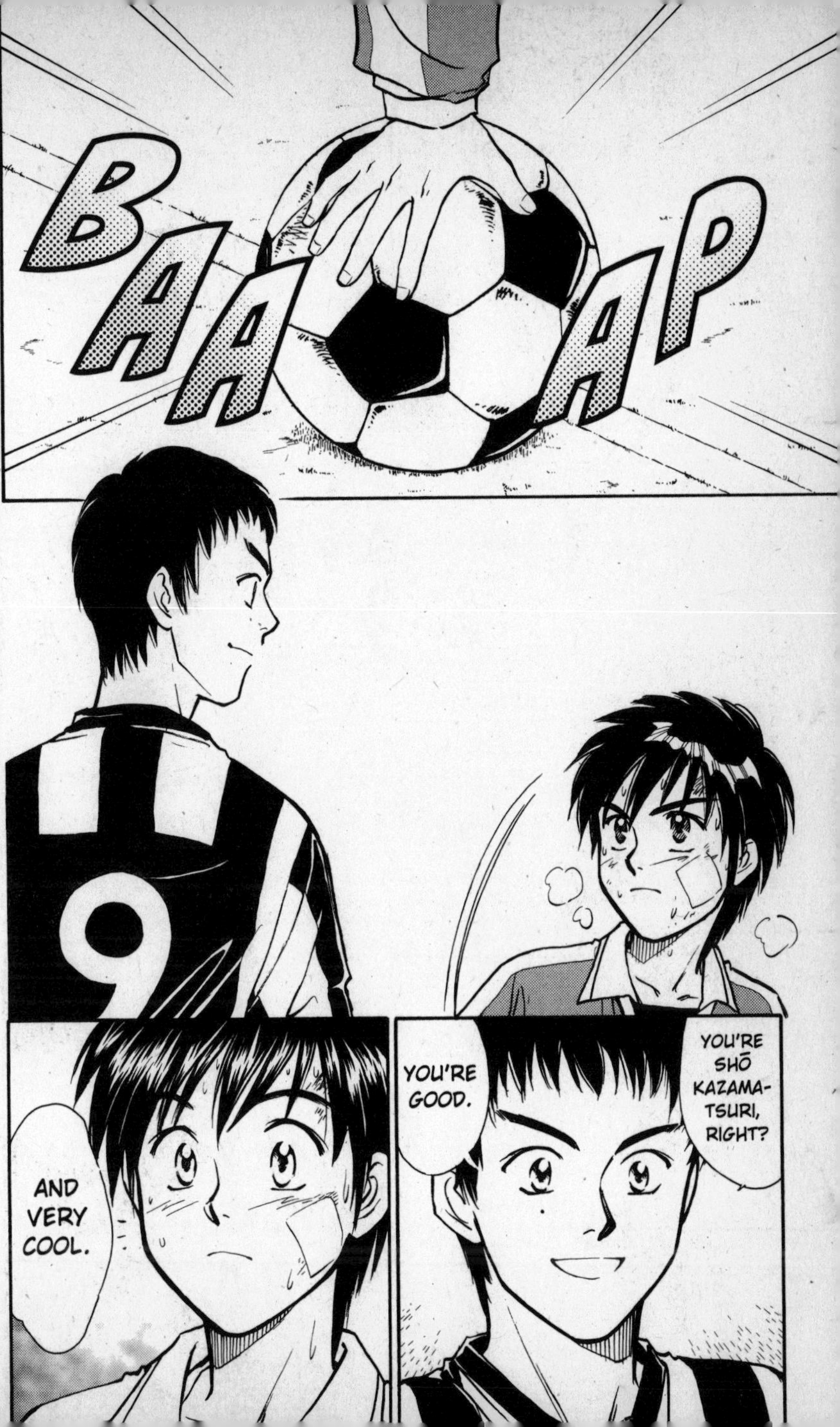
BAAAP
YOU'RE SHŌ KAZAMA-TSURI, RIGHT?
YOU'RE GOOD.
AND VERY COOL.

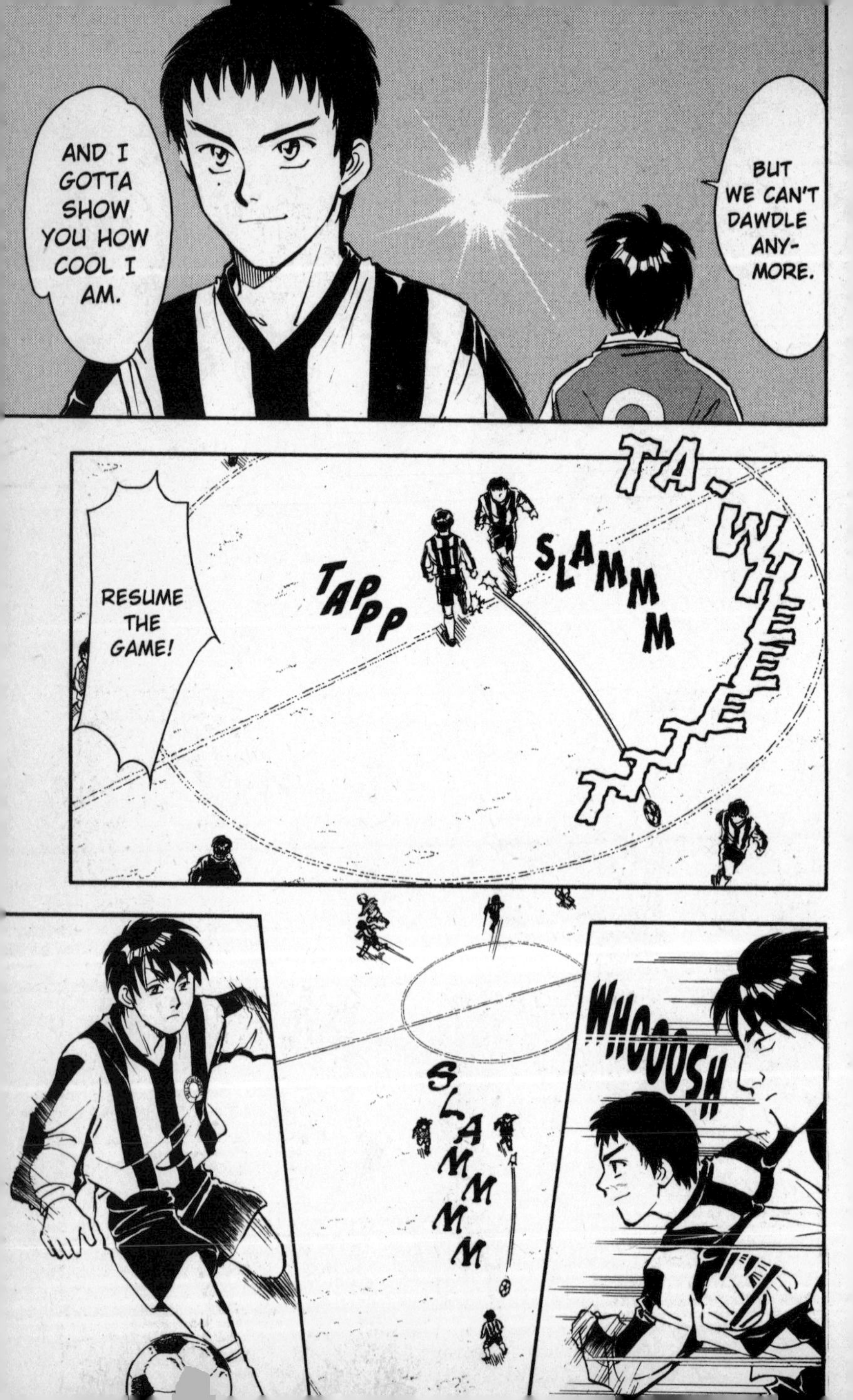
BUT WE CAN'T DAWDLE ANY-MORE.
AND I GOTTA SHOW YOU HOW COOL I AM.
TA-WHEEEEET
SLAMMM
TAPPP
RESUME THE GAME!
WHOOOSH
SLAMMMMM

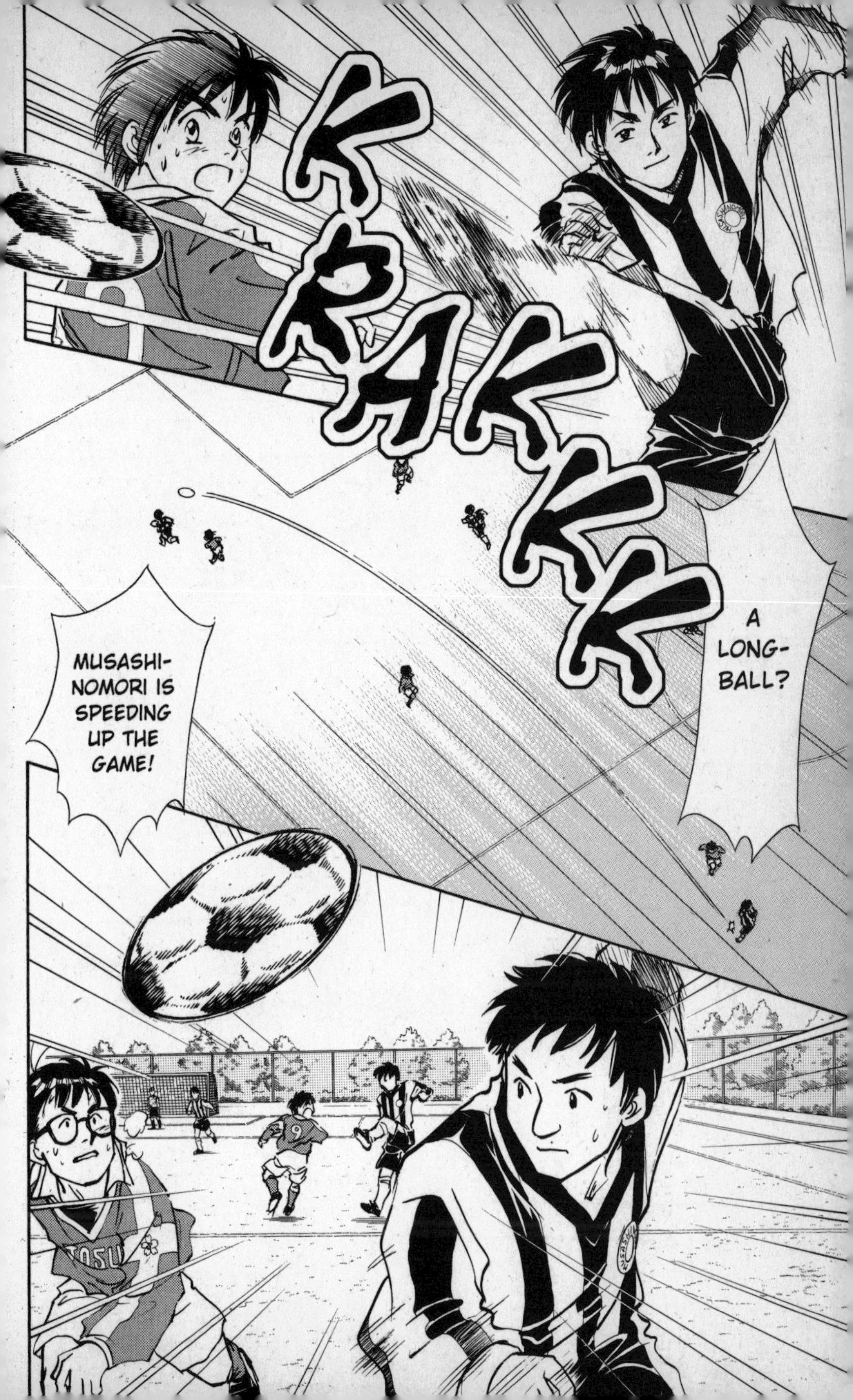
KRAKKK
A LONG-BALL?
MUSASHI-NOMORI IS SPEEDING UP THE GAME!

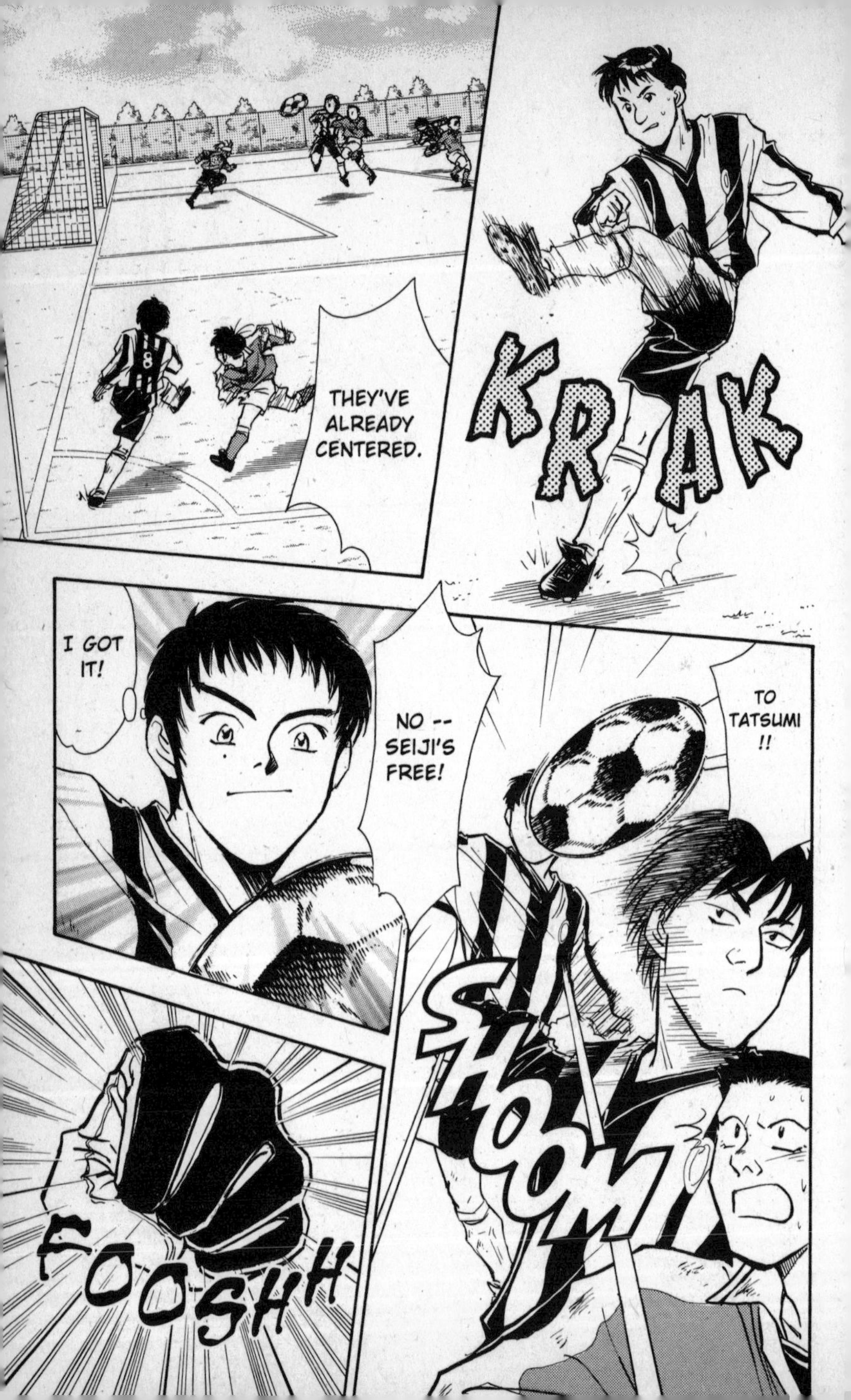
KRAK
THEY'VE ALREADY CENTERED.
TO TATSUMI !!
NO -- SEIJI'S FREE!
SHOOM
I GOT IT!
FOOSHH

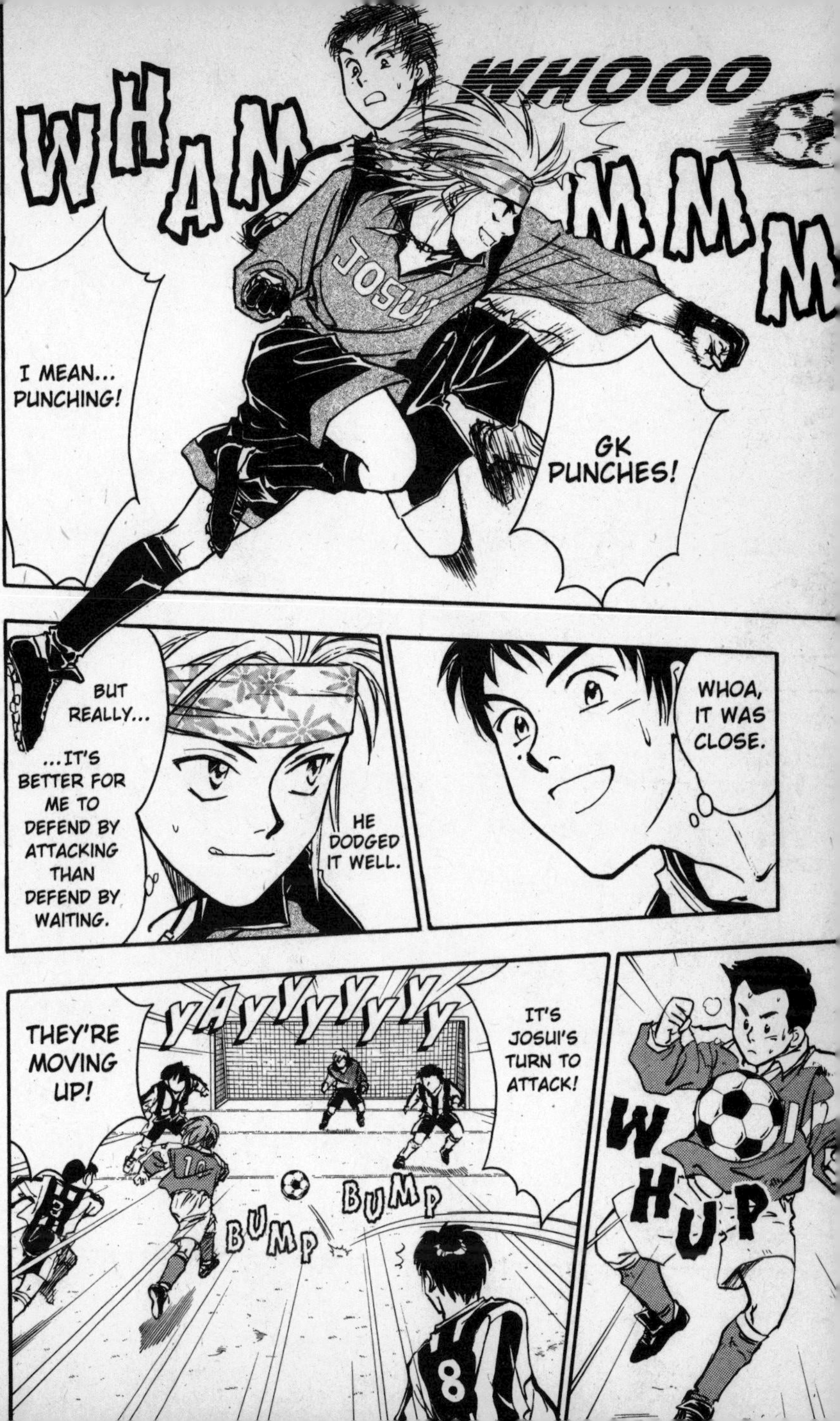
WHOOO
WHAMMMMM
GK PUNCHES!
I MEAN... PUNCHING!
WHOA, IT WAS CLOSE.
HE DODGED IT WELL.
BUT REALLY...
...IT'S BETTER FOR ME TO DEFEND BY ATTACKING THAN DEFEND BY WAITING.
WHUP
IT'S JOSUI'S TURN TO ATTACK!
YAYYYYYYY
THEY'RE MOVING UP!
BUMP
BUMP

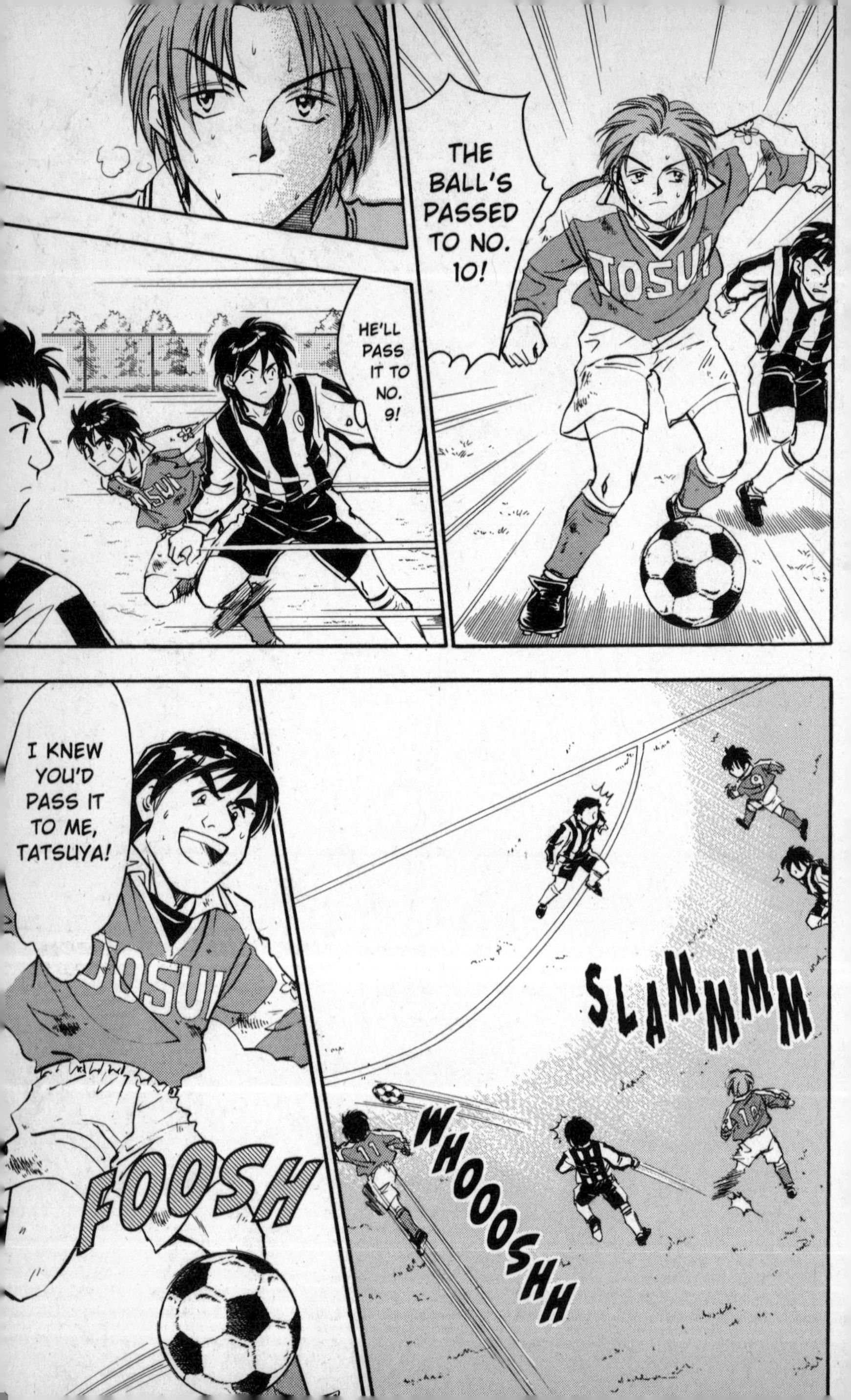
THE BALL'S PASSED TO NO. 10!
HE'LL PASS IT TO NO. 9!
SLAMMMM
WHOOOSHH
I KNEW YOU'D PASS IT TO ME, TATSUYA!
FOOSH

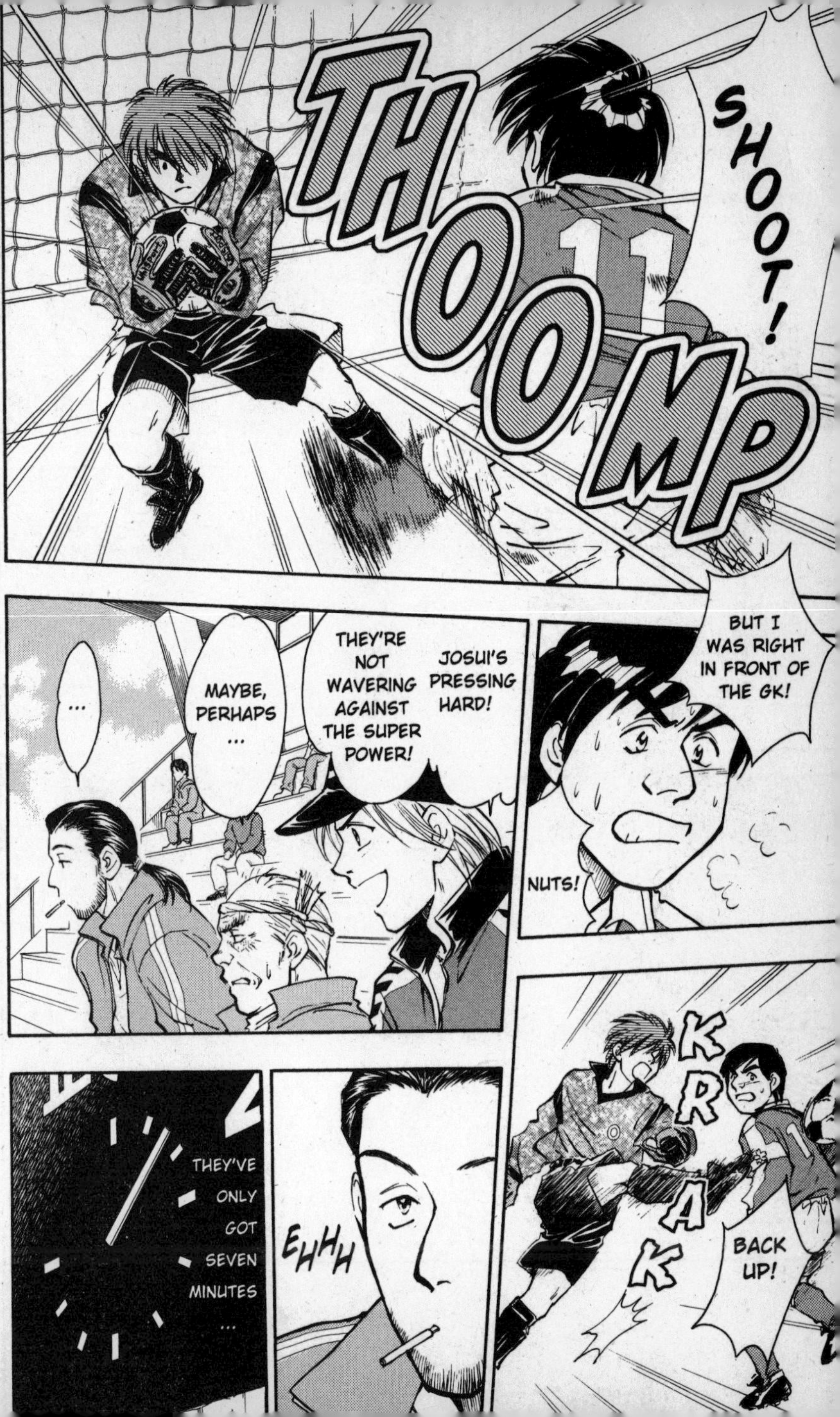
SHOOT!
THOOMP
BUT I WAS RIGHT IN FRONT OF THE GK!
NUTS!
JOSUI'S PRESSING HARD!
THEY'RE NOT WAVERING AGAINST THE SUPER POWER!
MAYBE, PERHAPS ...
...
KRAK
BACK UP!
EHHH
THEY'VE ONLY GOT SEVEN MINUTES ...

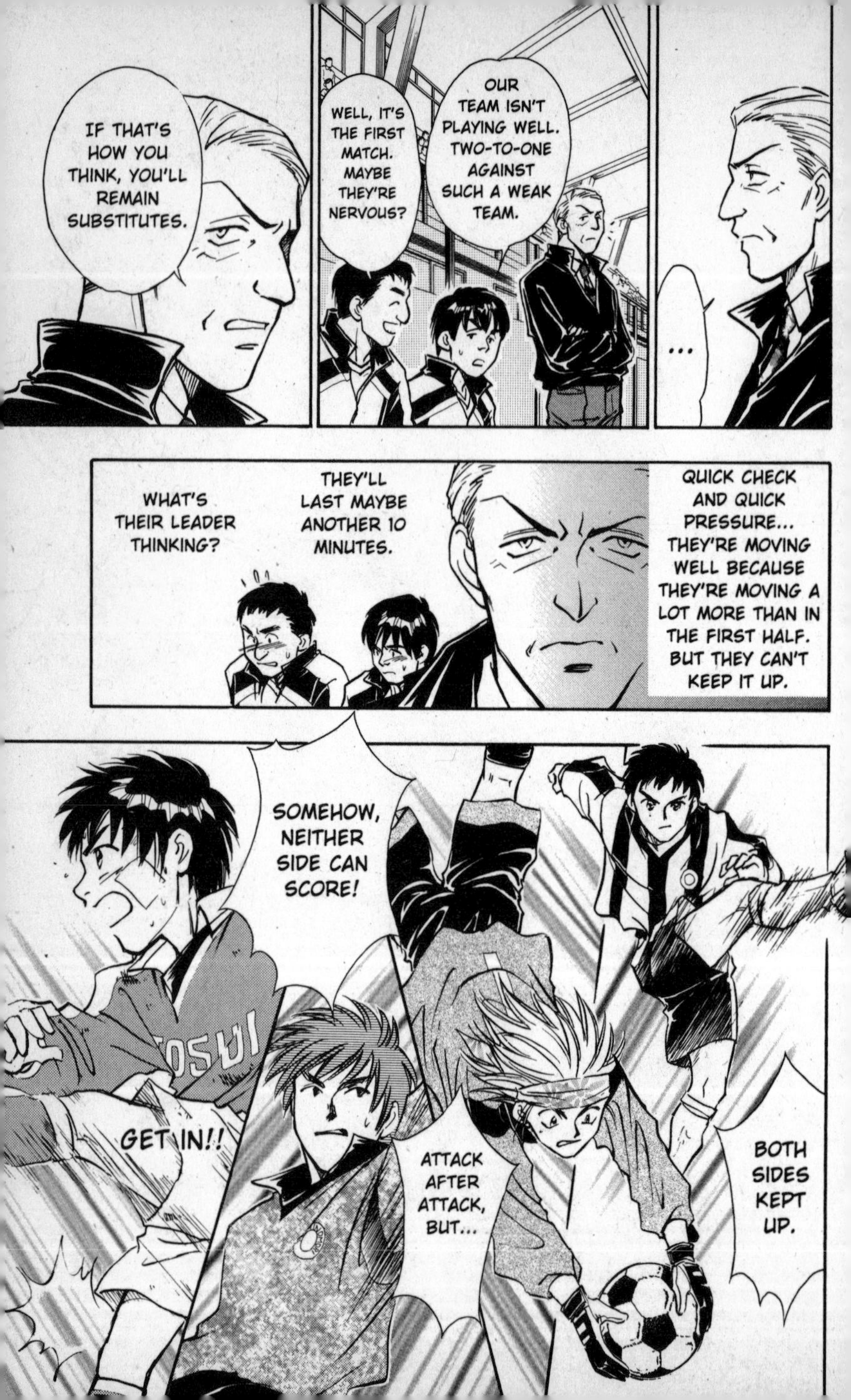
...
OUR TEAM ISN'T PLAYING WELL. TWO-TO-ONE AGAINST SUCH A WEAK TEAM.
WELL, IT'S THE FIRST MATCH. MAYBE THEY'RE NERVOUS?
IF THAT'S HOW YOU THINK, YOU'LL REMAIN SUBSTITUTES.
QUICK CHECK AND QUICK PRESSURE... THEY'RE MOVING WELL BECAUSE THEY'RE MOVING A LOT MORE THAN IN THE FIRST HALF. BUT THEY CAN'T KEEP IT UP.
THEY'LL LAST MAYBE ANOTHER 10 MINUTES.
WHAT'S THEIR LEADER THINKING?
BOTH SIDES KEPT UP.
ATTACK AFTER ATTACK, BUT...
SOMEHOW, NEITHER SIDE CAN SCORE!
GET IN!!

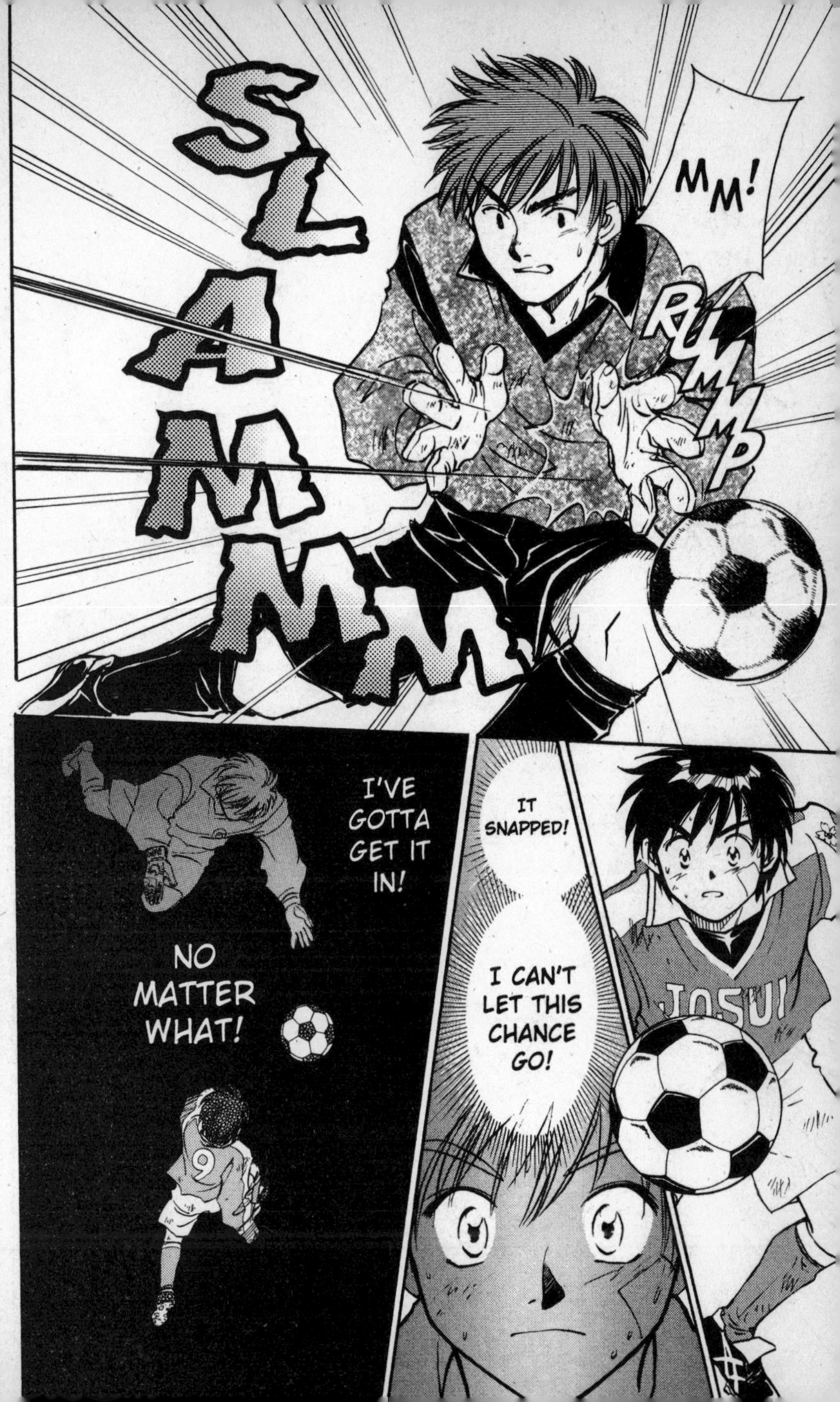
MM!
RUMMMP
SLAMMM
IT SNAPPED!
I CAN'T LET THIS CHANCE GO!
I'VE GOTTA GET IT IN!
NO MATTER WHAT!

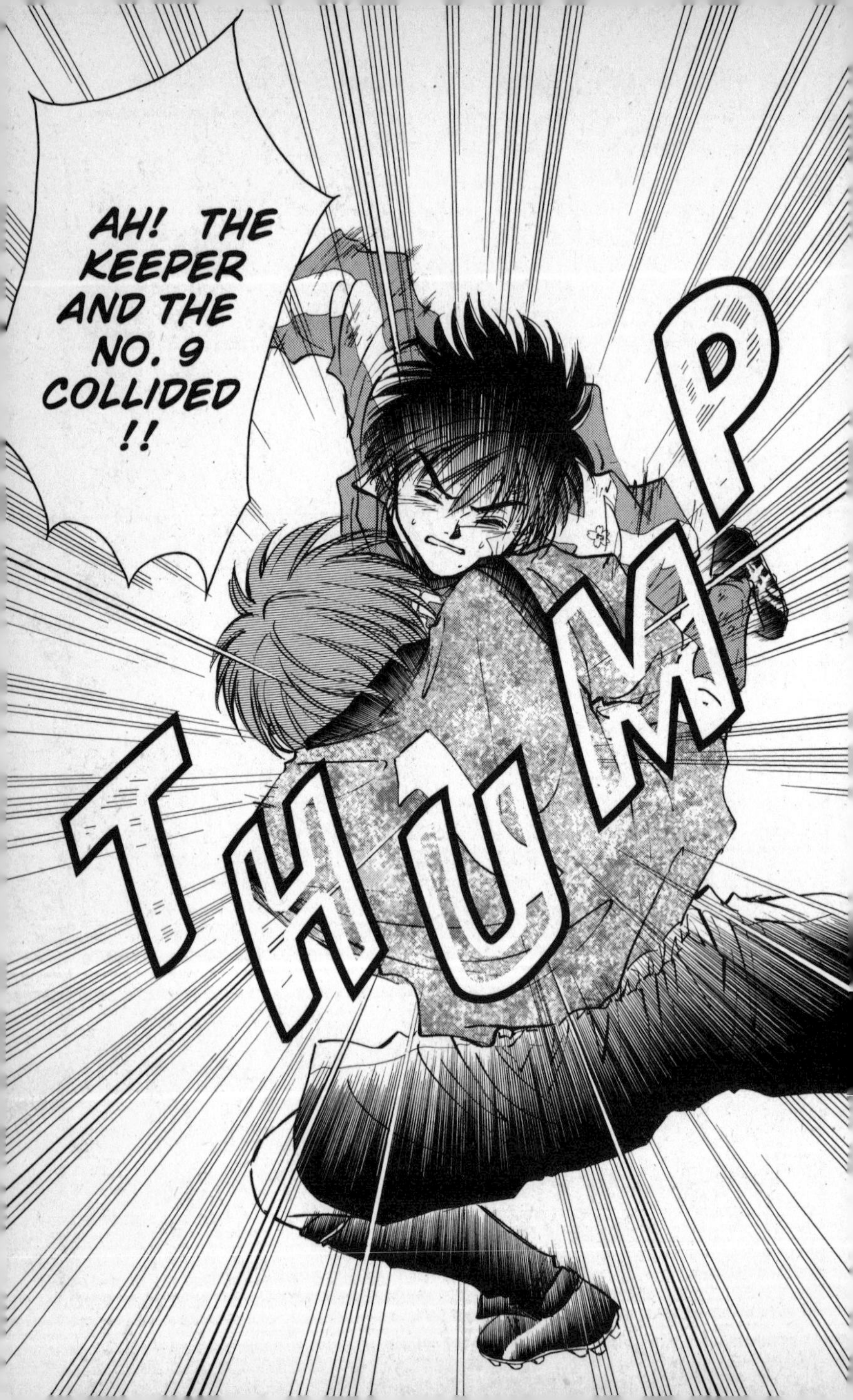
AH! THE KEEPER AND THE NO. 9 COLLIDED !!
THUMP

● BIOGRAPHIES OF GOAL KEEPERS

DINO ZOFF OF THE ITALY TEAM IS CALLED A LEGENDARY GOAL KEEPER. SINCE THE MEXICAN WORLD CUP OF 1970, HE PLAYED CONTINUOUSLY FOR THE FOUR WORLD CUPS. DURING THE SPANISH WORLD CUP OF 1982, AT THE AGE OF 40, HE LEAD THE ITALY TEAM TO VICTORY. TO TOP IT OFF, HE HAS THE RECORD LENGTH OF TIME BEFORE A FIRST SCORE IS MADE - 1,143 MINUTES IN THE INTERNATIONAL GAMES AND 903 MINUTES IN THE DOMESTIC GAMES. INDEED, HE WAS A GREAT GOAL KEEPER.

JUST LIKE ZOFF, AT THE AGE OF 40, PETER SHELTON OF THE ENGLAND TEAM PLAYED IN THE WORLD CUP. IT WAS THE ITALIAN WORLD CUP OF 1990, AND HE LEAD THE ENGLISH TEAM TO THE BEST FOUR. HE PLAYED FROM 1970 THROUGH 1990, FOR 20 YEARS AS A REPRESENTATIVE PLAYER FOR ENGLAND, AND THE NUMBER OF GAMES HE PLAYED WAS 125. THAT, OF COURSE, IS A RECORD FOR A PLAYER ON THE ENGLAND TEAM... AND NO ONE HAS BROKEN THE RECORD SO FAR.

WALTER ZENGA OF THE ITALY TEAM IS ANOTHER GOAL KEEPER WE CAN'T FORGET. AT THE ITALIAN WORLD CUP OF 1990, DURING THE SEMI-FINAL, HE DID NOT ALLOW THE OPPONENT, ARGENTINA, TO SCORE FOR THE FIRST 517 MINUTES, ESTABLISHING THE NEW RECORD FOR THE WORLD CUP. WITH HIS UNYIELDING AND SHOWY PERSONALITY, HE MADE BIG DEALS OUT OF AVERAGE SITUATIONS AND ATTRACTED MANY FEMALE FANS.

THE ATTRIBUTES REQUIRED FOR A GOAL KEEPER ARE NOT ONLY THE REFLEXES BUT ALSO STABILITY. IN ADDITION, THE ABILITY TO READ THE OVERALL FLOW OF THE GAME AND DIRECT THE TEAM FROM BEHIND. THAT'S WHY, IN THE GAME OF SOCCER, THE VOICE OF THE GOAL KEEPER IS CALLED THE "VOICE OF GOD."

--TATSUYA WATANABE (WINNING RUN)

STAGE.22 The Limit

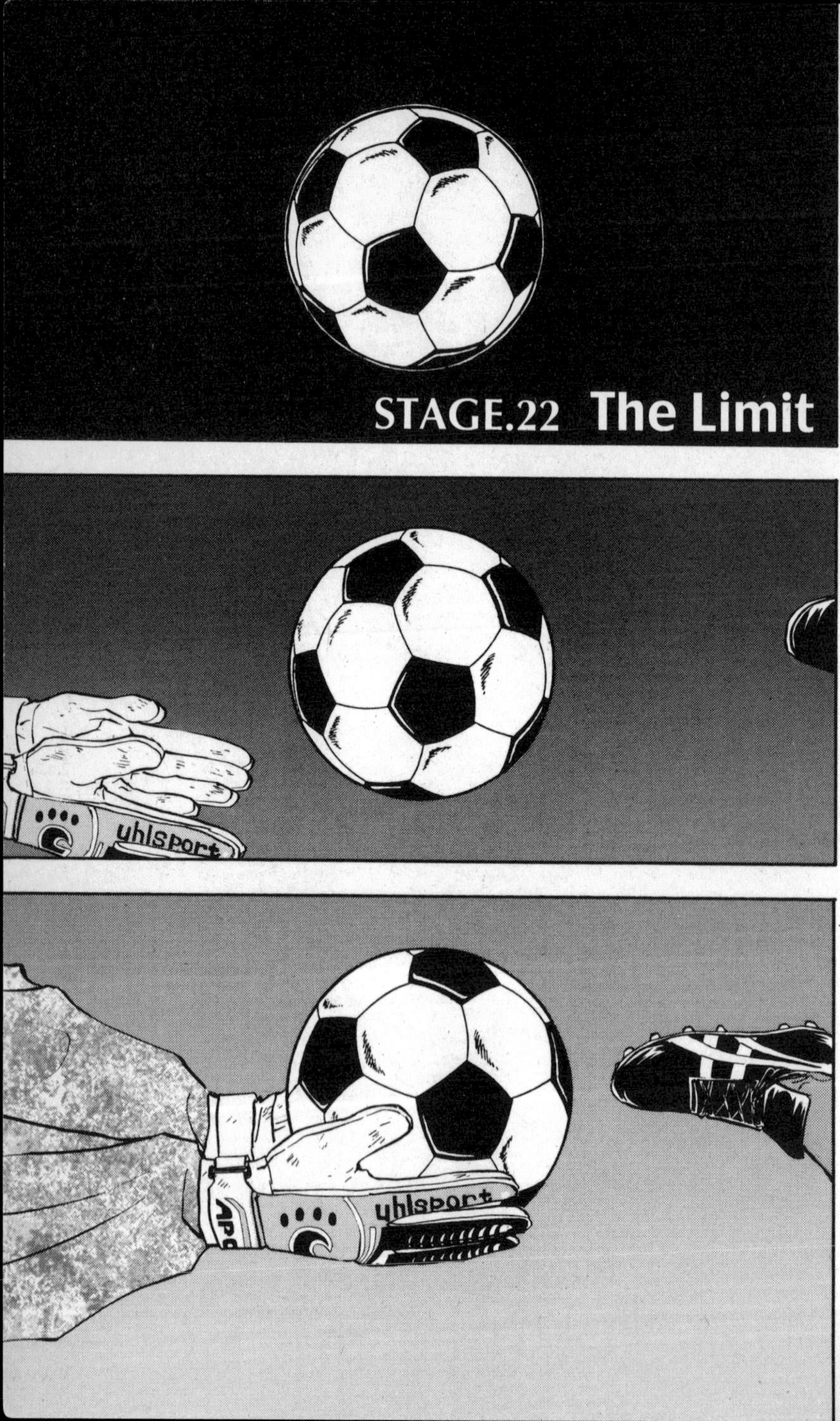
uhlsport
uhlsport

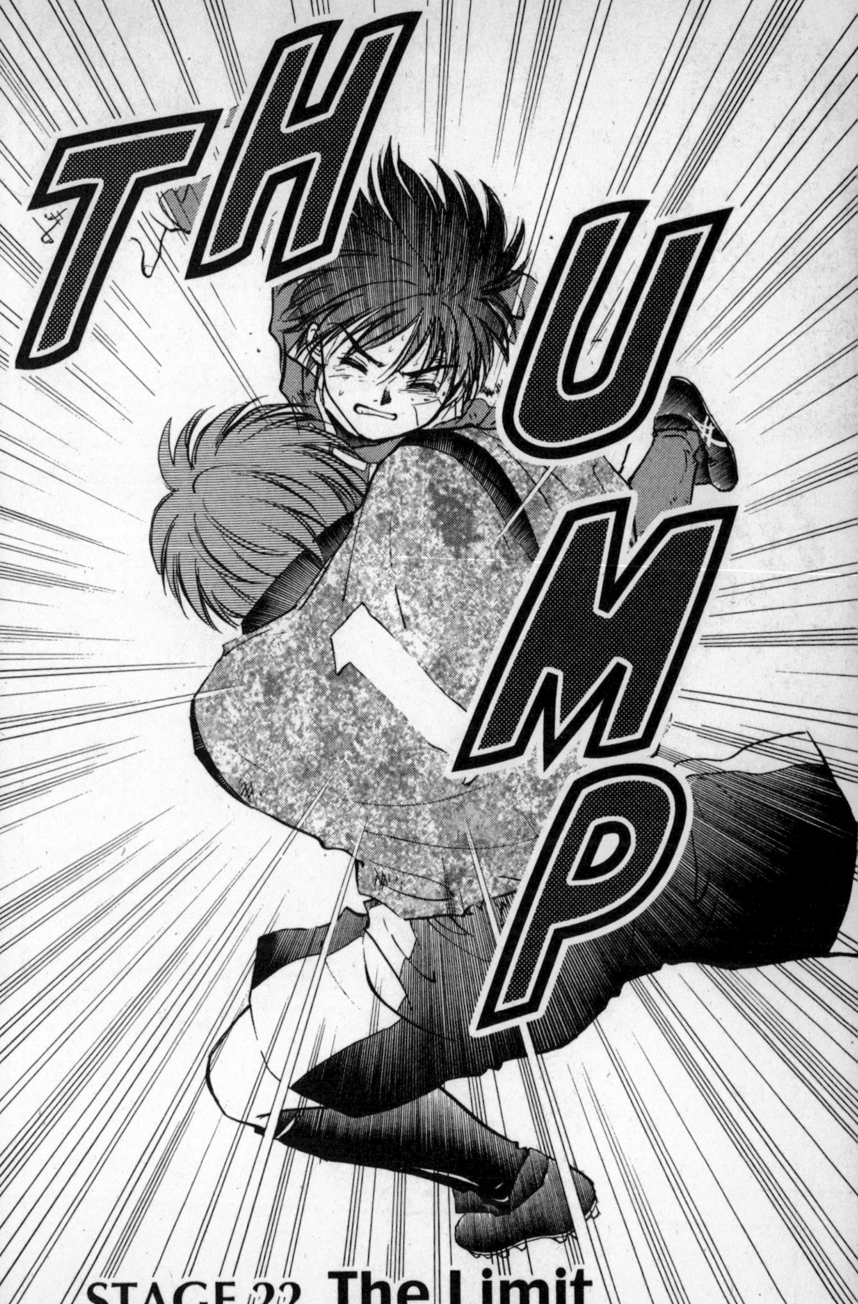
THUMP

STAGE.22 The Limit

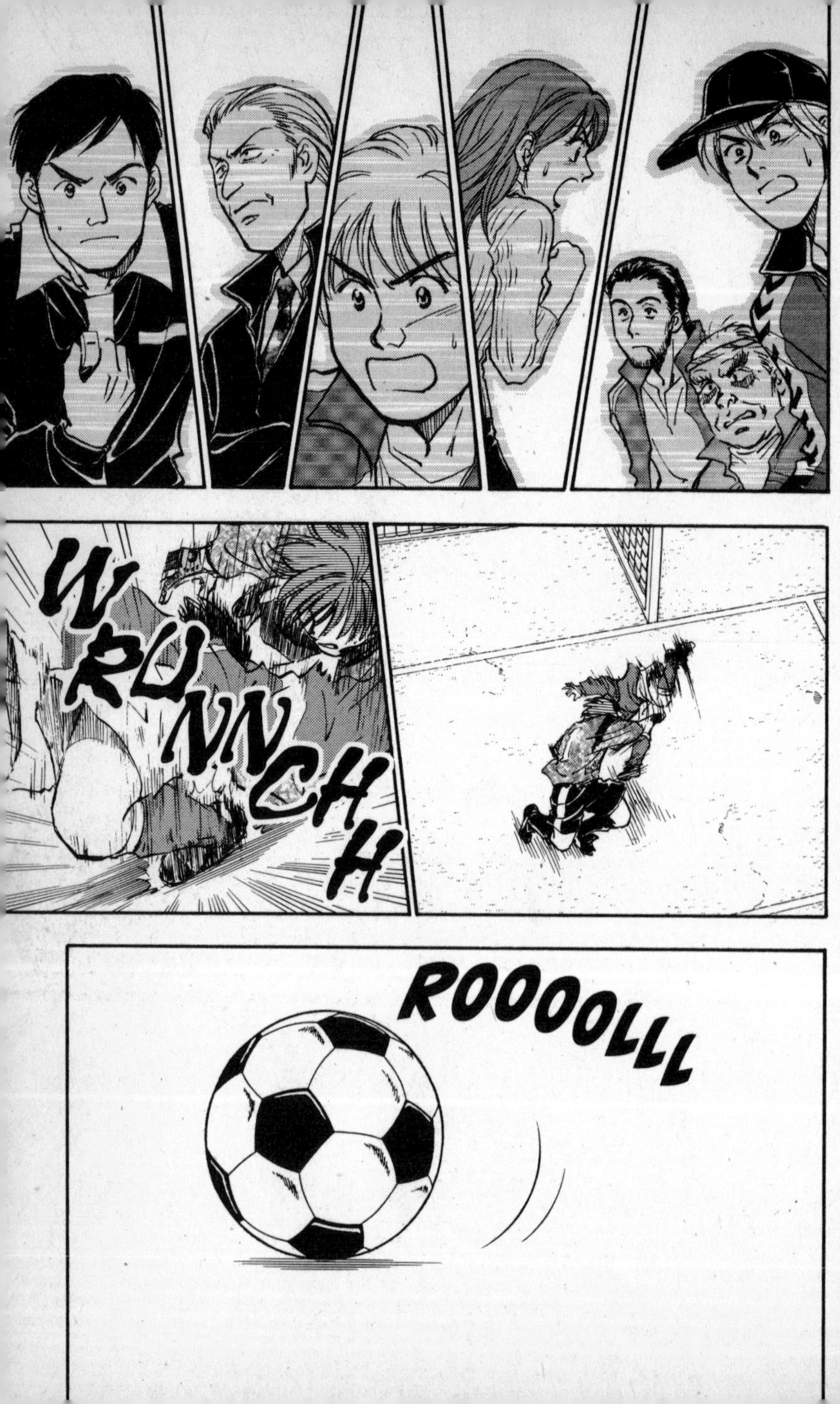
WRUNNCHH
ROOOOLLL

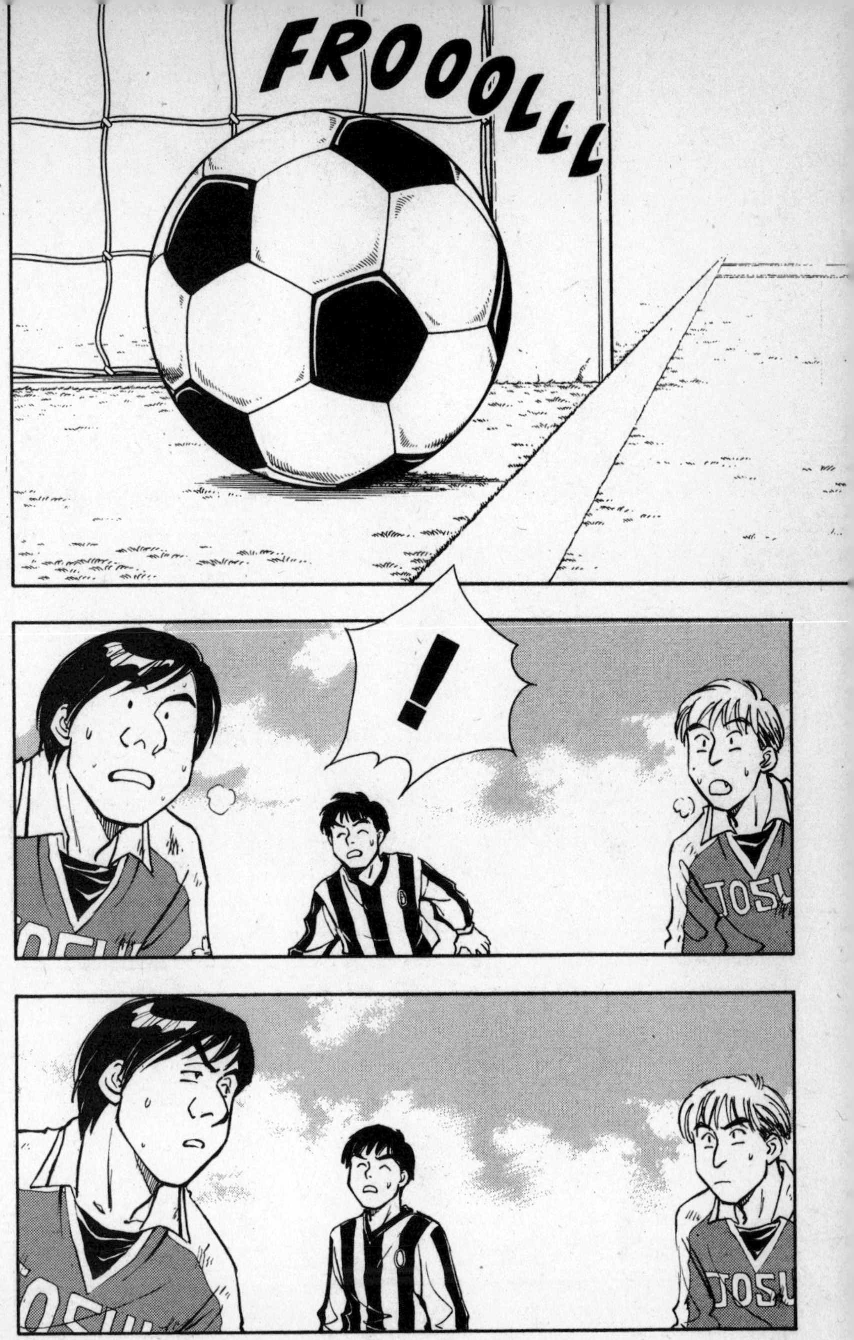
FROOOLLL
!

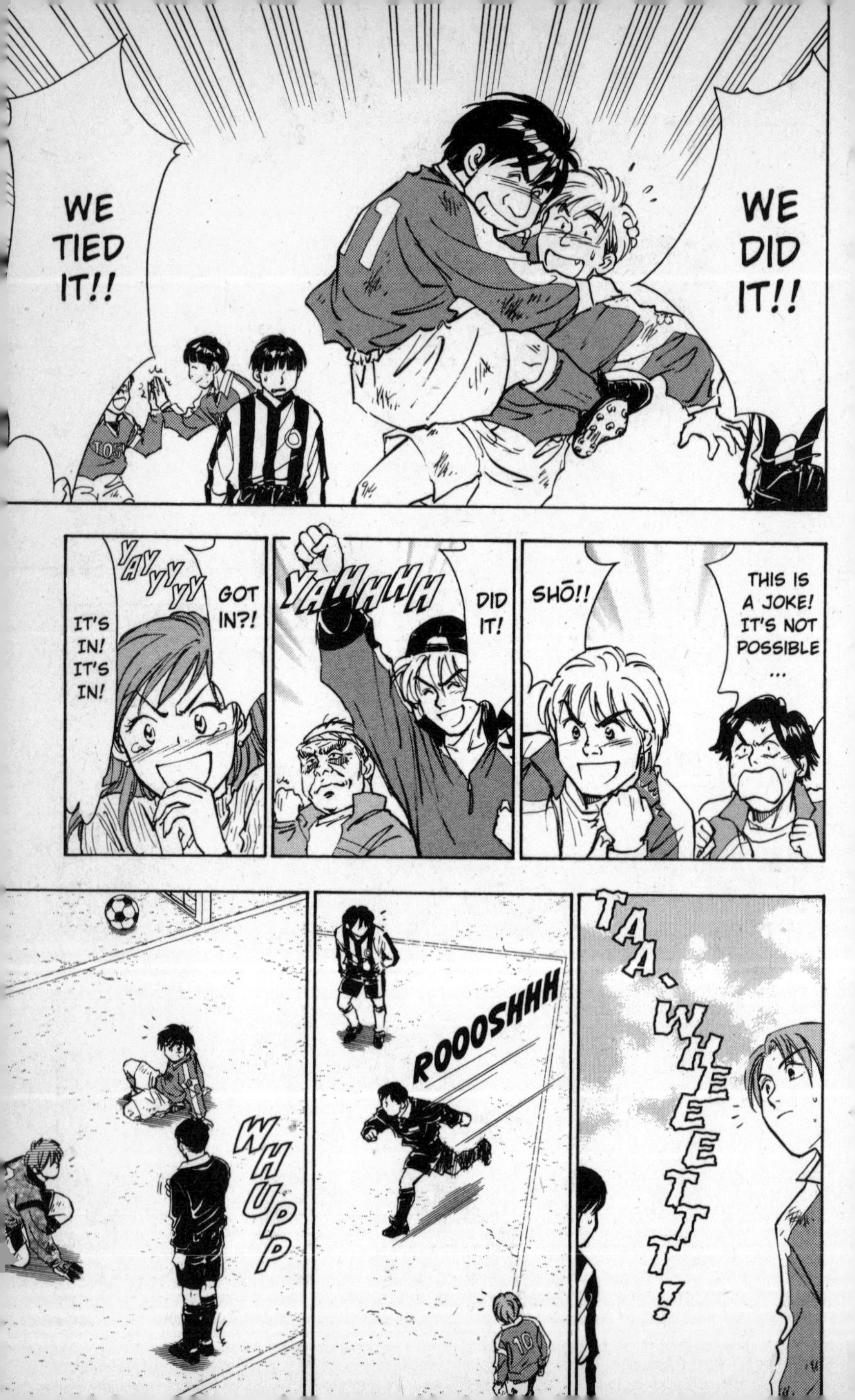
WE DID IT!!
WE TIED IT!!
THIS IS A JOKE! IT'S NOT POSSIBLE ...
SHŌ!!
DID IT!
YAHHHHH
GOT IN?!
YAYYYYY
IT'S IN! IT'S IN!
TAA-WHEEETTT!
ROOOSHHH
WHUPP

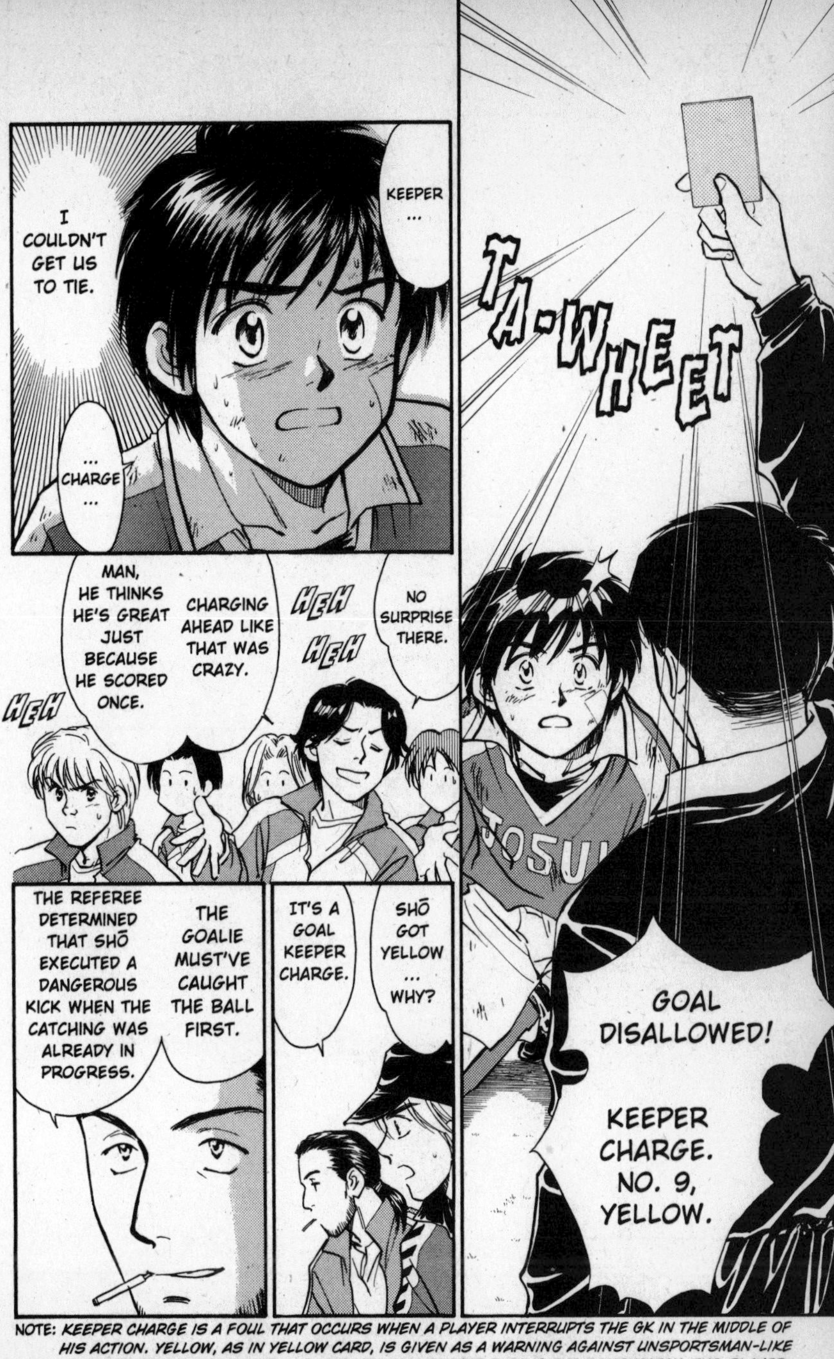
TA-WHEET
GOAL DISALLOWED!
KEEPER CHARGE. NO. 9, YELLOW.
KEEPER ...
I COULDN'T GET US TO TIE.
... CHARGE ...
NO SURPRISE THERE.
HEH
HEH
CHARGING AHEAD LIKE THAT WAS CRAZY.
MAN, HE THINKS HE'S GREAT JUST BECAUSE HE SCORED ONCE.
HEH
SHŌ GOT YELLOW ... WHY?
IT'S A GOAL KEEPER CHARGE.
THE GOALIE MUST'VE CAUGHT THE BALL FIRST.
THE REFEREE DETERMINED THAT SHŌ EXECUTED A DANGEROUS KICK WHEN THE CATCHING WAS ALREADY IN PROGRESS.

NOTE: *KEEPER CHARGE IS A FOUL THAT OCCURS WHEN A PLAYER INTERRUPTS THE GK IN THE MIDDLE OF HIS ACTION. YELLOW, AS IN YELLOW CARD, IS GIVEN AS A WARNING AGAINST UNSPORTSMAN-LIKE CONDUCT. IF A SECOND WARNING IS GIVEN TO A PLAYER DURING THE SAME MATCH, THE PLAYER IS KICKED OUT OF THE GAME.*

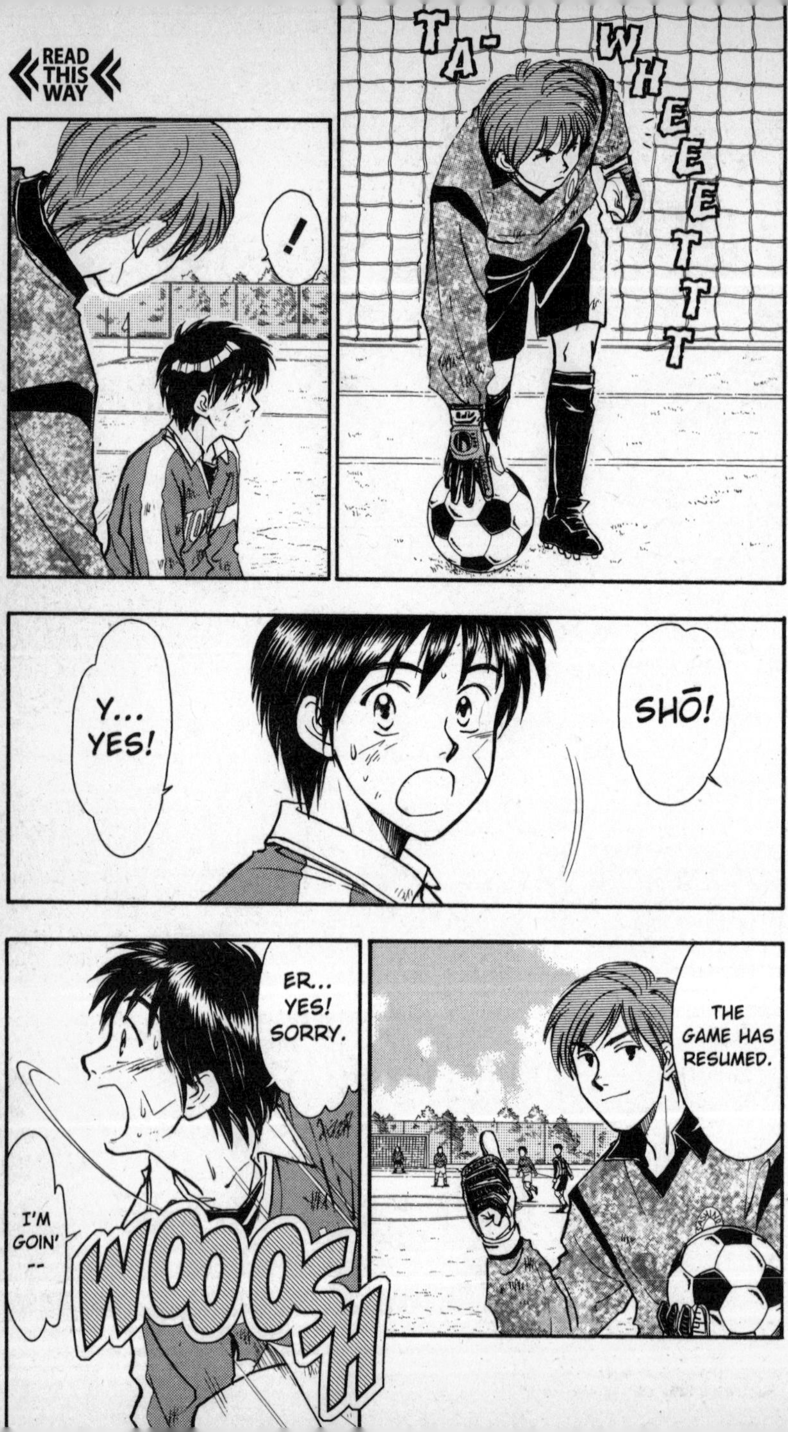
READ THIS WAY
TA-WHEEETTT
!
SHŌ!
Y... YES!
THE GAME HAS RESUMED.
ER... YES! SORRY.
I'M GOIN' --
WOOOSH

READ THIS WAY

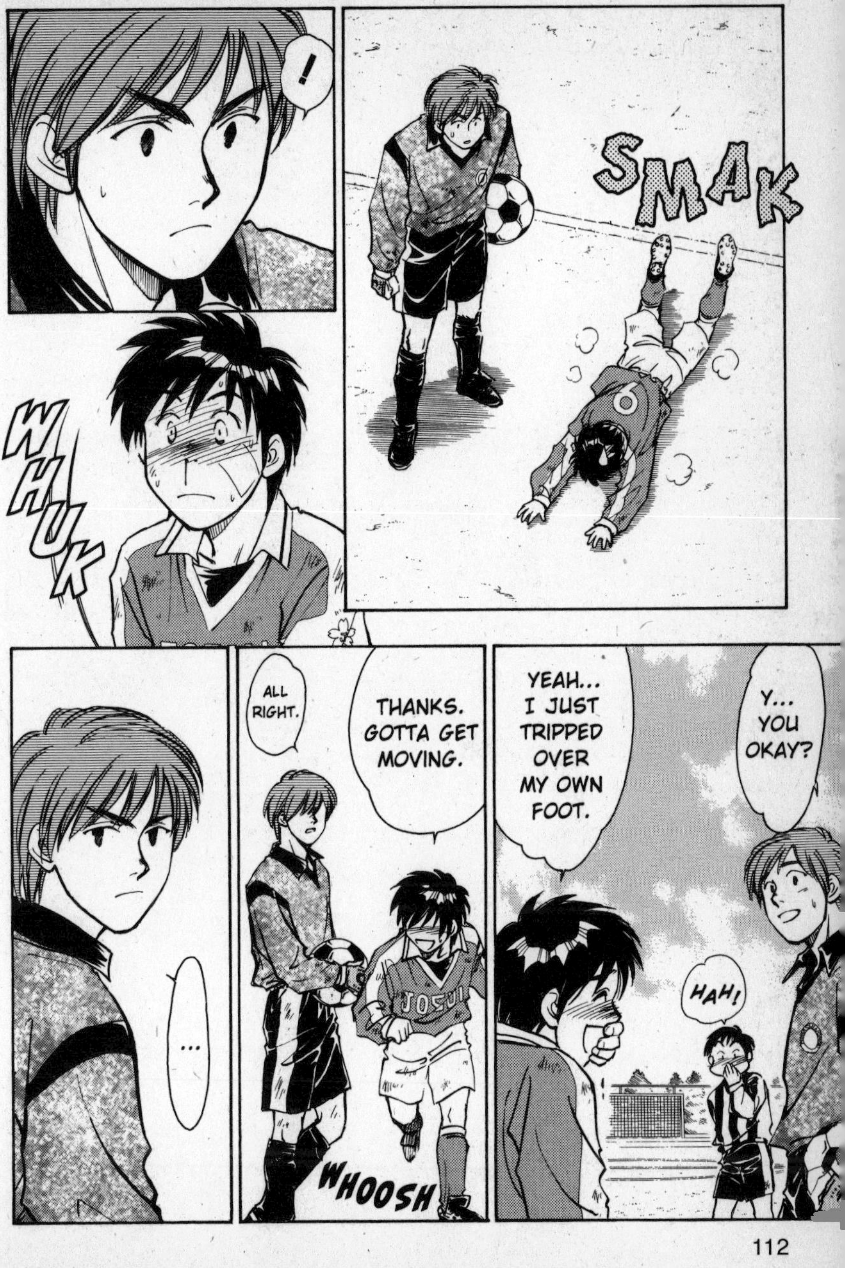

SMAK
!
WHUK
Y... YOU OKAY?
YEAH... I JUST TRIPPED OVER MY OWN FOOT.
HAH!
THANKS. GOTTA GET MOVING.
ALL RIGHT.
WHOOSH
...

READ THIS WAY

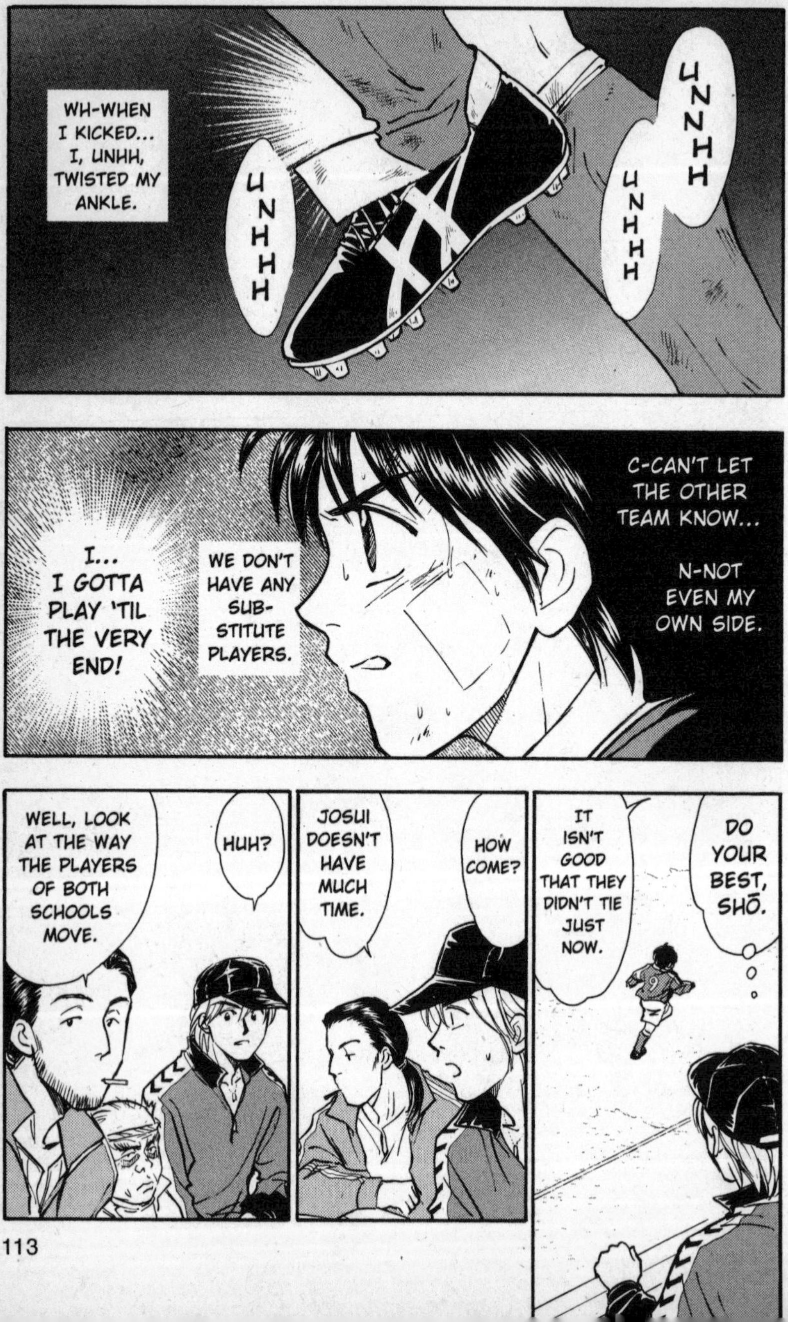

UNNHH
UNHHH
UNHHH
WH-WHEN I KICKED... I, UNHH, TWISTED MY ANKLE.
C-CAN'T LET THE OTHER TEAM KNOW...
N-NOT EVEN MY OWN SIDE.
WE DON'T HAVE ANY SUB-STITUTE PLAYERS.
I... I GOTTA PLAY 'TIL THE VERY END!
DO YOUR BEST, SHŌ.
IT ISN'T GOOD THAT THEY DIDN'T TIE JUST NOW.
HOW COME?
JOSUI DOESN'T HAVE MUCH TIME.
HUH?
WELL, LOOK AT THE WAY THE PLAYERS OF BOTH SCHOOLS MOVE.

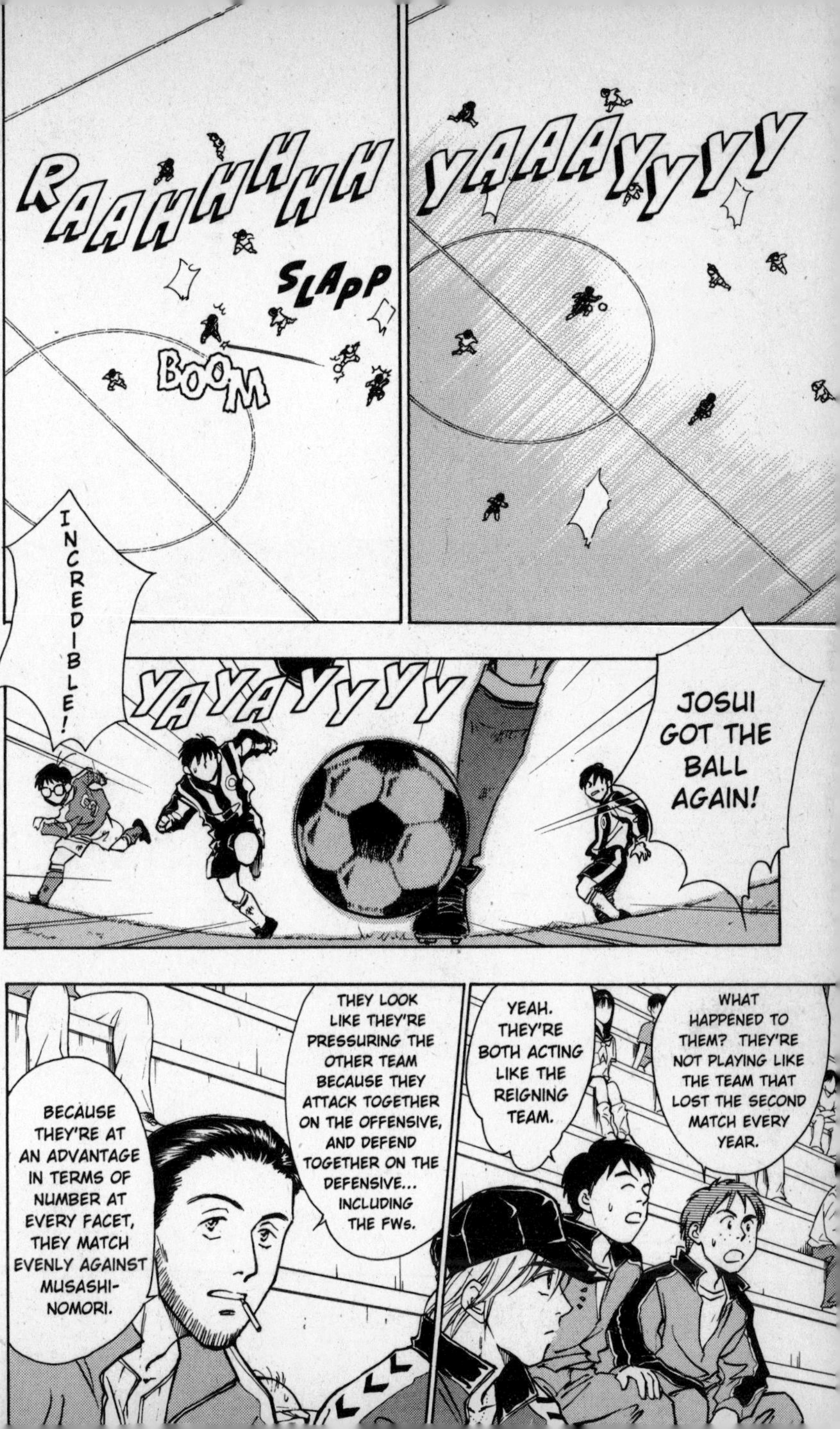
YAAAAYYYY
RAAHHHHHH
SLAPP
BOOM
JOSUI GOT THE BALL AGAIN!
YAYAYYYY
INCREDIBLE!
WHAT HAPPENED TO THEM? THEY'RE NOT PLAYING LIKE THE TEAM THAT LOST THE SECOND MATCH EVERY YEAR.
YEAH. THEY'RE BOTH ACTING LIKE THE REIGNING TEAM.
THEY LOOK LIKE THEY'RE PRESSURING THE OTHER TEAM BECAUSE THEY ATTACK TOGETHER ON THE OFFENSIVE, AND DEFEND TOGETHER ON THE DEFENSIVE... INCLUDING THE FWs.
BECAUSE THEY'RE AT AN ADVANTAGE IN TERMS OF NUMBER AT EVERY FACET, THEY MATCH EVENLY AGAINST MUSASHI-NOMORI.

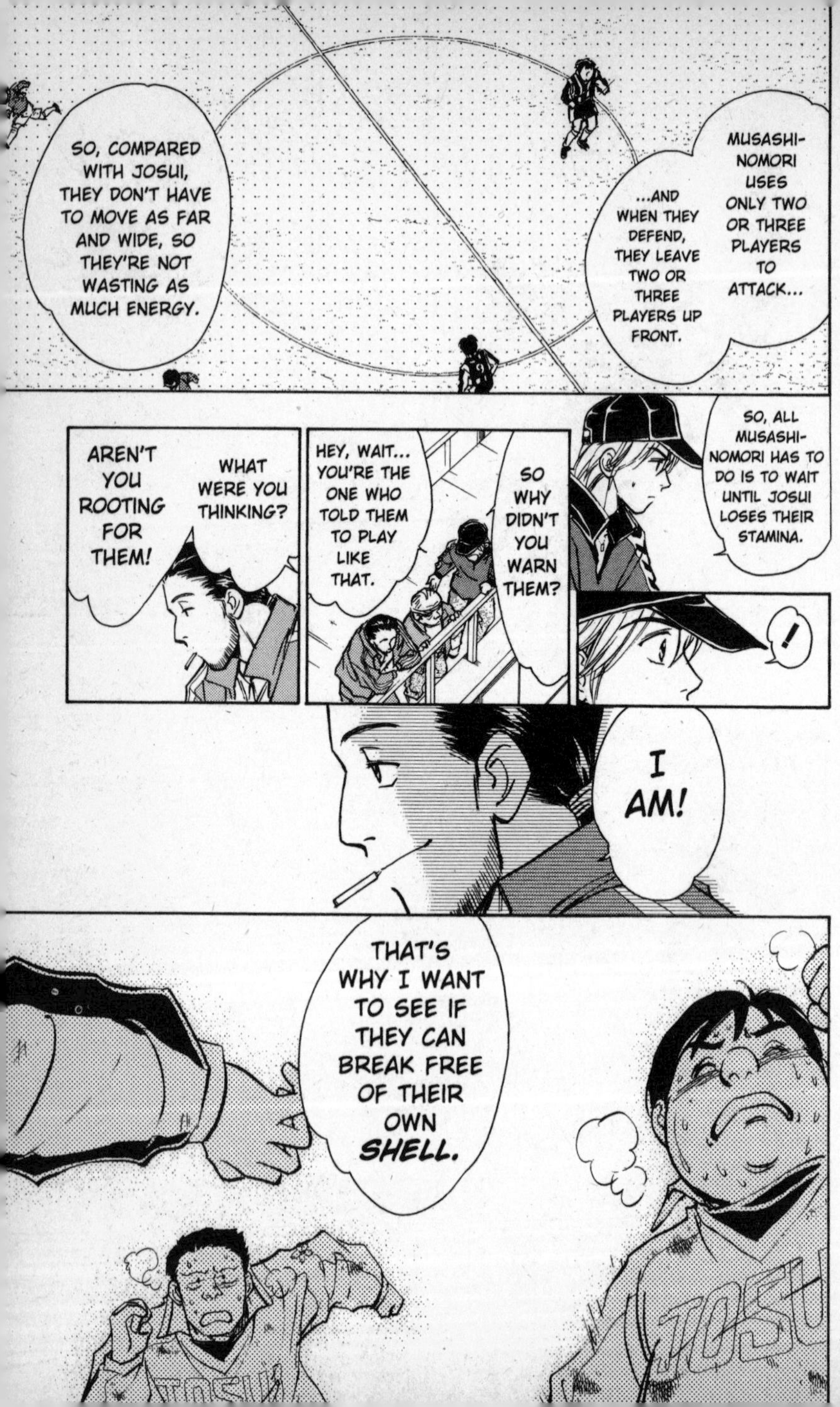
MUSASHI-NOMORI USES ONLY TWO OR THREE PLAYERS TO ATTACK...
...AND WHEN THEY DEFEND, THEY LEAVE TWO OR THREE PLAYERS UP FRONT.
SO, COMPARED WITH JOSUI, THEY DON'T HAVE TO MOVE AS FAR AND WIDE, SO THEY'RE NOT WASTING AS MUCH ENERGY.
SO, ALL MUSASHI-NOMORI HAS TO DO IS TO WAIT UNTIL JOSUI LOSES THEIR STAMINA.
!
SO WHY DIDN'T YOU WARN THEM?
HEY, WAIT... YOU'RE THE ONE WHO TOLD THEM TO PLAY LIKE THAT.
WHAT WERE YOU THINKING?
AREN'T YOU ROOTING FOR THEM!
I AM!
THAT'S WHY I WANT TO SEE IF THEY CAN BREAK FREE OF THEIR OWN SHELL.

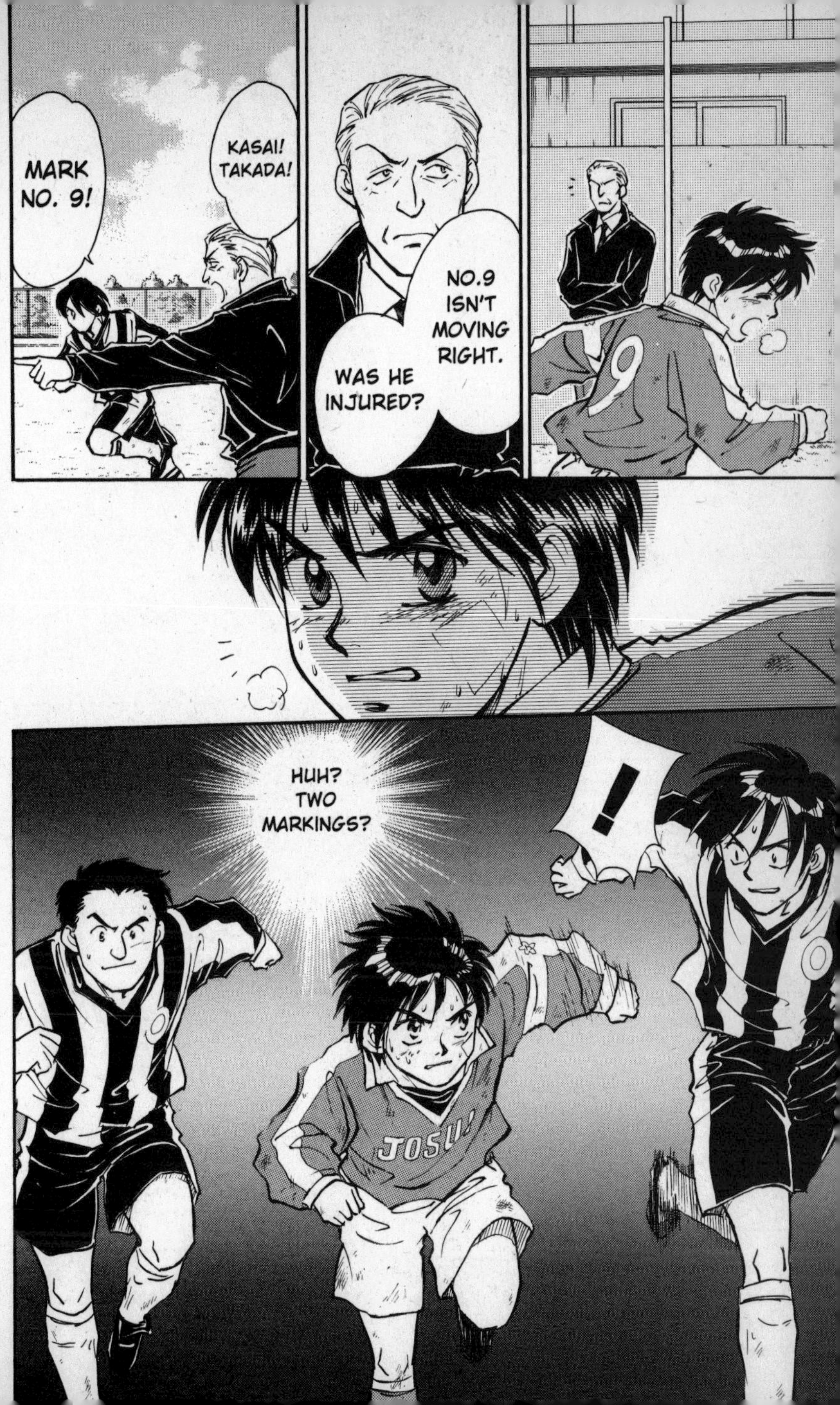
NO.9 ISN'T MOVING RIGHT.
WAS HE INJURED?
KASAI! TAKADA!
MARK NO. 9!
!
HUH? TWO MARKINGS?

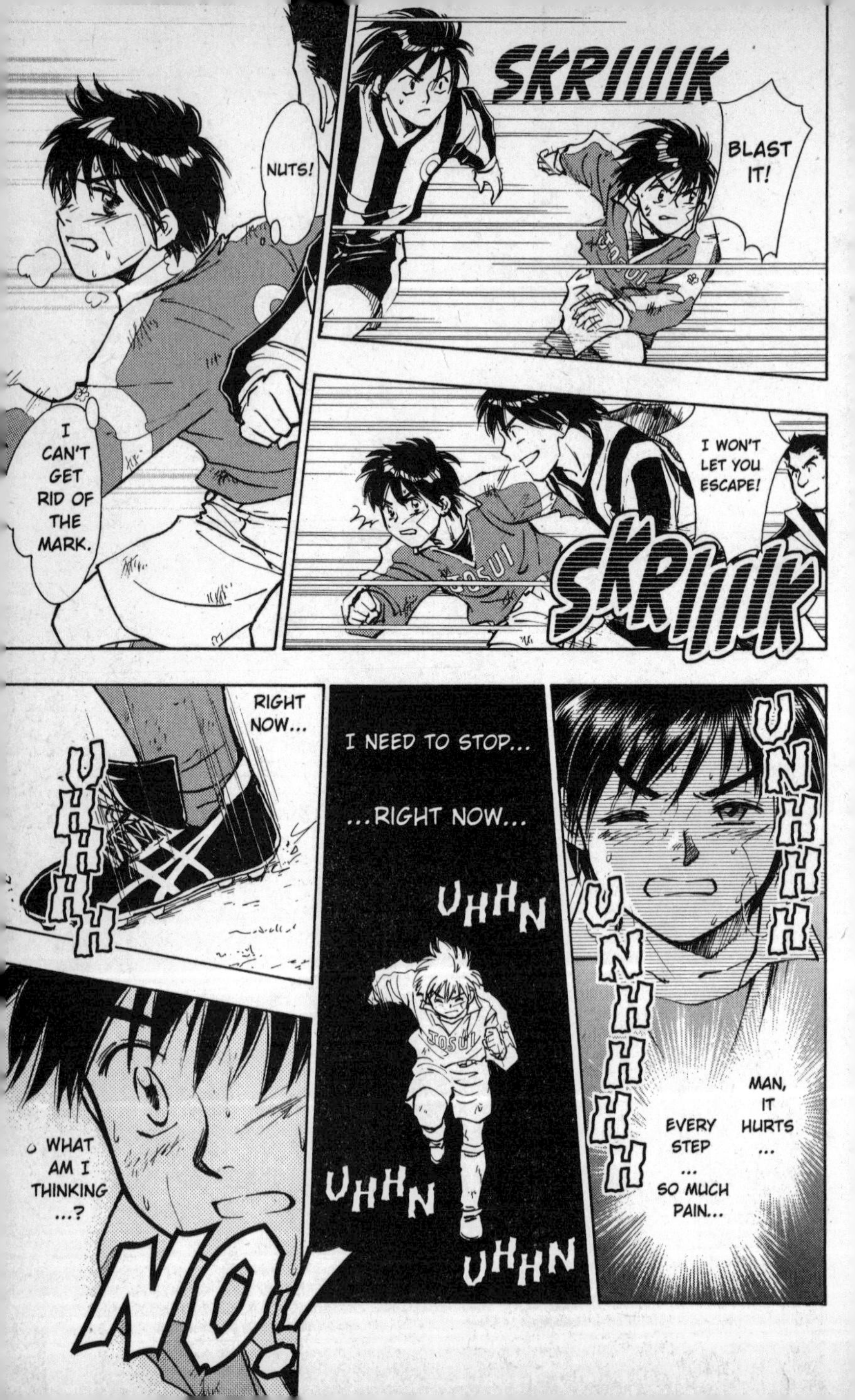
SKRIIIIK
BLAST IT!
NUTS!
I WON'T LET YOU ESCAPE!
SKRIIIK
I CAN'T GET RID OF THE MARK.
UNHHHH
UNHHHHH
MAN, IT HURTS...
EVERY STEP... SO MUCH PAIN...
I NEED TO STOP...
...RIGHT NOW...
UHHN
UHHN
UHHN
RIGHT NOW...
UHHHHH
WHAT AM I THINKING...?
NO!

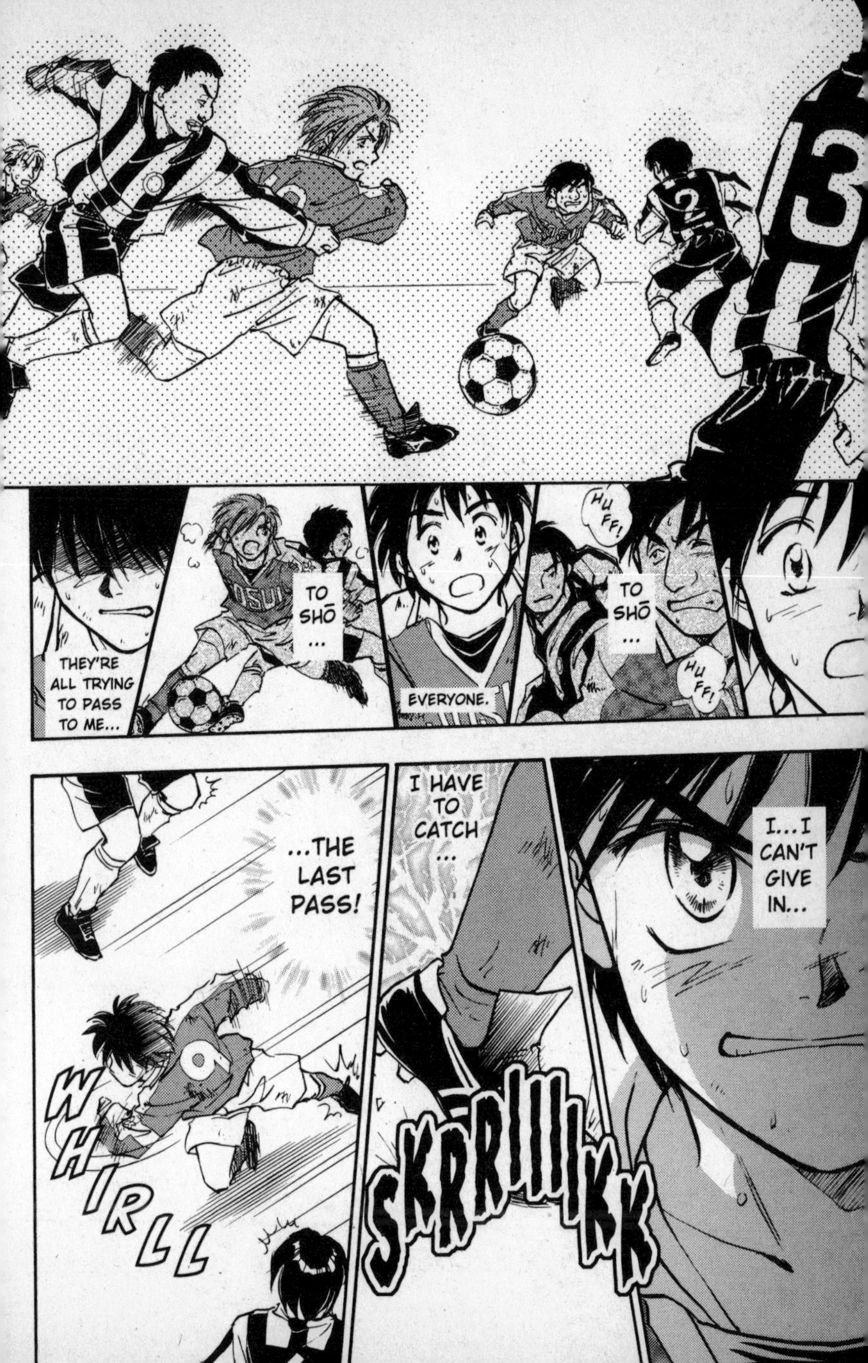
HUFF!
TO SHŌ ...
HUFF!
EVERYONE.
TO SHŌ ...
THEY'RE ALL TRYING TO PASS TO ME...
I...I CAN'T GIVE IN...
SKRIIIIKK
I HAVE TO CATCH ...
...THE LAST PASS!
WHIRLL

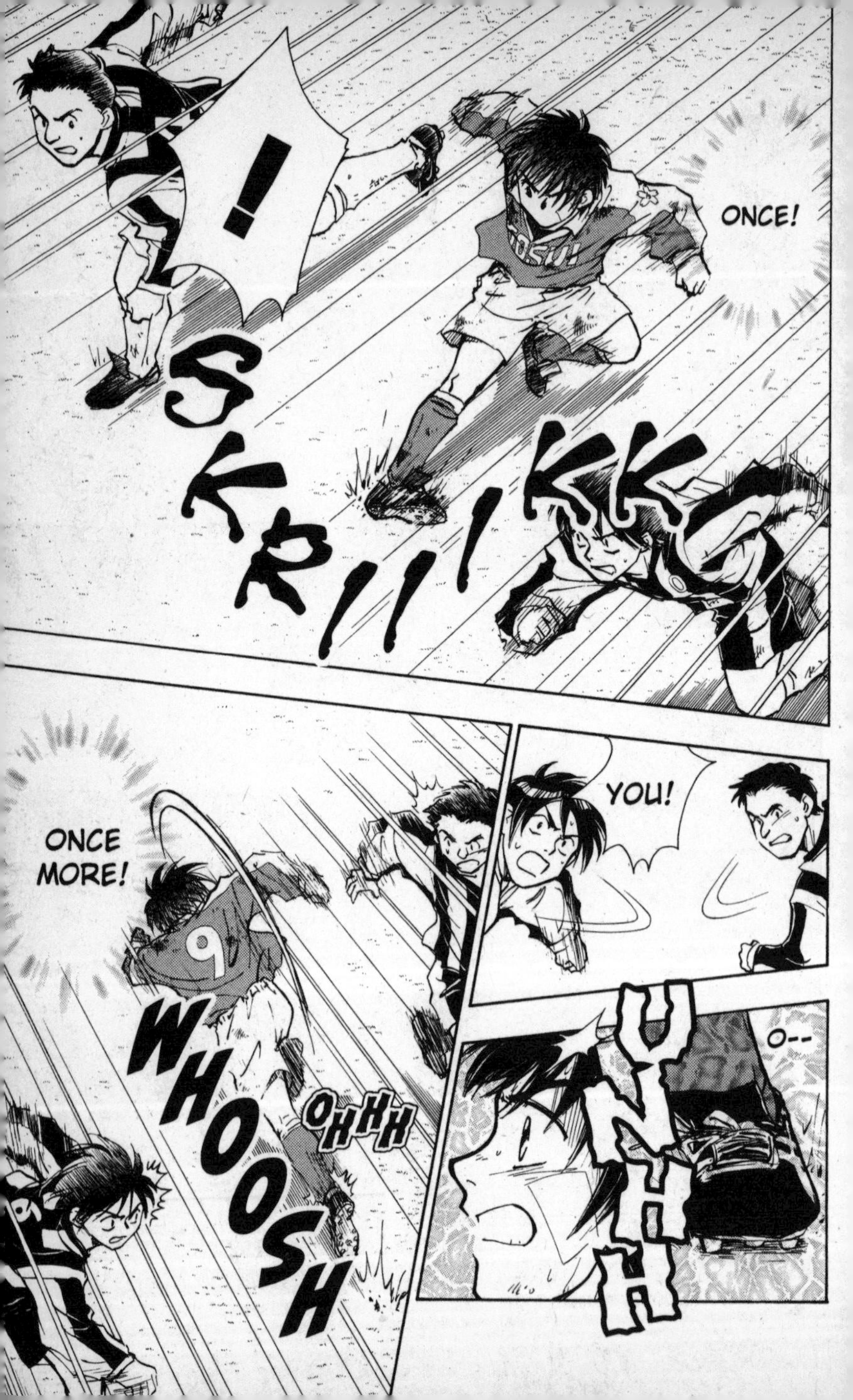
ONCE!
!
SKRIIIKK
YOU!
O--
UNH
ONCE MORE!
WHOOSH
OHHH

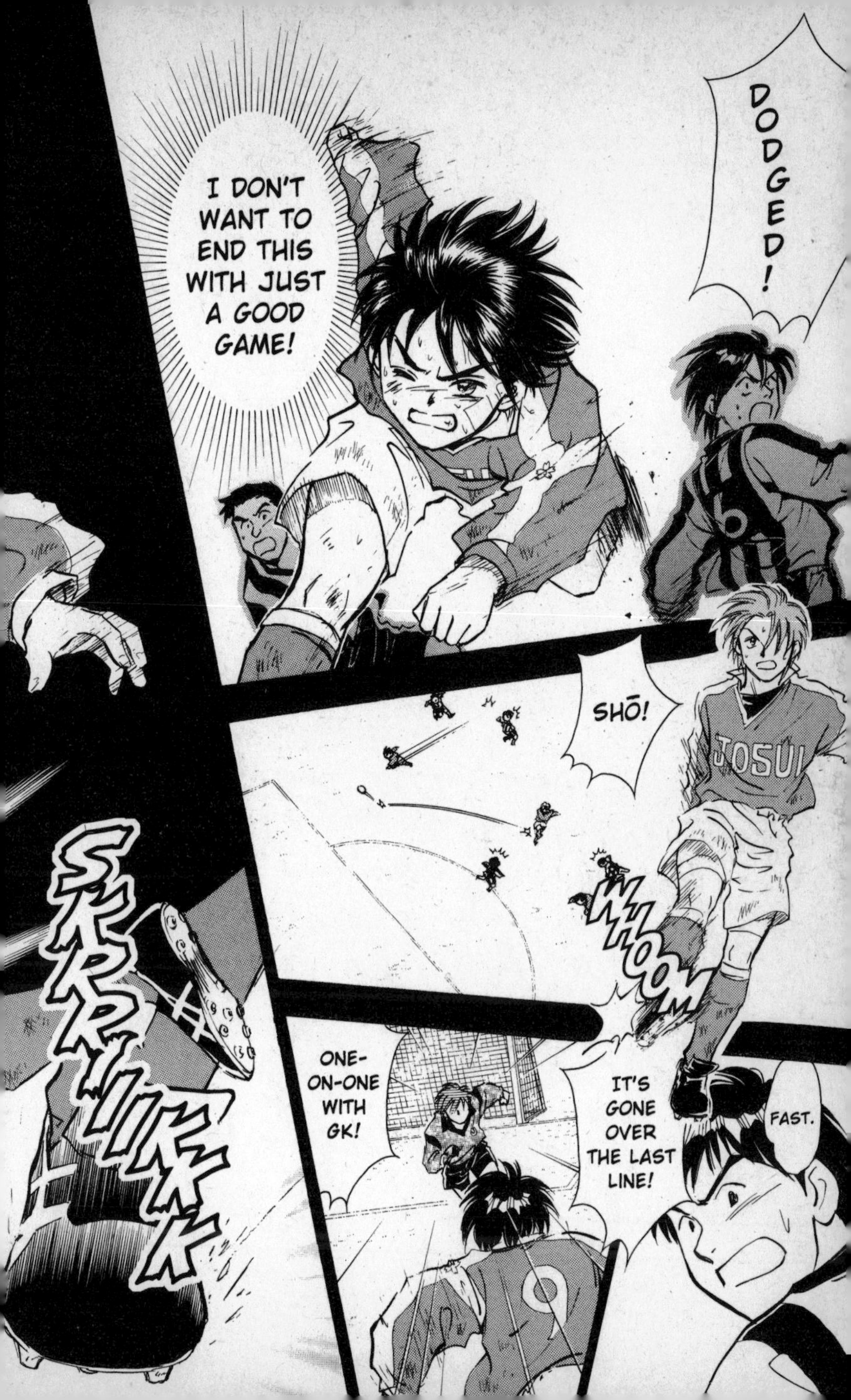
DODGED!
I DON'T WANT TO END THIS WITH JUST A GOOD GAME!
JOSUI
SHŌ!
WHOOM
FAST.
IT'S GONE OVER THE LAST LINE!
ONE-ON-ONE WITH GK!

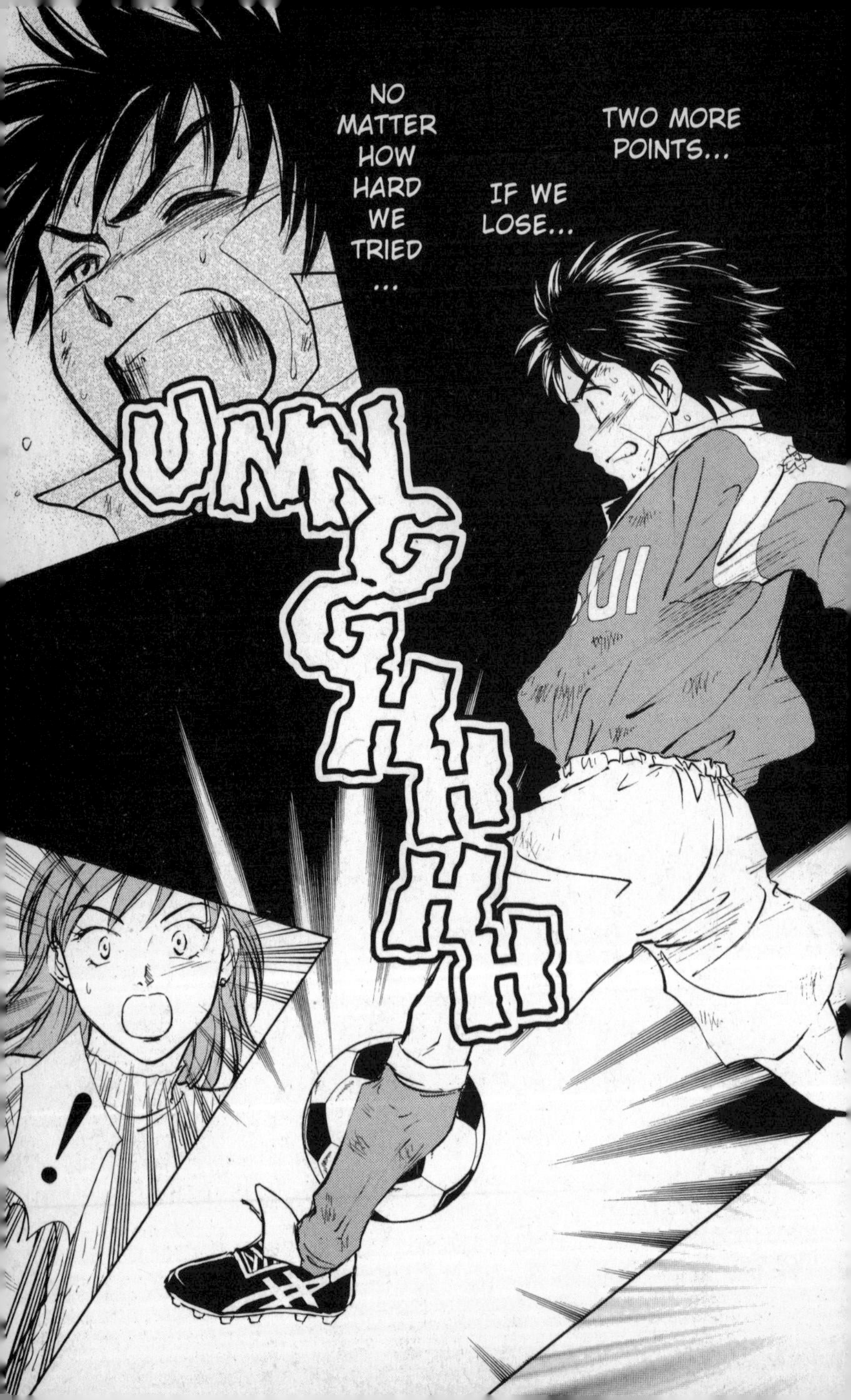
TWO MORE POINTS...
IF WE LOSE...
NO MATTER HOW HARD WE TRIED ...
UNNGGHHHH
!

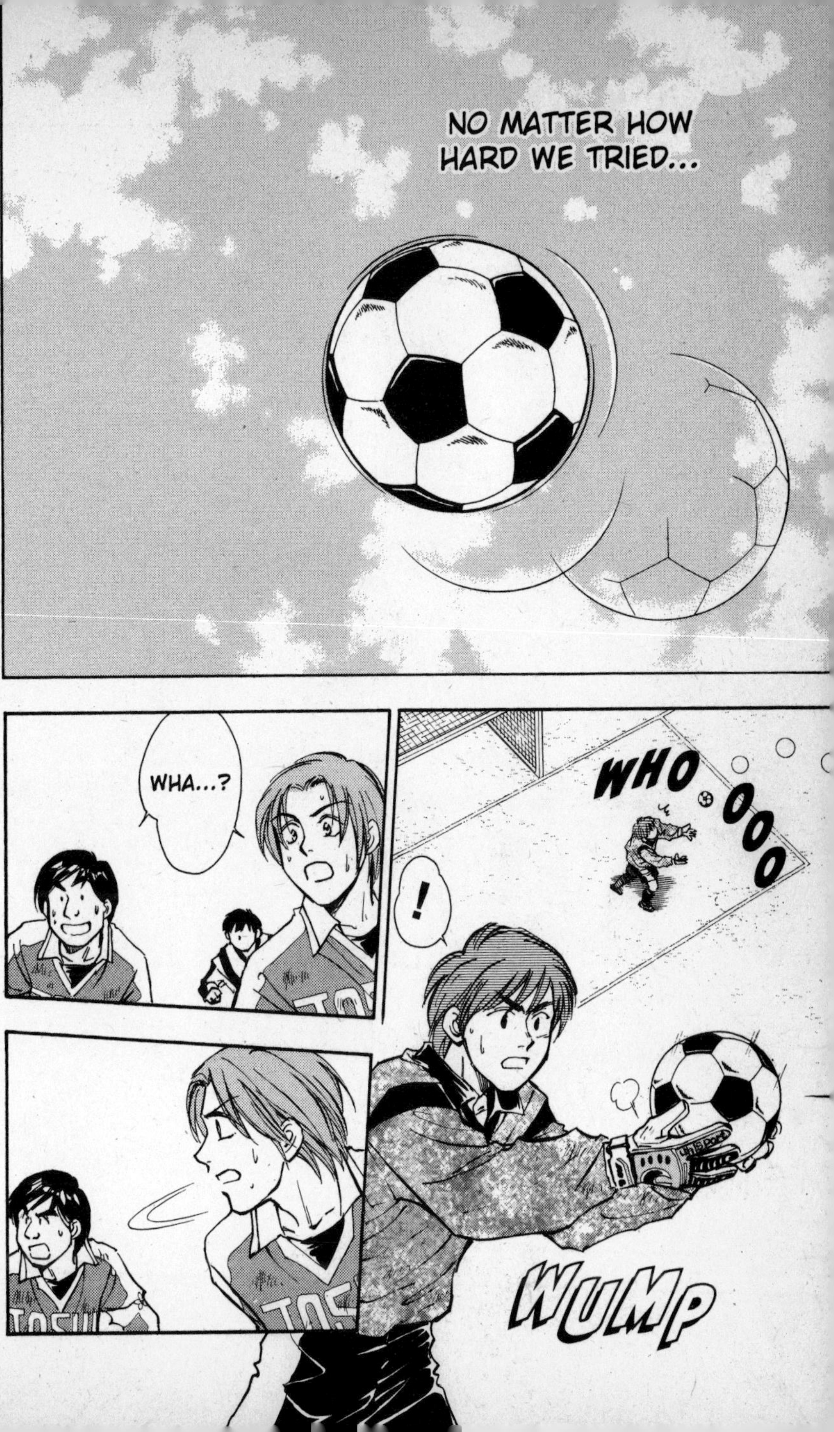
NO MATTER HOW HARD WE TRIED...
WHOOOO
!
WHA...?
WUMP

READ THIS WAY

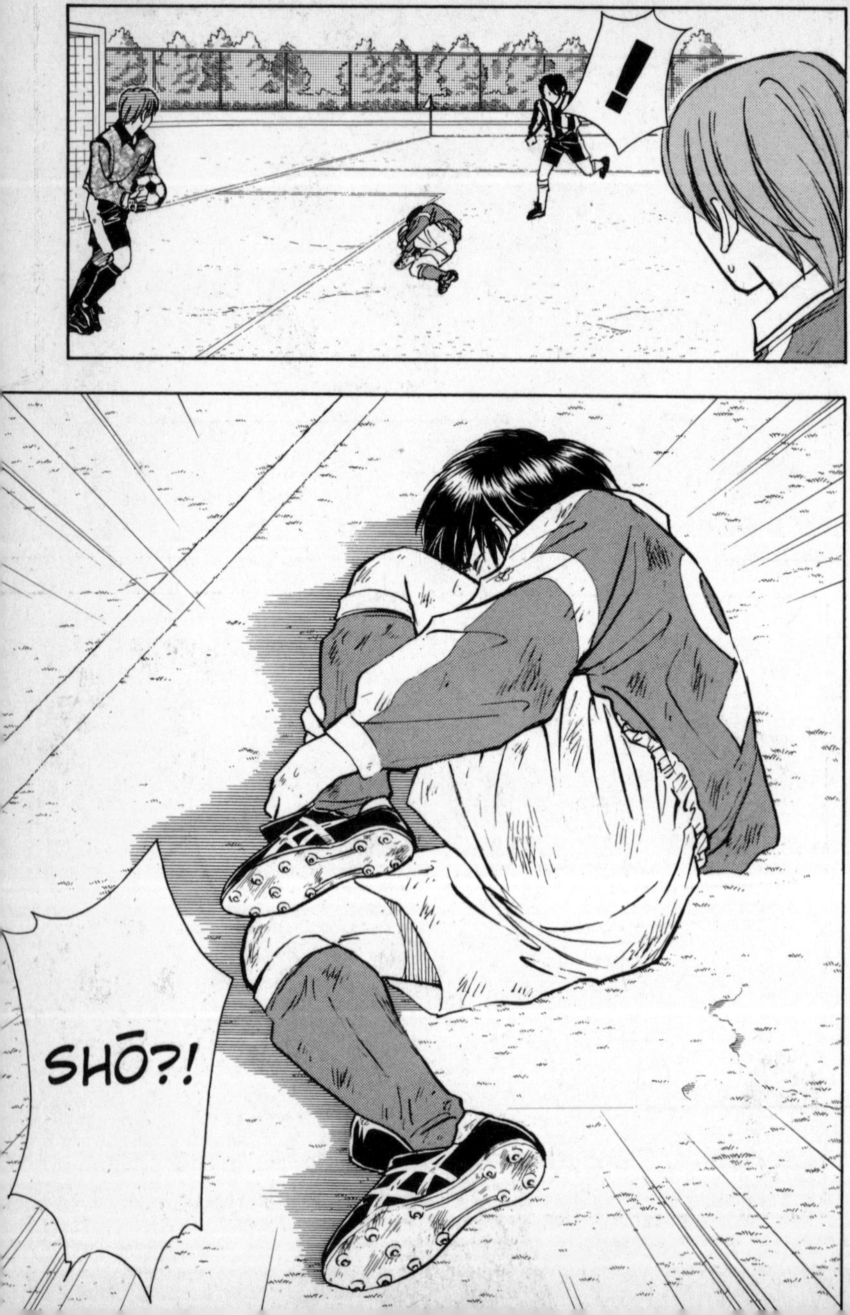
!
SHŌ?!

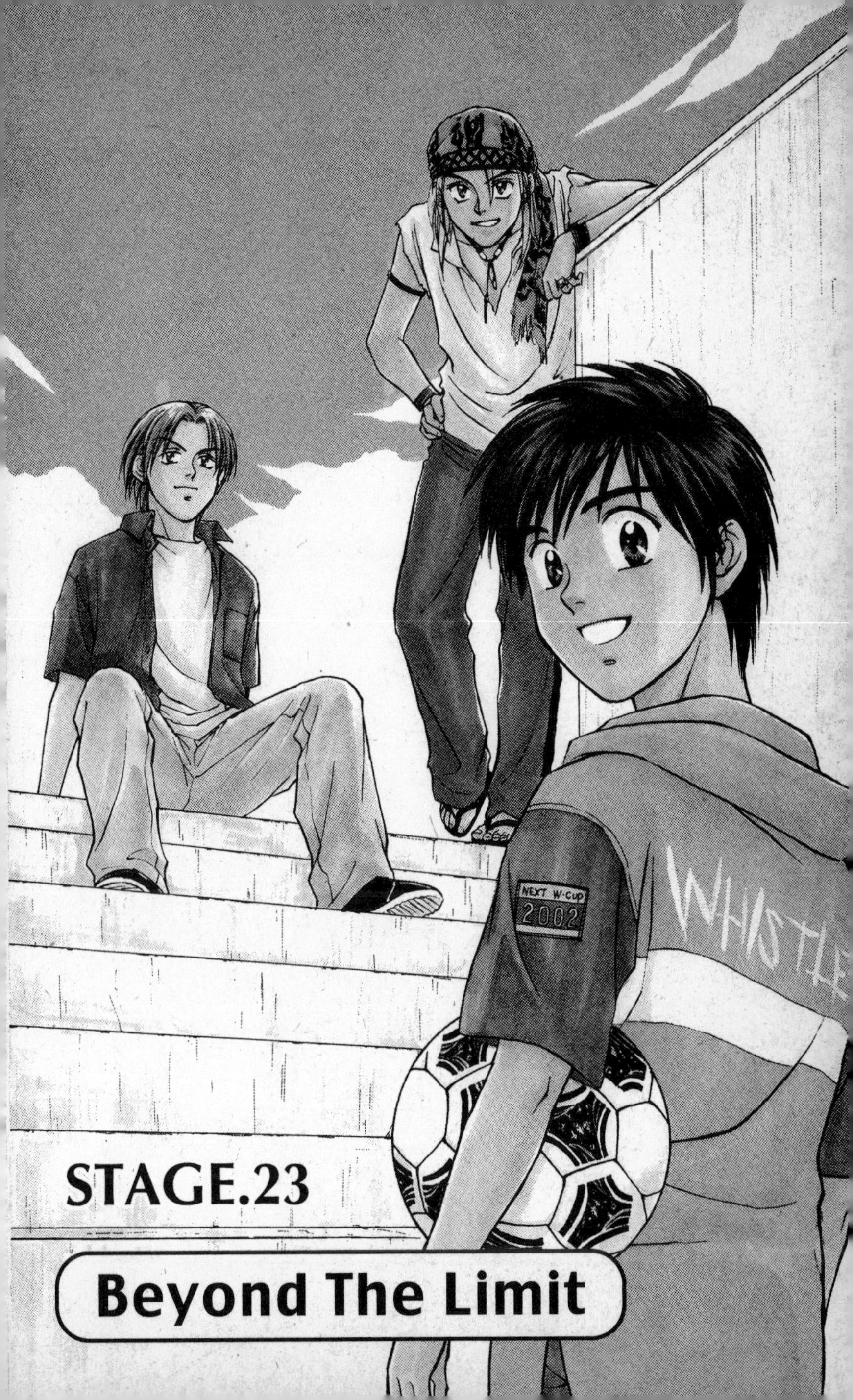
NEXT W-cup
2002
WHISTLE
STAGE.23
Beyond The Limit

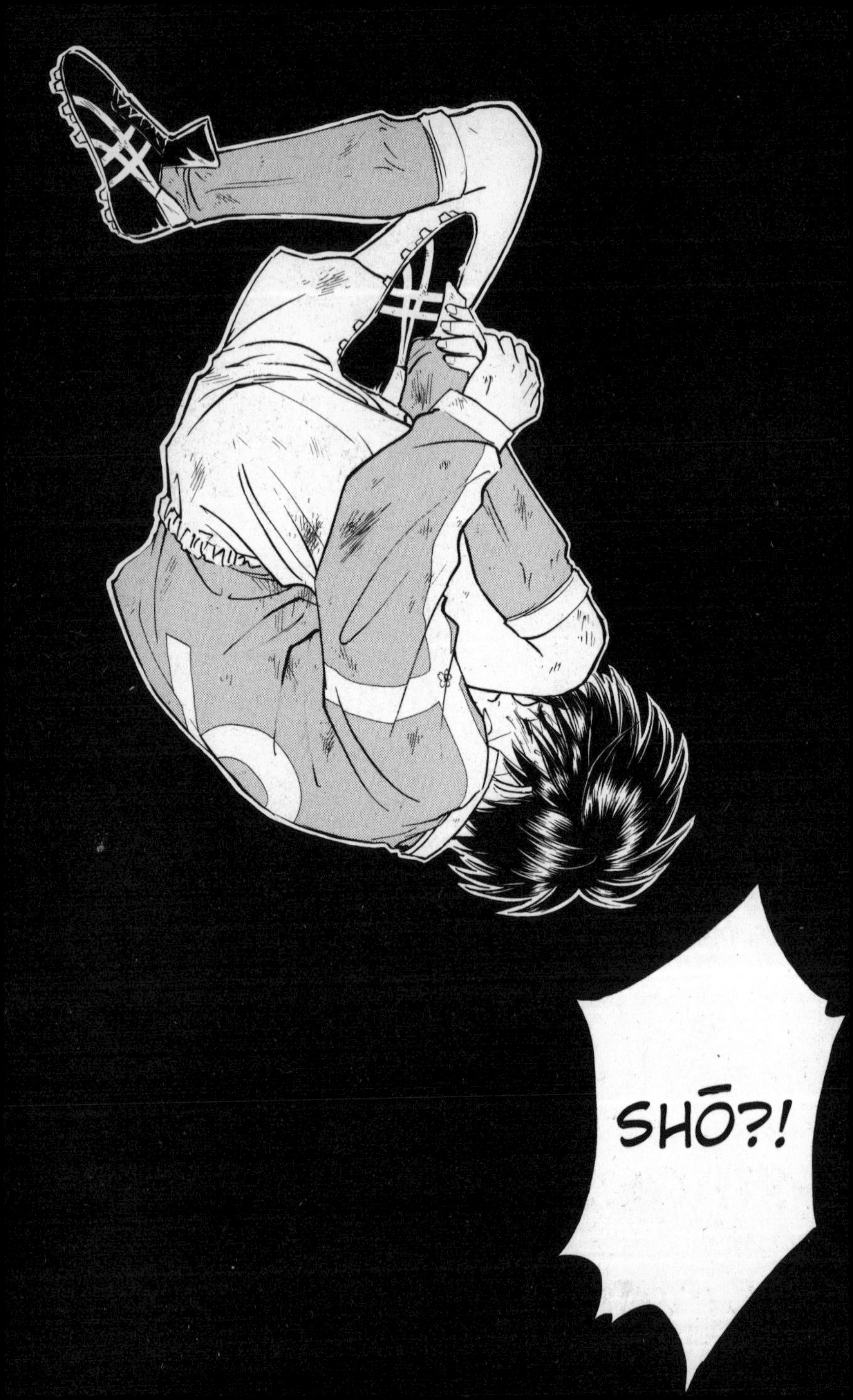
SHŌ?!

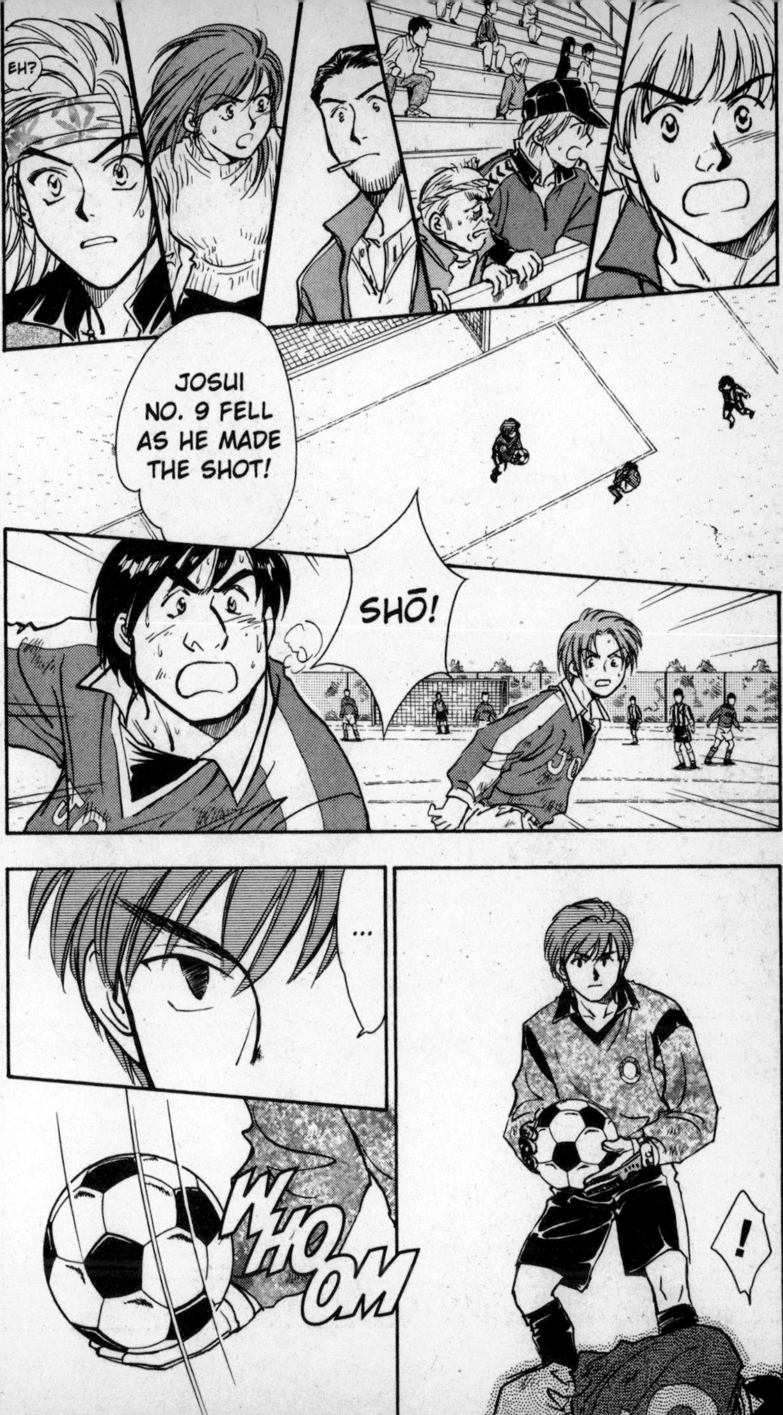
EH?
JOSUI NO. 9 FELL AS HE MADE THE SHOT!
SHŌ!
...
!
WHOOM

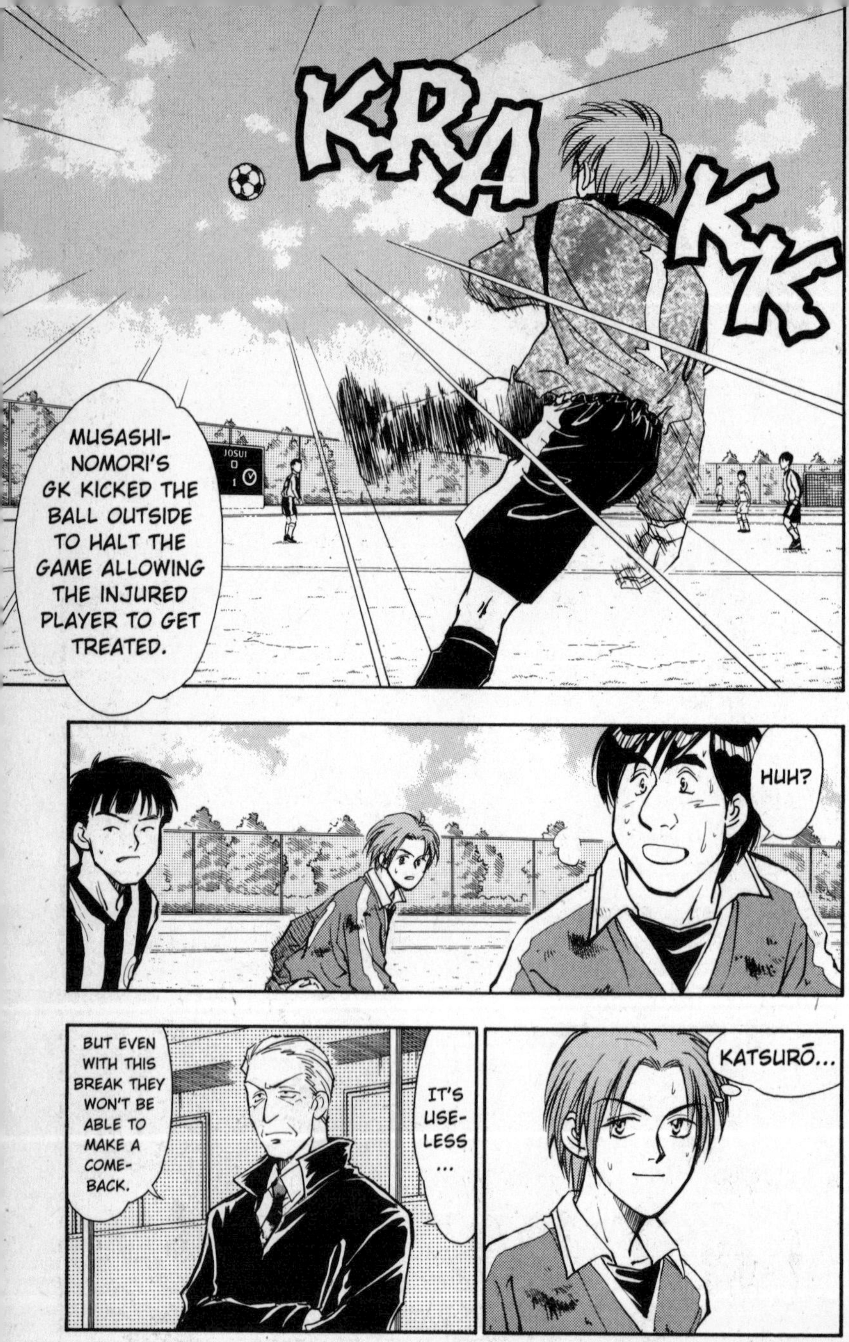
KRAKK
MUSASHINOMORI'S GK KICKED THE BALL OUTSIDE TO HALT THE GAME ALLOWING THE INJURED PLAYER TO GET TREATED.
HUH?
KATSURŌ...
IT'S USELESS...
BUT EVEN WITH THIS BREAK THEY WON'T BE ABLE TO MAKE A COMEBACK.

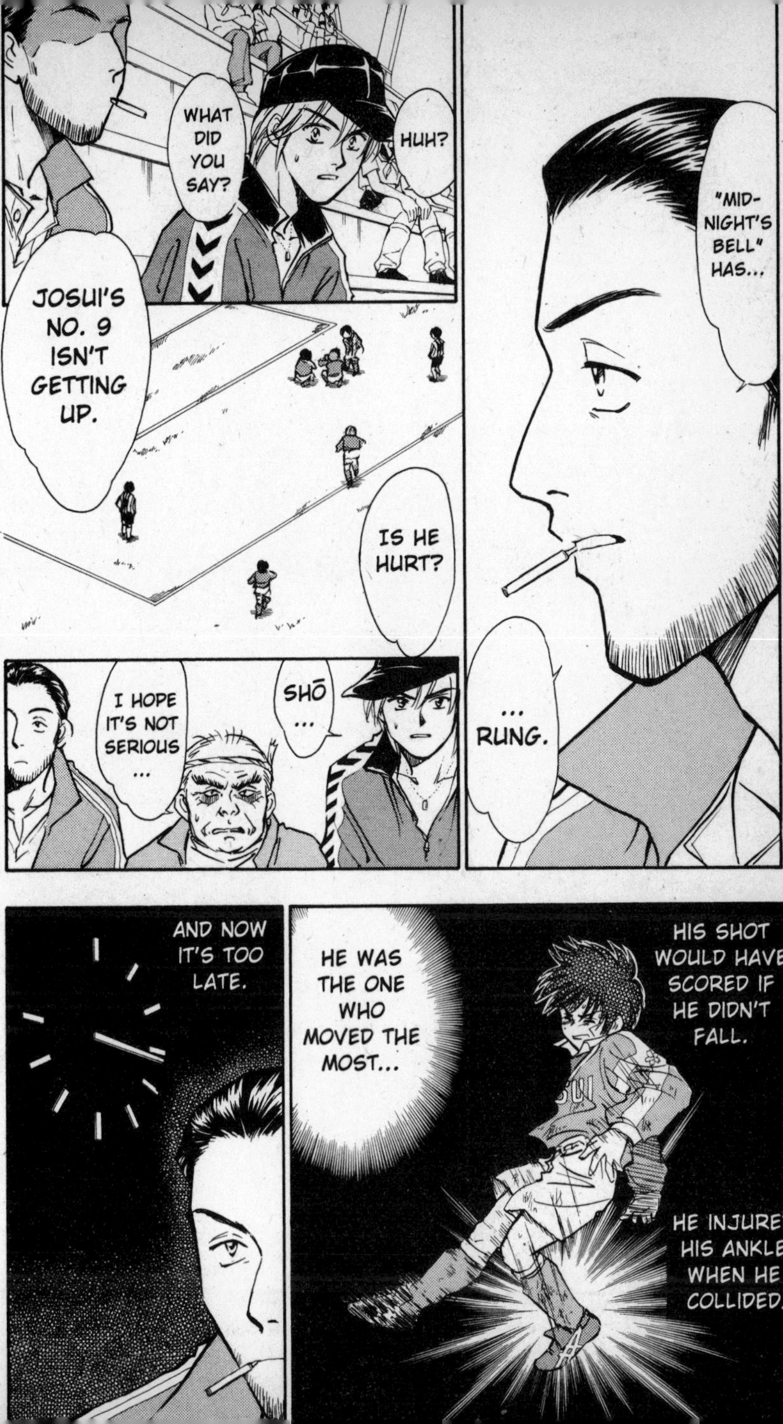
"MID-NIGHT'S BELL" HAS...
... RUNG.
HUH?
WHAT DID YOU SAY?
JOSUI'S NO. 9 ISN'T GETTING UP.
IS HE HURT?
SHŌ ...
I HOPE IT'S NOT SERIOUS ...
HIS SHOT WOULD HAVE SCORED IF HE DIDN'T FALL.
HE WAS THE ONE WHO MOVED THE MOST...
HE INJURED HIS ANKLE WHEN HE COLLIDED.
AND NOW IT'S TOO LATE.

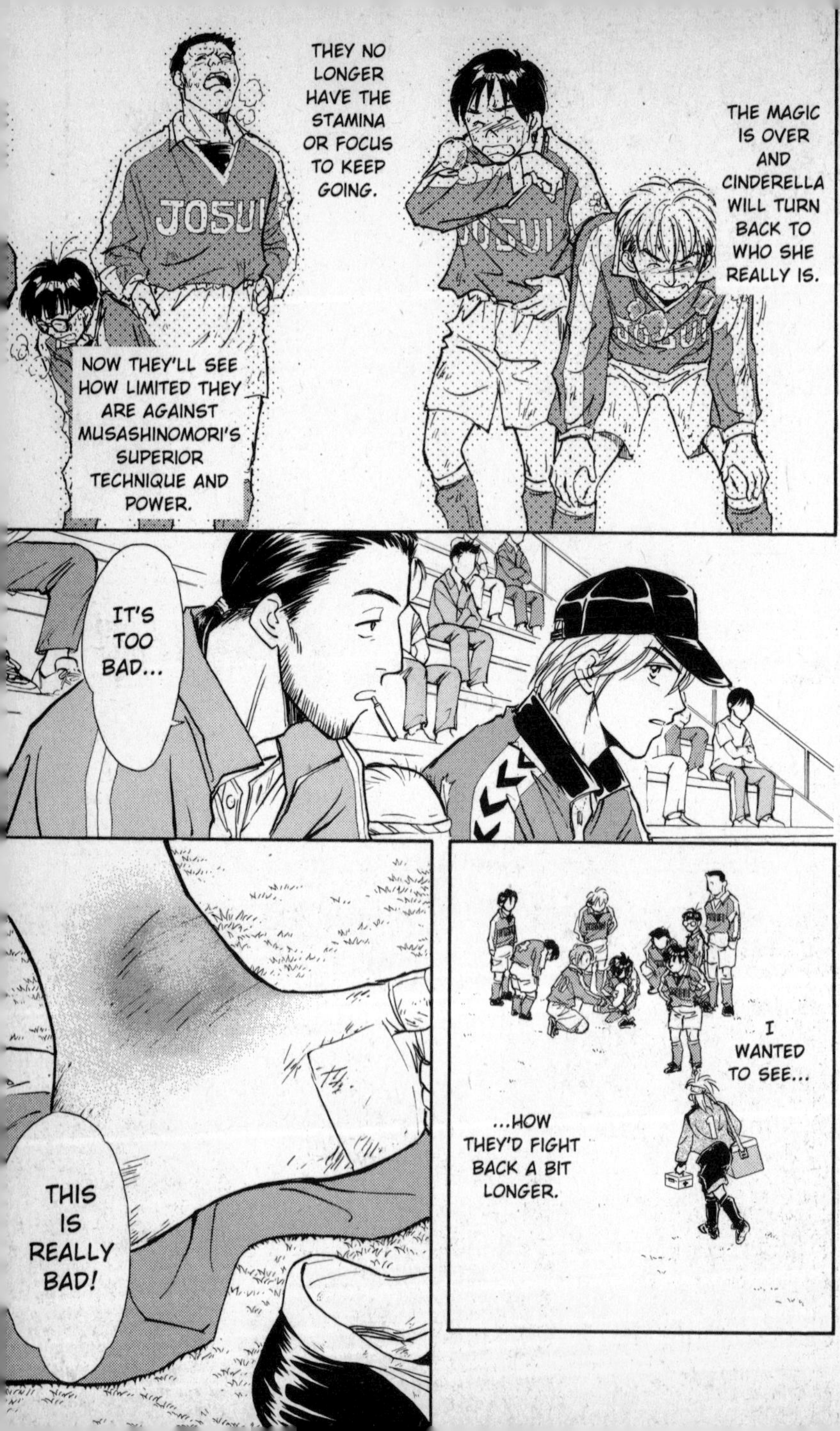
THE MAGIC IS OVER AND CINDERELLA WILL TURN BACK TO WHO SHE REALLY IS.
THEY NO LONGER HAVE THE STAMINA OR FOCUS TO KEEP GOING.
NOW THEY'LL SEE HOW LIMITED THEY ARE AGAINST MUSASHINOMORI'S SUPERIOR TECHNIQUE AND POWER.
JOSUI
IT'S TOO BAD...
I WANTED TO SEE...
...HOW THEY'D FIGHT BACK A BIT LONGER.
THIS IS REALLY BAD!

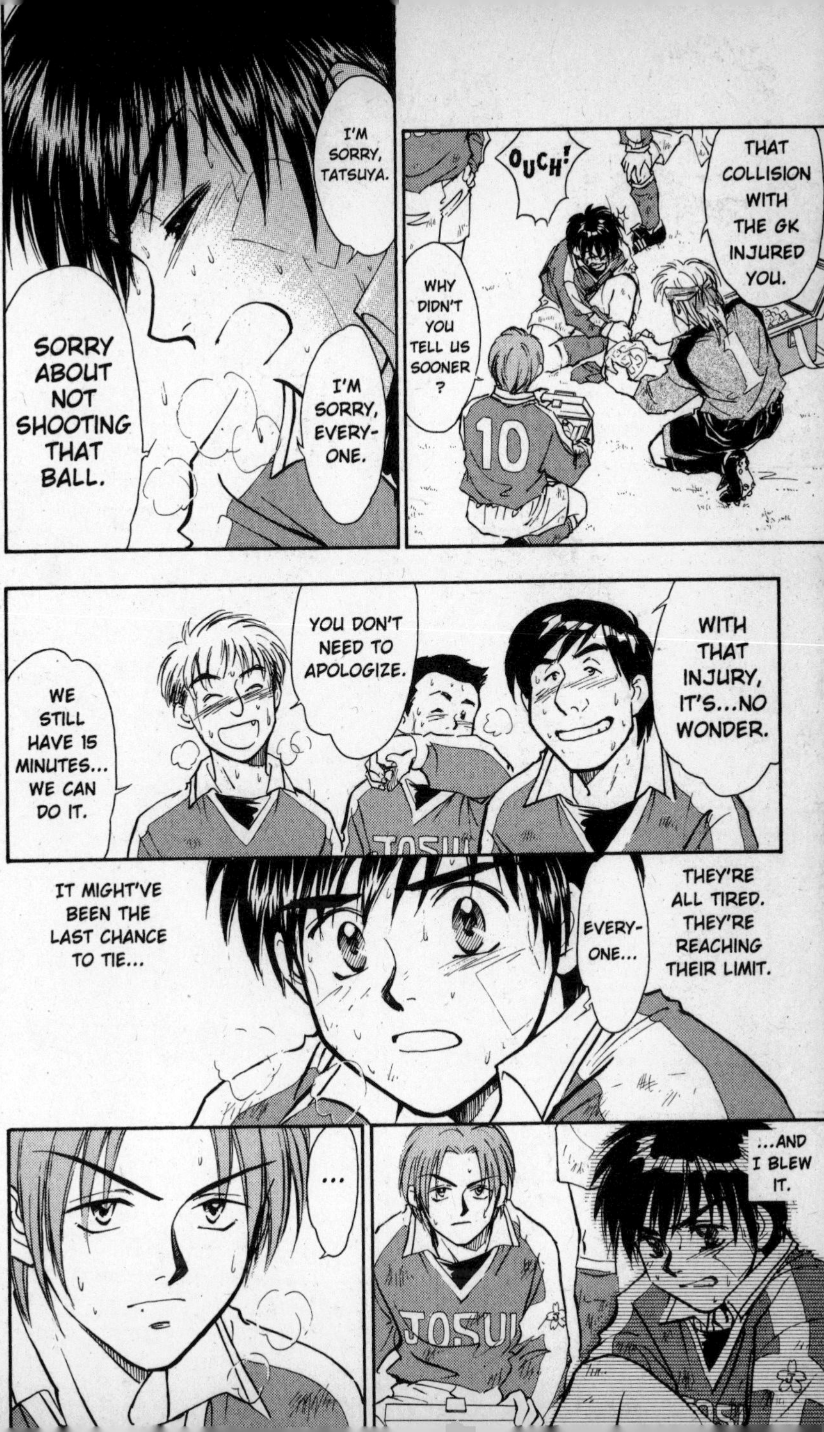
THAT COLLISION WITH THE GK INJURED YOU.
OUCH!
WHY DIDN'T YOU TELL US SOONER?
I'M SORRY, TATSUYA.
I'M SORRY, EVERY-ONE.
SORRY ABOUT NOT SHOOTING THAT BALL.
WITH THAT INJURY, IT'S...NO WONDER.
YOU DON'T NEED TO APOLOGIZE.
WE STILL HAVE 15 MINUTES... WE CAN DO IT.
JOSUI
THEY'RE ALL TIRED. THEY'RE REACHING THEIR LIMIT.
EVERY-ONE...
IT MIGHT'VE BEEN THE LAST CHANCE TO TIE...
...AND I BLEW IT.
JOSUI
...

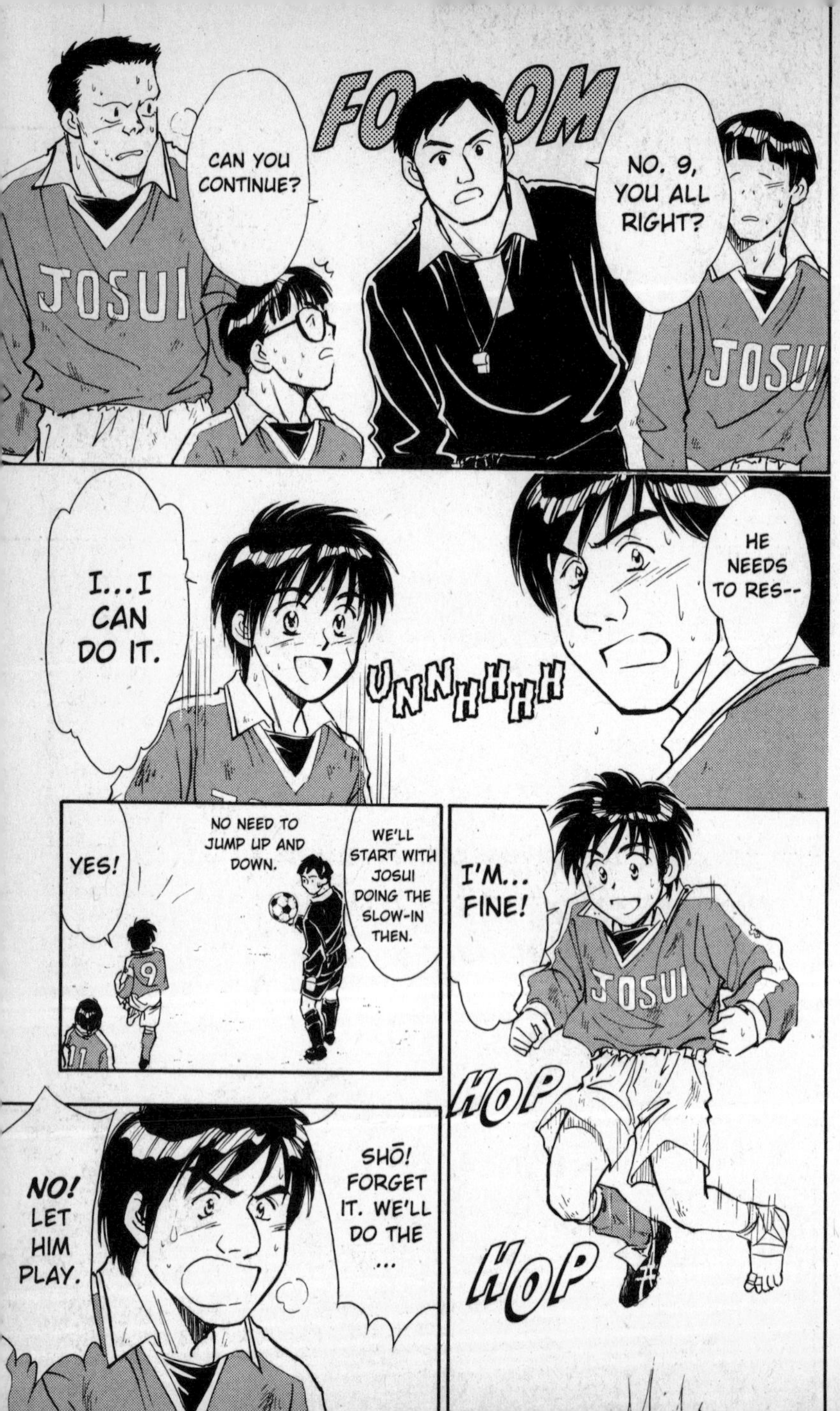
FO OM
NO. 9, YOU ALL RIGHT?
CAN YOU CONTINUE?
HE NEEDS TO RES--
UNNHHHH
I...I CAN DO IT.
I'M... FINE!
HOP
HOP
WE'LL START WITH JOSUI DOING THE SLOW-IN THEN.
NO NEED TO JUMP UP AND DOWN.
YES!
SHŌ! FORGET IT. WE'LL DO THE ...
NO! LET HIM PLAY.

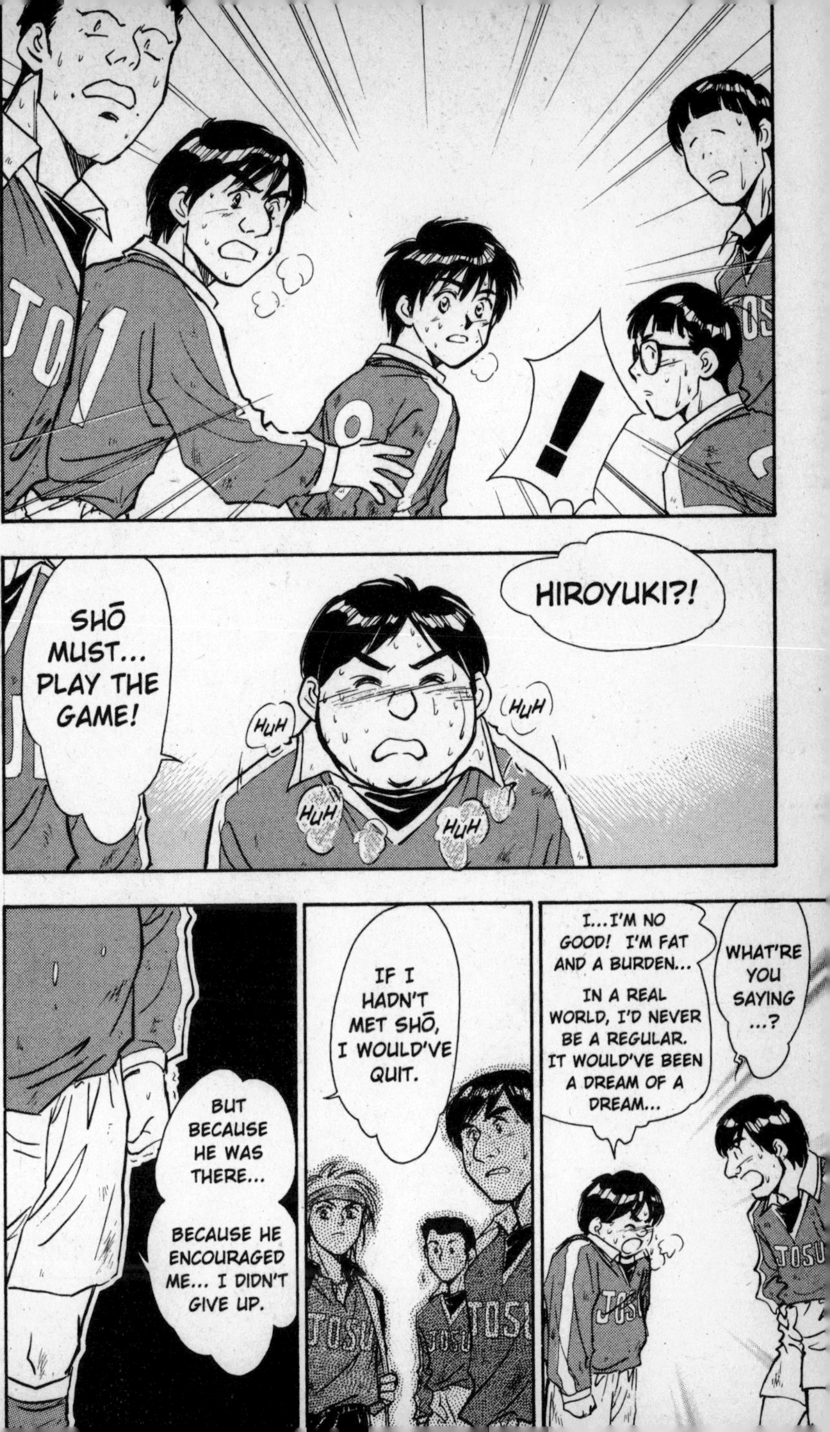
!
HIROYUKI?!
HUH
HUH
HUH
HUH
SHŌ MUST... PLAY THE GAME!
WHAT'RE YOU SAYING ...?
I...I'M NO GOOD! I'M FAT AND A BURDEN...
IN A REAL WORLD, I'D NEVER BE A REGULAR. IT WOULD'VE BEEN A DREAM OF A DREAM...
IF I HADN'T MET SHŌ, I WOULD'VE QUIT.
BUT BECAUSE HE WAS THERE...
BECAUSE HE ENCOURAGED ME... I DIDN'T GIVE UP.

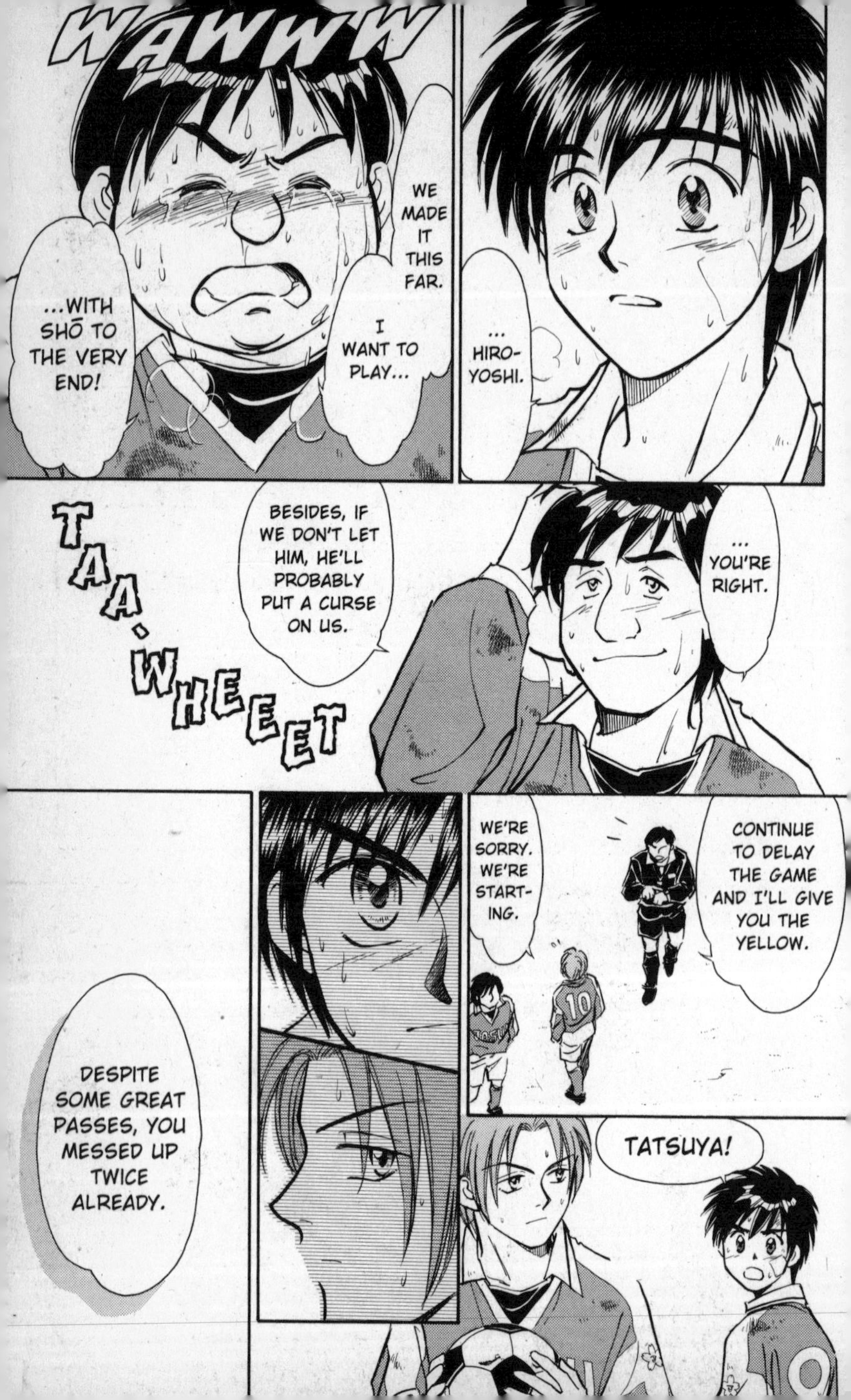
...
HIRO-YOSHI.
WAWWW
WE MADE IT THIS FAR.
I WANT TO PLAY...
...WITH SHŌ TO THE VERY END!
...
YOU'RE RIGHT.
BESIDES, IF WE DON'T LET HIM, HE'LL PROBABLY PUT A CURSE ON US.
TAA-WHEEET
CONTINUE TO DELAY THE GAME AND I'LL GIVE YOU THE YELLOW.
WE'RE SORRY. WE'RE STARTING.
TATSUYA!
DESPITE SOME GREAT PASSES, YOU MESSED UP TWICE ALREADY.

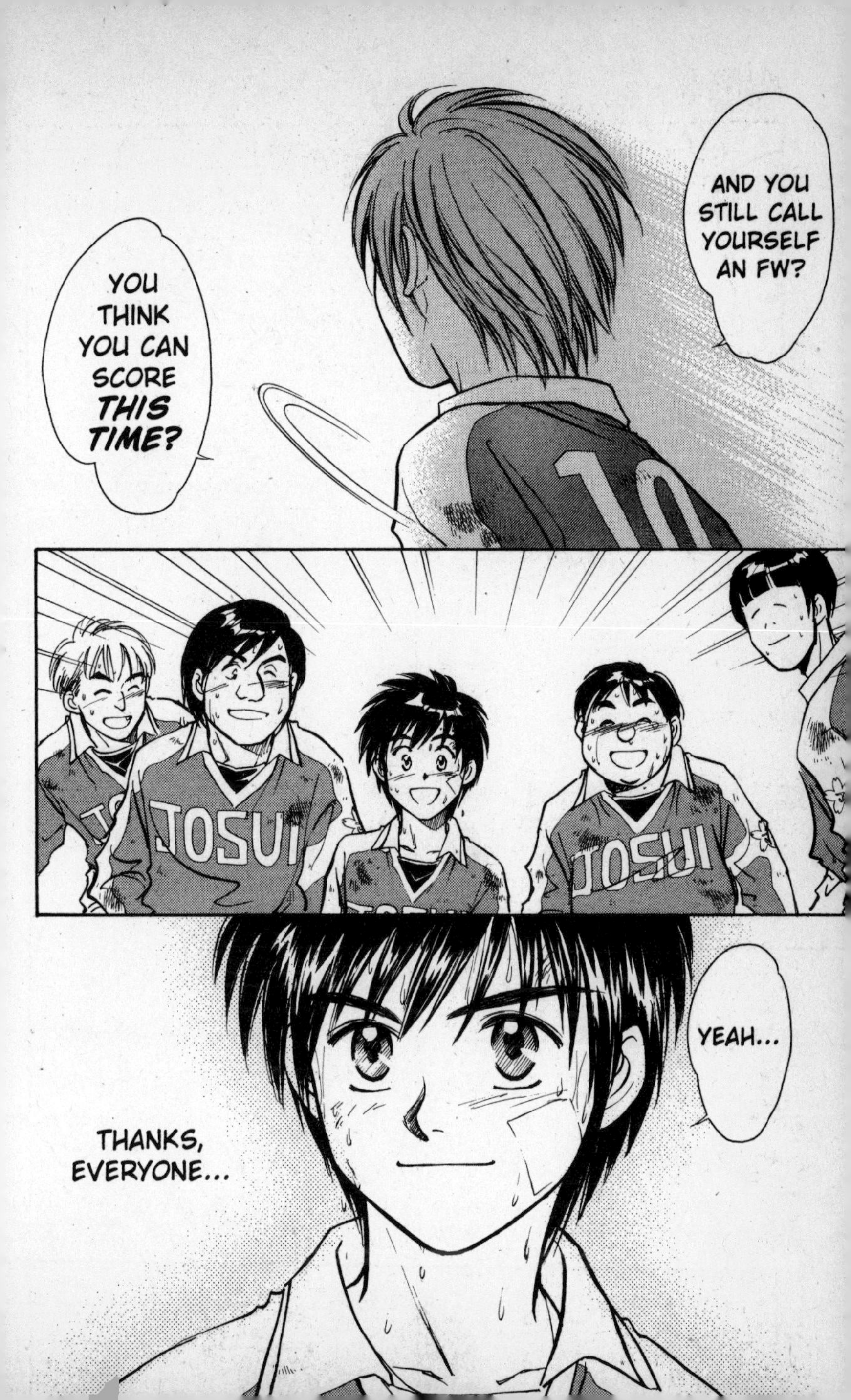
AND YOU STILL CALL YOURSELF AN FW?
YOU THINK YOU CAN SCORE *THIS TIME?*
JOSUI
JOSUI
YEAH...
THANKS, EVERYONE...

READ THIS WAY

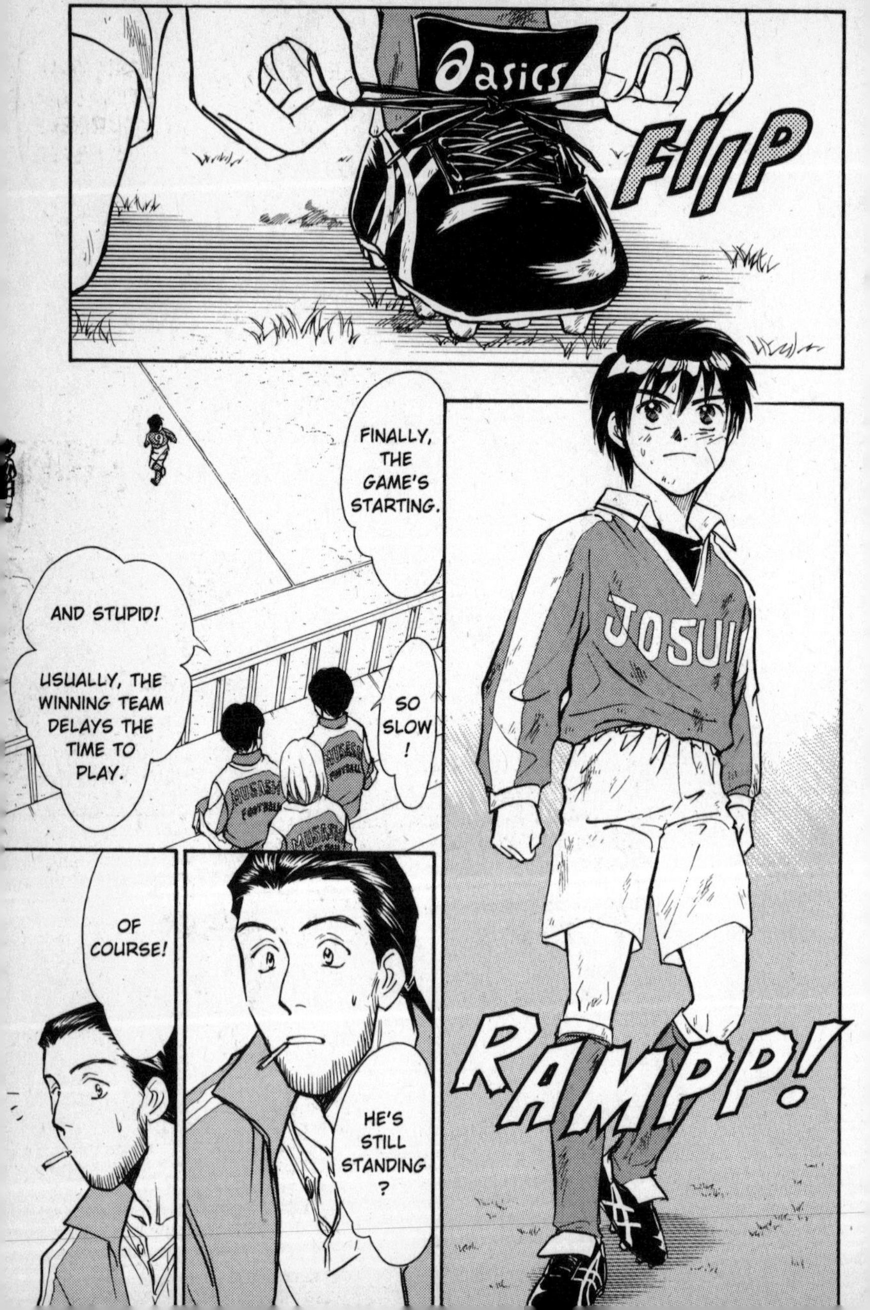
FLIP
RAMPP!
FINALLY, THE GAME'S STARTING.
SO SLOW!
AND STUPID!
USUALLY, THE WINNING TEAM DELAYS THE TIME TO PLAY.
HE'S STILL STANDING?
OF COURSE!

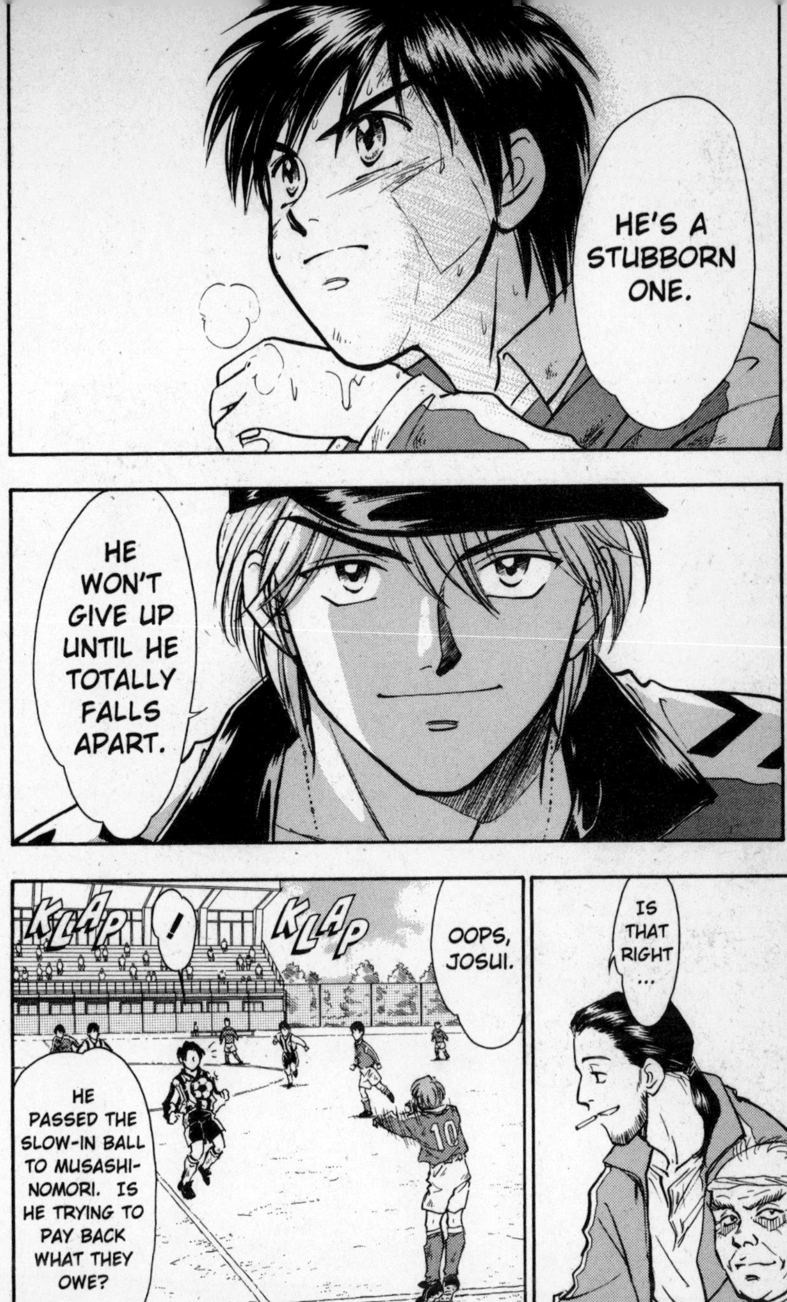
HE'S A STUBBORN ONE.
HE WON'T GIVE UP UNTIL HE TOTALLY FALLS APART.
IS THAT RIGHT ...
OOPS, JOSUI.
KLAP
!
KLAP
HE PASSED THE SLOW-IN BALL TO MUSASHI-NOMORI. IS HE TRYING TO PAY BACK WHAT THEY OWE?

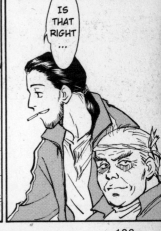

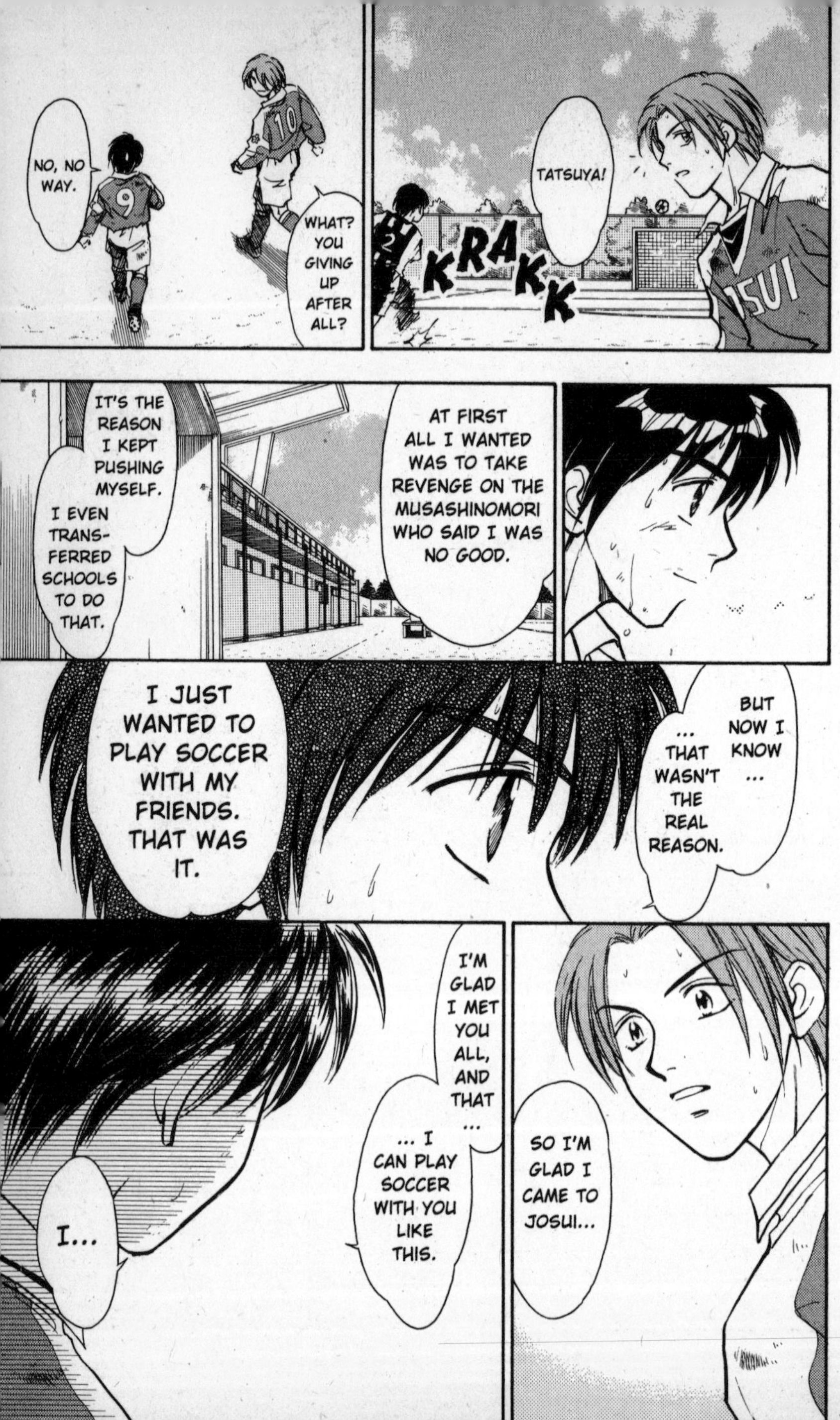
TATSUYA!
KRAKK
WHAT? YOU GIVING UP AFTER ALL?
NO, NO WAY.
AT FIRST ALL I WANTED WAS TO TAKE REVENGE ON THE MUSASHINOMORI WHO SAID I WAS NO GOOD.
IT'S THE REASON I KEPT PUSHING MYSELF.
I EVEN TRANS-FERRED SCHOOLS TO DO THAT.
BUT NOW I KNOW ...
... THAT WASN'T THE REAL REASON.
I JUST WANTED TO PLAY SOCCER WITH MY FRIENDS. THAT WAS IT.
SO I'M GLAD I CAME TO JOSUI...
I'M GLAD I MET YOU ALL, AND THAT ...
... I CAN PLAY SOCCER WITH YOU LIKE THIS.
I...

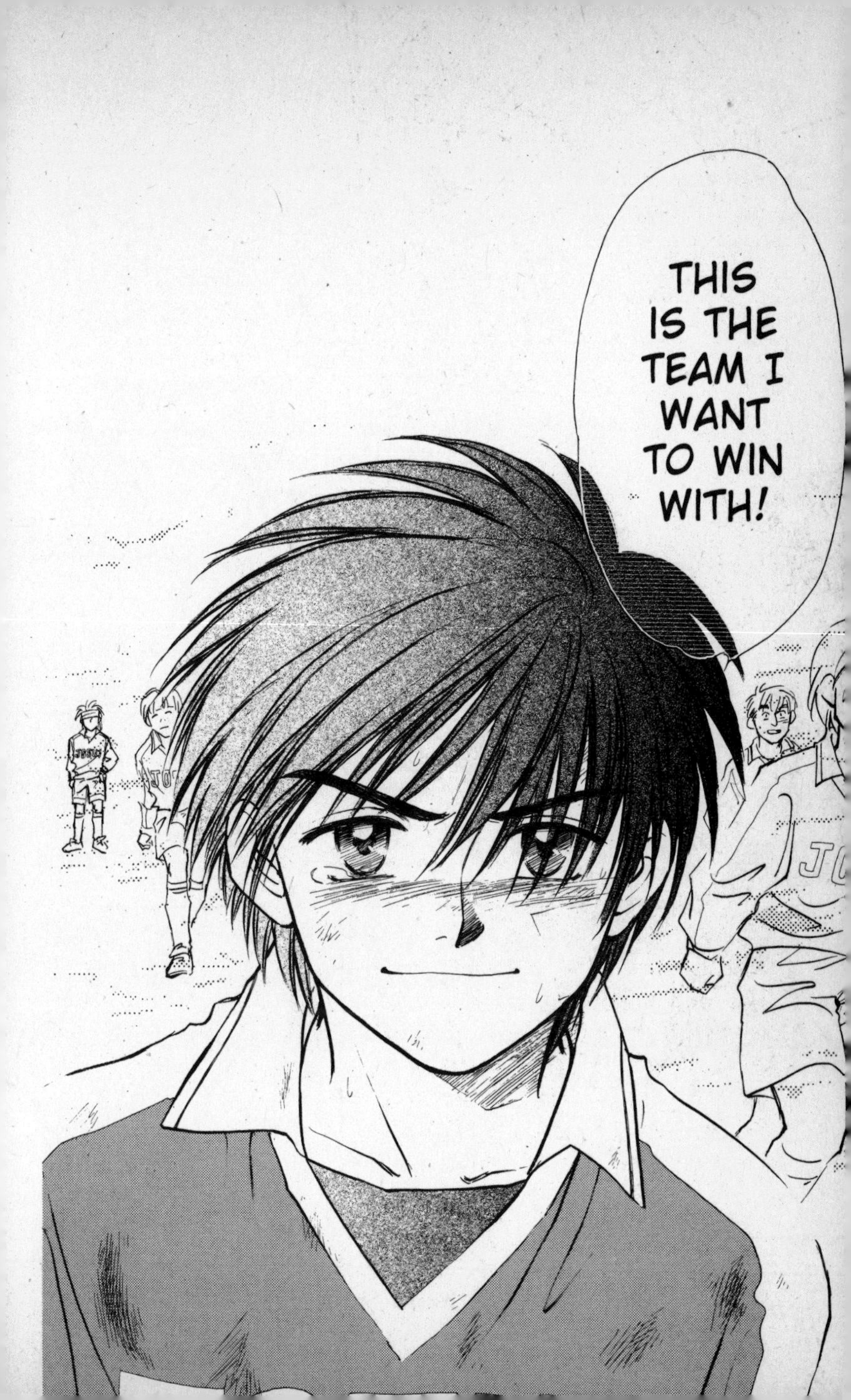
THIS IS THE TEAM I WANT TO WIN WITH!

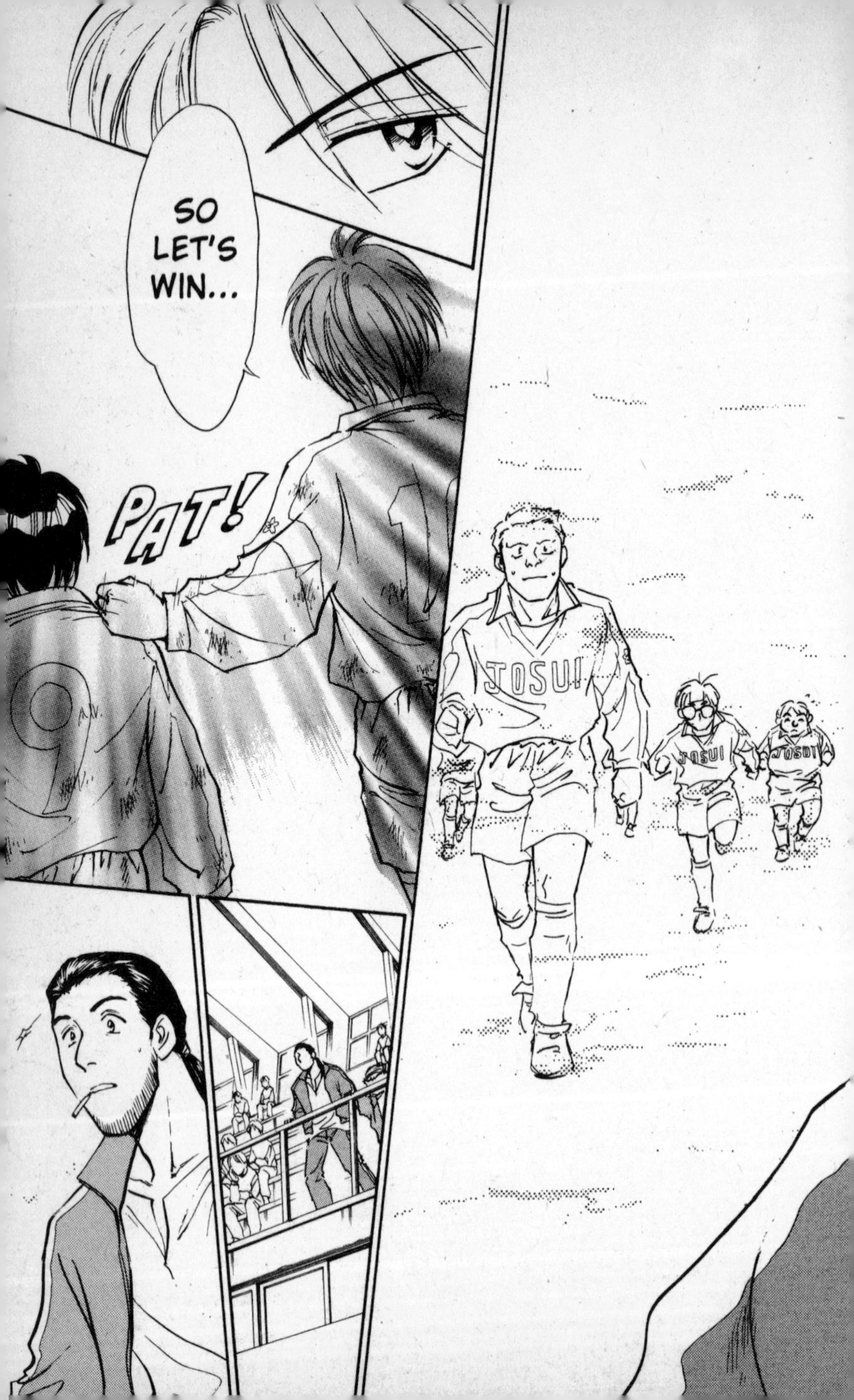
SO LET'S WIN...
PAT!
JOSUI
JOSUI
JOSUI

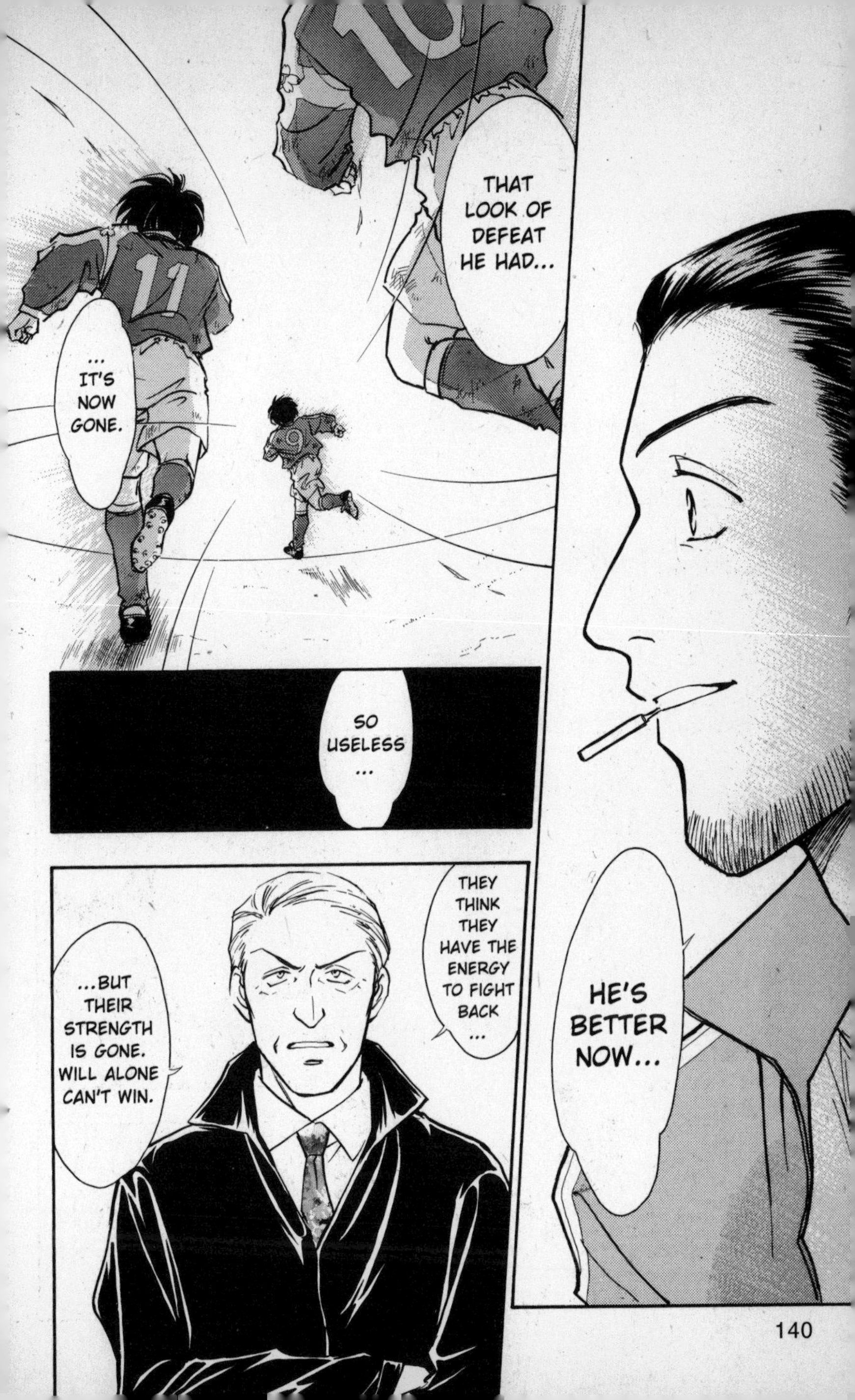

HE'S BETTER NOW...
THAT LOOK OF DEFEAT HE HAD...
... IT'S NOW GONE.
SO USELESS ...
THEY THINK THEY HAVE THE ENERGY TO FIGHT BACK ...
...BUT THEIR STRENGTH IS GONE. WILL ALONE CAN'T WIN.

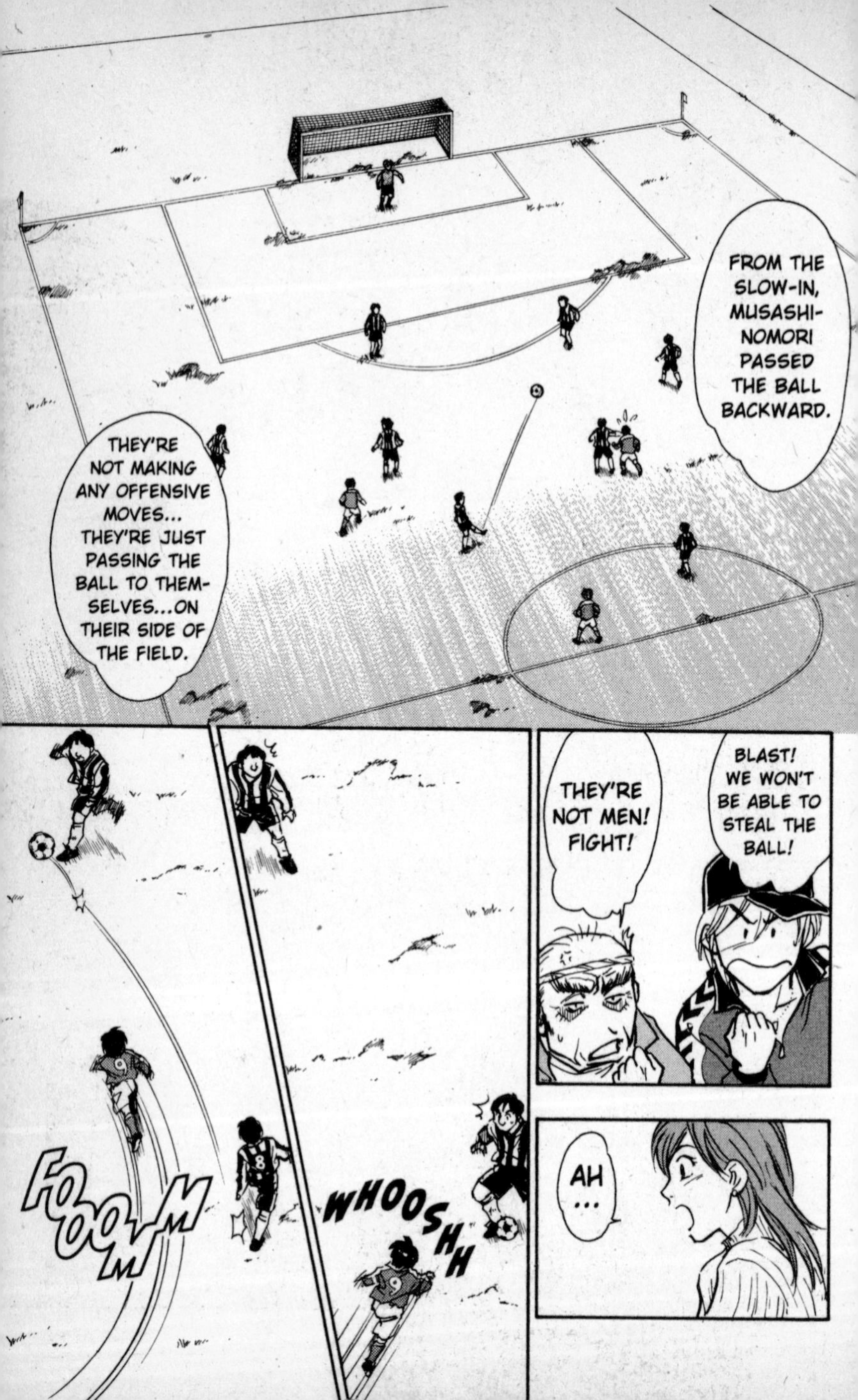
FROM THE SLOW-IN, MUSASHI-NOMORI PASSED THE BALL BACKWARD.
THEY'RE NOT MAKING ANY OFFENSIVE MOVES... THEY'RE JUST PASSING THE BALL TO THEM-SELVES...ON THEIR SIDE OF THE FIELD.
BLAST! WE WON'T BE ABLE TO STEAL THE BALL!
THEY'RE NOT MEN! FIGHT!
AH ...
WHOOSHH
FOOOMM

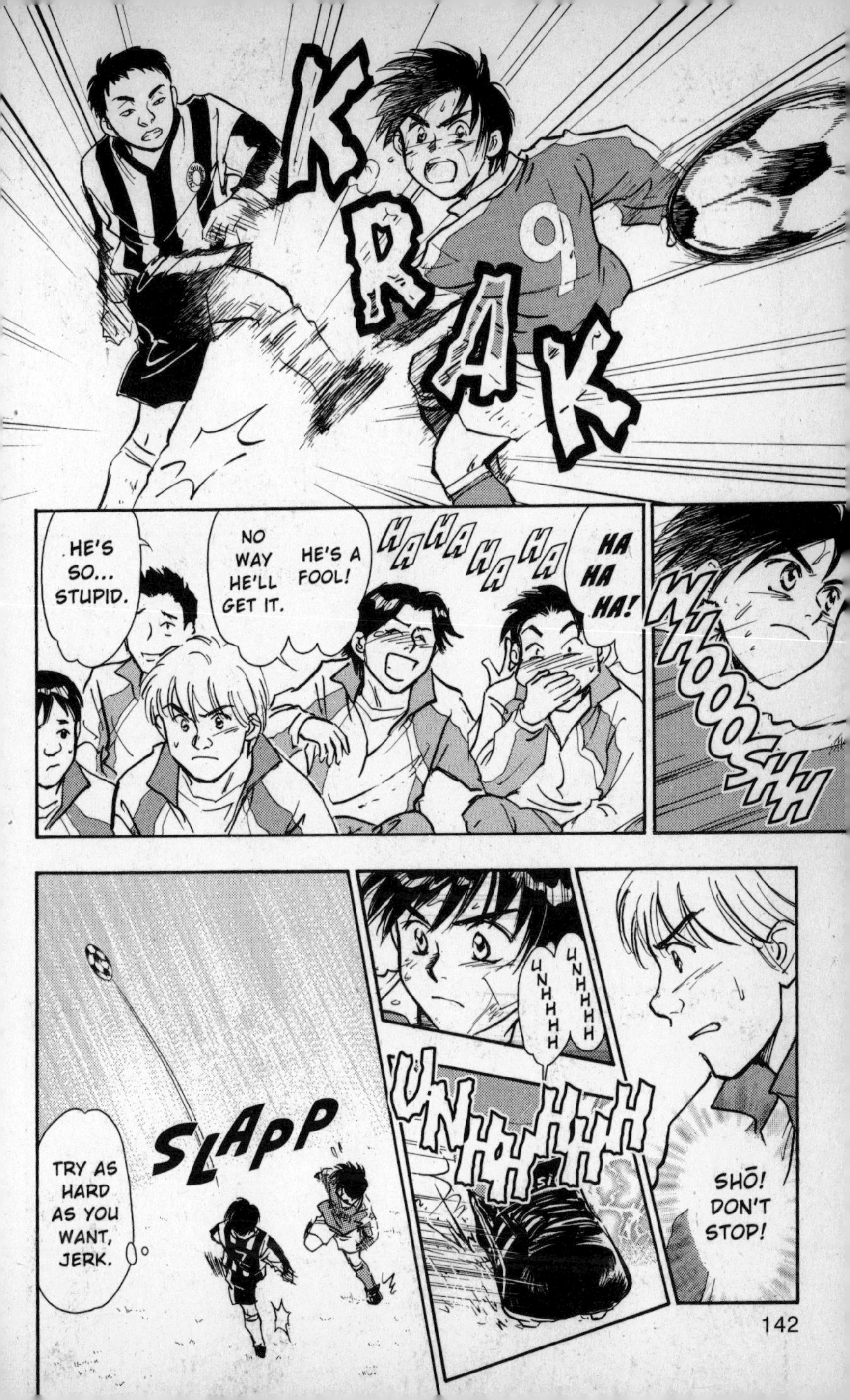
KRAK
WHOOOSHH
HA HA HA!
HAHAHAHAHA
HE'S A FOOL!
NO WAY HE'LL GET IT.
HE'S SO... STUPID.
SHŌ! DON'T STOP!
UNHHHHHH
UNHHHH
UNHHHHHH
SLAPP
TRY AS HARD AS YOU WANT, JERK.

READ THIS WAY

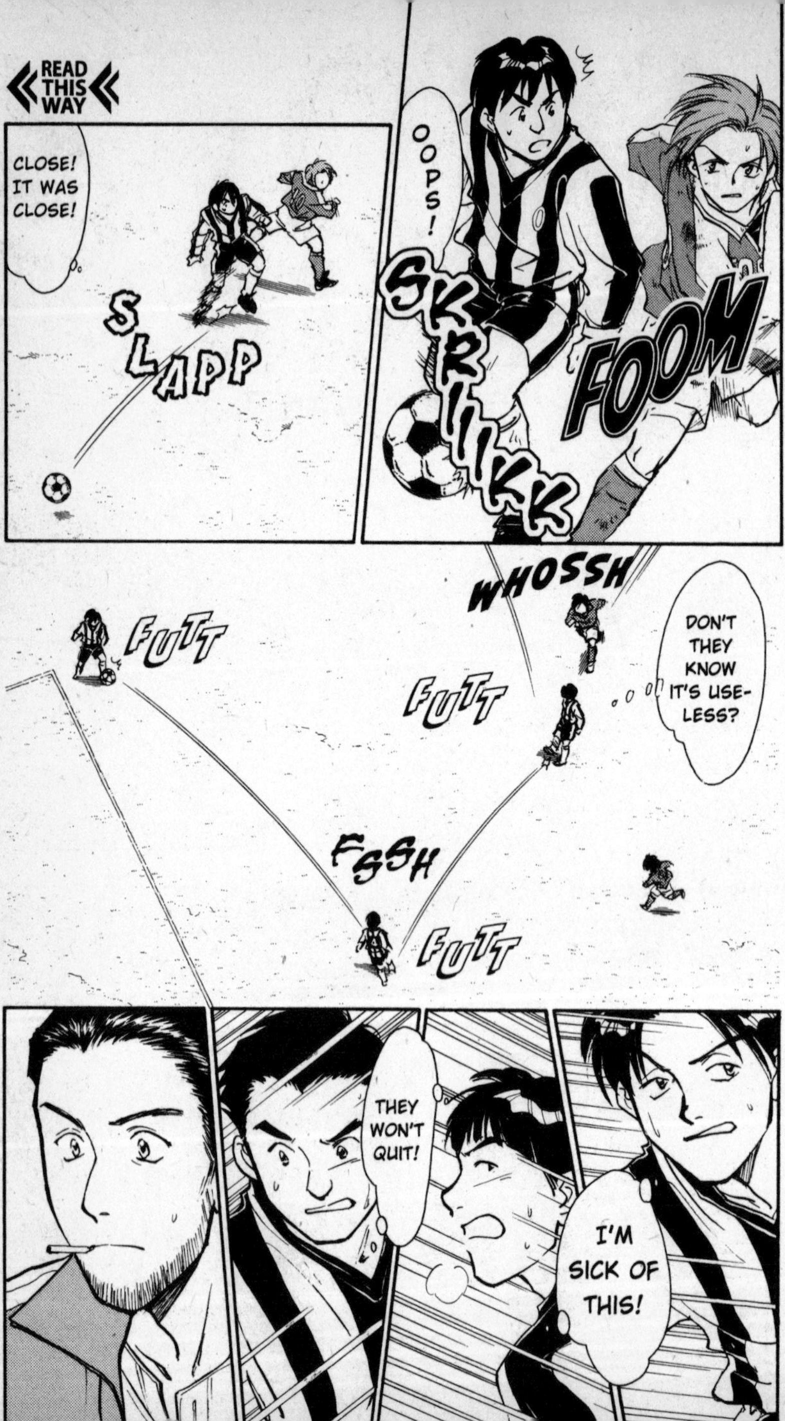
OOPS!
SKRIIIKK
FOOM
CLOSE! IT WAS CLOSE!
SLAPP
WHOSSH
DON'T THEY KNOW IT'S USE-LESS?
FUTT
FUTT
FSSH
FUTT
I'M SICK OF THIS!
THEY WON'T QUIT!

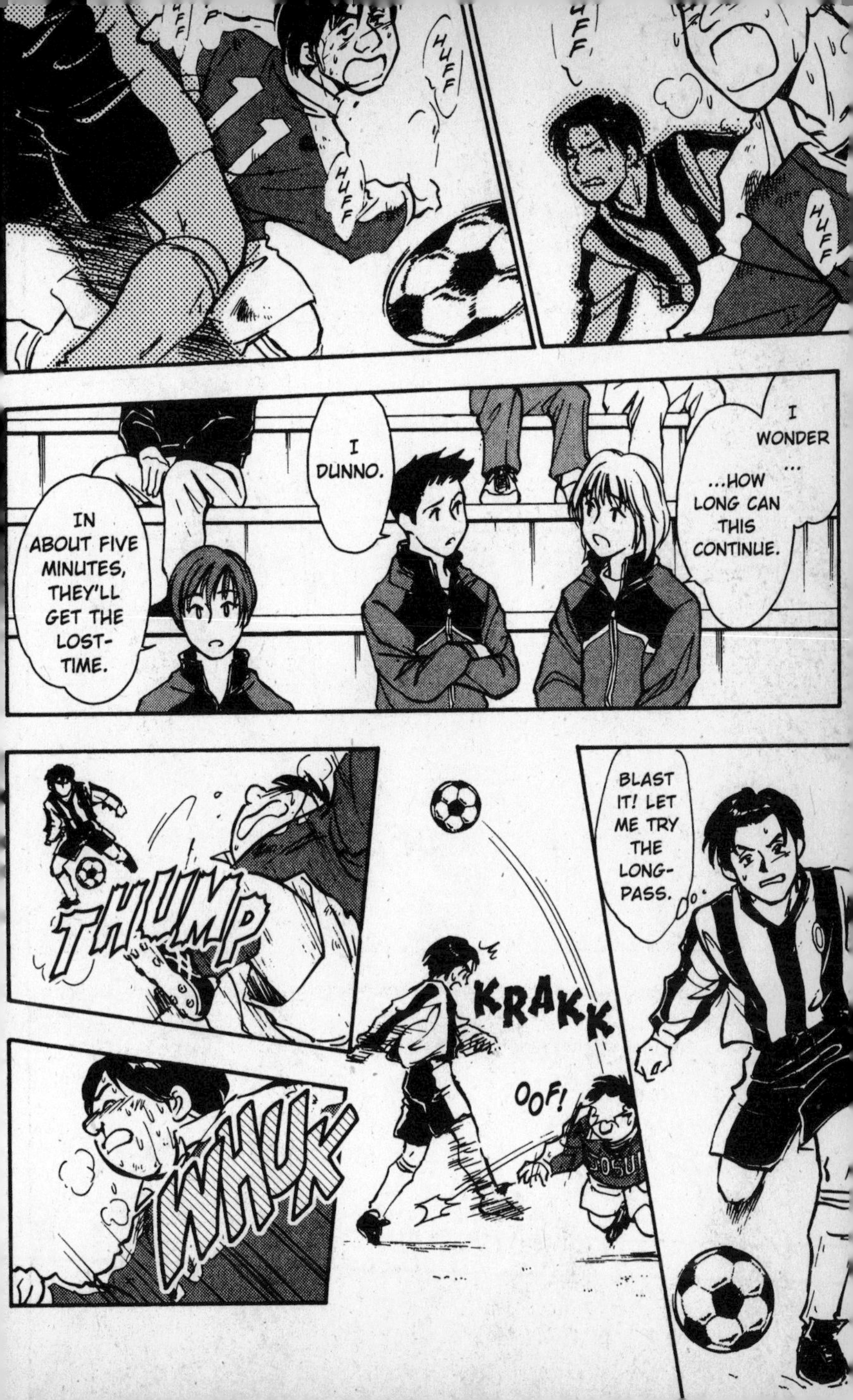
HUFF
HUFF
HUFF
HUFF
HUFF
I WONDER ...
...HOW LONG CAN THIS CONTINUE.
I DUNNO.
IN ABOUT FIVE MINUTES, THEY'LL GET THE LOST-TIME.
BLAST IT! LET ME TRY THE LONG-PASS.
KRAKK
OOF!
THUMP
WHUK

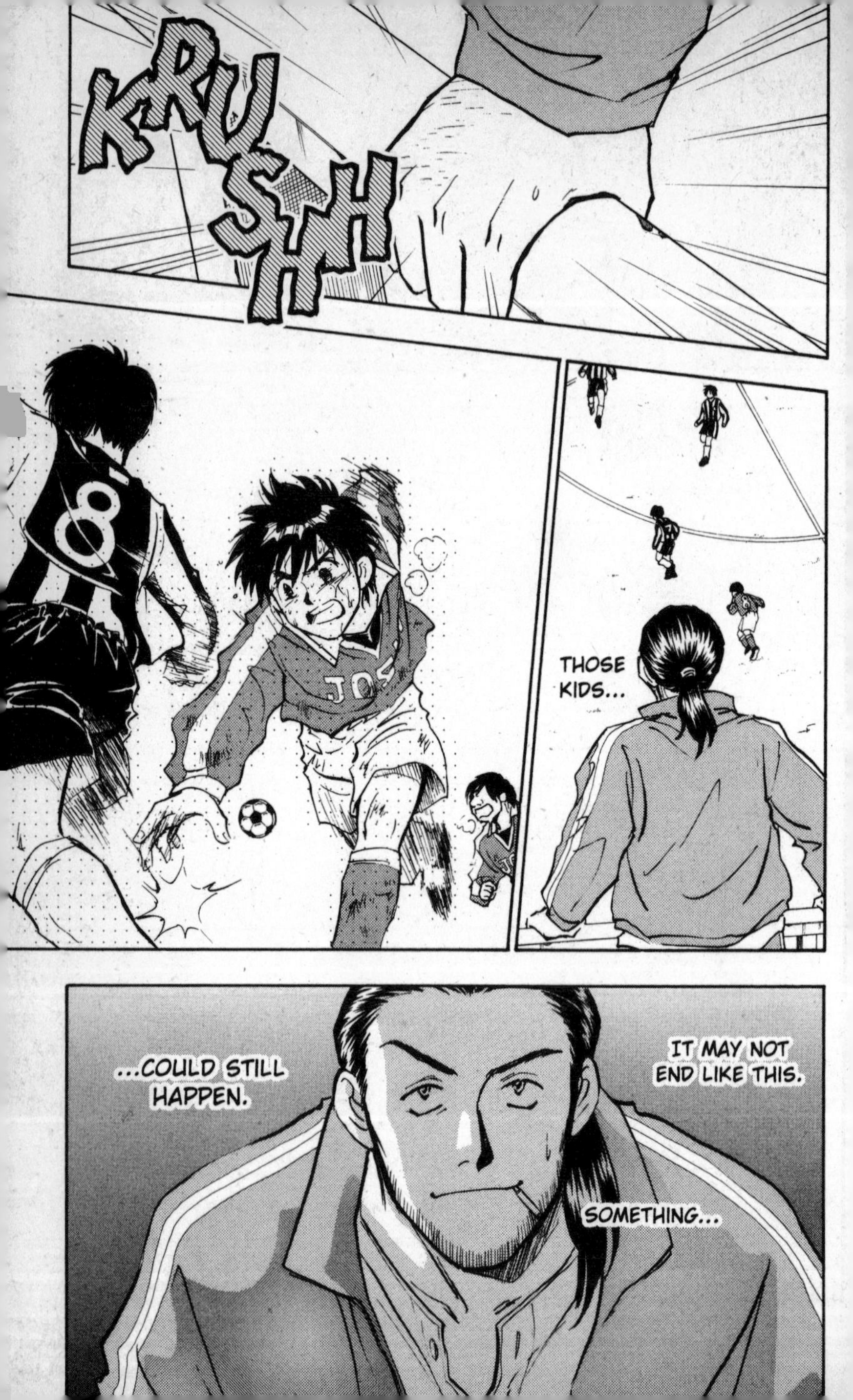
KRUSH
THOSE KIDS...
IT MAY NOT END LIKE THIS.
SOMETHING...
...COULD STILL HAPPEN.

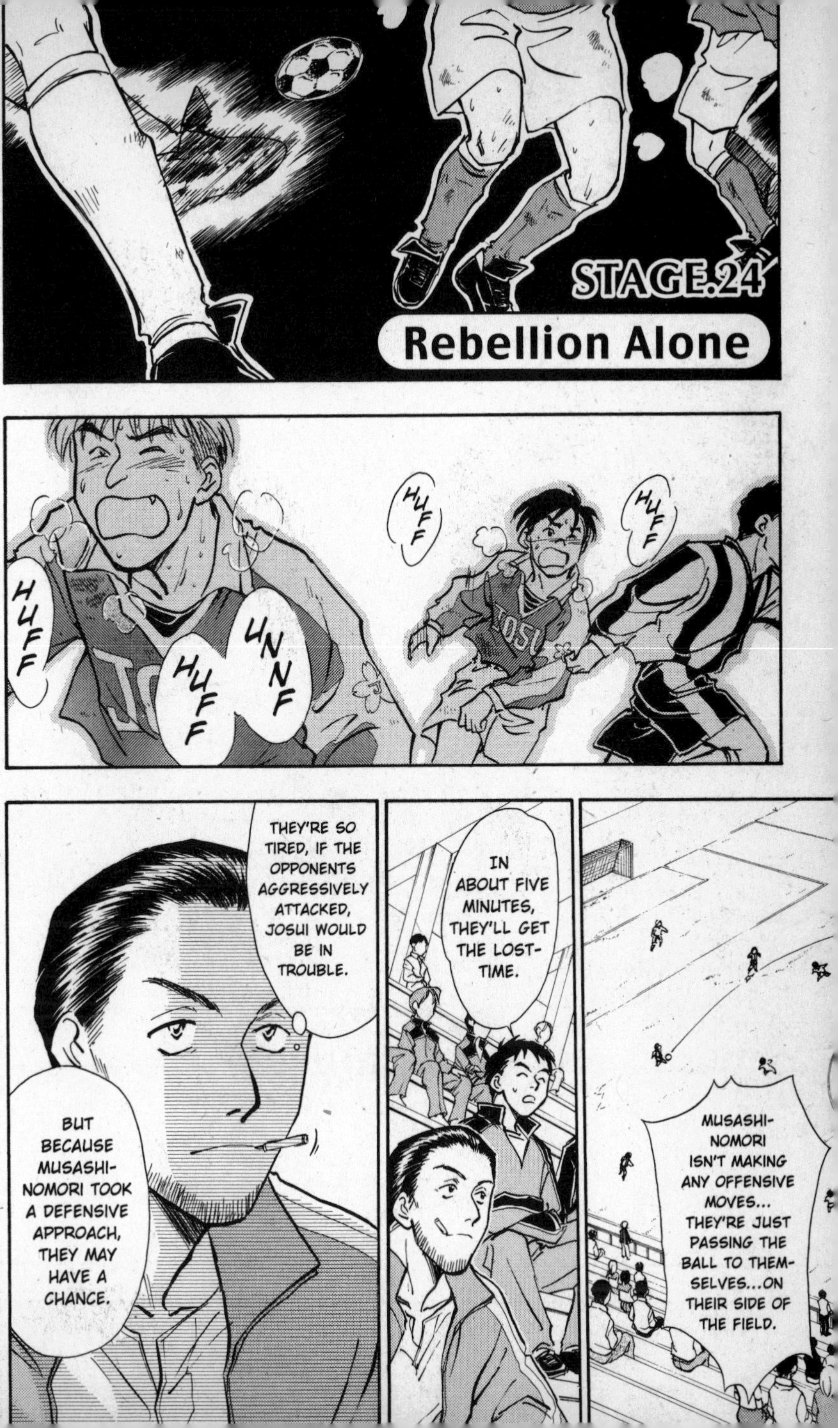
STAGE.24
Rebellion Alone
HUFF HUFF
HUFF HUFF
UNNF
HUFF HUFF
HUFF HUFF
MUSASHI-NOMORI ISN'T MAKING ANY OFFENSIVE MOVES... THEY'RE JUST PASSING THE BALL TO THEM-SELVES...ON THEIR SIDE OF THE FIELD.
IN ABOUT FIVE MINUTES, THEY'LL GET THE LOST-TIME.
THEY'RE SO TIRED, IF THE OPPONENTS AGGRESSIVELY ATTACKED, JOSUI WOULD BE IN TROUBLE.
BUT BECAUSE MUSASHI-NOMORI TOOK A DEFENSIVE APPROACH, THEY MAY HAVE A CHANCE.

STAGE.24
Rebellion Alone

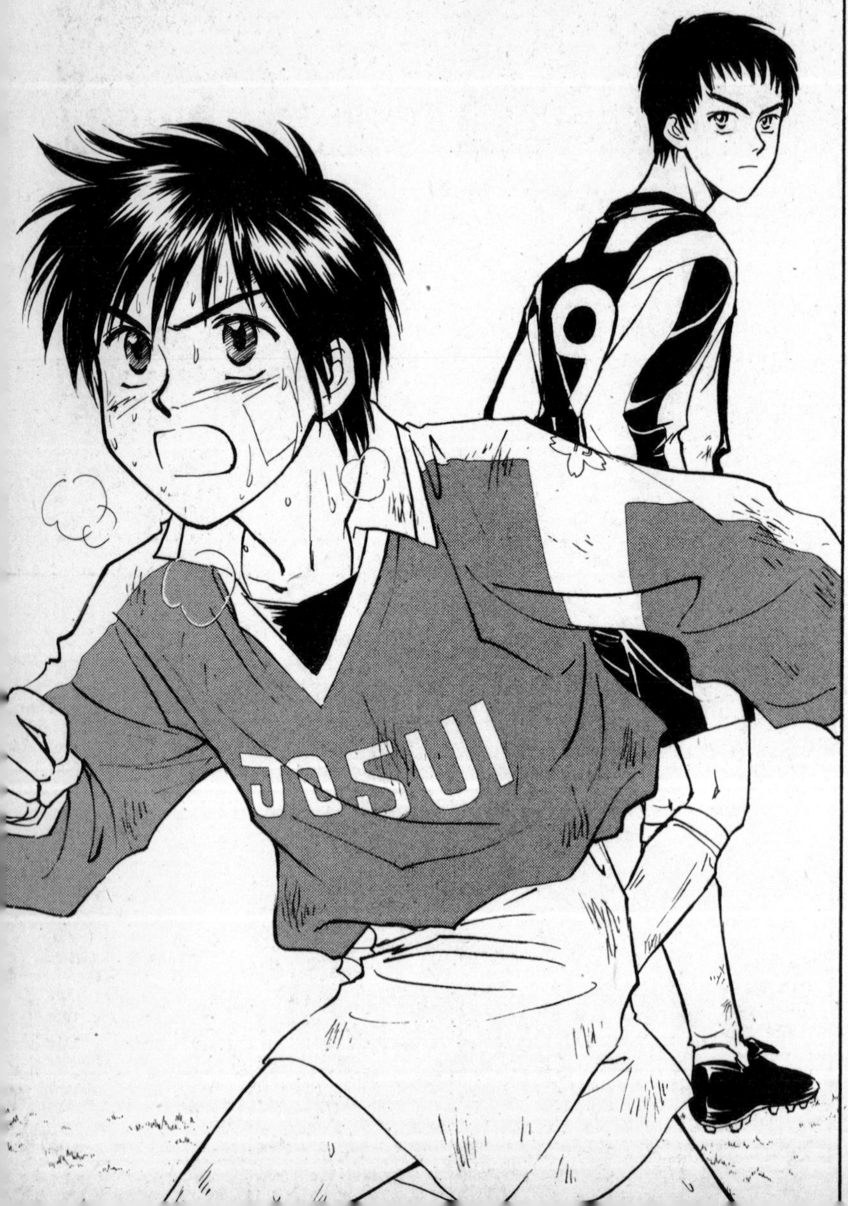
JOSUI

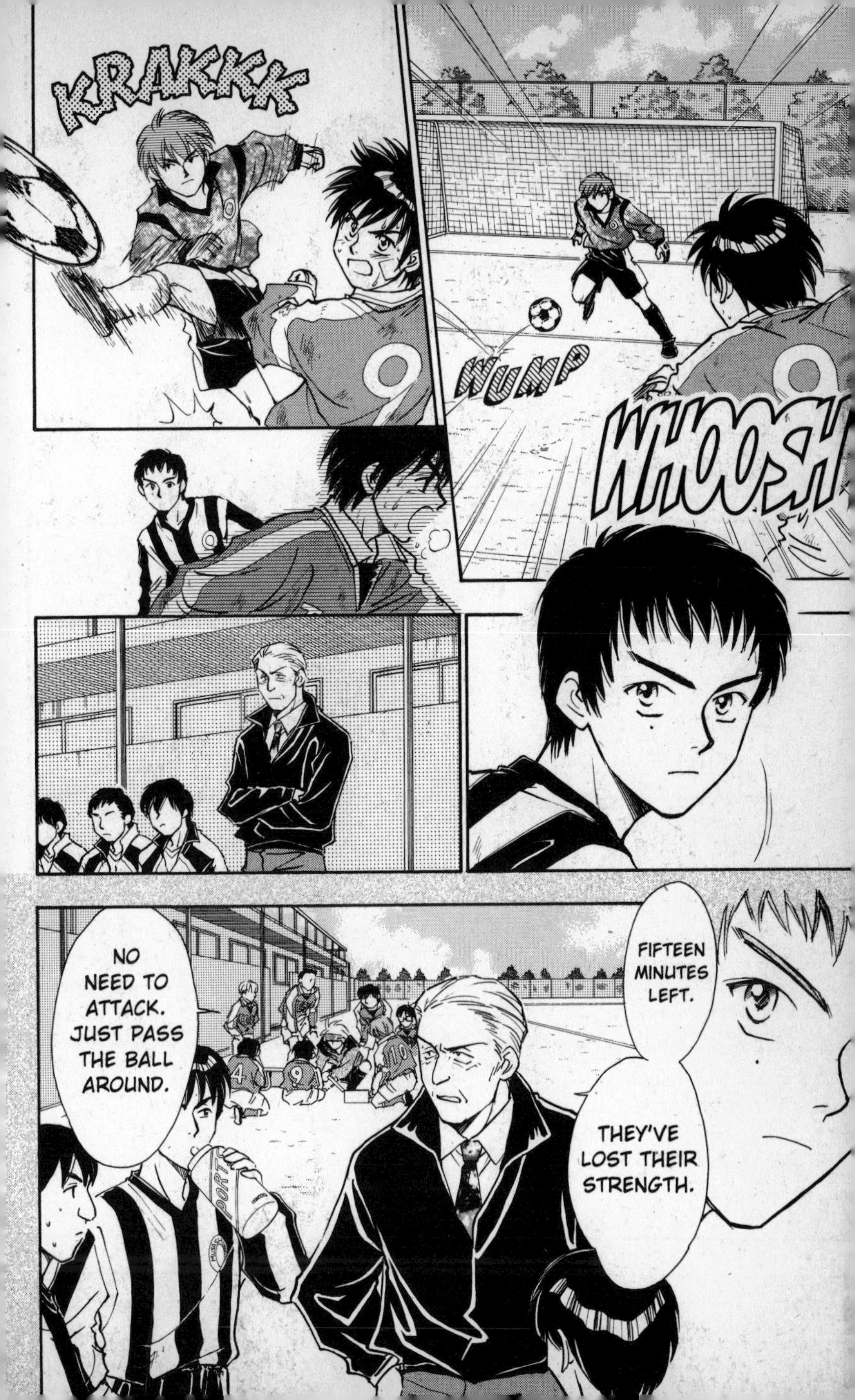
WUMP
WHOOSH
KRAKKK
FIFTEEN MINUTES LEFT.
THEY'VE LOST THEIR STRENGTH.
NO NEED TO ATTACK. JUST PASS THE BALL AROUND.

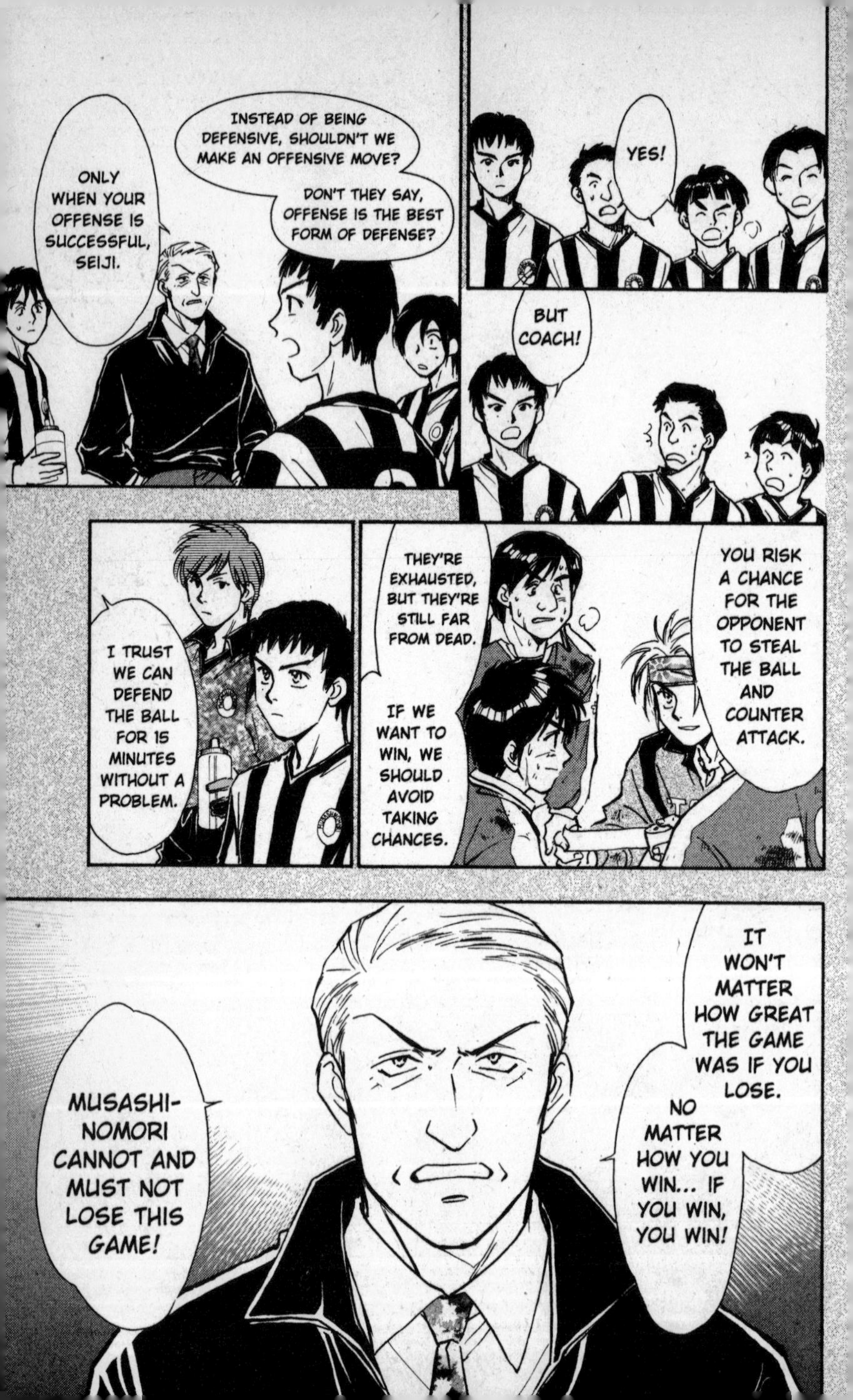
YES!
BUT COACH!
INSTEAD OF BEING DEFENSIVE, SHOULDN'T WE MAKE AN OFFENSIVE MOVE?
DON'T THEY SAY, OFFENSE IS THE BEST FORM OF DEFENSE?
ONLY WHEN YOUR OFFENSE IS SUCCESSFUL, SEIJI.
YOU RISK A CHANCE FOR THE OPPONENT TO STEAL THE BALL AND COUNTER ATTACK.
THEY'RE EXHAUSTED, BUT THEY'RE STILL FAR FROM DEAD.
IF WE WANT TO WIN, WE SHOULD AVOID TAKING CHANCES.
I TRUST WE CAN DEFEND THE BALL FOR 15 MINUTES WITHOUT A PROBLEM.
IT WON'T MATTER HOW GREAT THE GAME WAS IF YOU LOSE.
NO MATTER HOW YOU WIN... IF YOU WIN, YOU WIN!
MUSASHI-NOMORI CANNOT AND MUST NOT LOSE THIS GAME!

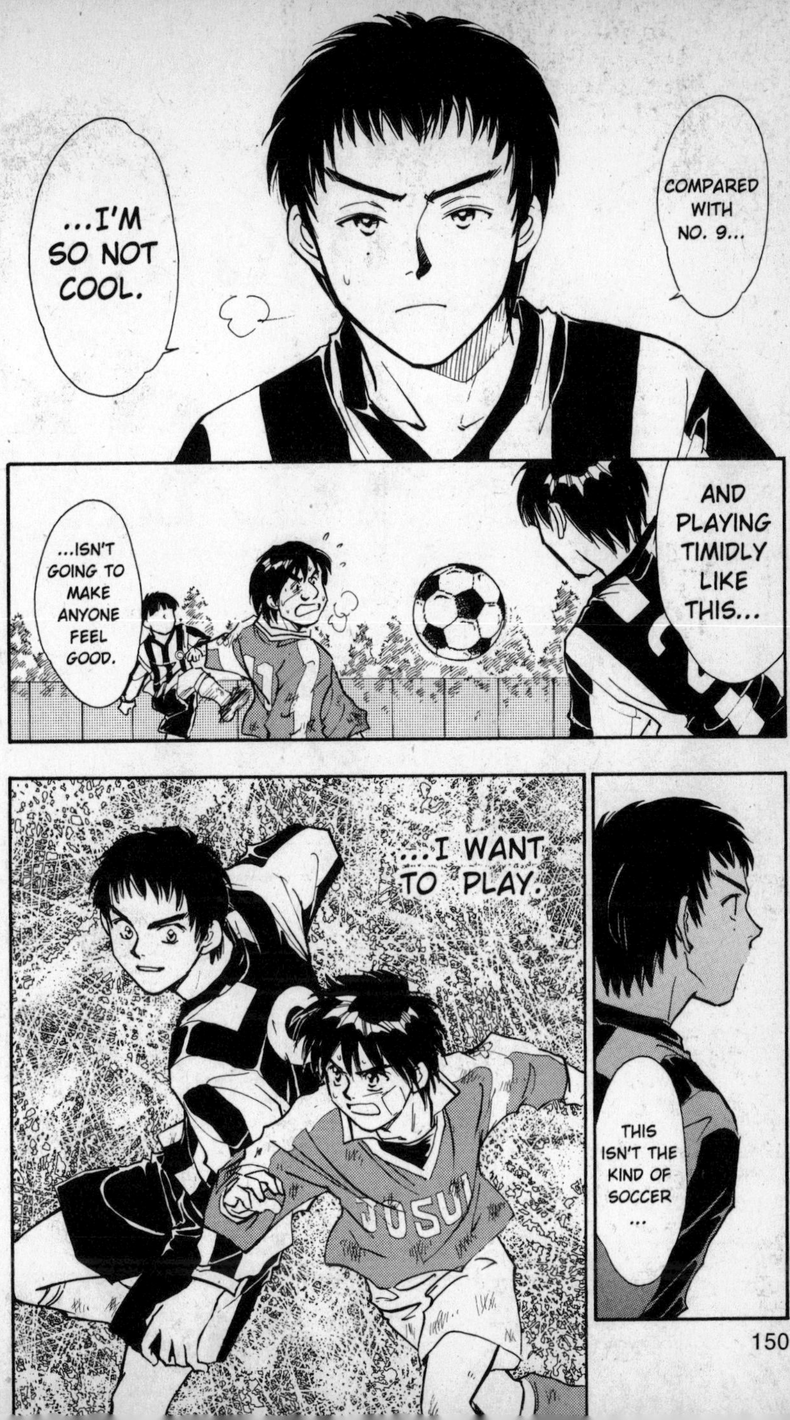
COMPARED WITH NO. 9...
...I'M SO NOT COOL.
AND PLAYING TIMIDLY LIKE THIS...
...ISN'T GOING TO MAKE ANYONE FEEL GOOD.
THIS ISN'T THE KIND OF SOCCER ...
...I WANT TO PLAY.

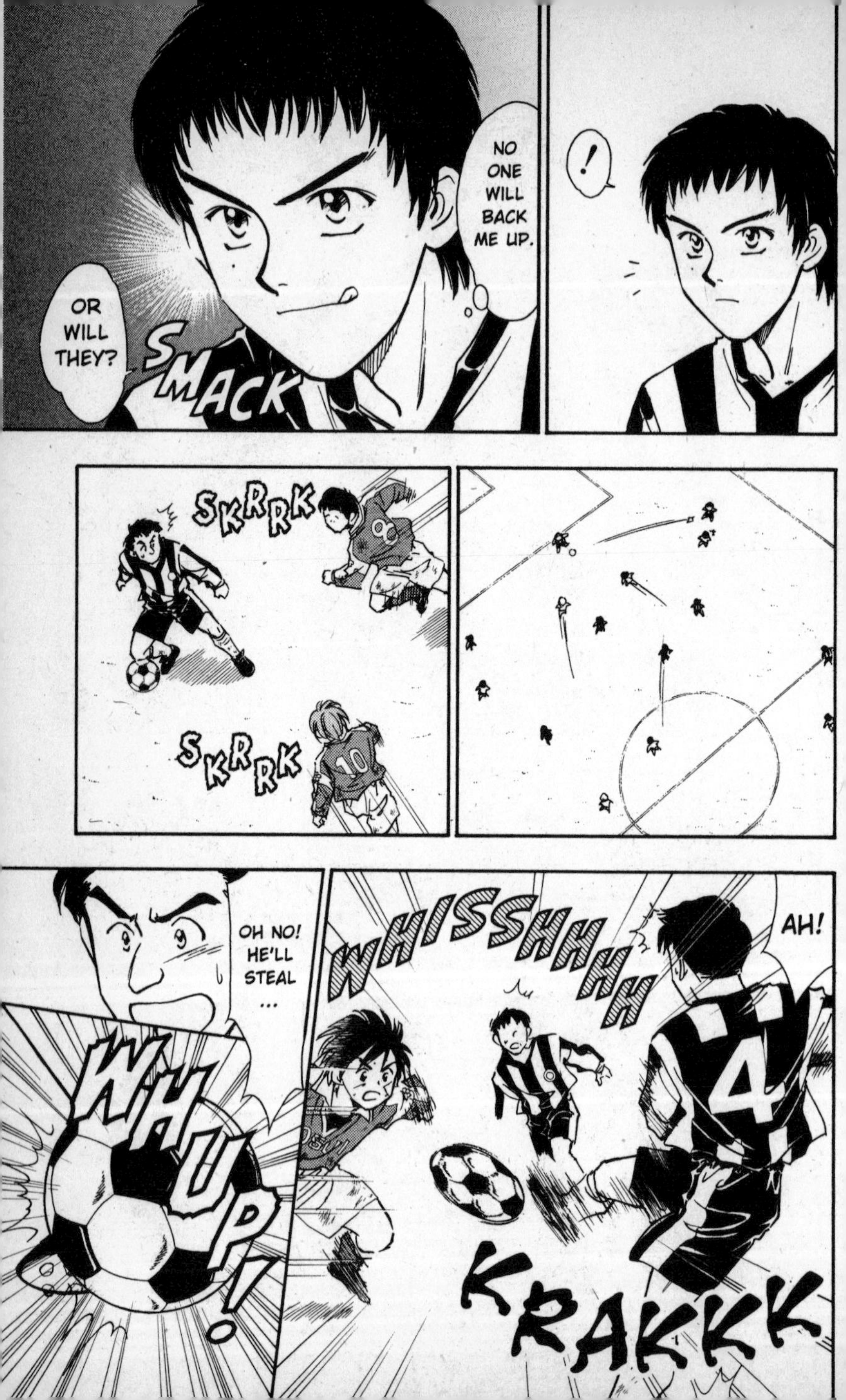
!
NO ONE WILL BACK ME UP.
OR WILL THEY?
SMACK
SKRRK
SKRRK
AH!
WHISSHHHHH
KRAKKK
OH NO! HE'LL STEAL ...
WHUP!!

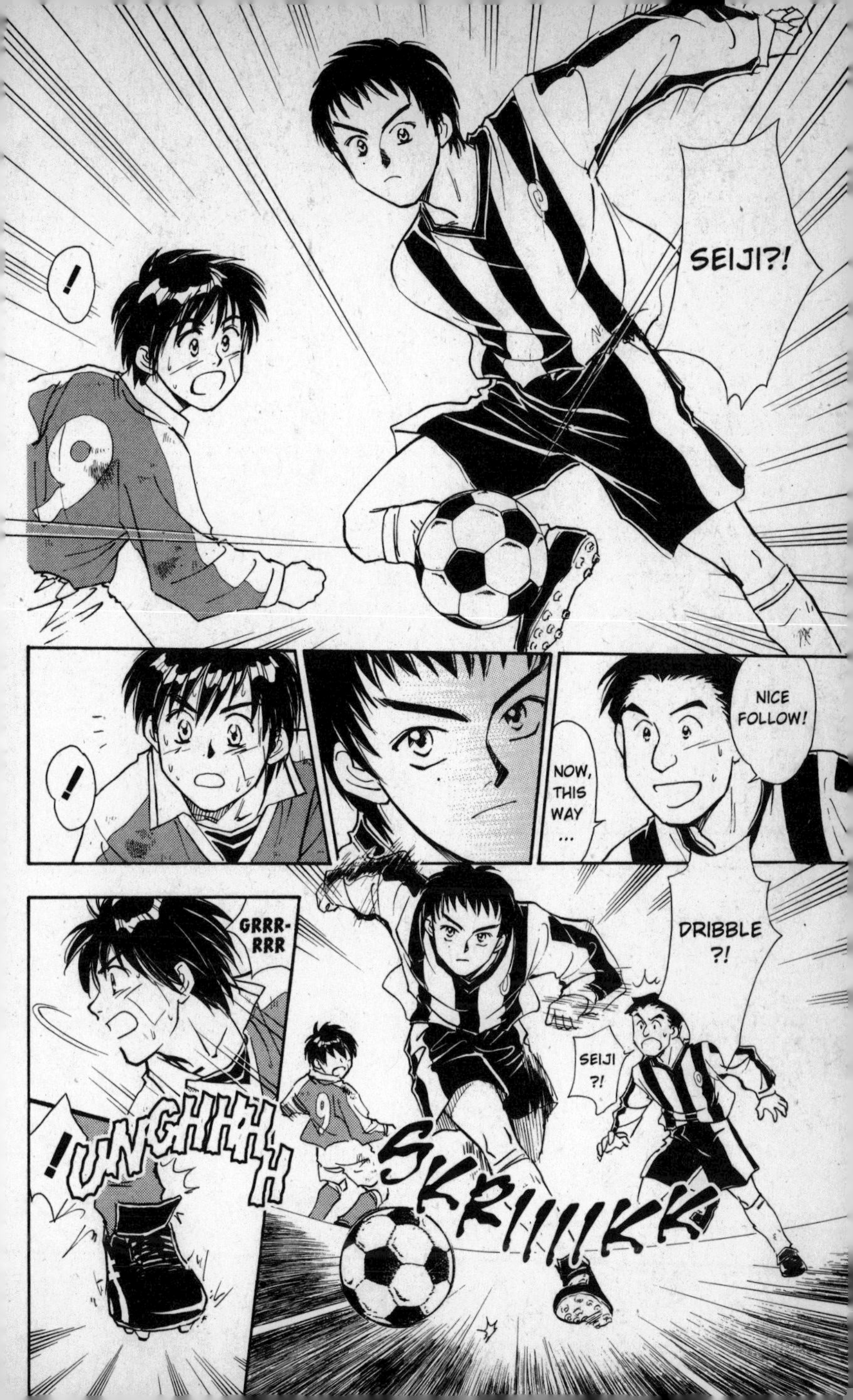
SEIJI?!
!
NICE FOLLOW!
NOW, THIS WAY ...
!
DRIBBLE ?!
SEIJI ?!
SKRIIIIKK
GRRR-RRR
!UNGHHHH

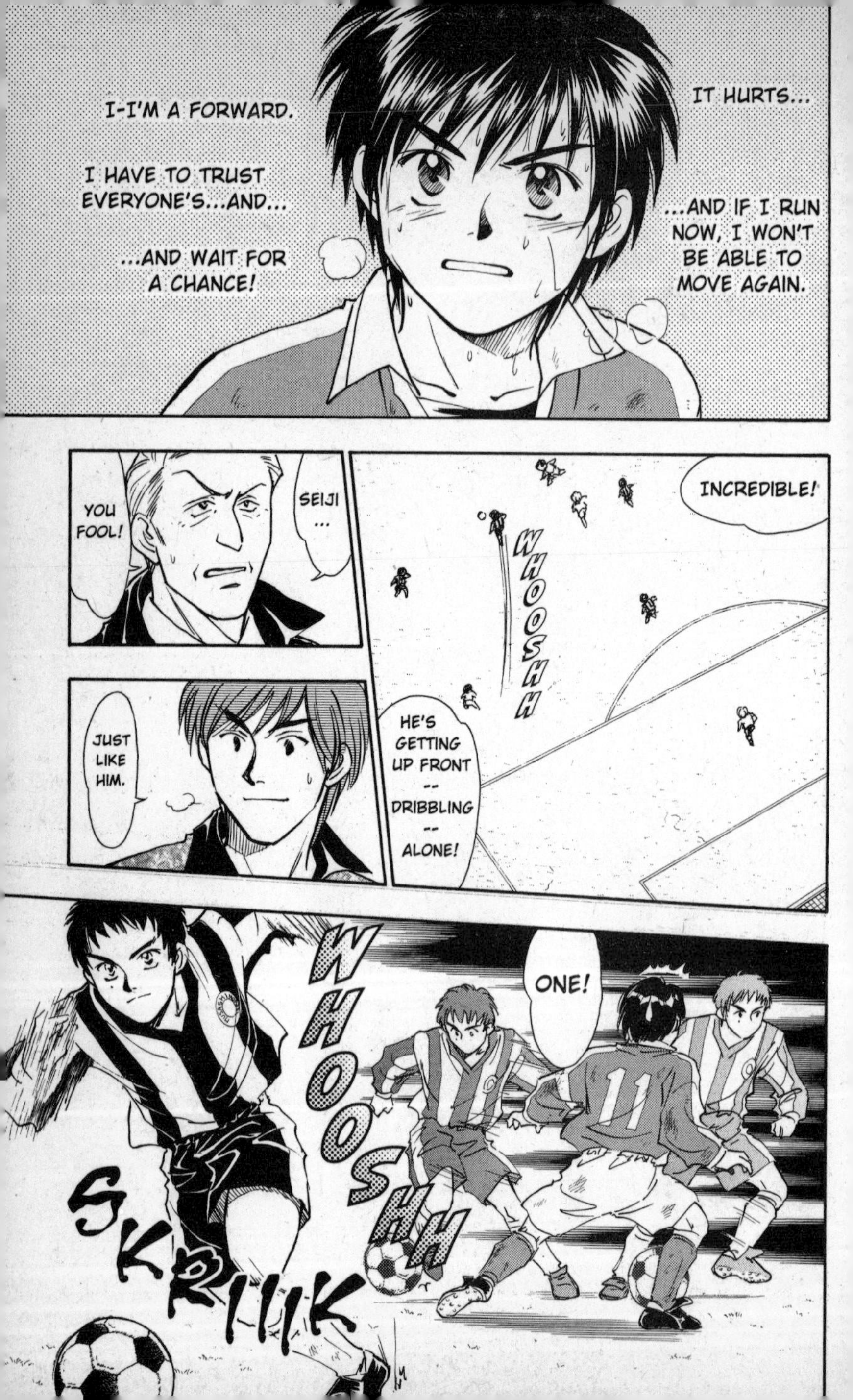
IT HURTS...
...AND IF I RUN NOW, I WON'T BE ABLE TO MOVE AGAIN.
I-I'M A FORWARD.
I HAVE TO TRUST EVERYONE'S...AND...
...AND WAIT FOR A CHANCE!
INCREDIBLE!
WHOOSHH
HE'S GETTING UP FRONT -- DRIBBLING -- ALONE!
SEIJI ...
YOU FOOL!
JUST LIKE HIM.
ONE!
WHOOOSHH
SKRIIIK

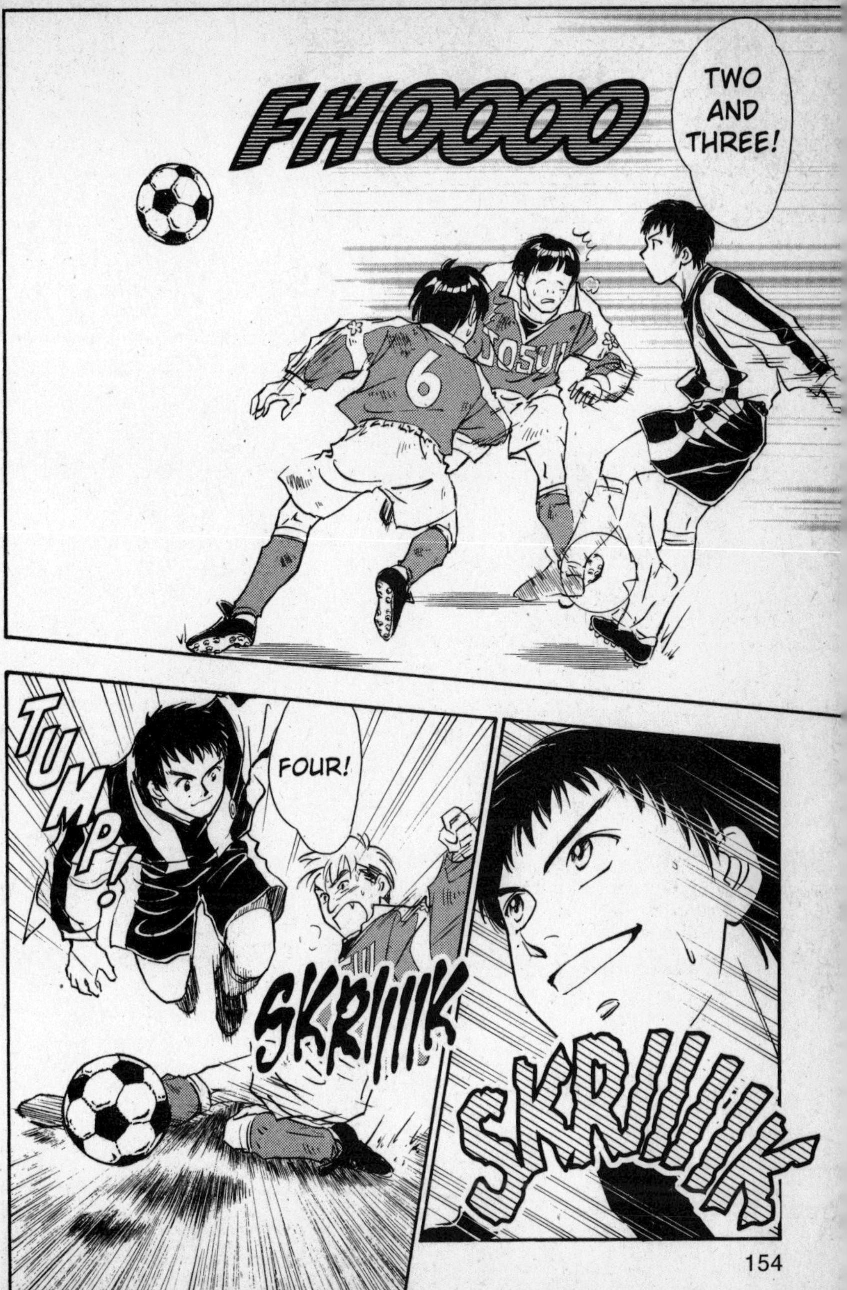
TWO AND THREE!
FHOOOO
SKRIIIK
FOUR!
TUMP!
SKRIIIK

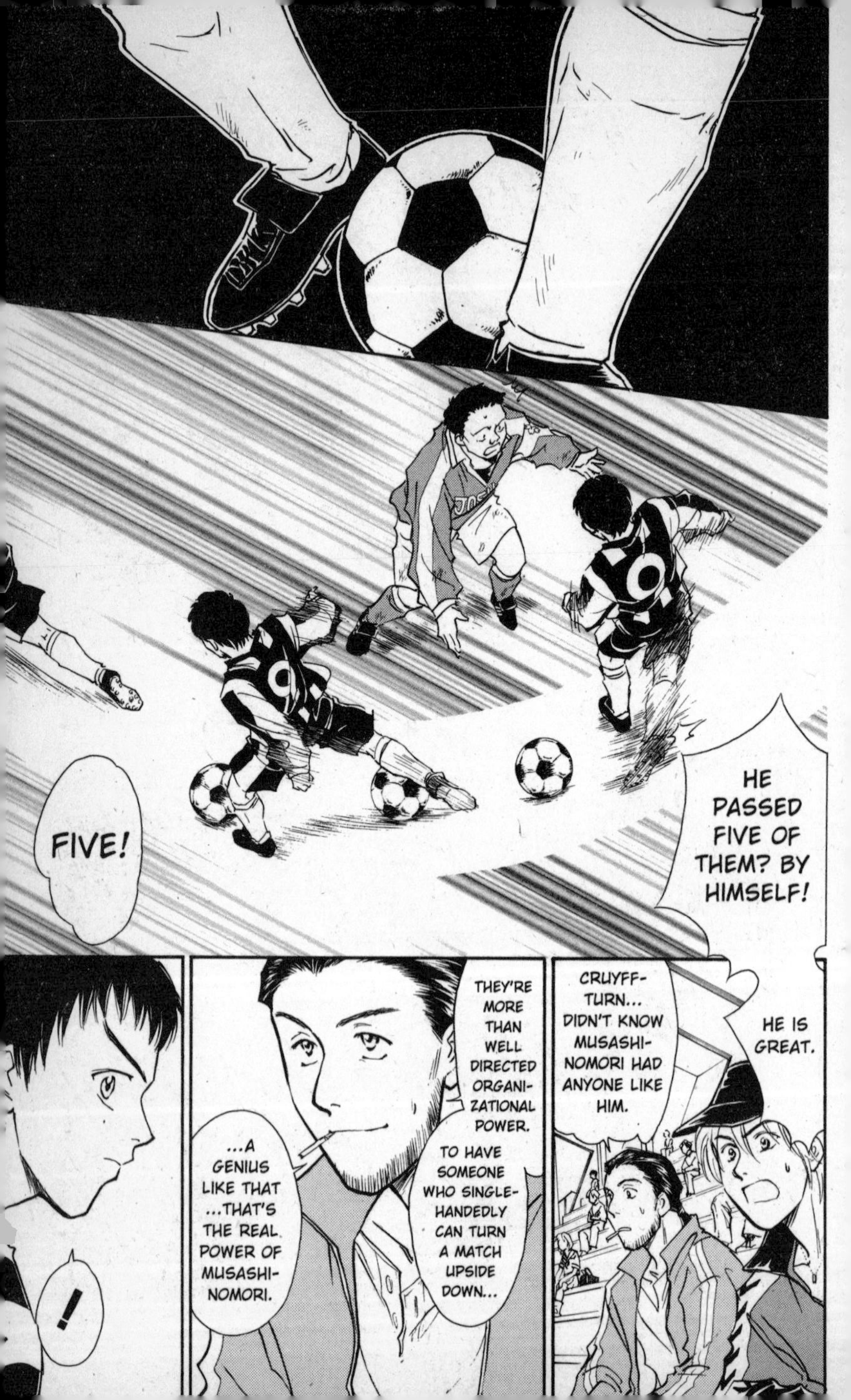
HE PASSED FIVE OF THEM? BY HIMSELF!
FIVE!
HE IS GREAT.
CRUYFF-TURN... DIDN'T KNOW MUSASHI-NOMORI HAD ANYONE LIKE HIM.
THEY'RE MORE THAN WELL DIRECTED ORGANIZATIONAL POWER.
TO HAVE SOMEONE WHO SINGLE-HANDEDLY CAN TURN A MATCH UPSIDE DOWN...
...A GENIUS LIKE THAT ...THAT'S THE REAL POWER OF MUSASHI-NOMORI.
!

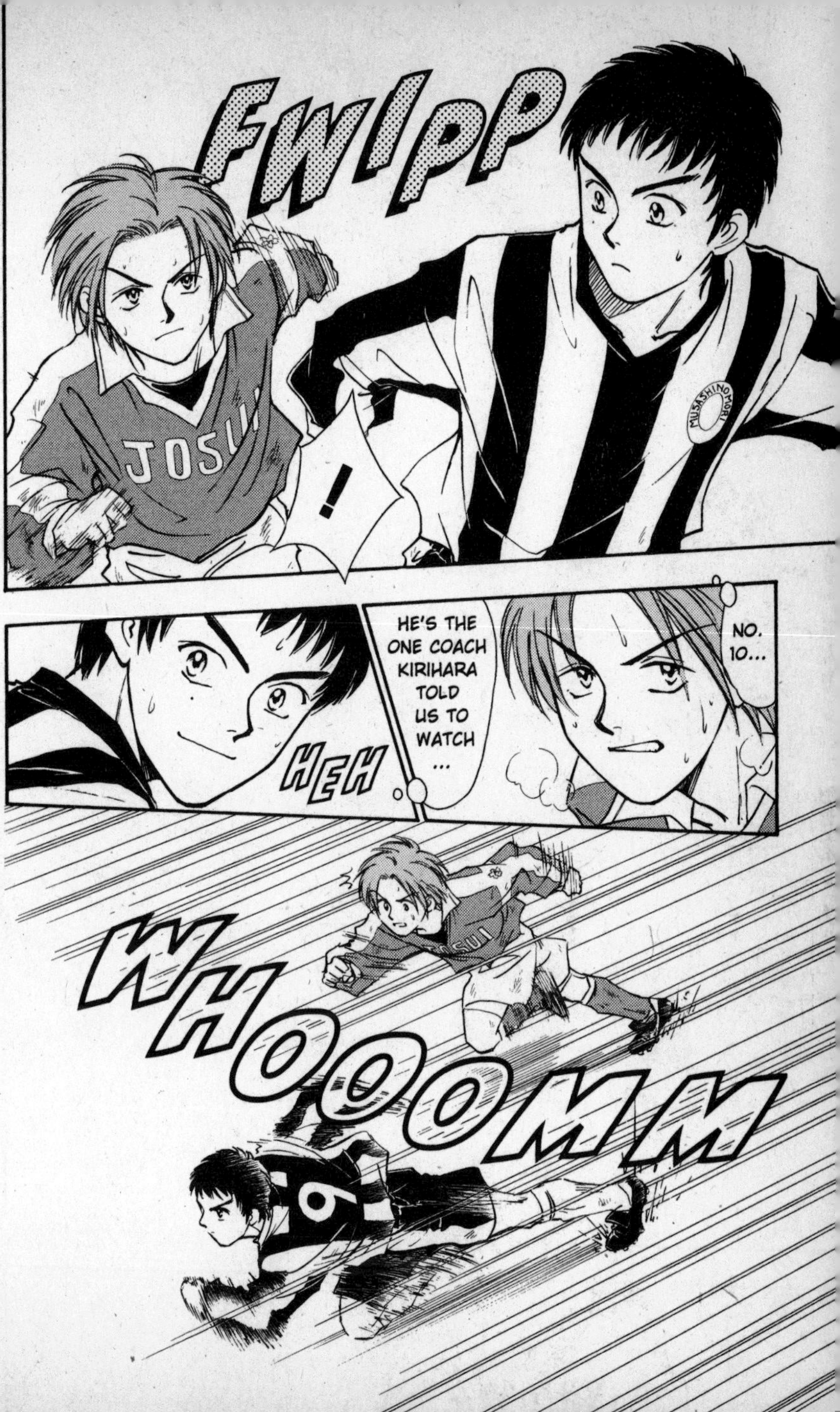
FWIPP
!
NO. 10...
HE'S THE ONE COACH KIRIHARA TOLD US TO WATCH ...
HEH
WHOOOMM

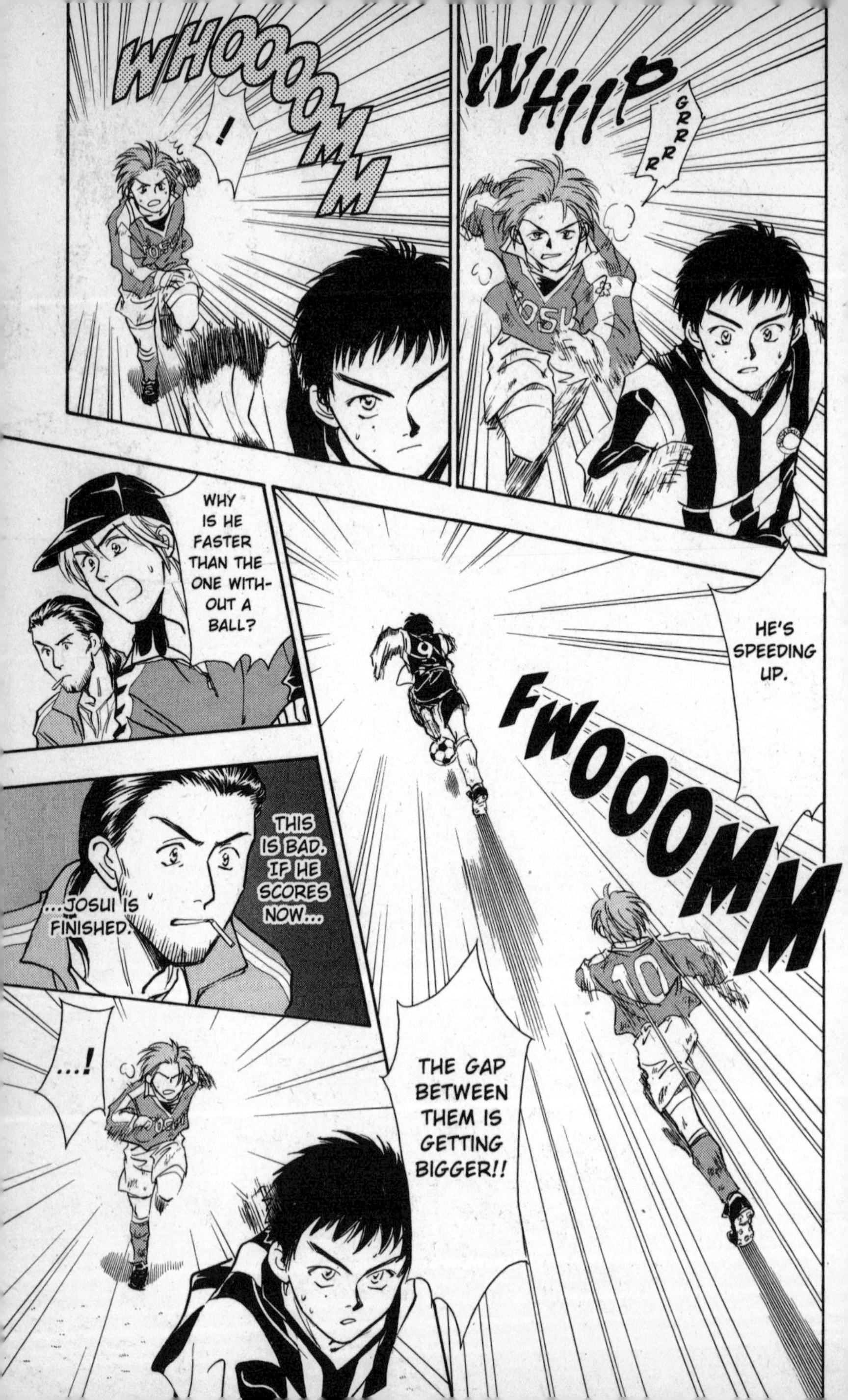
WHIIP
GRRRR
WHOOOOMM
!
HE'S SPEEDING UP.
FWOOOMM
THE GAP BETWEEN THEM IS GETTING BIGGER!!
WHY IS HE FASTER THAN THE ONE WITH-OUT A BALL?
THIS IS BAD. IF HE SCORES NOW...
...JOSUI IS FINISHED.
...!

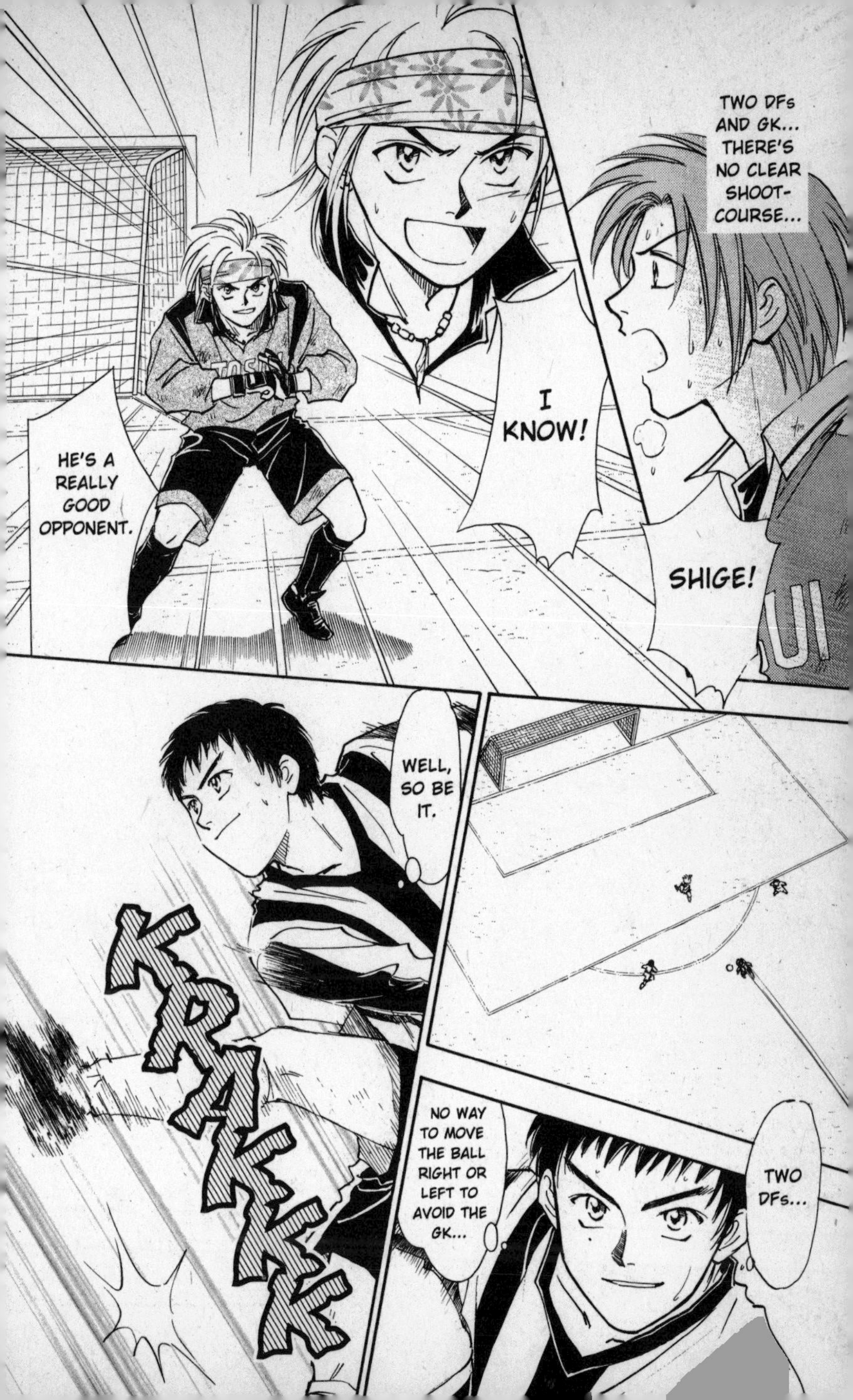
TWO DFs AND GK... THERE'S NO CLEAR SHOOT-COURSE...
SHIGE!
I KNOW!
HE'S A REALLY GOOD OPPONENT.
TWO DFs...
NO WAY TO MOVE THE BALL RIGHT OR LEFT TO AVOID THE GK...
WELL, SO BE IT.
KRAKK

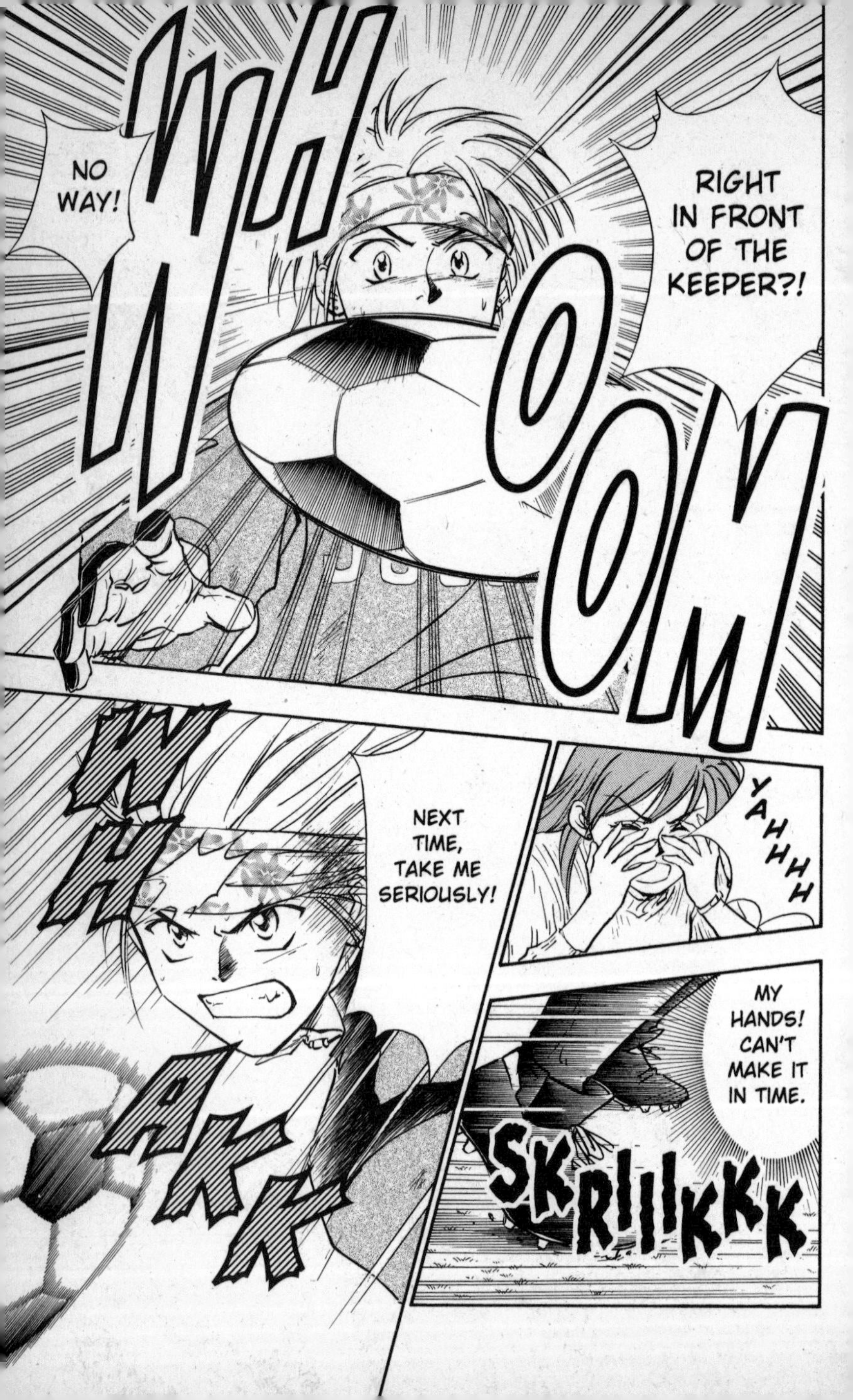
RIGHT IN FRONT OF THE KEEPER?!
WHOOM
NO WAY!
YAHHHH
MY HANDS! CAN'T MAKE IT IN TIME.
SKRIIKKK
NEXT TIME, TAKE ME SERIOUSLY!
WHAKK

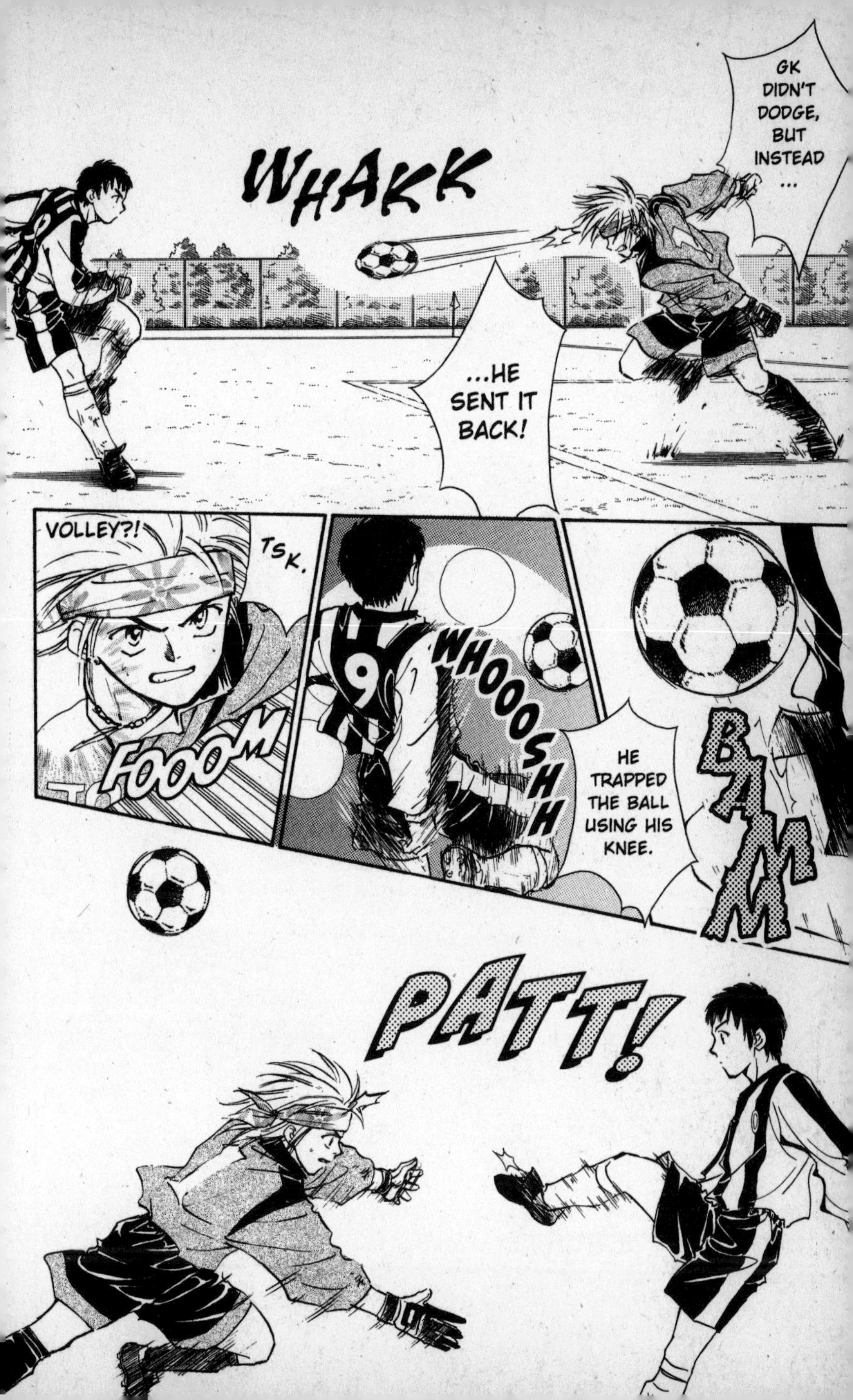
GK DIDN'T DODGE, BUT INSTEAD ...
WHAKK
...HE SENT IT BACK!
BAMM
HE TRAPPED THE BALL USING HIS KNEE.
WHOOOSHH
VOLLEY?!
TSK.
FOOOM
PATT!

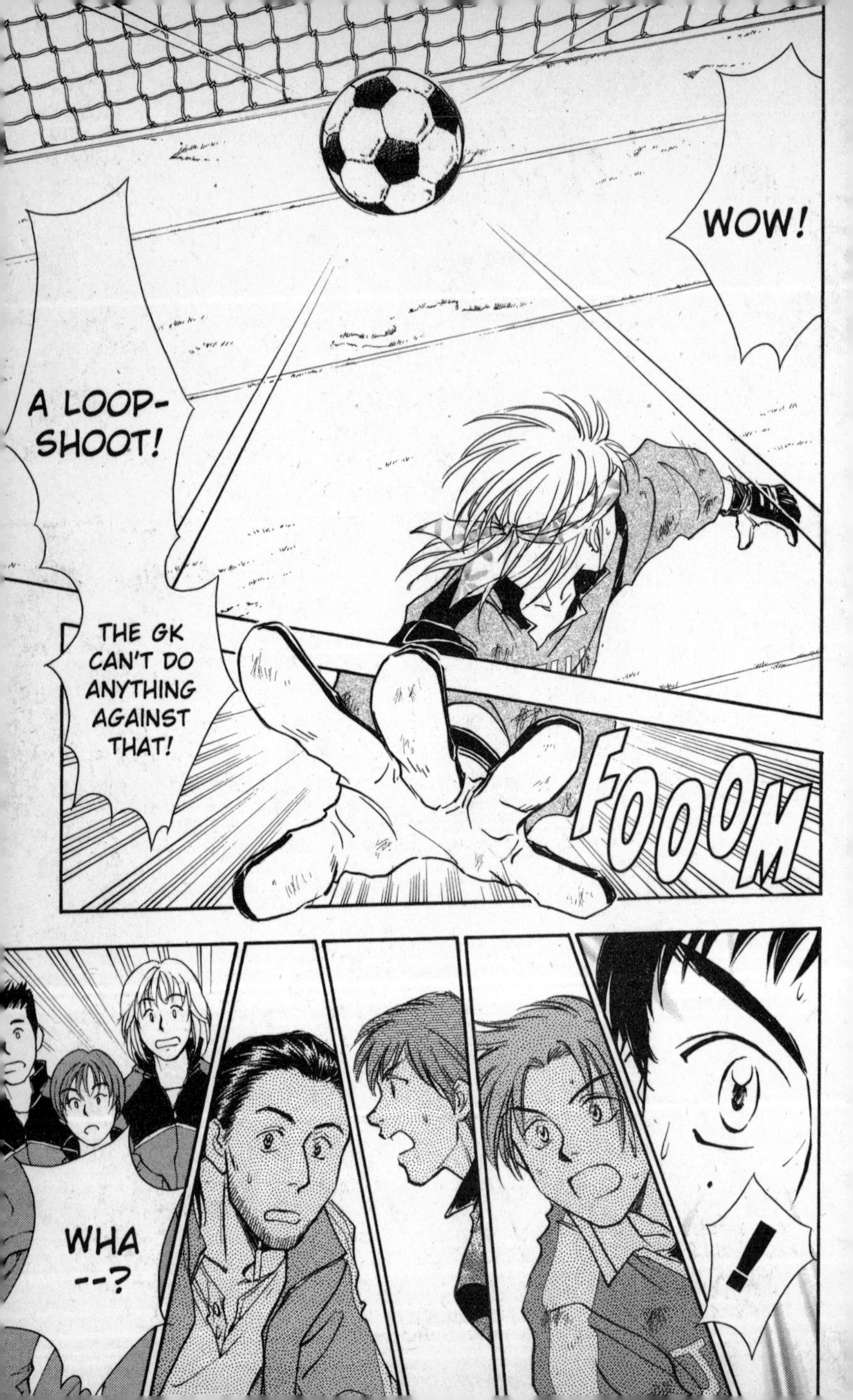
WOW!
A LOOP-SHOOT!
THE GK CAN'T DO ANYTHING AGAINST THAT!
FOOOM
!
WHA --?

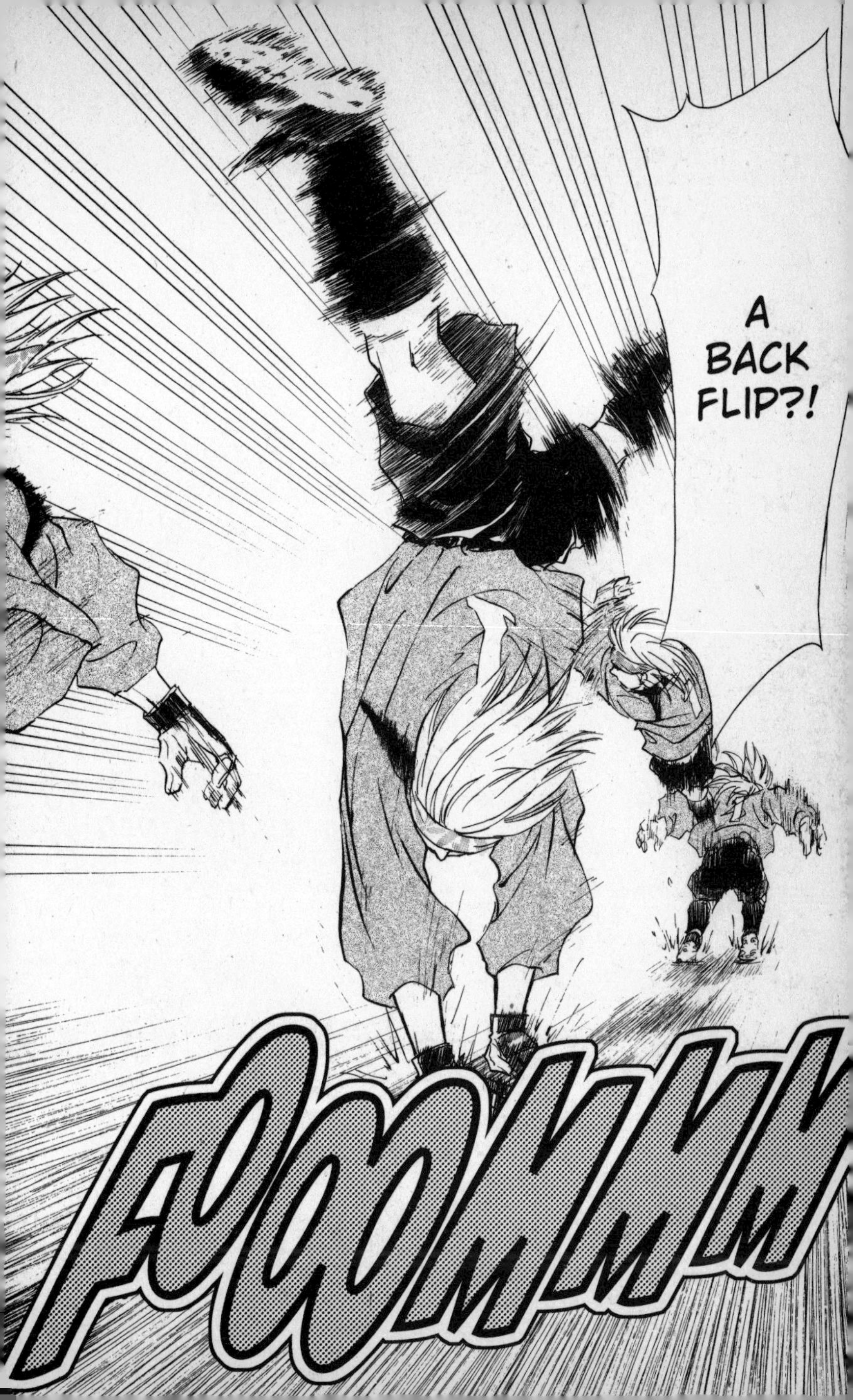
A BACK FLIP?!
FOOMMM

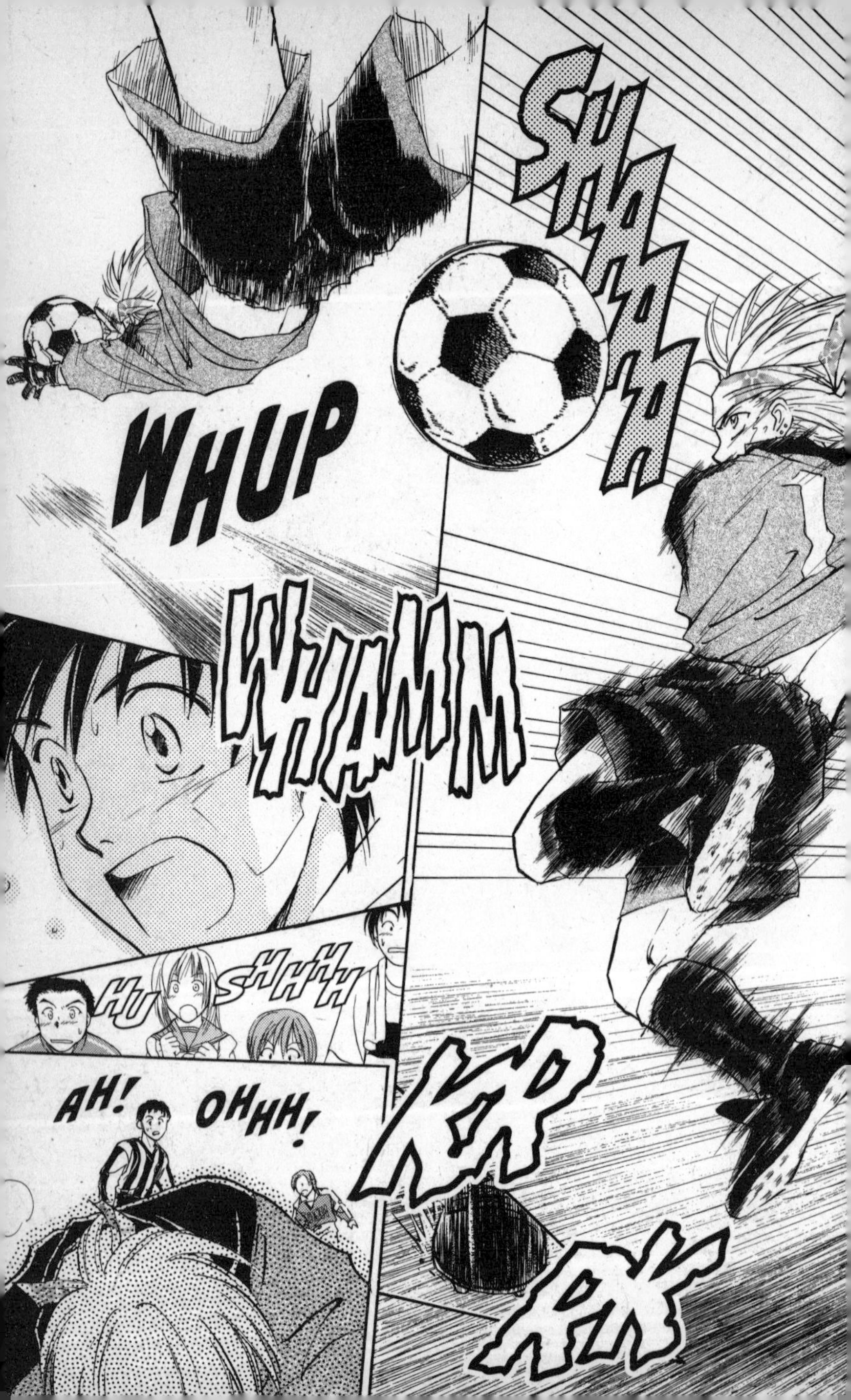
SHAAAA
KRAK
WHUP
WHAMM
HUSHHH
AH!
OHHH!

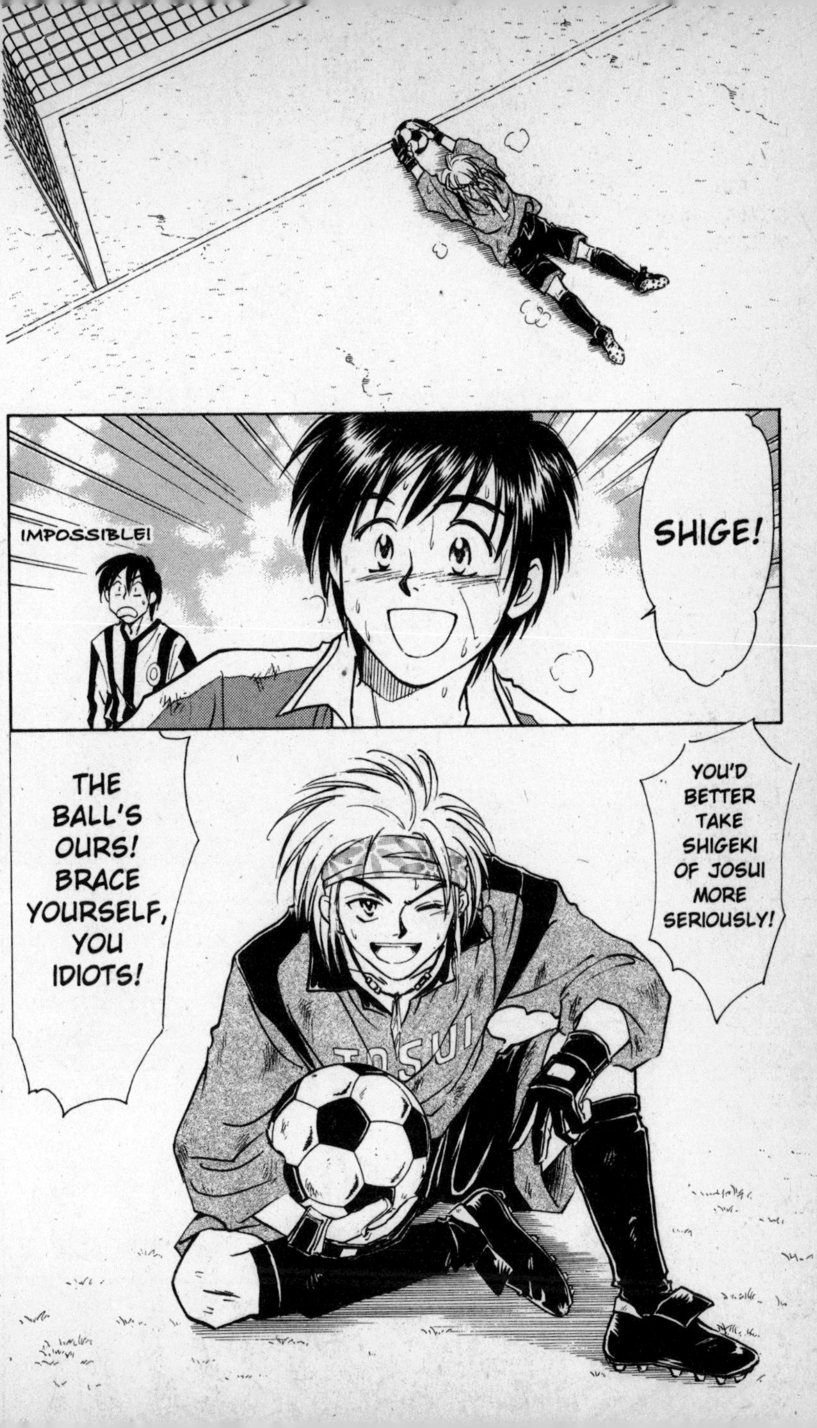
SHIGE!
IMPOSSIBLE!
YOU'D BETTER TAKE SHIGEKI OF JOSUI MORE SERIOUSLY!
THE BALL'S OURS! BRACE YOURSELF, YOU IDIOTS!
JOSUI

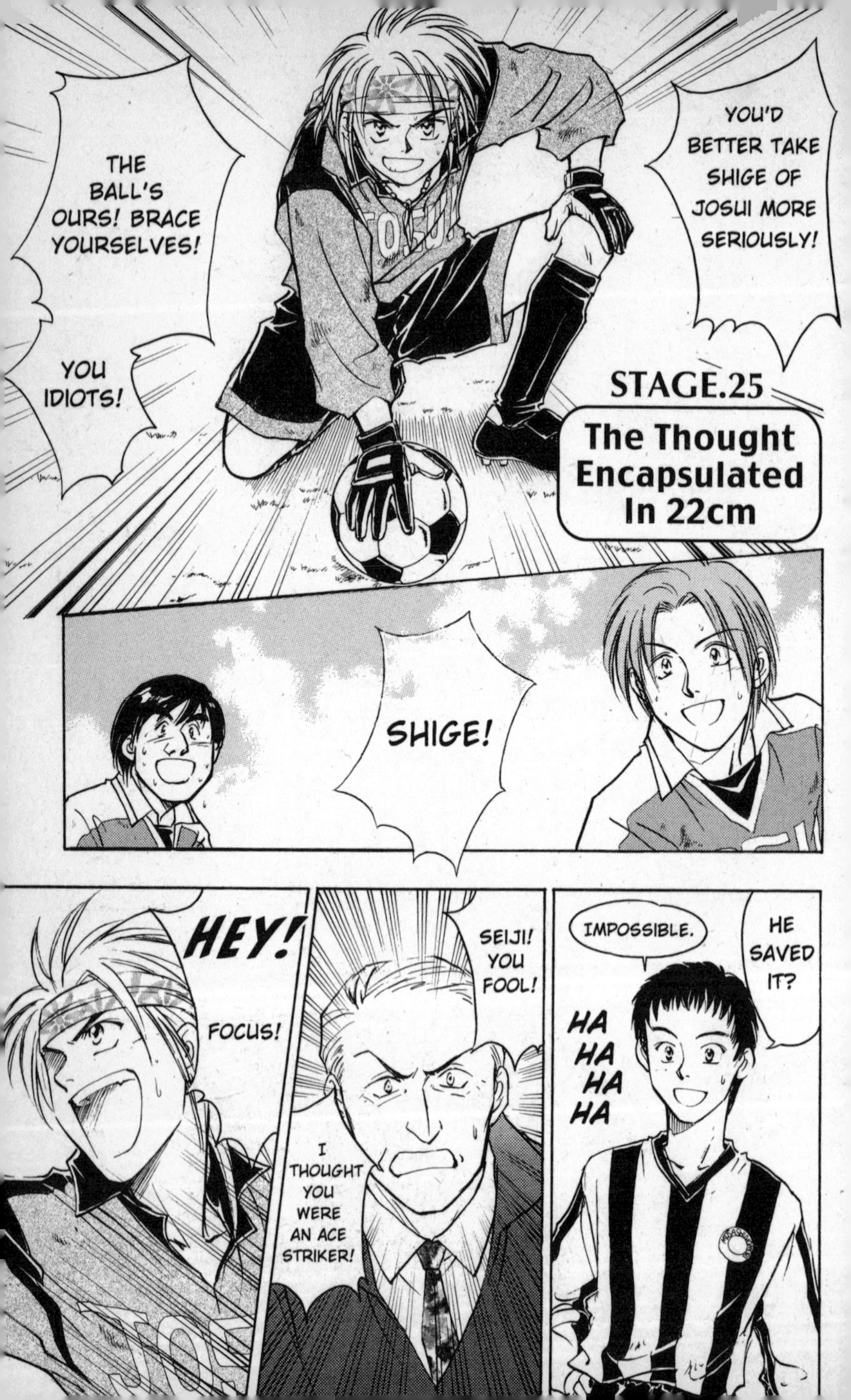
YOU'D BETTER TAKE SHIGE OF JOSUI MORE SERIOUSLY!
THE BALL'S OURS! BRACE YOURSELVES!
STAGE.25
The Thought Encapsulated In 22cm
YOU IDIOTS!
SHIGE!
HE SAVED IT?
IMPOSSIBLE.
HA HA HA HA HA
SEIJI! YOU FOOL!
I THOUGHT YOU WERE AN ACE STRIKER!
HEY!
FOCUS!

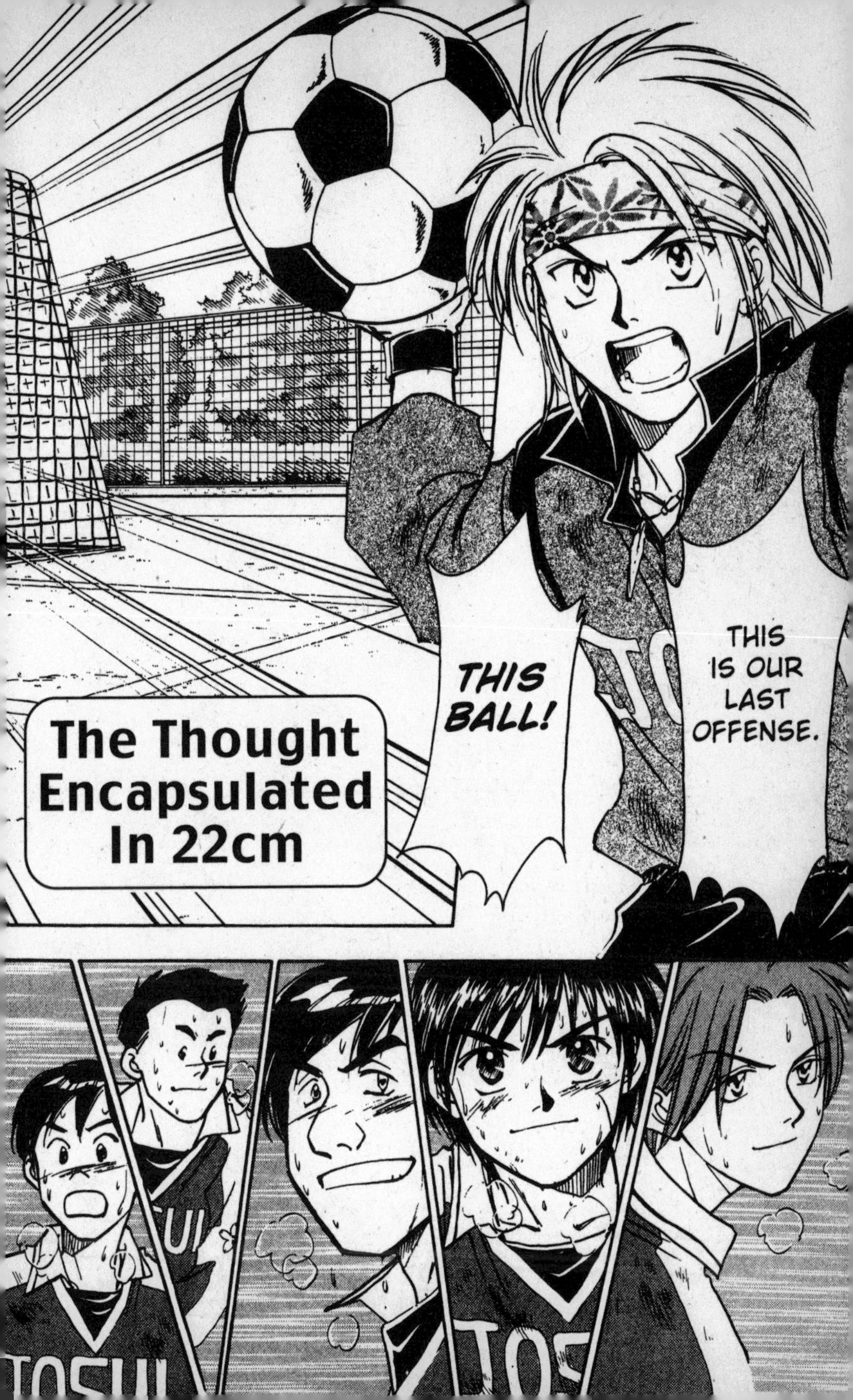
THIS IS OUR LAST OFFENSE.
THIS BALL!
The Thought Encapsulated In 22cm

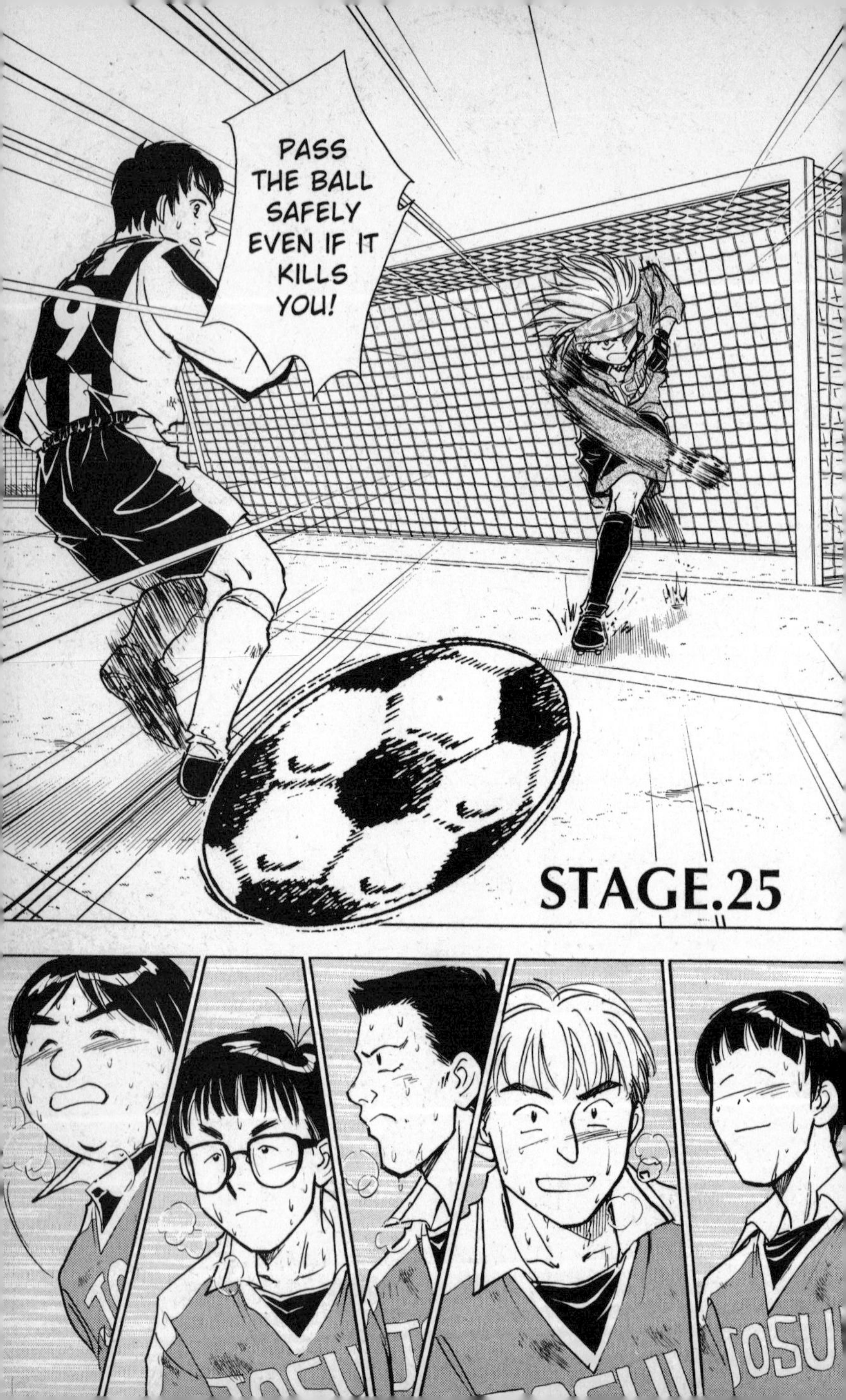
PASS THE BALL SAFELY EVEN IF IT KILLS YOU!
STAGE.25

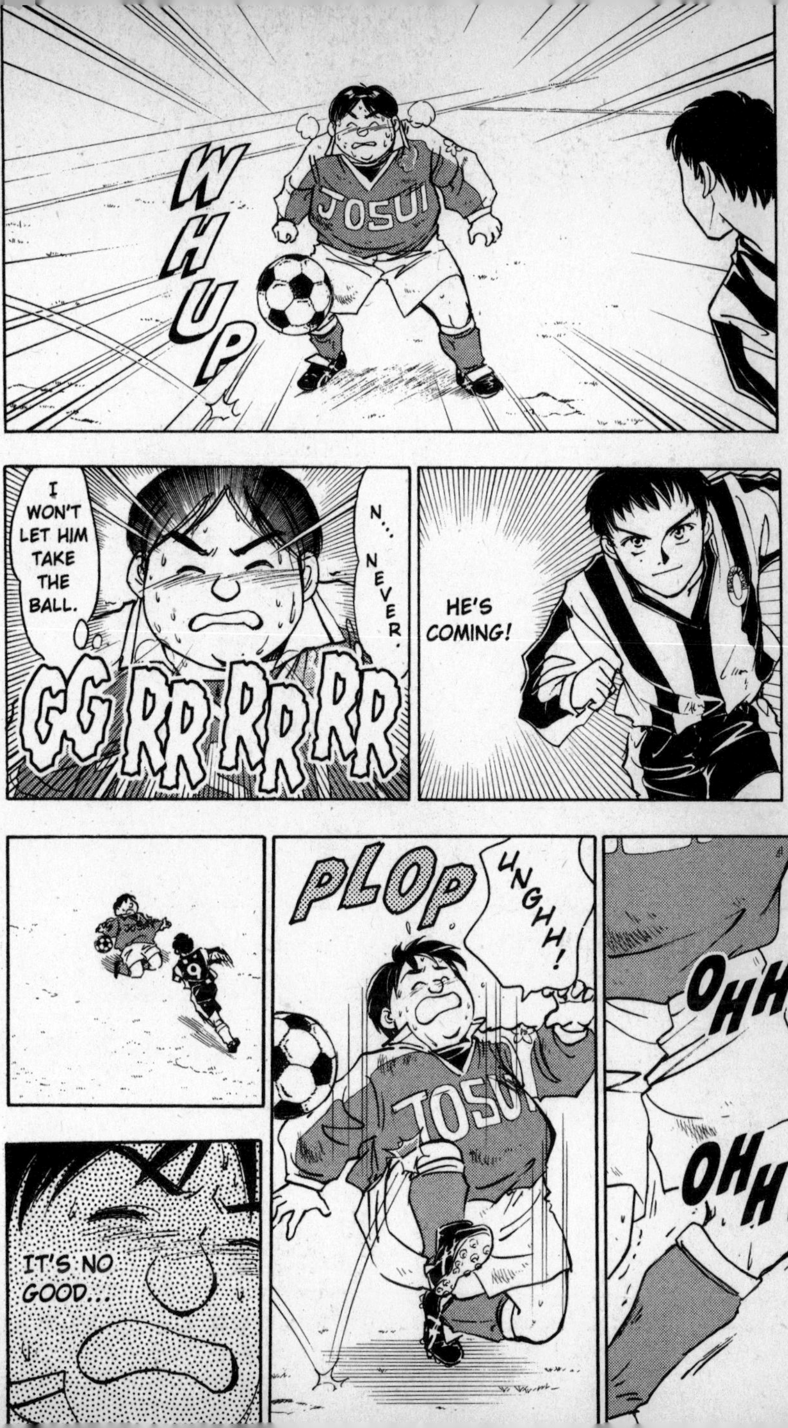
WHUP
HE'S COMING!
N... NEVER.
I WON'T LET HIM TAKE THE BALL.
GGRRRRRRR
OHH
OHH
UNGHH!
PLOP
IT'S NO GOOD...

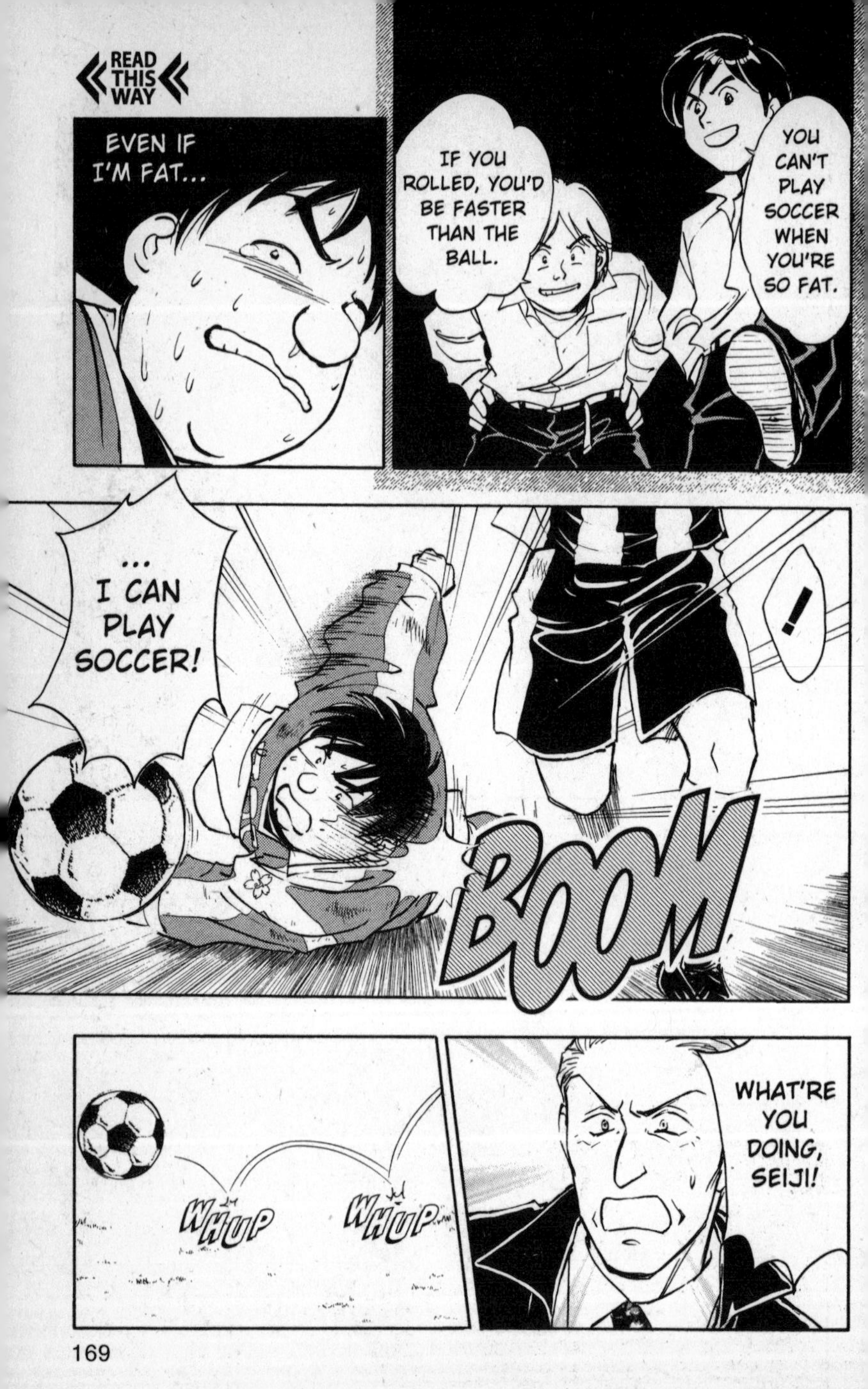
READ THIS WAY
YOU CAN'T PLAY SOCCER WHEN YOU'RE SO FAT.
IF YOU ROLLED, YOU'D BE FASTER THAN THE BALL.
EVEN IF I'M FAT...
!
... I CAN PLAY SOCCER!
BOOM
WHAT'RE YOU DOING, SEIJI!
WHUP
WHUP

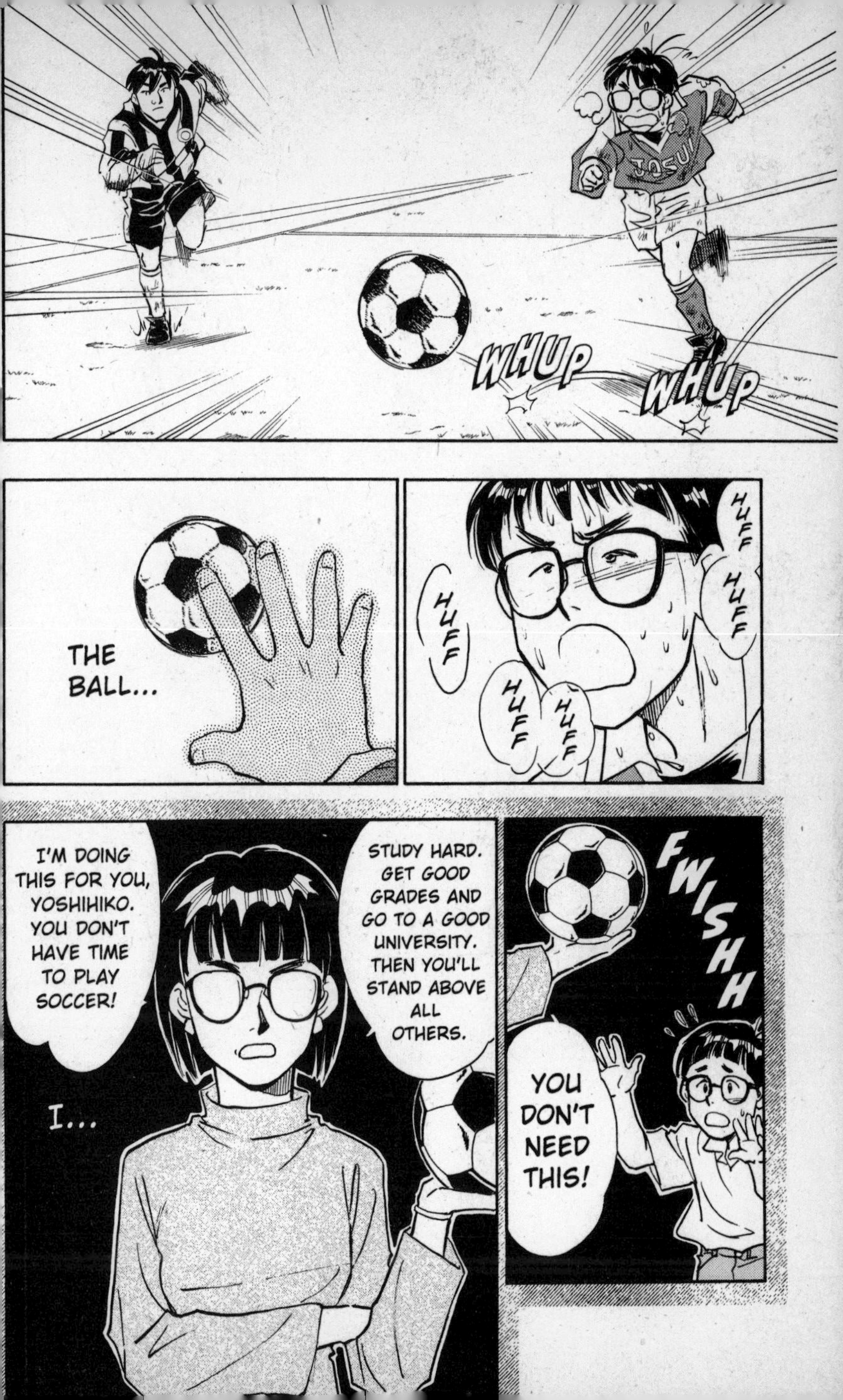
WHUP
WHUP
HUFF
HUFF
HUFF
HUFF
HUFF
THE BALL...
FWISHH
YOU DON'T NEED THIS!
I'M DOING THIS FOR YOU, YOSHIHIKO. YOU DON'T HAVE TIME TO PLAY SOCCER!
STUDY HARD. GET GOOD GRADES AND GO TO A GOOD UNIVERSITY. THEN YOU'LL STAND ABOVE ALL OTHERS.
I...

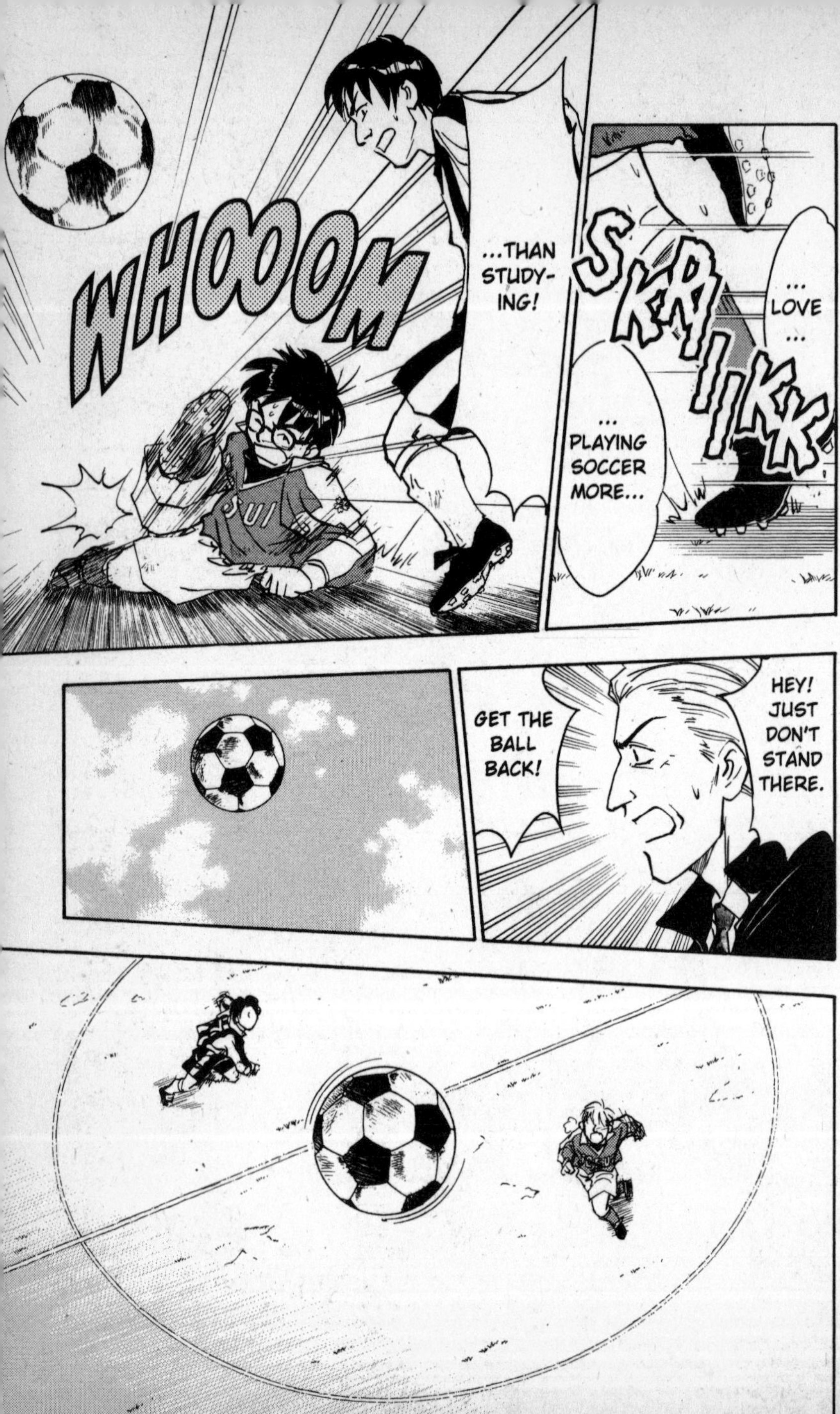
SKRIIKK
... LOVE ...
... PLAYING SOCCER MORE...
...THAN STUDYING!
WHOOOM
HEY! JUST DON'T STAND THERE.
GET THE BALL BACK!

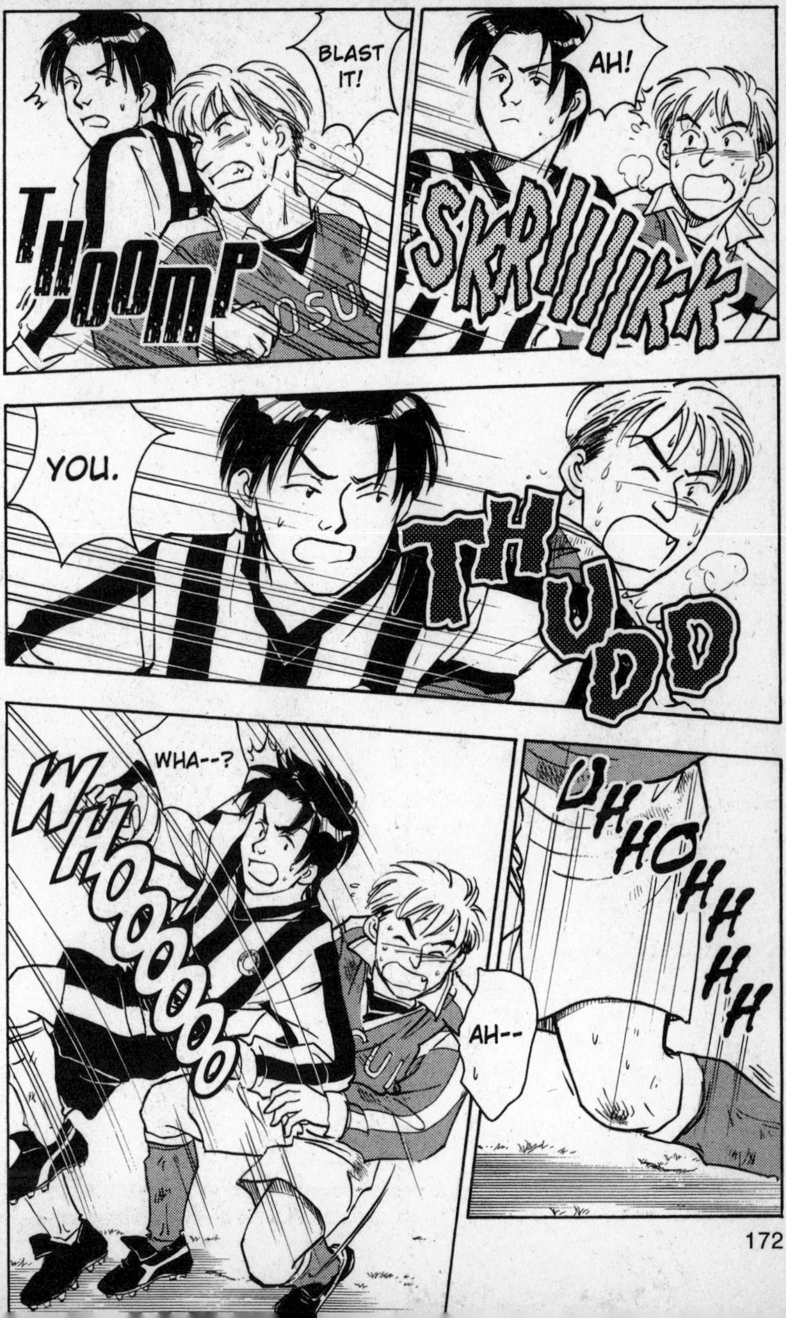
AH!
SKRIIIIKK
BLAST IT!
THOOMP
OSU
THUDD
YOU.
UHHOHHHHH
AH--
WHA--?
WHOOOOOOO

READ THIS WAY

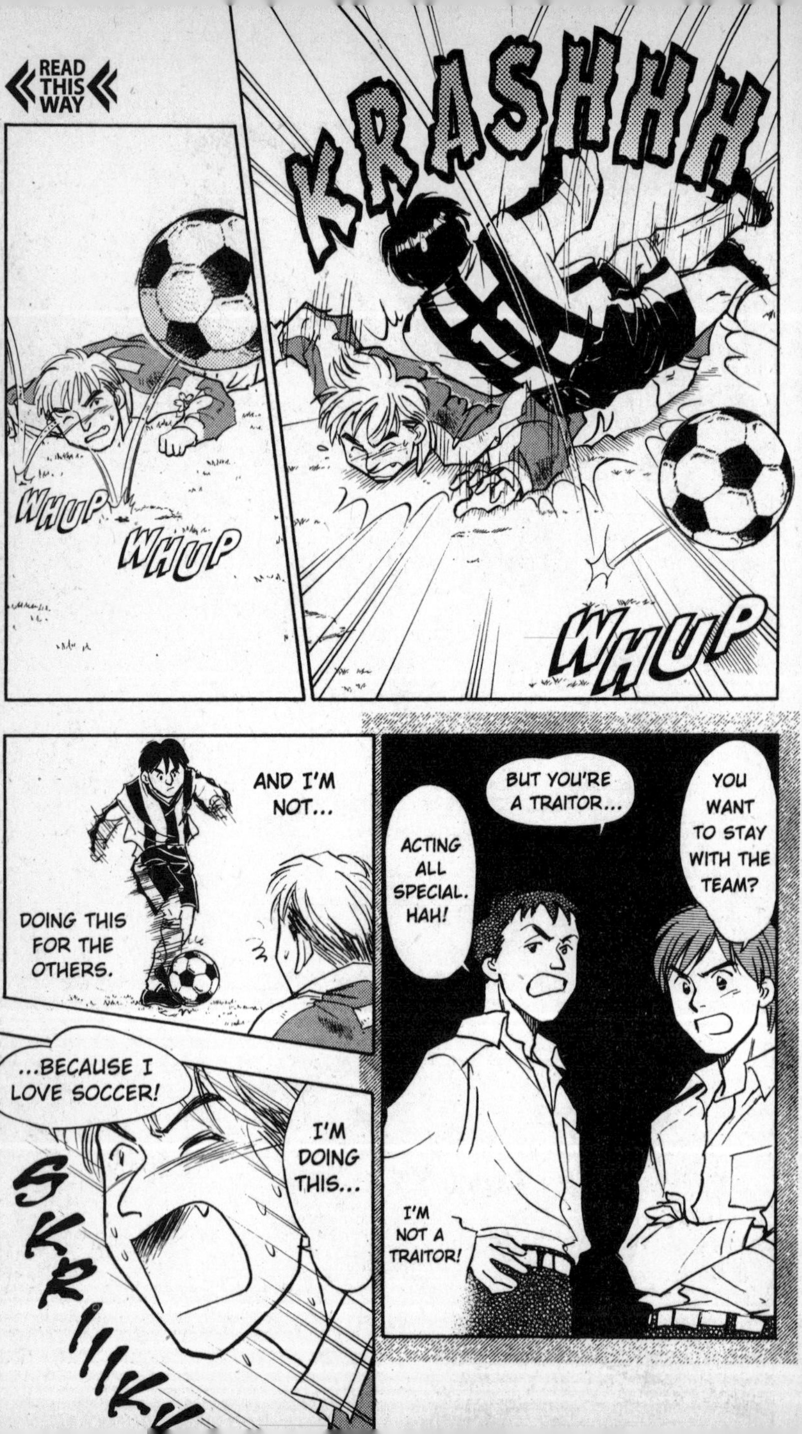
KRASHHH
WHUP
WHUP
WHUP
YOU WANT TO STAY WITH THE TEAM?
BUT YOU'RE A TRAITOR...
ACTING ALL SPECIAL. HAH!
I'M NOT A TRAITOR!
AND I'M NOT...
DOING THIS FOR THE OTHERS.
I'M DOING THIS...
...BECAUSE I LOVE SOCCER!
SKRIIIK

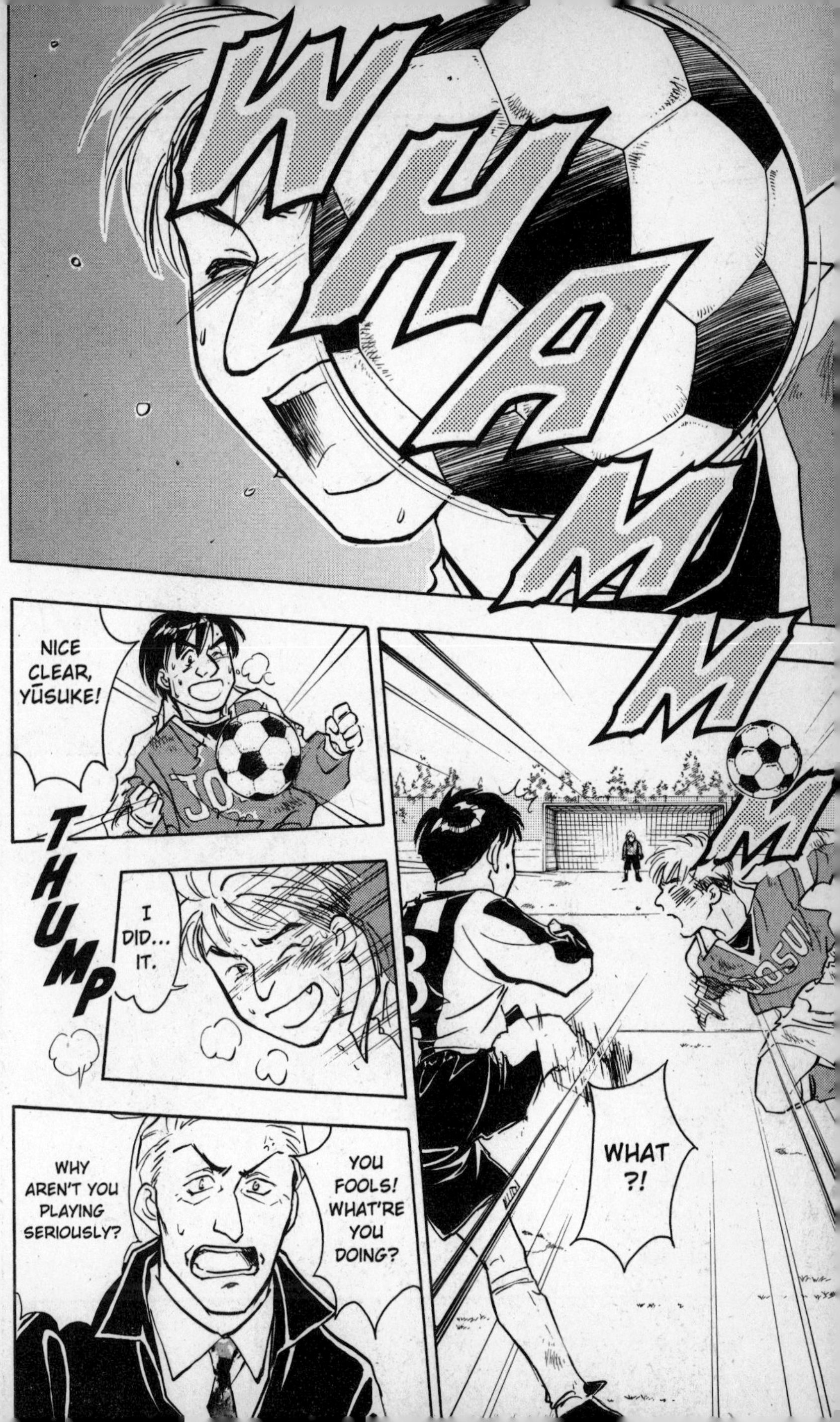
WHAMMM
WHAT ?!
NICE CLEAR, YŪSUKE!
THUMP
I DID... IT.
YOU FOOLS! WHAT'RE YOU DOING?
WHY AREN'T YOU PLAYING SERIOUSLY?

READ THIS WAY

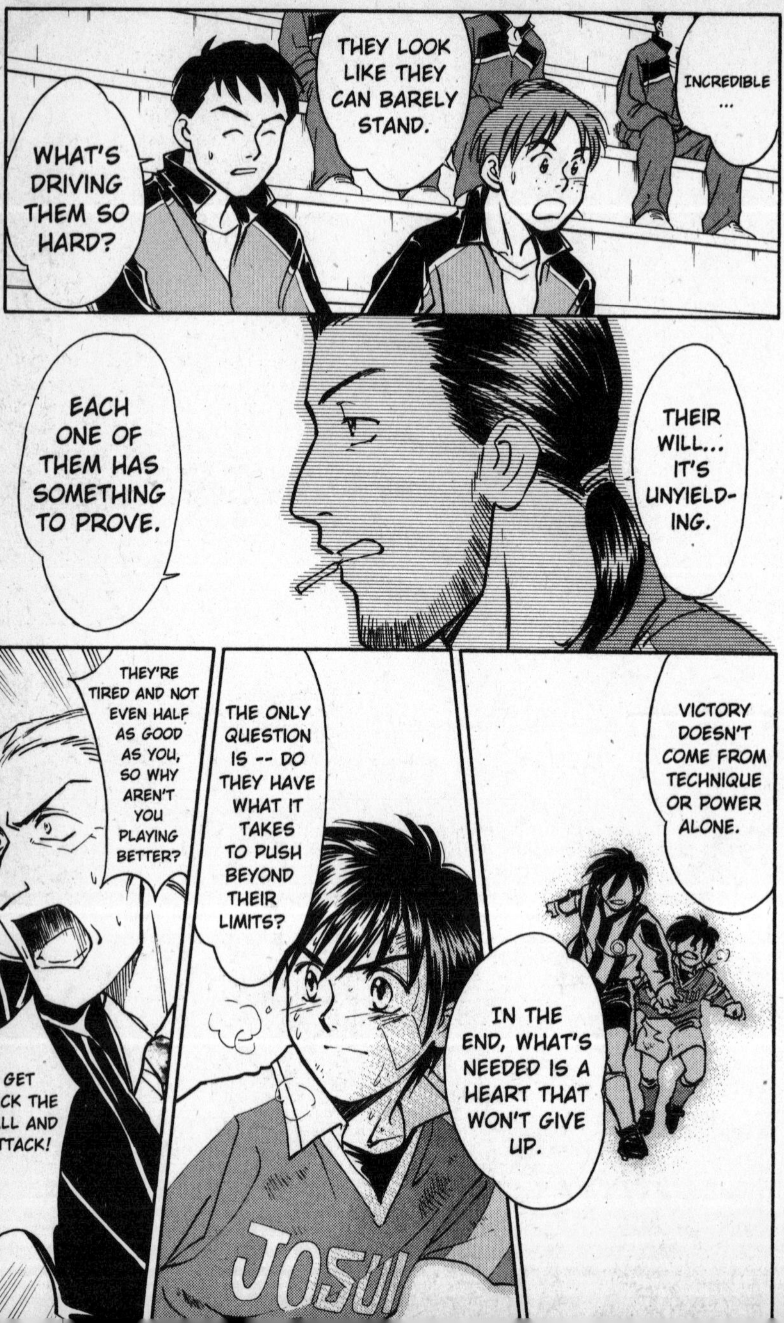
INCREDIBLE...
THEY LOOK LIKE THEY CAN BARELY STAND.
WHAT'S DRIVING THEM SO HARD?
THEIR WILL... IT'S UNYIELDING.
EACH ONE OF THEM HAS SOMETHING TO PROVE.
VICTORY DOESN'T COME FROM TECHNIQUE OR POWER ALONE.
IN THE END, WHAT'S NEEDED IS A HEART THAT WON'T GIVE UP.
THE ONLY QUESTION IS -- DO THEY HAVE WHAT IT TAKES TO PUSH BEYOND THEIR LIMITS?
JOSUI
THEY'RE TIRED AND NOT EVEN HALF AS GOOD AS YOU, SO WHY AREN'T YOU PLAYING BETTER?
GET BACK THE BALL AND ATTACK!

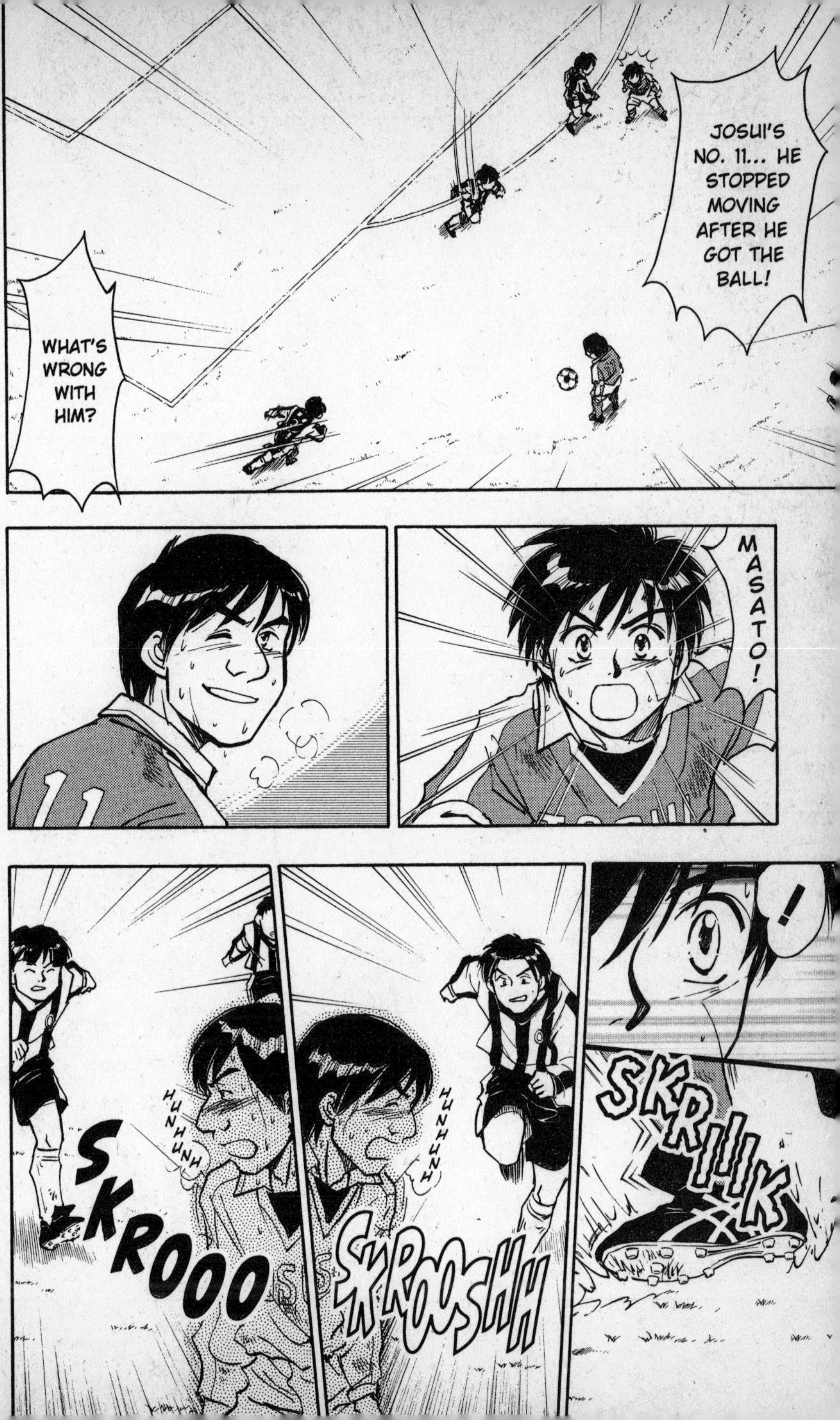
JOSUI'S NO. 11... HE STOPPED MOVING AFTER HE GOT THE BALL!
WHAT'S WRONG WITH HIM?
MASATO!
!
SKRUUK
HUNHUNH
SKROOSHH
HUNHUNH
SKROOO

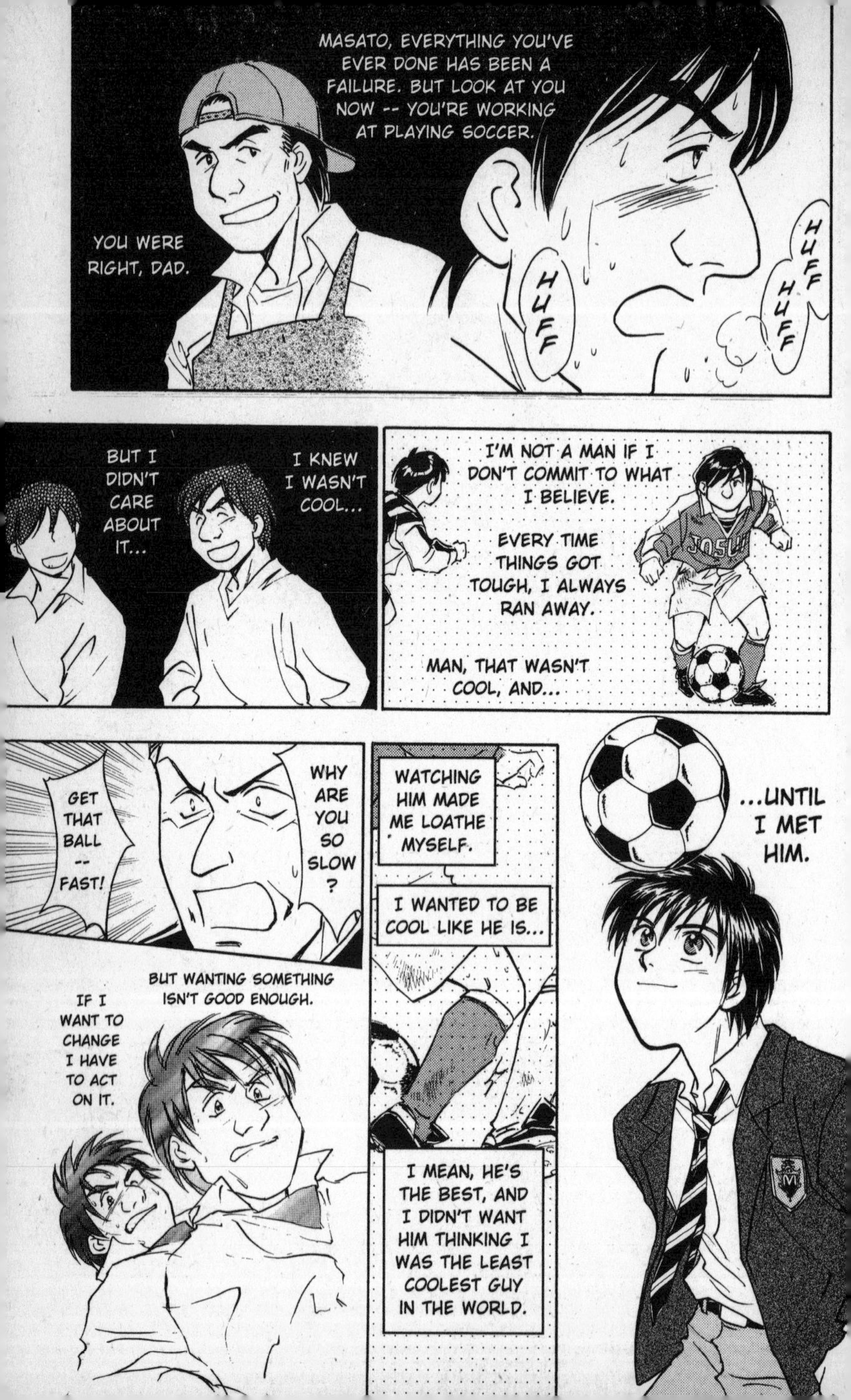
MASATO, EVERYTHING YOU'VE EVER DONE HAS BEEN A FAILURE. BUT LOOK AT YOU NOW -- YOU'RE WORKING AT PLAYING SOCCER.
HUFF HUFF HUFF
HUFF
YOU WERE RIGHT, DAD.
I'M NOT A MAN IF I DON'T COMMIT TO WHAT I BELIEVE.
EVERY TIME THINGS GOT TOUGH, I ALWAYS RAN AWAY.
MAN, THAT WASN'T COOL, AND...
I KNEW I WASN'T COOL...
BUT I DIDN'T CARE ABOUT IT...
...UNTIL I MET HIM.
WATCHING HIM MADE ME LOATHE MYSELF.
I WANTED TO BE COOL LIKE HE IS...
I MEAN, HE'S THE BEST, AND I DIDN'T WANT HIM THINKING I WAS THE LEAST COOLEST GUY IN THE WORLD.
WHY ARE YOU SO SLOW?
GET THAT BALL -- FAST!
BUT WANTING SOMETHING ISN'T GOOD ENOUGH.
IF I WANT TO CHANGE I HAVE TO ACT ON IT.

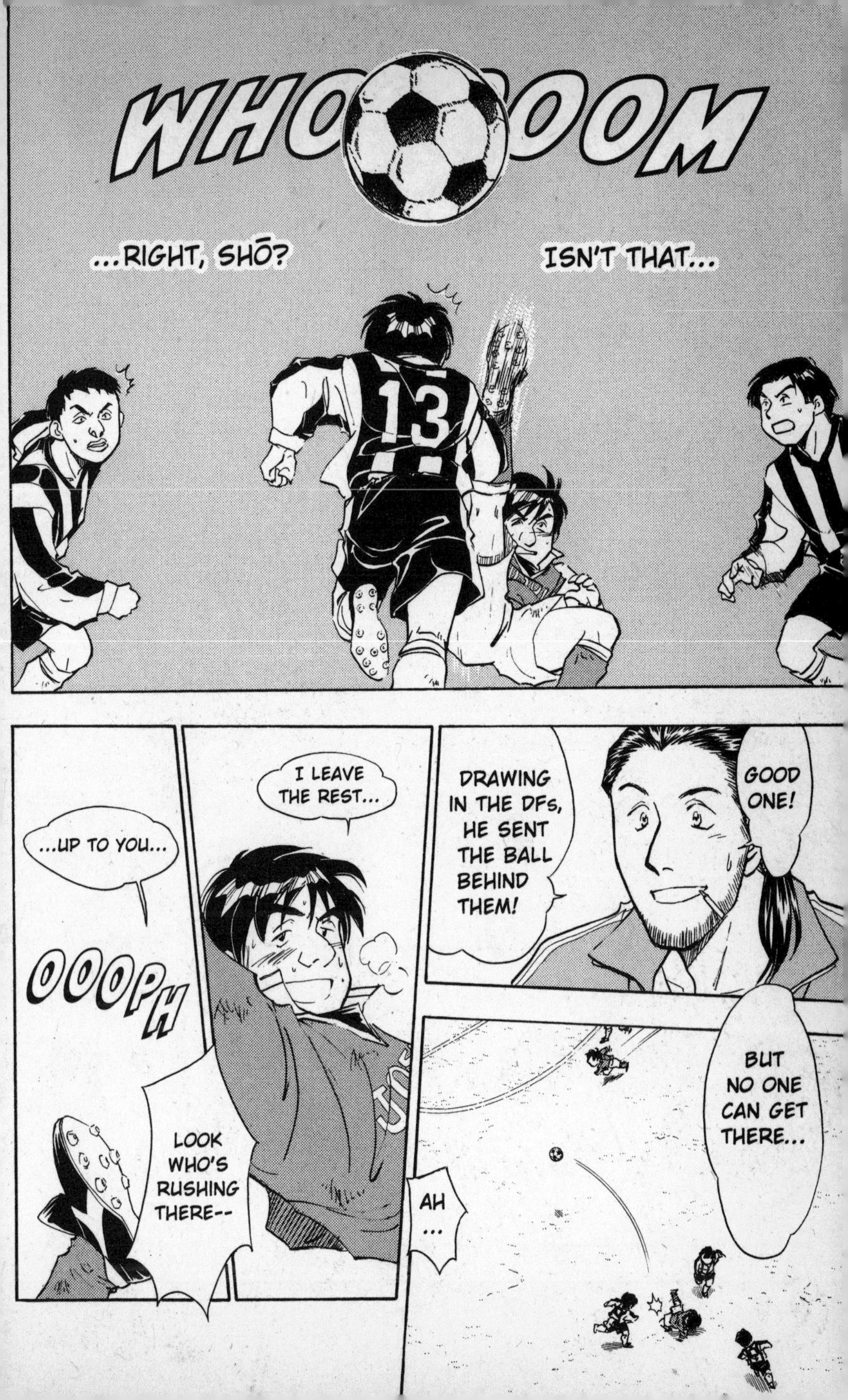
WHO OOM
ISN'T THAT...
...RIGHT, SHŌ?
GOOD ONE!
DRAWING IN THE DFs, HE SENT THE BALL BEHIND THEM!
BUT NO ONE CAN GET THERE...
AH...
I LEAVE THE REST...
...UP TO YOU...
OOOPH
LOOK WHO'S RUSHING THERE--

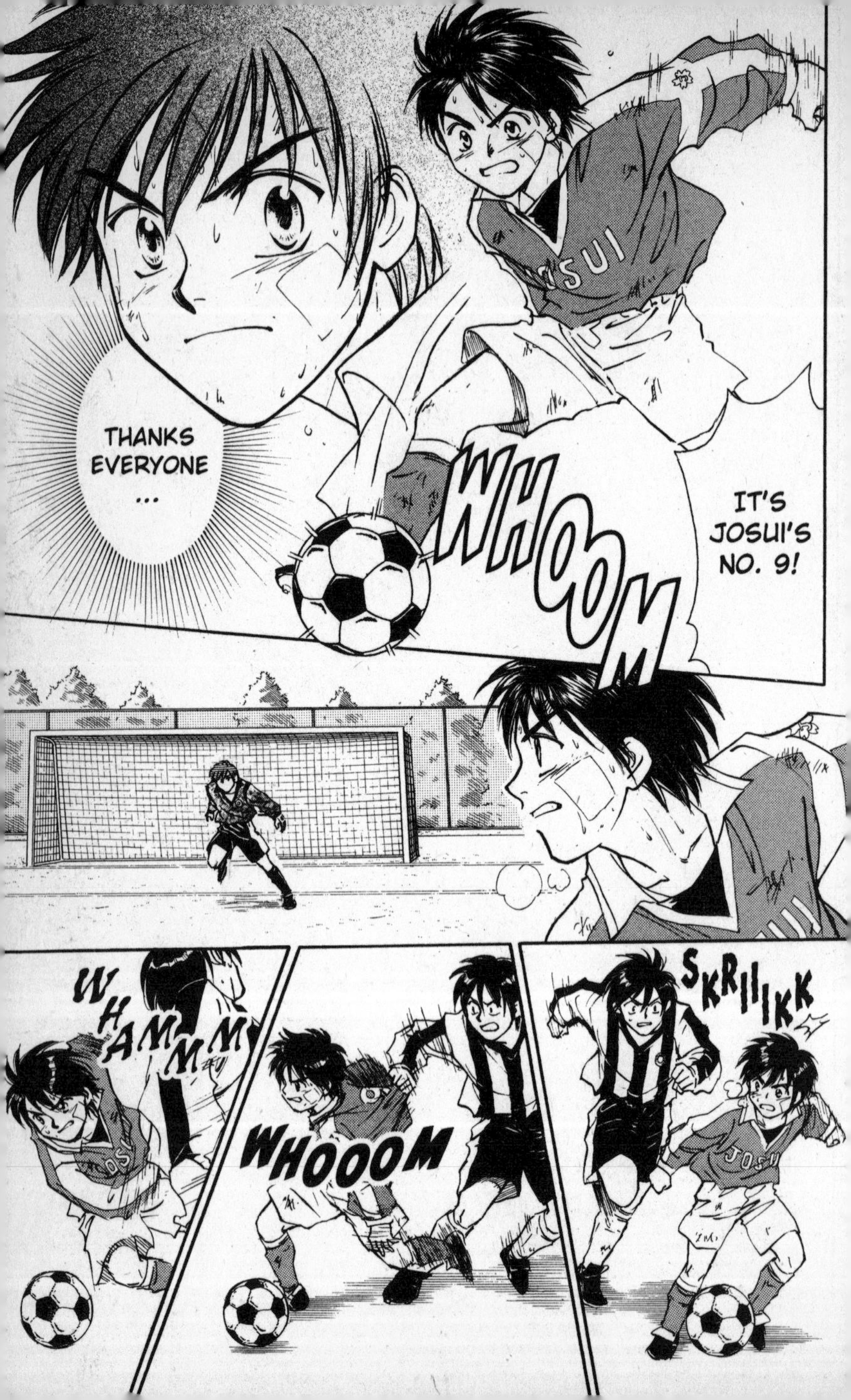
IT'S JOSUI'S NO. 9!
WHOOOM
THANKS EVERYONE ...
SKRIIIKK
WHOOOM
WHAMMM

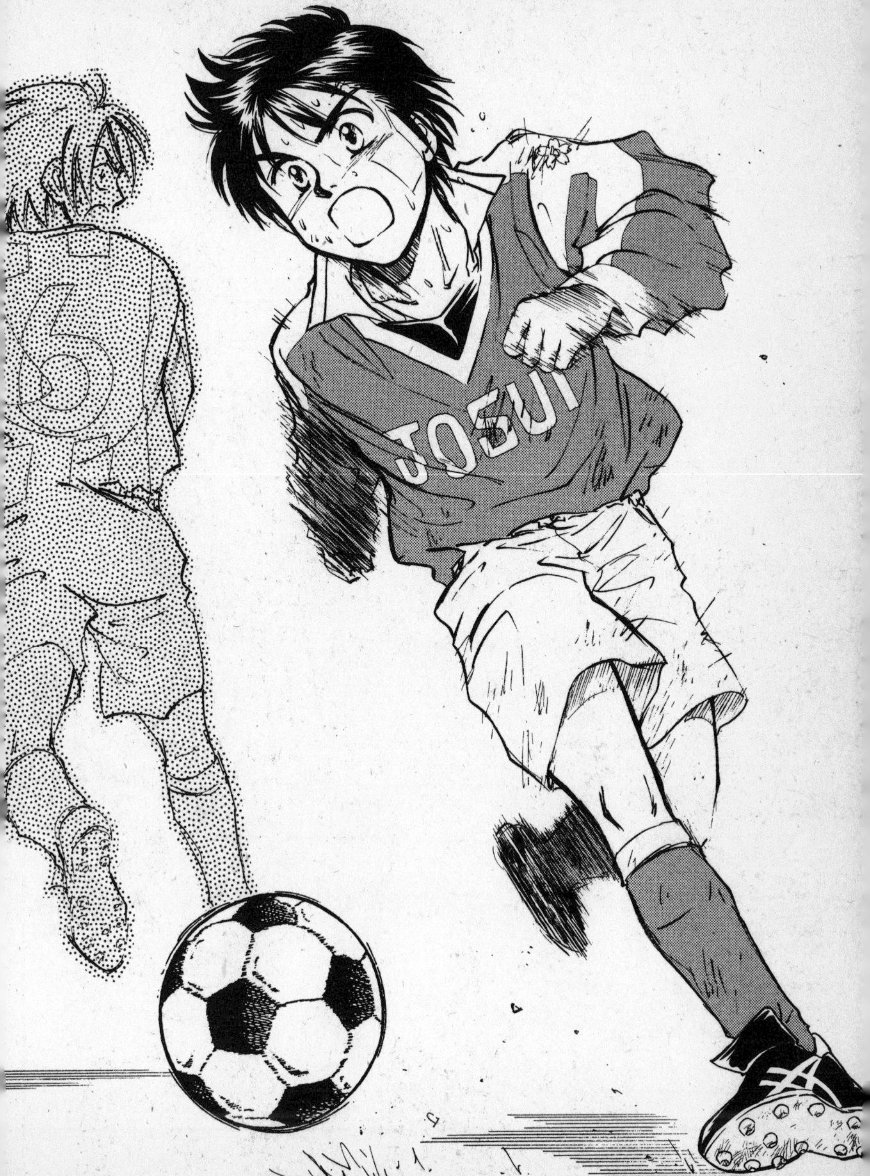
JOSUI

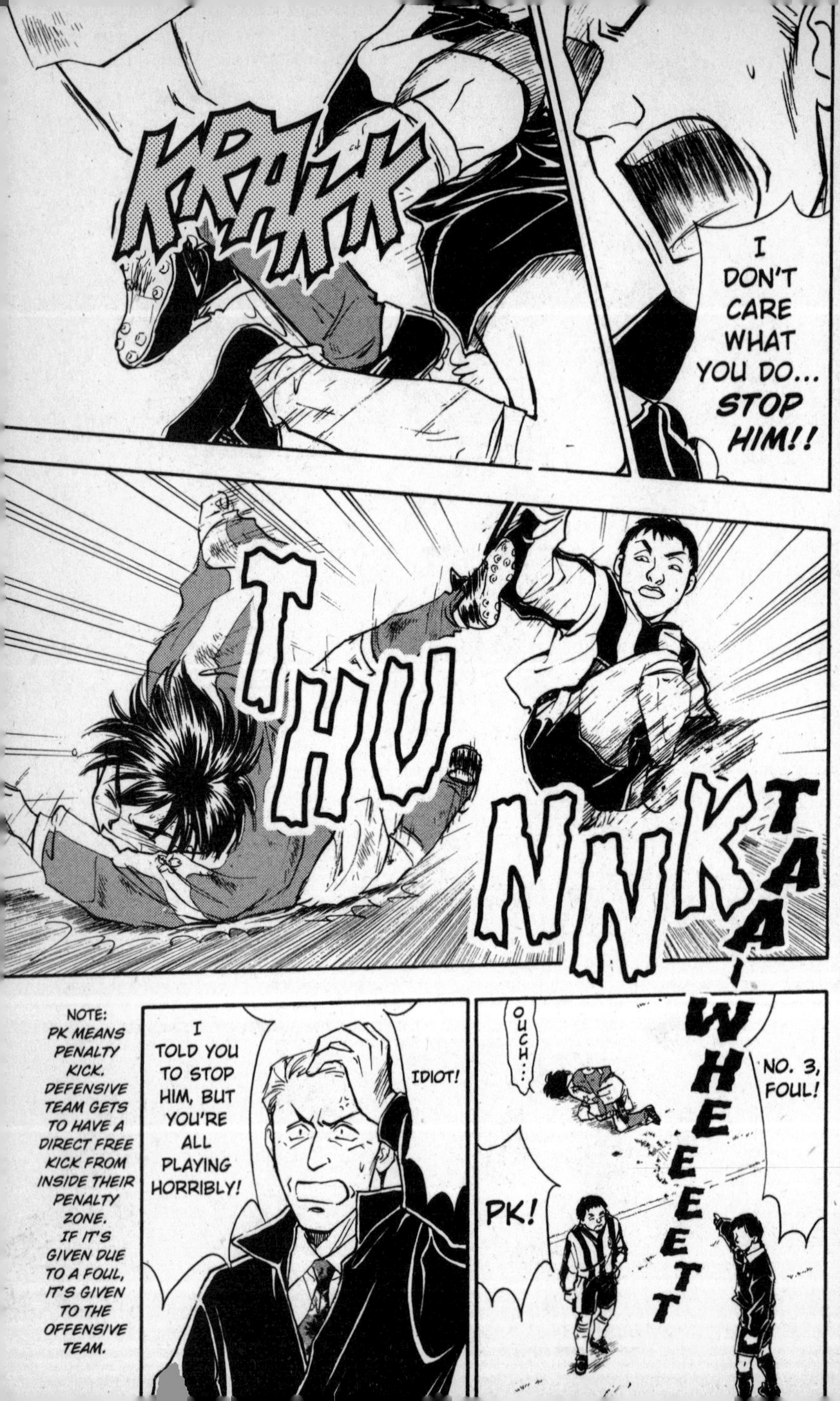
I DON'T CARE WHAT YOU DO... STOP HIM!!
KRACK
THUNNK
NO. 3, FOUL!
TA-WHEEEETT
PK!
OUCH...
IDIOT!
I TOLD YOU TO STOP HIM, BUT YOU'RE ALL PLAYING HORRIBLY!

NOTE: PK MEANS PENALTY KICK. DEFENSIVE TEAM GETS TO HAVE A DIRECT FREE KICK FROM INSIDE THEIR PENALTY ZONE. IF IT'S GIVEN DUE TO A FOUL, IT'S GIVEN TO THE OFFENSIVE TEAM.

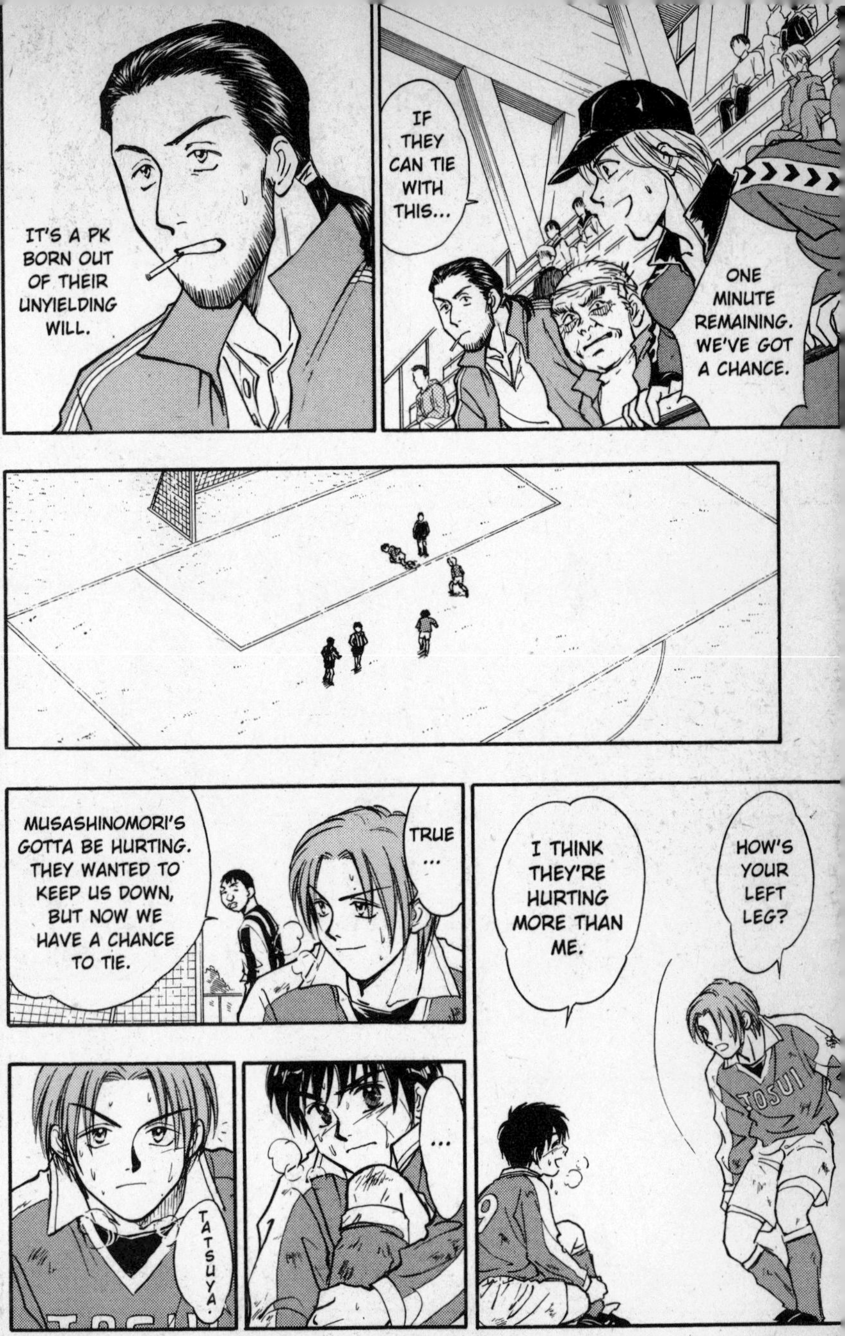
IF THEY CAN TIE WITH THIS...
ONE MINUTE REMAINING. WE'VE GOT A CHANCE.
IT'S A PK BORN OUT OF THEIR UNYIELDING WILL.
HOW'S YOUR LEFT LEG?
I THINK THEY'RE HURTING MORE THAN ME.
TRUE ...
MUSASHINOMORI'S GOTTA BE HURTING. THEY WANTED TO KEEP US DOWN, BUT NOW WE HAVE A CHANCE TO TIE.
...
TATSUYA.

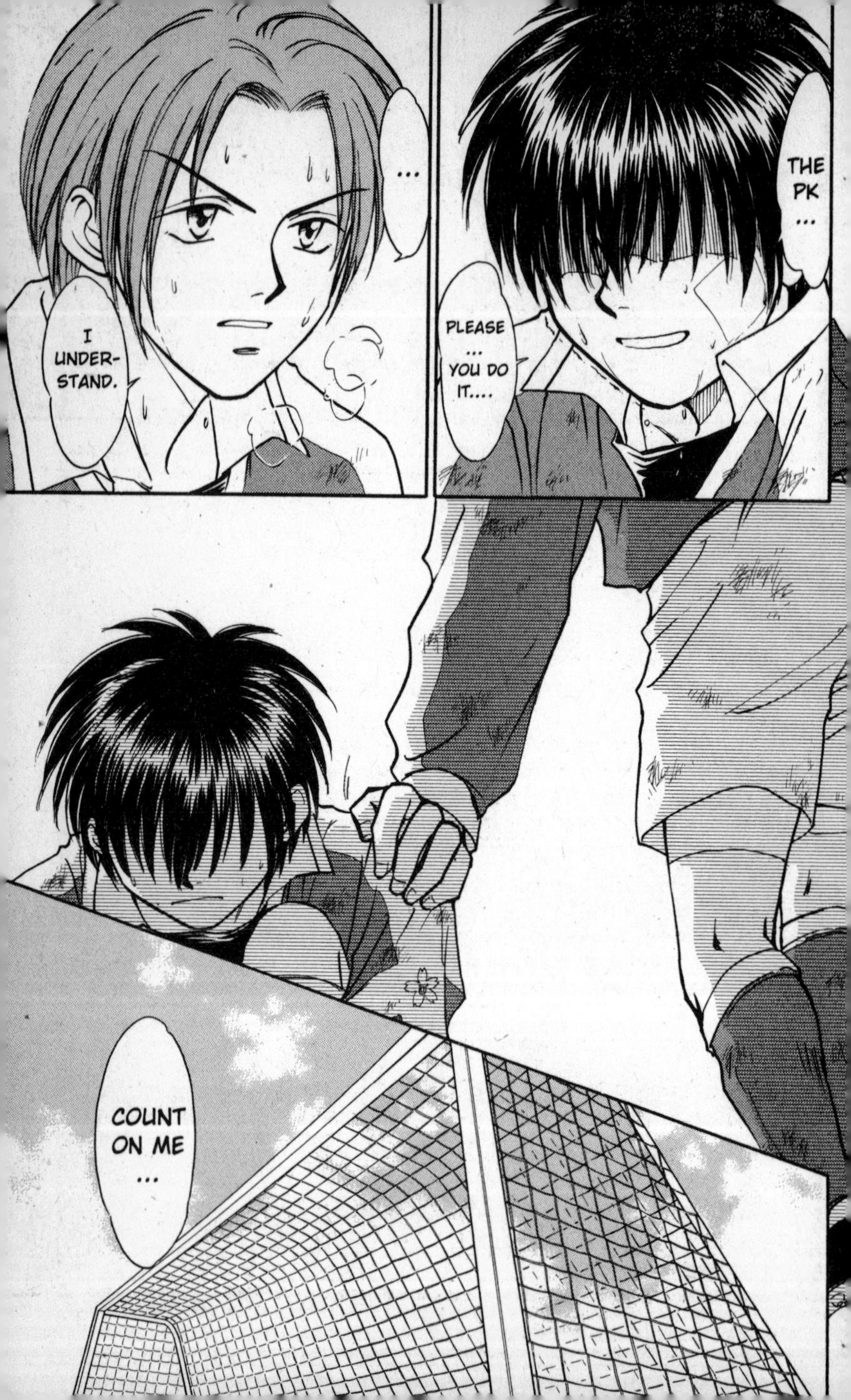
THE PK ...
PLEASE ... YOU DO IT....
...
I UNDER-STAND.
COUNT ON ME ...

● ANECDOTE SURROUNDING THE NO 9.

THE ACE NUMBER (NUMBER FOR AN ACE OF A TEAM) IN SOCCER IS "NO. 10." AND THE ACE STRIKER WHO SCORES POINTS IS "NO. 9." HOWEVER, IT'S HARD TO NAME AN INTERNATIONALLY FAMOUS PLAYER WHO'S ASSIGNED NO. 9.

THE GOD OF SOCCER, PELE, AS WELL AS MARADONA AND JEKO -- WORLD FAMOUS PLAYERS, ARE ALL NO. 10. THE ARGENTINA'S MARIO KENPES AND THE ENGLAND'S RYNEKAR, WHO ARE THE SUPERSTARS OF THE WORLD CUP AND ARE THE KING OF SCORERS, ARE ALSO ALL NO. 10. THE NETHERLAND'S CRUYFF, THE GENIUS PLAYER THAT TOOK THE WORLD BY SURPRISE, WAS NO. 14. THE GERMANY'S BECKENBAUER WAS FIVE. IT'S PROBABLY BECAUSE THE ACE STRIKERS ARE ALWAYS THOROUGHLY MARKED BY THE OPPONENTS THAT THEY CAN'T SCORE THAT MANY POINTS, AND AS A RESULT, IT IS VERY DIFFICULT FOR THEM TO BECOME A WORLD FAMOUS SUPERSTAR.

HOWEVER, WE HAD AN INCREDIBLE PLAYER IN JAPAN WHO CAN BE CONSIDERED AN ACE STRIKER. HE IS KUNISHIGE KAMAMOTO. DURING THE J-LEAGUE ERA, HE PLAYED 251 GAMES IN 16 YEARS, AND HE MADE 202 GOALS. THAT MEANS, ON AVERAGE, HE SCORED 0.8 GOALS PER GAME. IT'S AN INCREDIBLE AVERAGE. HE BECAME THE KING OF SCORERS SEVEN TIMES. WITHOUT A DOUBT HE WAS AN ACE STRIKER. AT THE OLYMPICS HELD IN MEXICO IN 1968, HE HELPED THE JAPAN TEAM SEIZE THE BRONZE MEDAL, AND HE RECEIVED THE HONOR OF BECOMING THE KING OF SCORERS OF THAT EVENT. AFTER THAT, HE WAS INVITED TO JOIN THE GERMAN PROFESSIONAL TEAM, BUT DUE TO THE ACUTE HEPATITIS HE SUFFERED, HE HAD TO GIVE IT UP. LATER ON, HE WAS INJURED AND SEVERED HIS ACHILLES TENDON TWICE, AND YET, DESPITE ALL THAT, HE MADE THAT RECORD. HE WAS, NO DOUBT, AN ACE STRIKER.

I WONDER IF A WORLD FAMOUS ACE STRIKER WOULD EVER APPEAR? I HAVE A GREAT HOPE FOR RONALDO, THE PLAYER FOR THE BRAZIL TEAM.

--TATSUYA WATANABE (WINNING RUN)

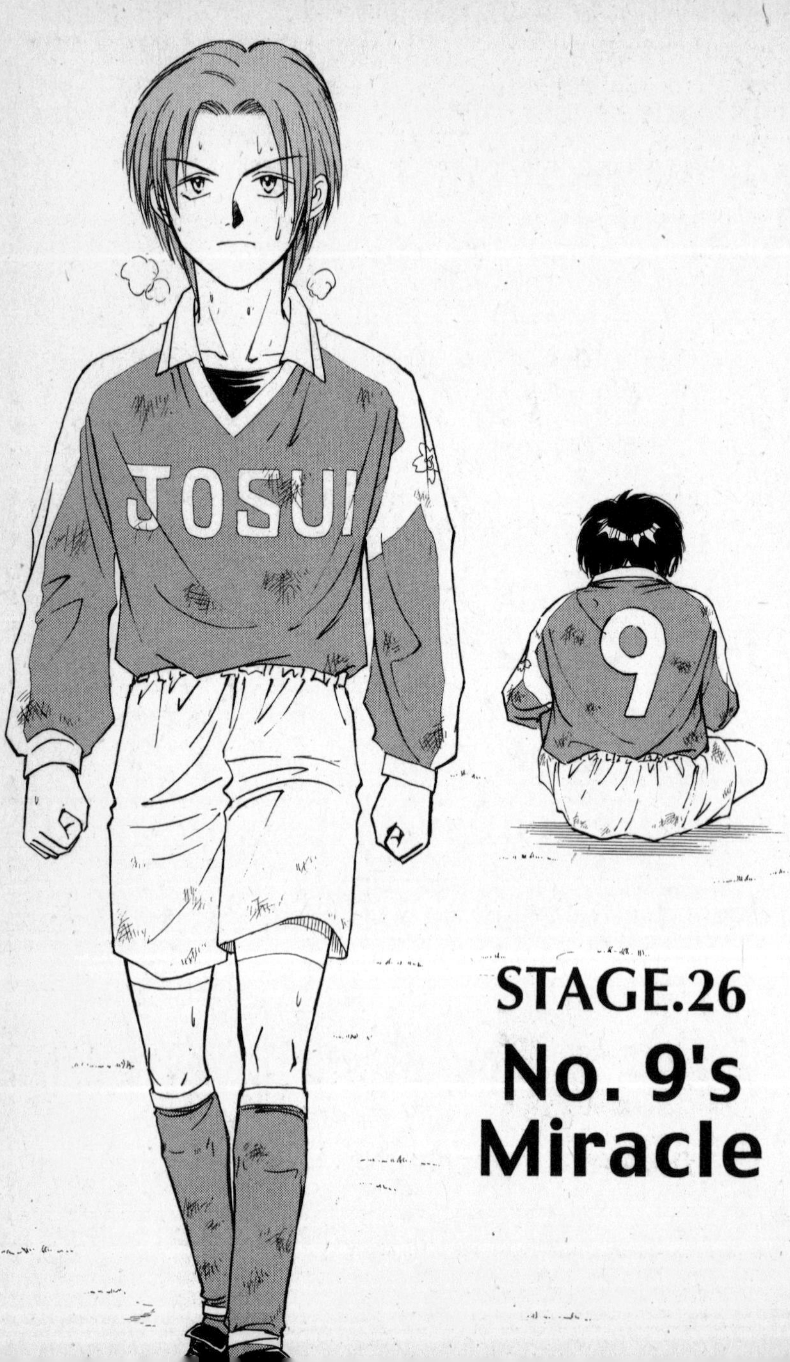
JOSUI
9

STAGE.26

No. 9's Miracle

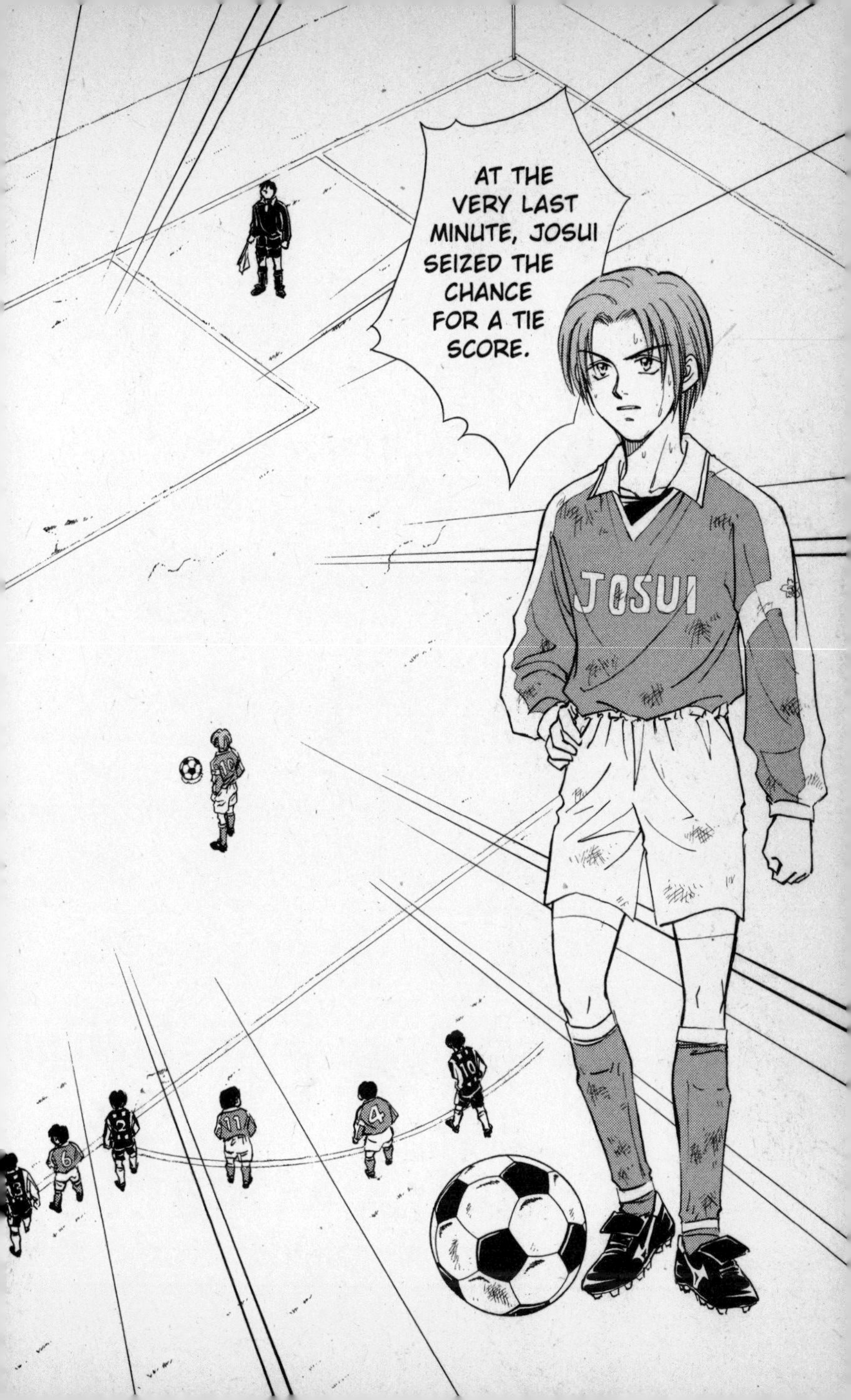
AT THE VERY LAST MINUTE, JOSUI SEIZED THE CHANCE FOR A TIE SCORE.
JOSUI

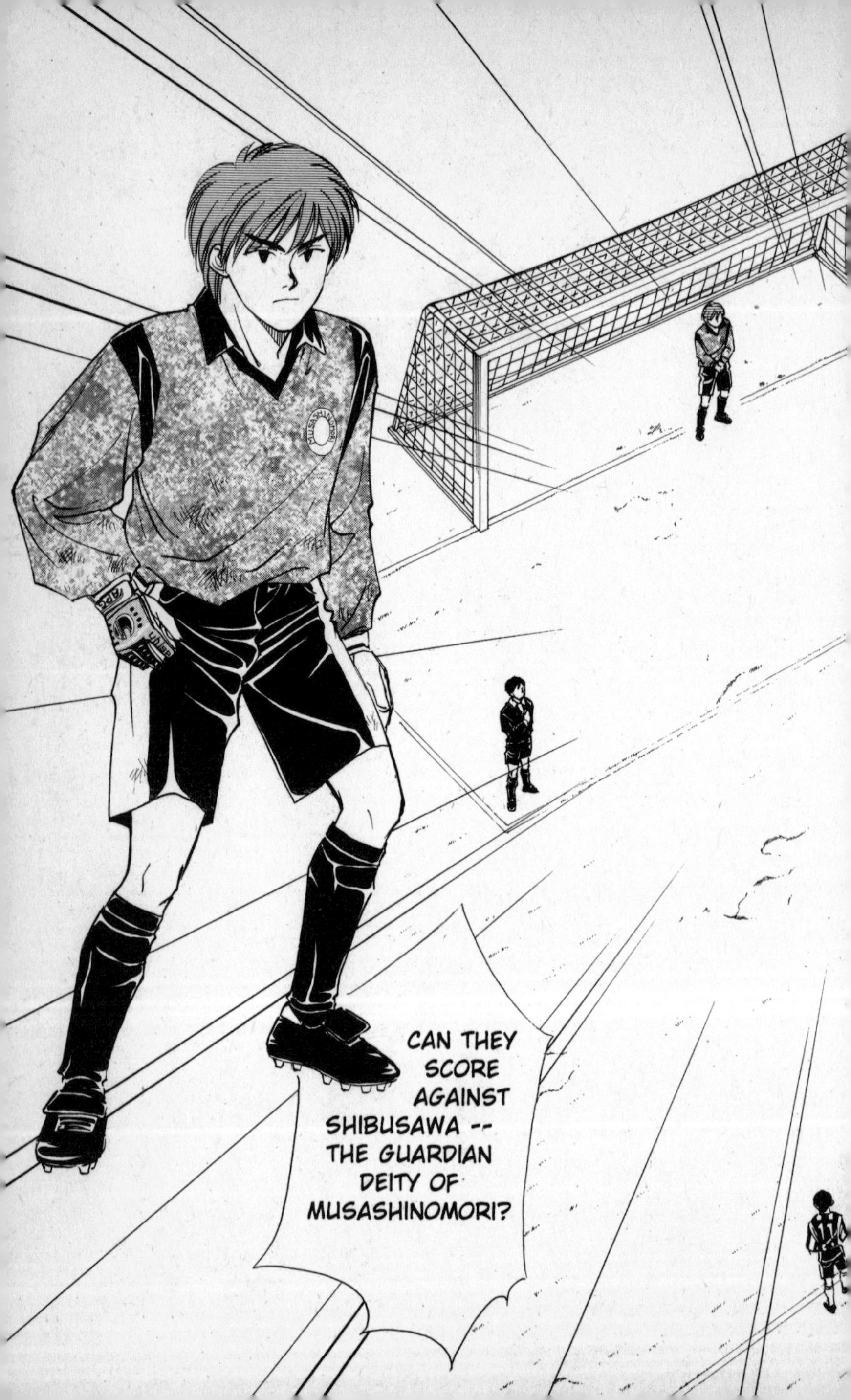
CAN THEY SCORE AGAINST SHIBUSAWA -- THE GUARDIAN DEITY OF MUSASHINOMORI?

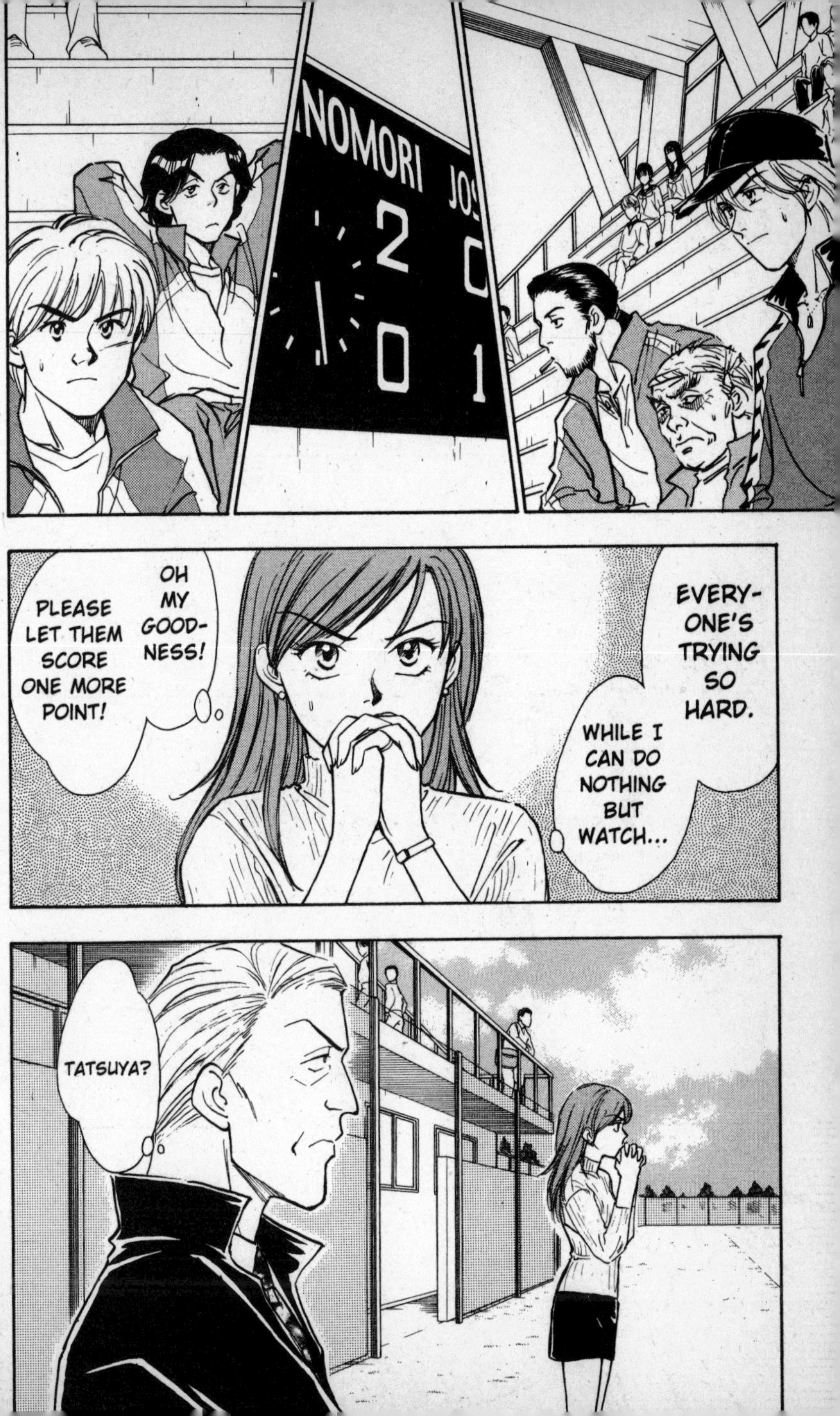
NOMORI JOS
2 0
0 1
EVERY-ONE'S TRYING SO HARD.
WHILE I CAN DO NOTHING BUT WATCH...
OH MY GOODNESS!
PLEASE LET THEM SCORE ONE MORE POINT!
TATSUYA?

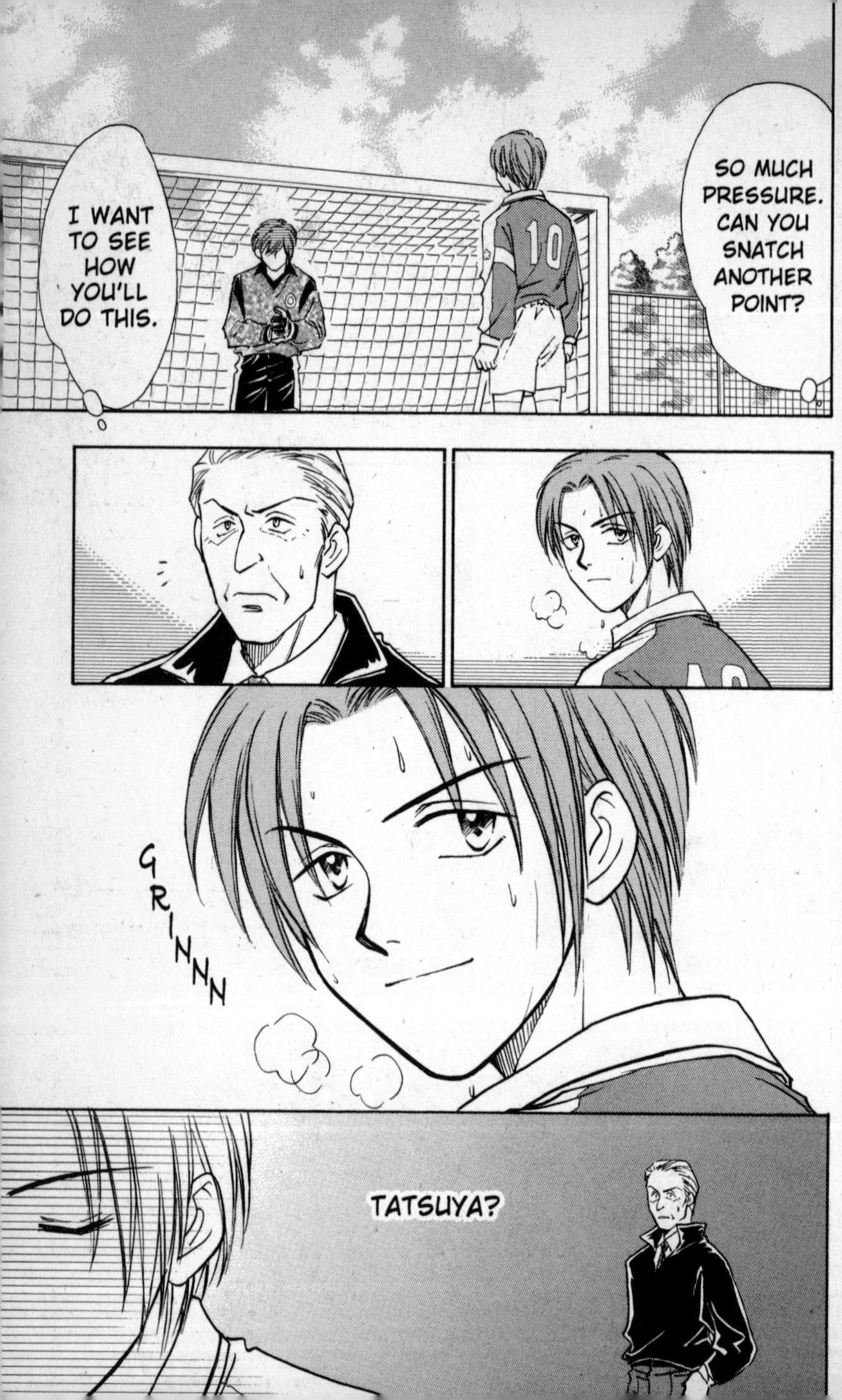
SO MUCH PRESSURE. CAN YOU SNATCH ANOTHER POINT?
I WANT TO SEE HOW YOU'LL DO THIS.
GRINNNN
TATSUYA?

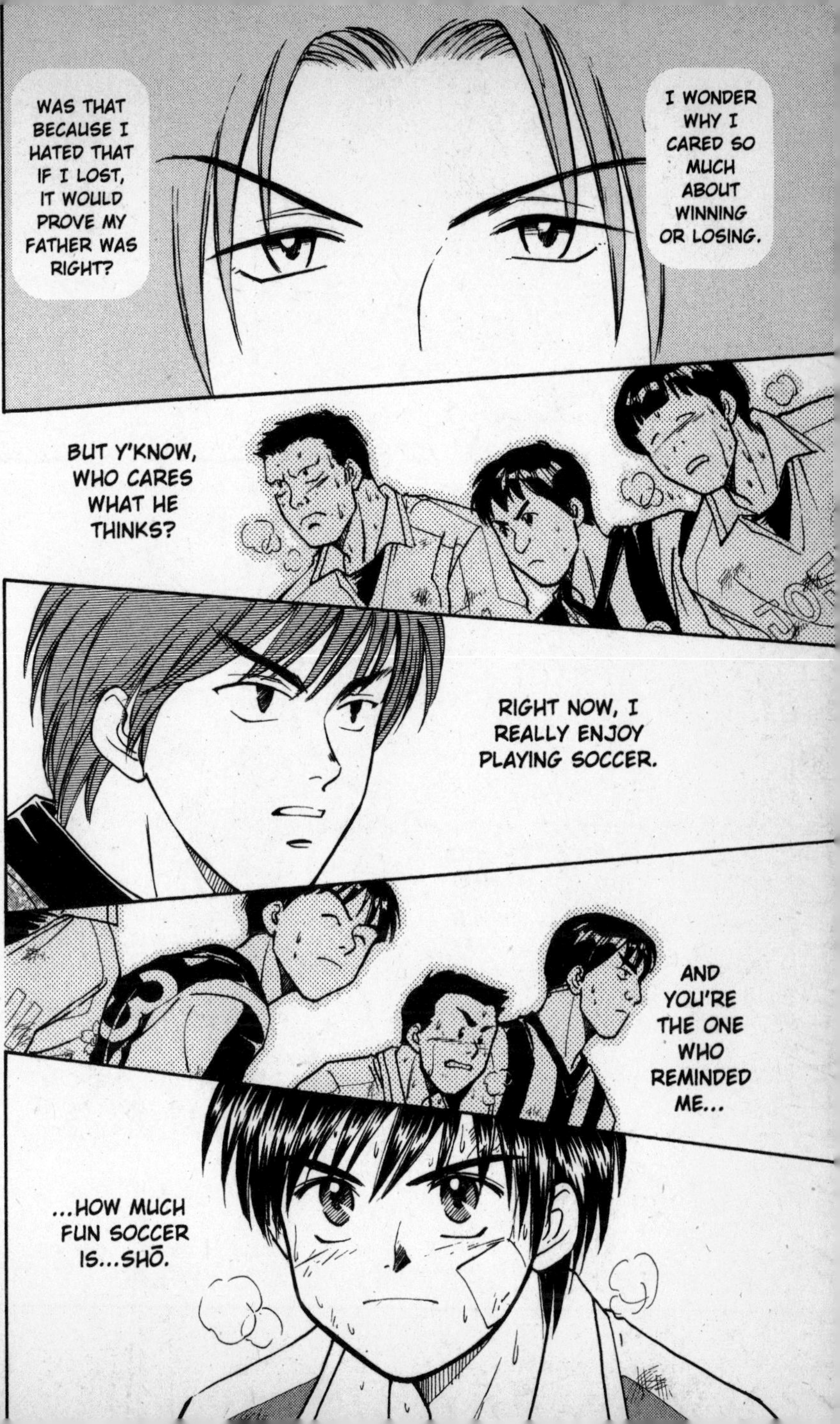
I WONDER WHY I CARED SO MUCH ABOUT WINNING OR LOSING.
WAS THAT BECAUSE I HATED THAT IF I LOST, IT WOULD PROVE MY FATHER WAS RIGHT?
BUT Y'KNOW, WHO CARES WHAT HE THINKS?
RIGHT NOW, I REALLY ENJOY PLAYING SOCCER.
AND YOU'RE THE ONE WHO REMINDED ME...
...HOW MUCH FUN SOCCER IS...SHŌ.

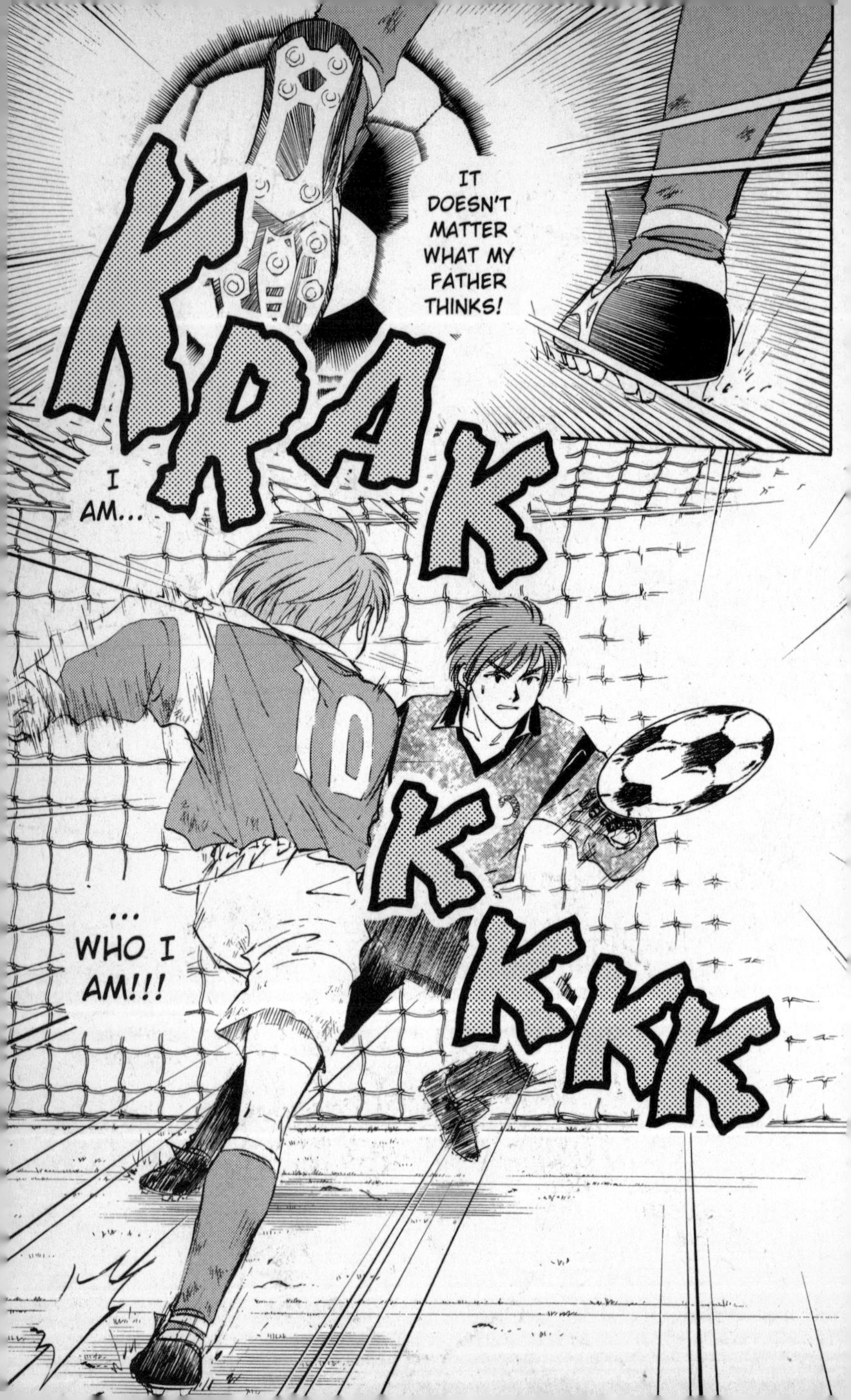
IT DOESN'T MATTER WHAT MY FATHER THINKS!
KRAK
I AM...
KKKK
... WHO I AM!!!

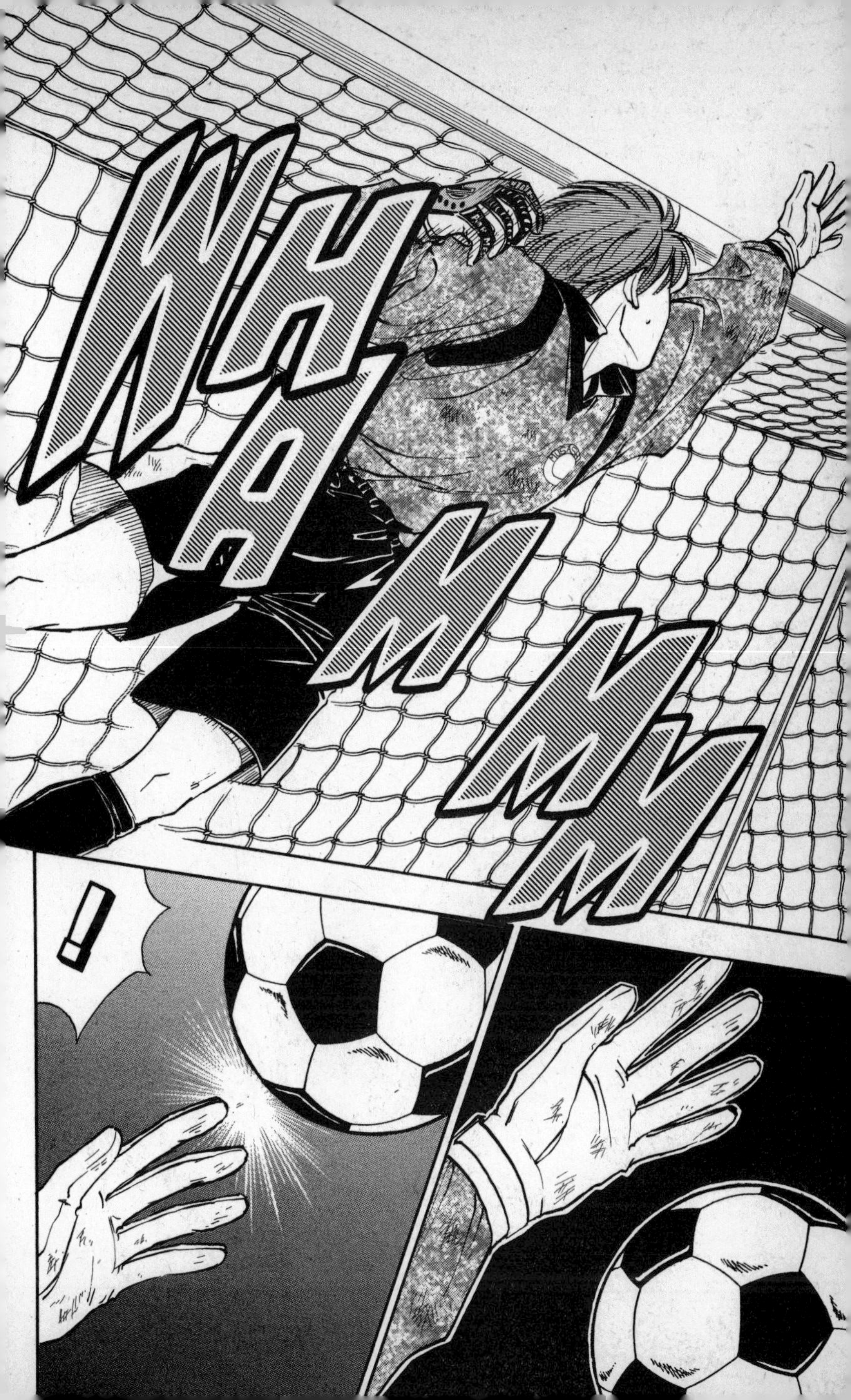
WHAMMM
!

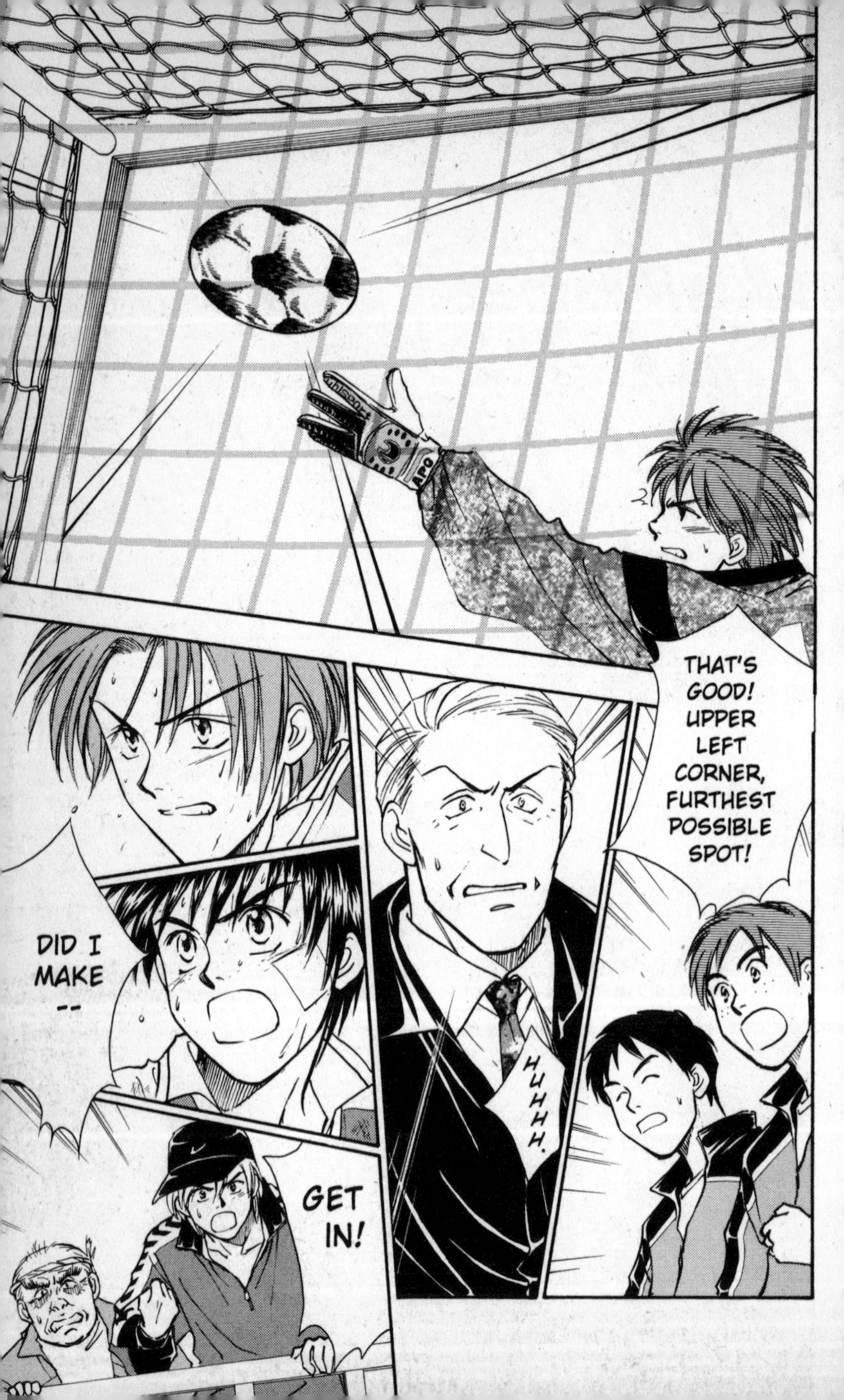
THAT'S GOOD! UPPER LEFT CORNER, FURTHEST POSSIBLE SPOT!
HUHHH.
DID I MAKE --
GET IN!

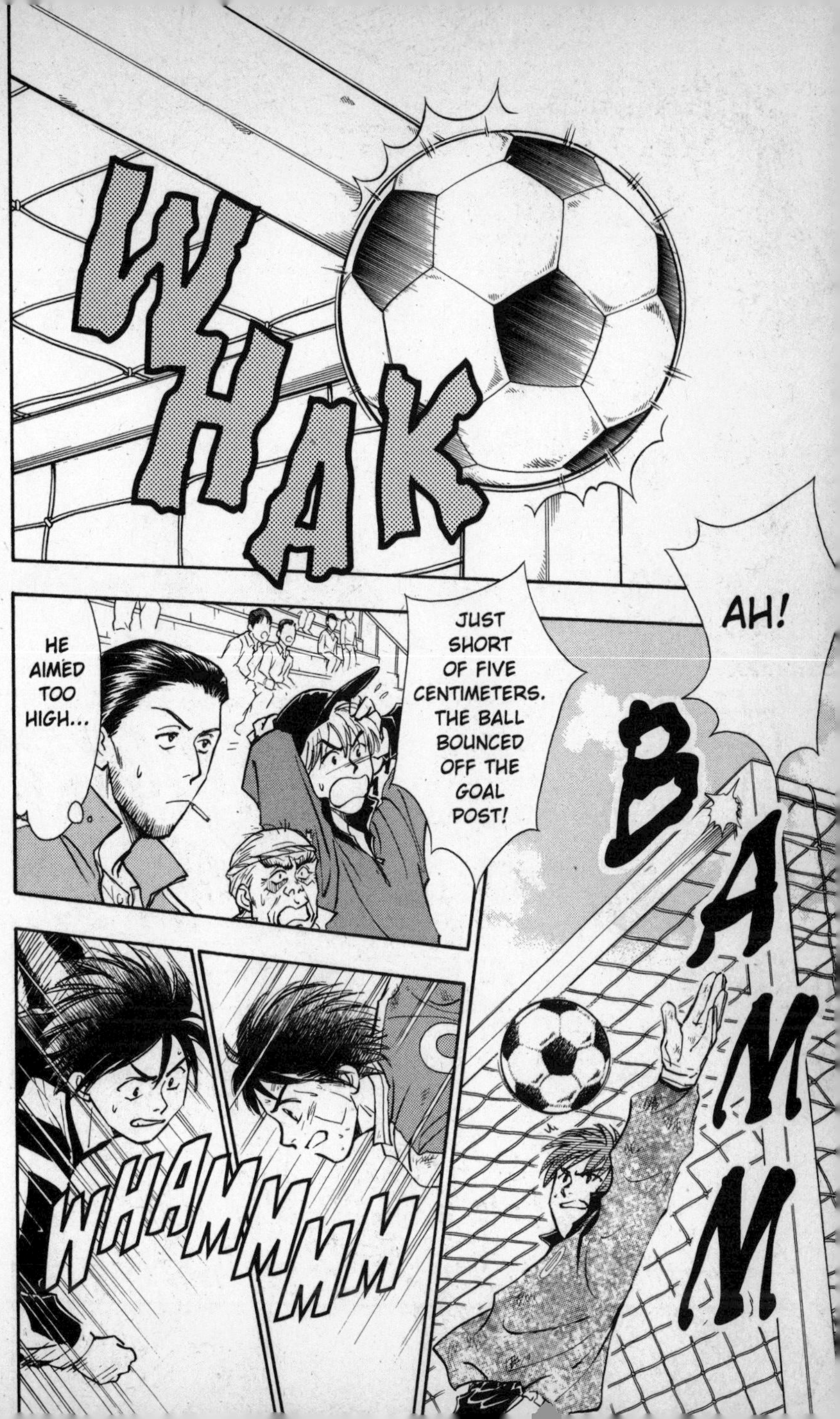
WHAK
AH!
BAMM
JUST SHORT OF FIVE CENTIMETERS. THE BALL BOUNCED OFF THE GOAL POST!
HE AIMED TOO HIGH...
WHAMMMMM

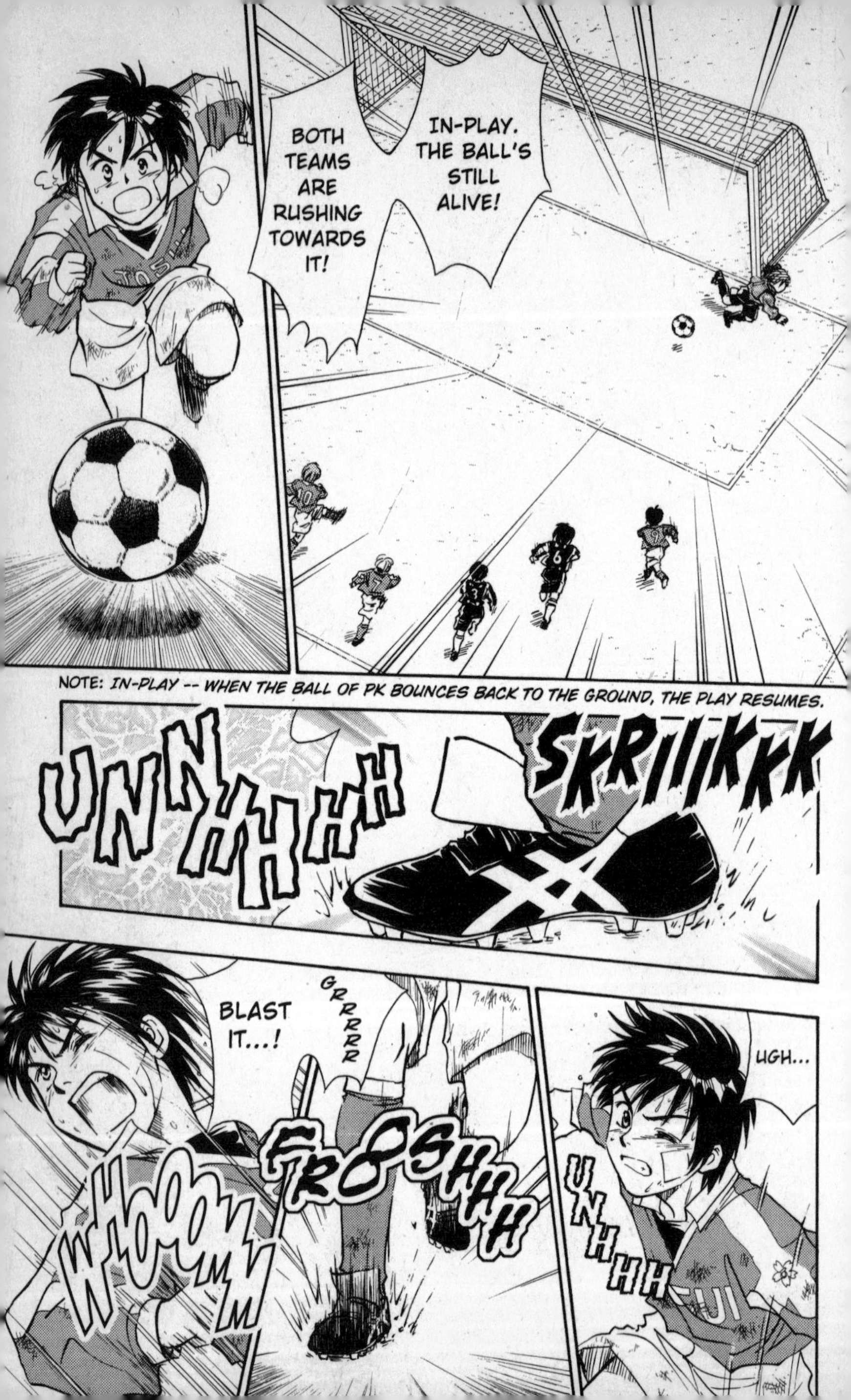
IN-PLAY. THE BALL'S STILL ALIVE!
BOTH TEAMS ARE RUSHING TOWARDS IT!
NOTE: IN-PLAY -- WHEN THE BALL OF PK BOUNCES BACK TO THE GROUND, THE PLAY RESUMES.
SKRIIIKKK
UNNHHHHH
UGH...
UNHHHH
GRRRRR
BLAST IT...!
FROSHHHH
WHOOOMMM

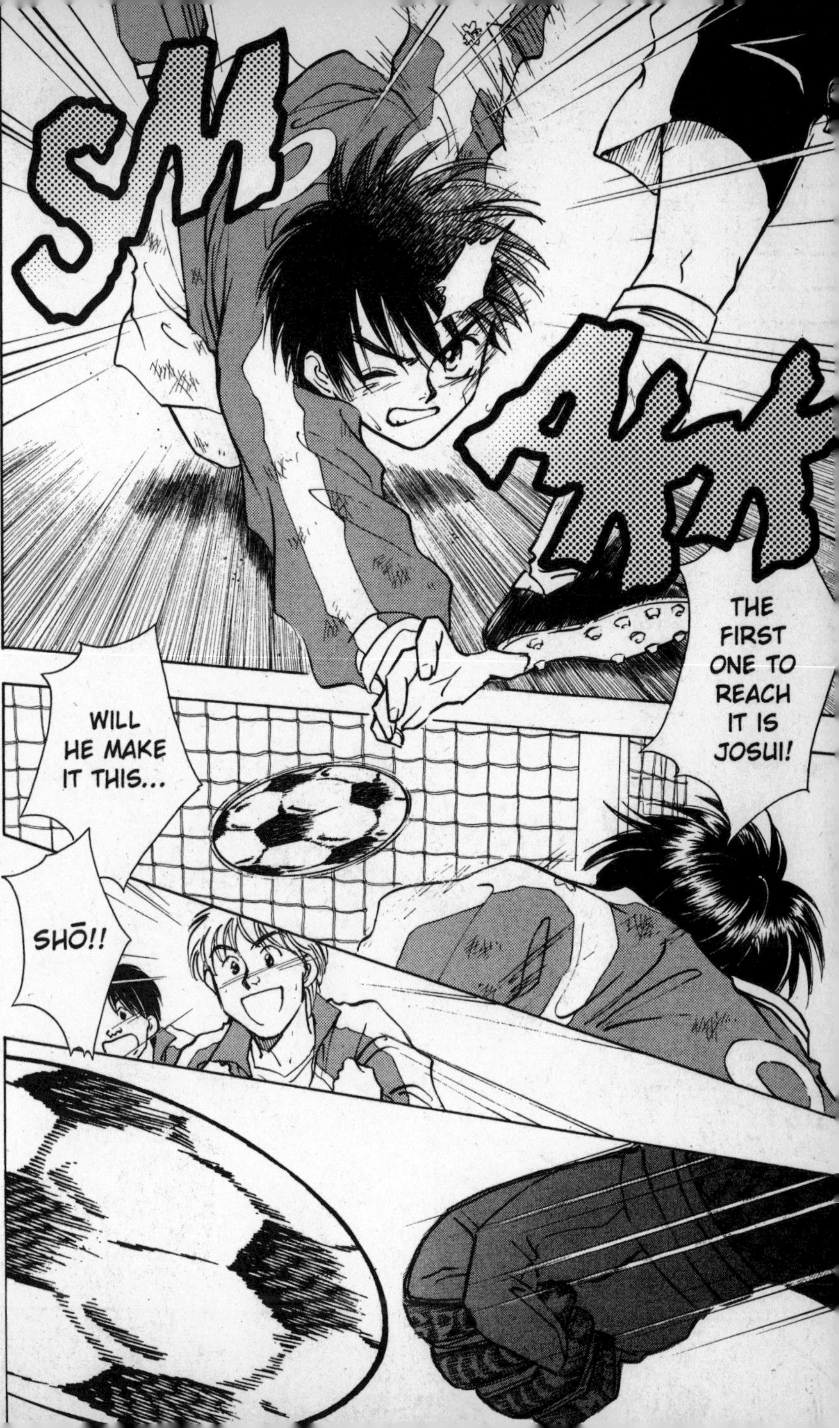
SMASH
THE FIRST ONE TO REACH IT IS JOSUI!
WILL HE MAKE IT THIS...
SHŌ!!

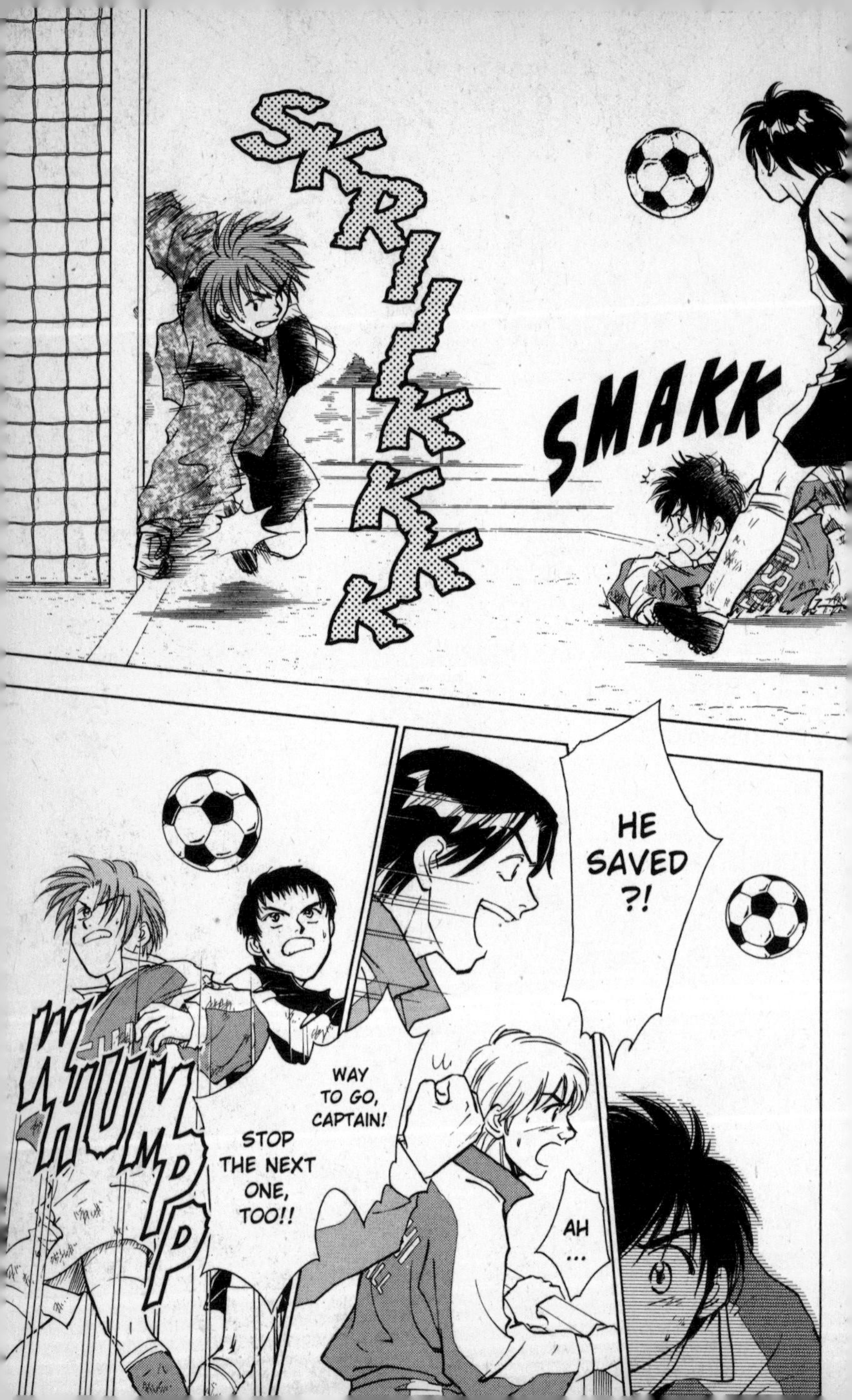
SMAKK
SKRIIKKKK
HE SAVED ?!
AH ...
WAY TO GO, CAPTAIN!
STOP THE NEXT ONE, TOO!!

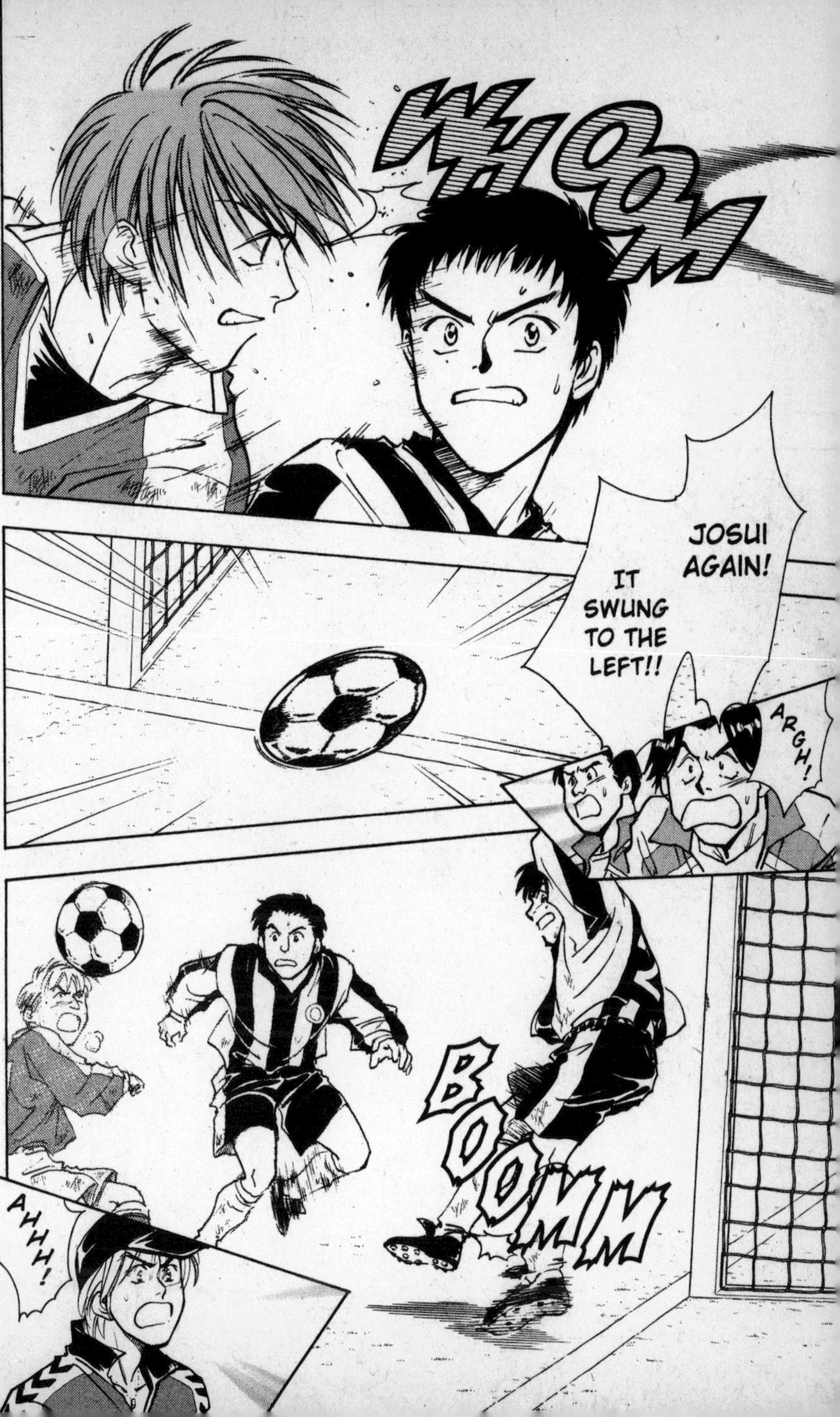
WHOOM
JOSUI AGAIN!
IT SWUNG TO THE LEFT!!
ARGH!
BOOMMM
AHHH!

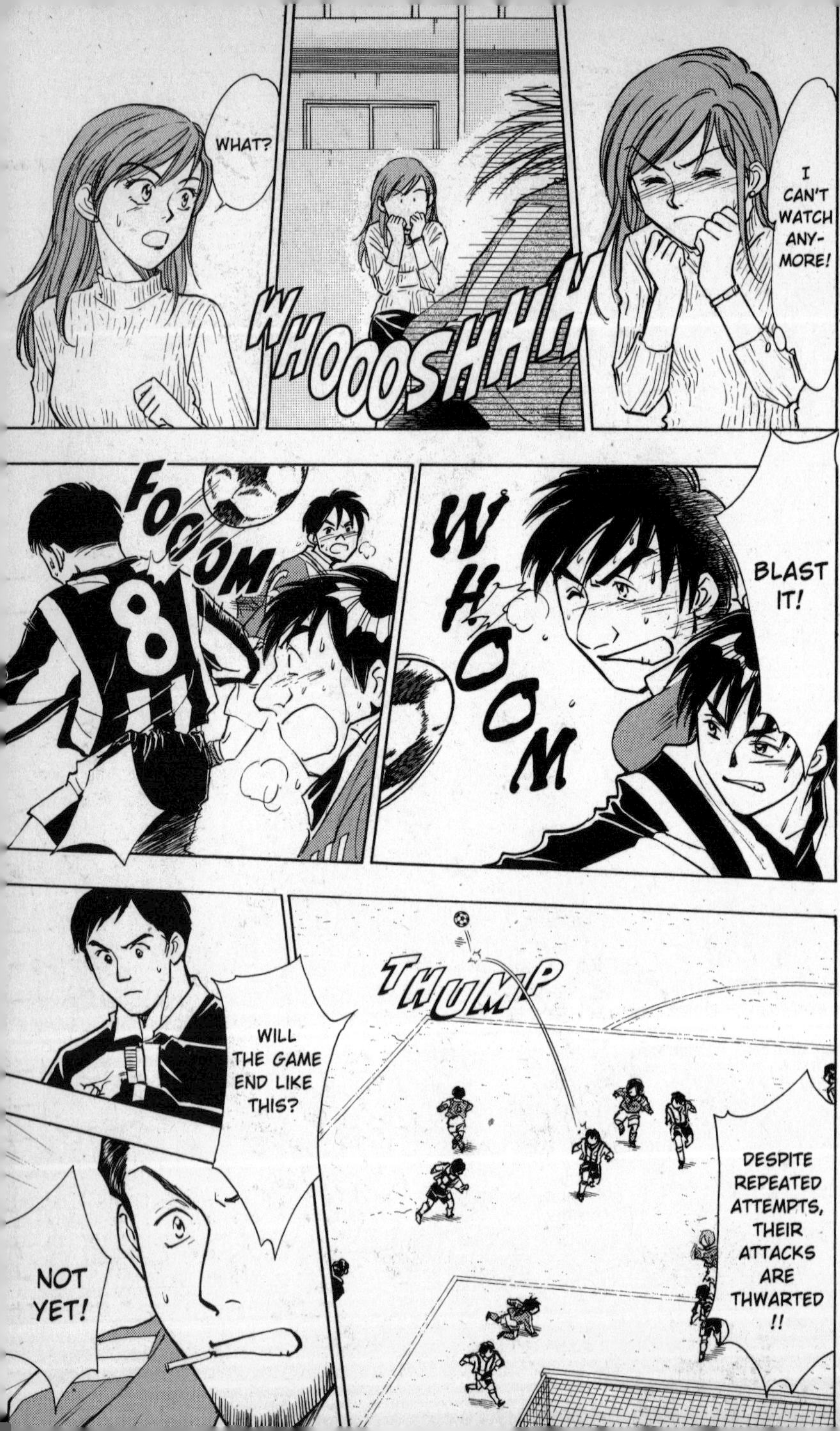

I CAN'T WATCH ANY-MORE!
WHOOOSHHH
WHAT?
WHOOOM
BLAST IT!
FOOOM
THUMP
DESPITE REPEATED ATTEMPTS, THEIR ATTACKS ARE THWARTED !!
WILL THE GAME END LIKE THIS?
NOT YET!

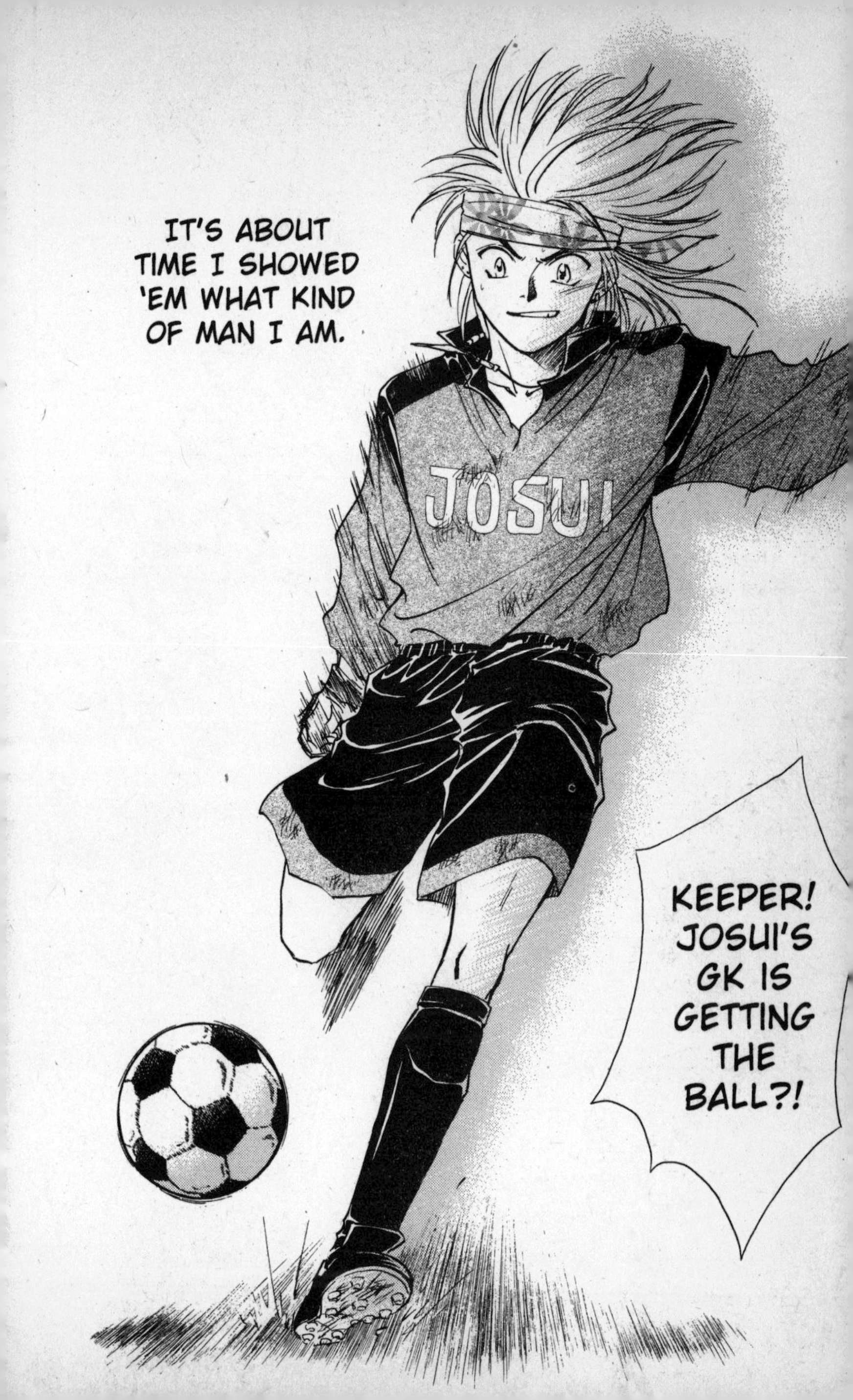
KEEPER! JOSUI'S GK IS GETTING THE BALL?!
IT'S ABOUT TIME I SHOWED 'EM WHAT KIND OF MAN I AM.
JOSUI

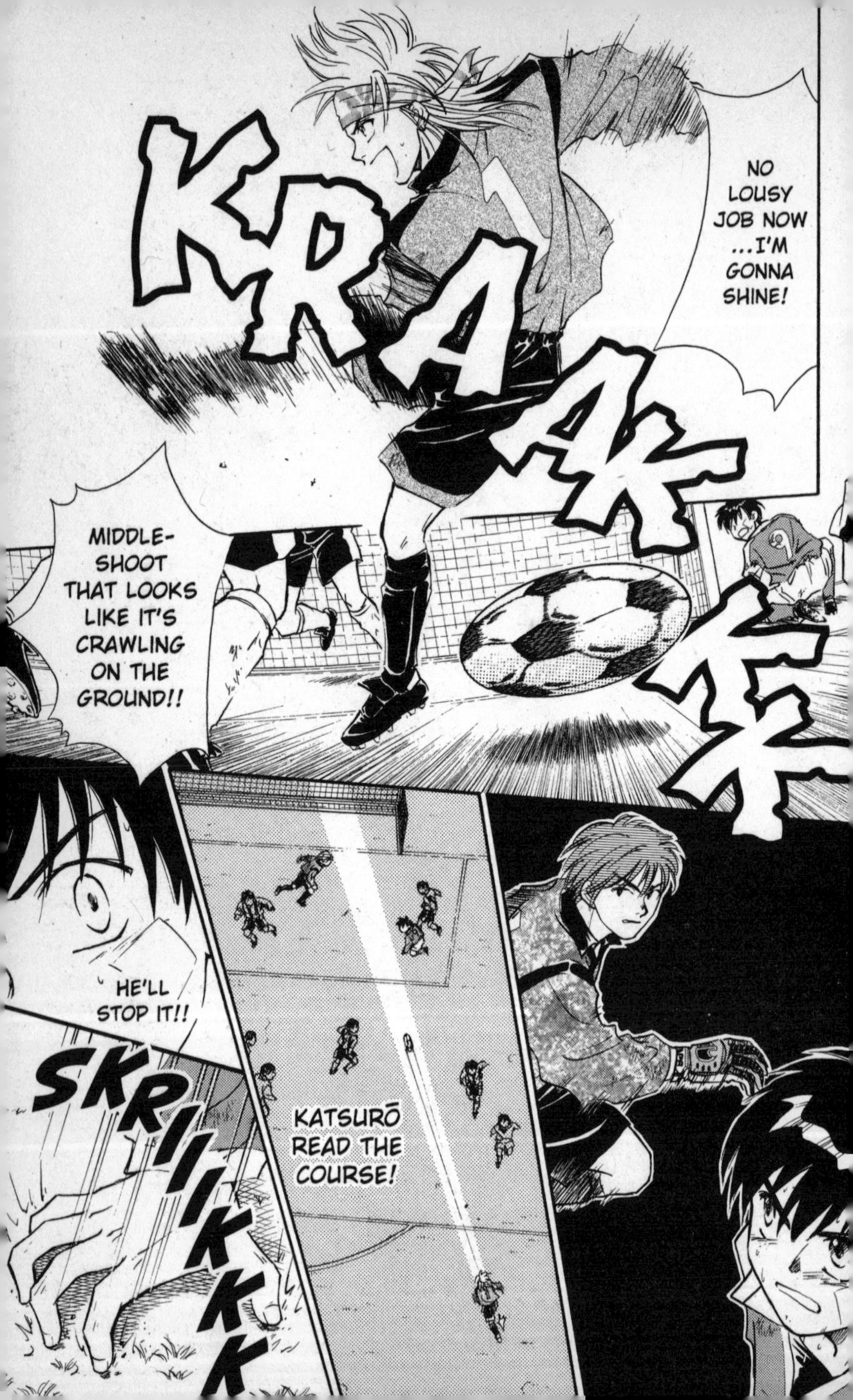
NO LOUSY JOB NOW ...I'M GONNA SHINE!
KRAAKK
MIDDLE-SHOOT THAT LOOKS LIKE IT'S CRAWLING ON THE GROUND!!
KATSURŌ READ THE COURSE!
HE'LL STOP IT!!
SKRIIIKKKK

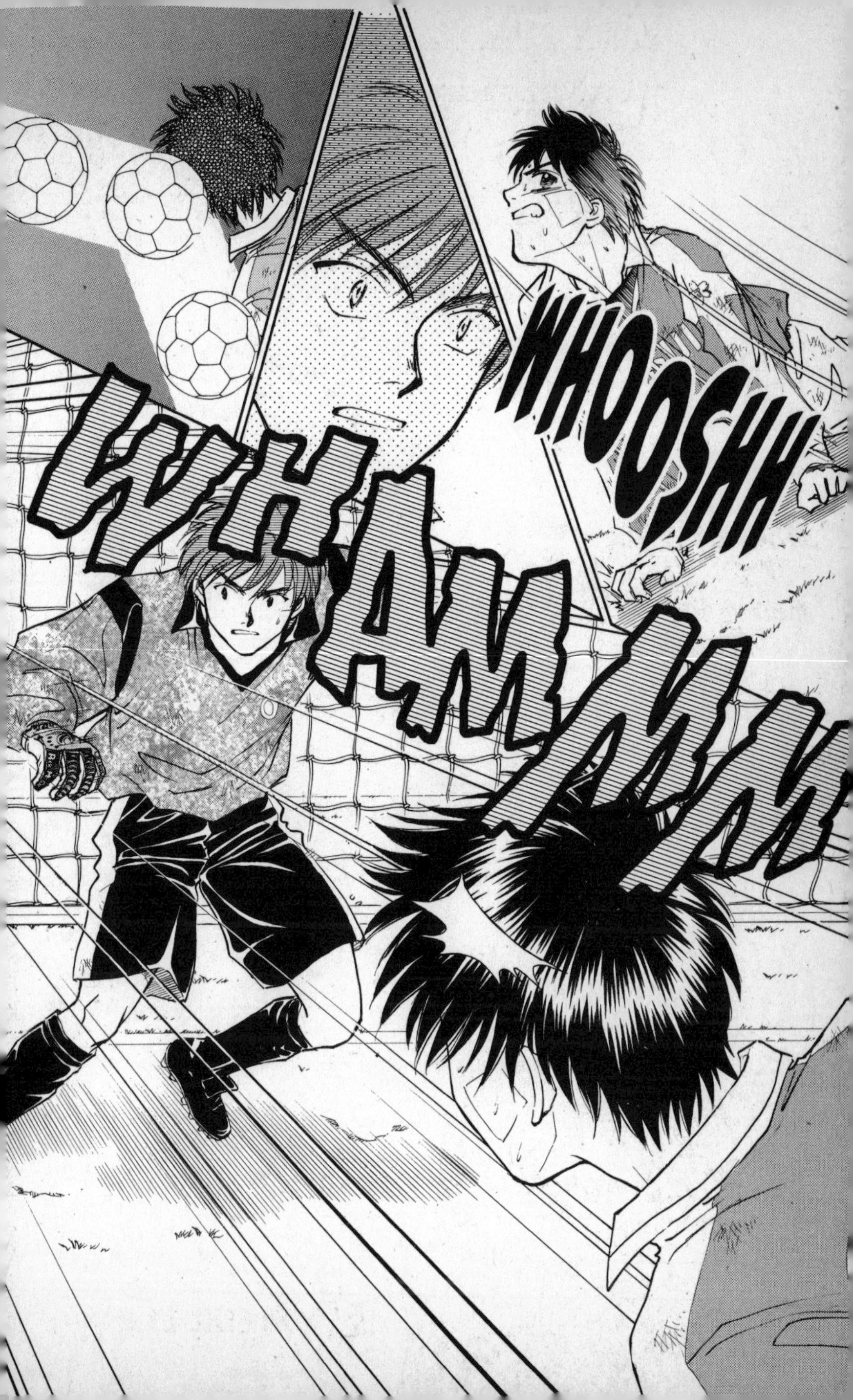

WHOOSH!
WHAMMMM

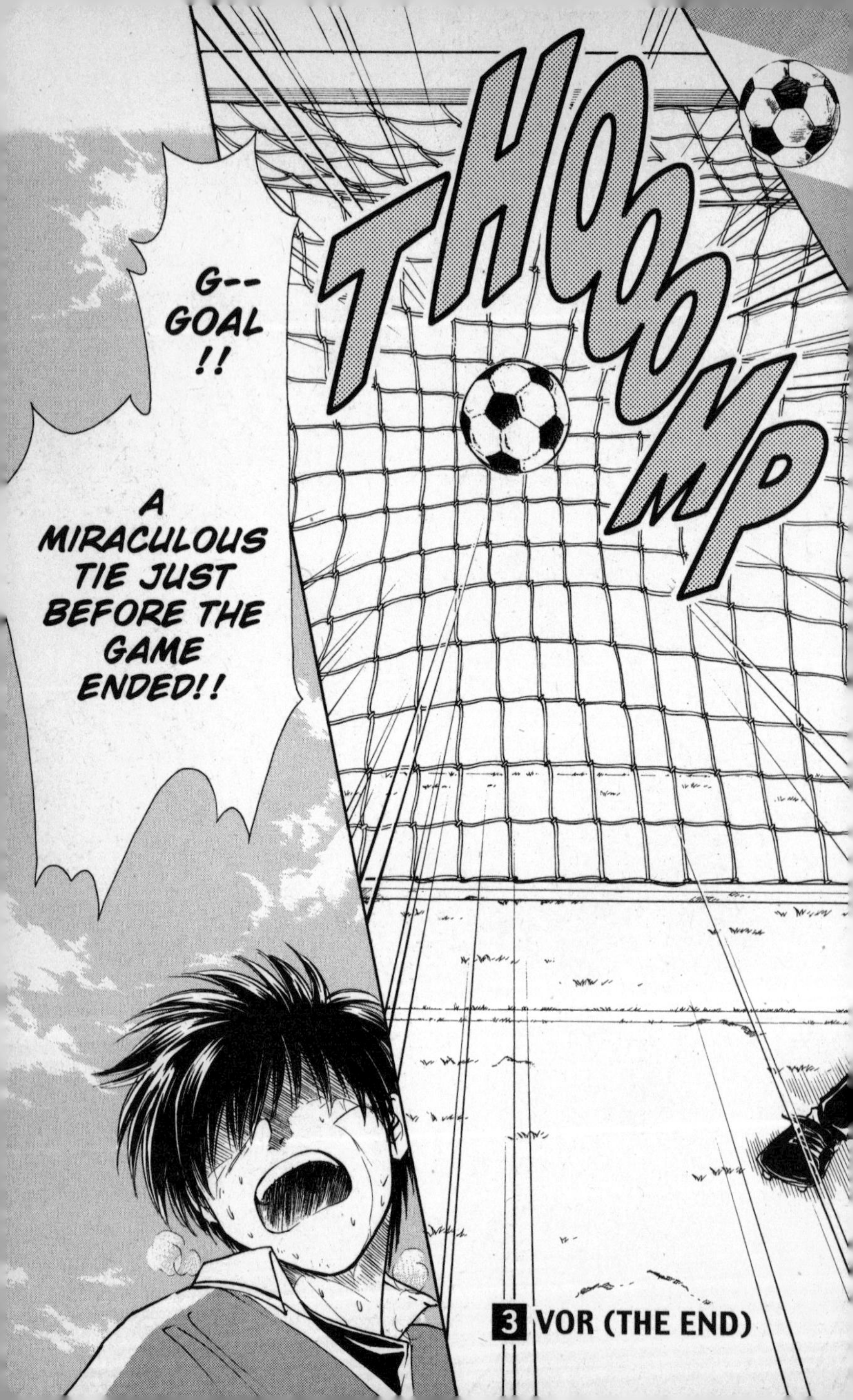
THOOOMP
G-- GOAL!!
A MIRACULOUS TIE JUST BEFORE THE GAME ENDED!!
3 VOR (THE END)

SMALL WHISTLE! THEATRE!!

HOW RUDE! THIS IS DELICIOUS...
PTUI!!

MANGA BY **SEKI**, ASSISTANT S

Whistle's ? minutes cooking.
PLOP PLOP
BUBBLE
ALL IT NEEDS NOW IS TO SIMMER...
♪
BOOBLE
I WONDER IF THE POT'S TOO SMALL?
TRY YŪKO'S SPECIAL DRINK, AND...
... STRAIGHTEN YOURSELVES UP!

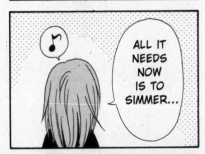

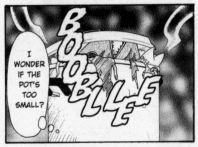

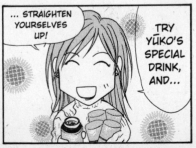

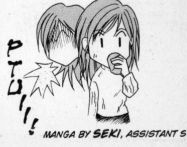

How about the dinner made by Katsurō Shibusawa?

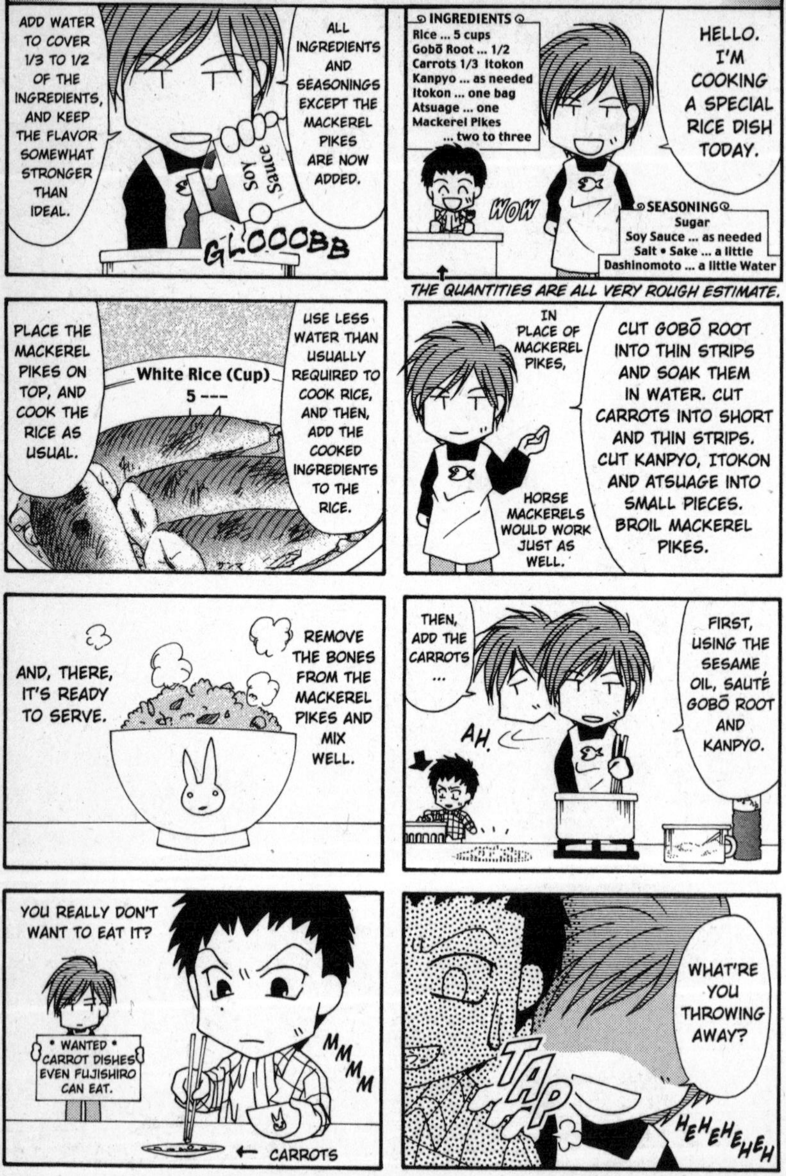
HELLO. I'M COOKING A SPECIAL RICE DISH TODAY.
INGREDIENTS
Rice ... 5 cups
Gobō Root ... 1/2
Carrots 1/3 Itokon
Kanpyo ... as needed
Itokon ... one bag
Atsuage ... one
Mackerel Pikes ... two to three
WOW
SEASONING
Sugar
Soy Sauce ... as needed
Salt • Sake ... a little
Dashinomoto ... a little Water
THE QUANTITIES ARE ALL VERY ROUGH ESTIMATE.
ALL INGREDIENTS AND SEASONINGS EXCEPT THE MACKEREL PIKES ARE NOW ADDED.
Soy Sauce
GLOOOBB
ADD WATER TO COVER 1/3 TO 1/2 OF THE INGREDIENTS, AND KEEP THE FLAVOR SOMEWHAT STRONGER THAN IDEAL.
CUT GOBŌ ROOT INTO THIN STRIPS AND SOAK THEM IN WATER. CUT CARROTS INTO SHORT AND THIN STRIPS. CUT KANPYO, ITOKON AND ATSUAGE INTO SMALL PIECES. BROIL MACKEREL PIKES.
IN PLACE OF MACKEREL PIKES,
HORSE MACKERELS WOULD WORK JUST AS WELL.
USE LESS WATER THAN USUALLY REQUIRED TO COOK RICE, AND THEN, ADD THE COOKED INGREDIENTS TO THE RICE.
White Rice (Cup)
5 ---
PLACE THE MACKEREL PIKES ON TOP, AND COOK THE RICE AS USUAL.
FIRST, USING THE SESAME OIL, SAUTÉ GOBŌ ROOT AND KANPYO.
THEN, ADD THE CARROTS ...
AH.
REMOVE THE BONES FROM THE MACKEREL PIKES AND MIX WELL.
AND, THERE, IT'S READY TO SERVE.
WHAT'RE YOU THROWING AWAY?
TAP
HEHEHEHEH
YOU REALLY DON'T WANT TO EAT IT?
• WANTED • CARROT DISHES EVEN FUJISHIRO CAN EAT.
MMMM
CARROTS

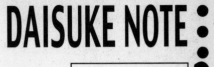

DAISUKE NOTE

MASATO TAKAI

IS THIS BRUCE LEE?

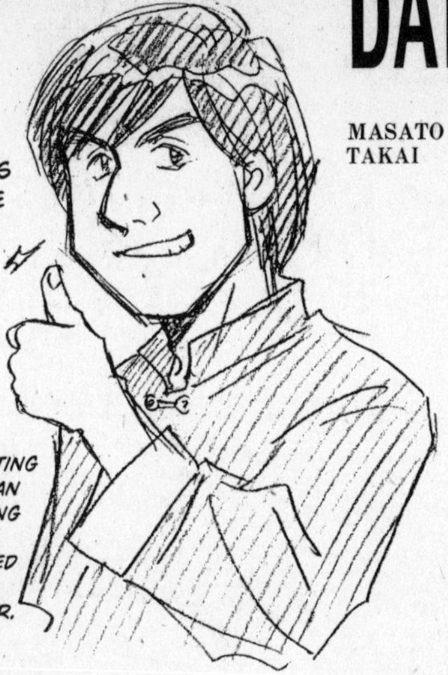

IMPERSONATING JACKIE CHAN AFTER BEING TOLD HE RESEMBLED THE CHARACTER.

PERSONAL DATA	
BIRTHDAY:	MARCH 29, 1985
SIZE:	158 cm 50 kg
BLOOD TYPE:	B
FAVORITE FOOD:	DRY FRIED CHICKEN
WHAT HE DISLIKES:	EGGPLANTS
HOBBY AND SPECIAL SKILLS:	JAPANESE CHESS AND IMPERSONATION

YŪSUKE MORINAGA

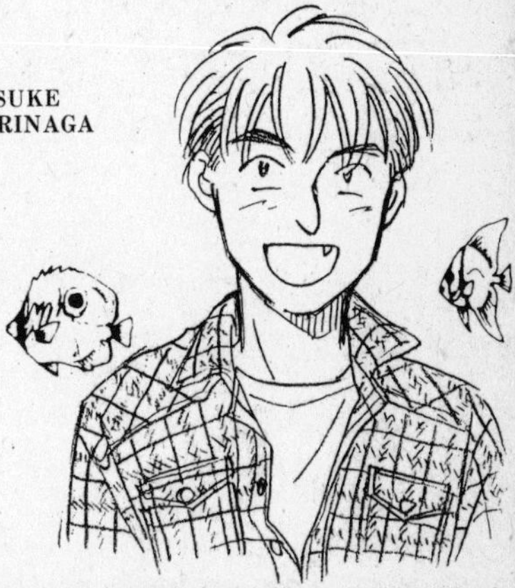

PERSONAL DATA	
BIRTHDAY:	MAY 30, 1984
SIZE:	159 cm 48 kg
BLOOD TYPE:	A
FAVORITE FOOD:	MELON BREAD
WHAT HE DISLIKES:	TOMATOES
HOBBY AND SPECIAL SKILLS:	VISITING AQUARIUMS & LOOKING AFTER OTHERS

ONCE UPON A TIME, THERE WAS A CAPTAIN CALLED "HONMA" AT JOSUI...

ILLUSTRATION BY MESO AIKO.

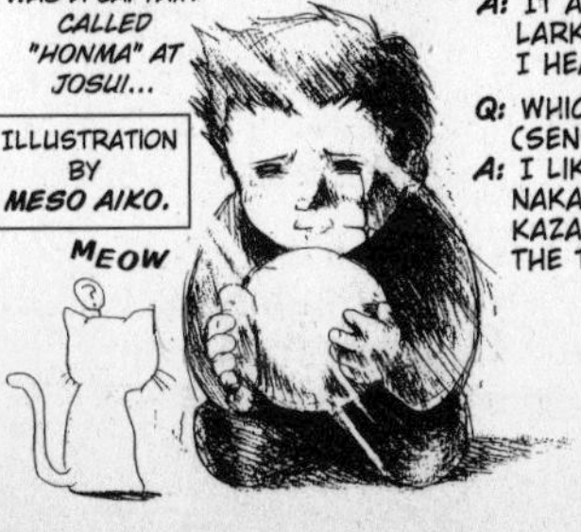
MEOW

THERE WERE A LOT OF QUESTIONS IN THE LETTERS WE RECEIVED *(PART 2)*

Q: WHAT DOES TATSUYA LIKE TO LISTEN TO?
A: IT APPEARS THAT HE LIKES B'Z (BREAK THROUGH. RUN~) LARK (DIVE TO BLUE, SHOUT AT THE DEVIL~). I HEAR HE LISTENS TO VARIOUS OTHER SONGS TOO.

Q: WHICH GAMES AND THE PLAYERS ARE SENSEI'S FAVORITES? (SENSEI = MANGA ARTIST = DAISUKE HIGUCHI)
A: I LIKE THAT MUDDY SORT OF PLAY THE PLAYER MASASHI NAKAYAMA, NICKNAMED GON NAKAYAMA, DOES. I DARE SAY KAZAMATSURI MAY POSSIBLY BE MODELED AFTER GON-CHAN. THE TEAM I LIKE IS JUBIRO IWATA.

JOSUI SIDE

Two side-kicks who're developing nicely, plus the x-captain.

AKIRA MIKAMI

PERSONAL DATA	
BIRTHDAY:	JANUARY 22, 1984
SIZE:	172 cm 58 kg
BLOOD TYPE:	AB
FAVORITE FOOD:	SUSHI (SEA URCHIN)
WHAT HE DISLIKES:	ANYTHING SWEET
HOBBY AND SPECIAL SKILLS:	INTERNET & MEMORIZED CIRCULAR CONSTANT UP TO 50 DIGITS

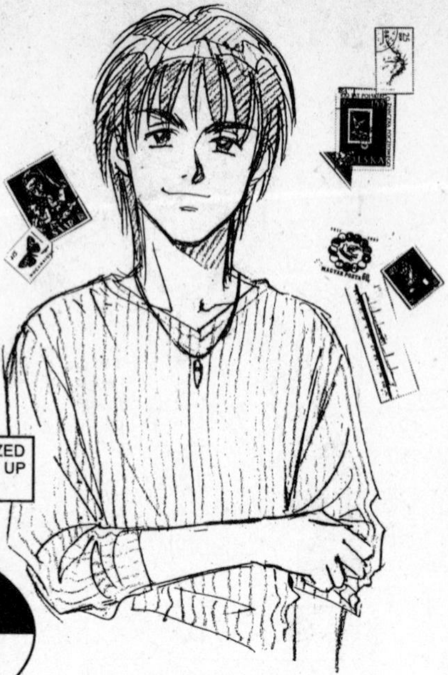

MUSASHINOMORI SIDE PROFILE

Two side-kicks who're popular for some unknown reason.

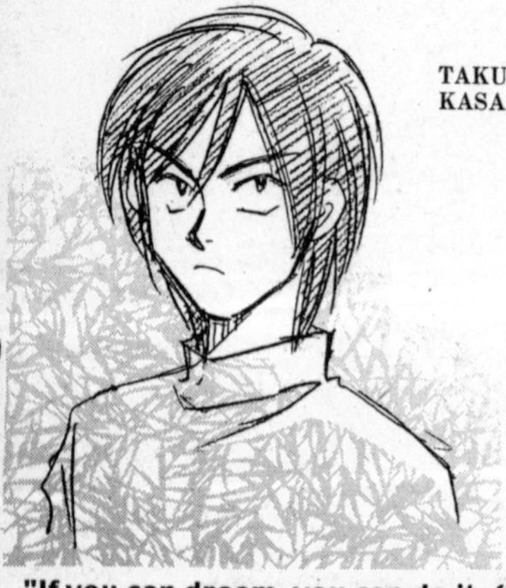

TAKUMI KASAI

PERSONAL DATA	
BIRTHDAY:	NOVEMBER 3, 1984
SIZE:	169 cm 56 kg
BLOOD TYPE:	O
FAVORITE FOOD:	SARDINES
WHAT HE DISLIKES:	CHICKEN SKINS
HOBBY AND SPECIAL SKILLS:	FISHING AND PLAYING PIANO

"If you can dream, you can do it. (If you wish, it'll come true.)" is a favorite American proverb of Coach Akira Nishino (Kashiwa Reisol), whom I like, and I took the opportunity to use it. It's a good proverb, don't you think? It has become one of my beliefs now.

Next in Whistle!

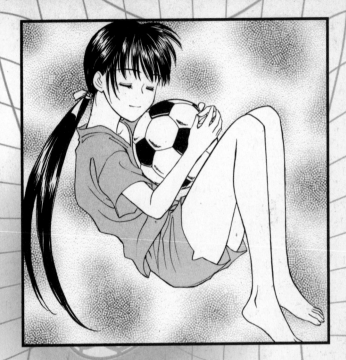

RE-START

After playing an incredible and inspirational soccer match against their cross-town rivals, the gang at Josui Junior High is now fielding queries from players who want to join their team. One of these hopefuls is Yuki Kojima, the team's pretty manager. She may be cute and sweet but she's also an awesome soccer player. In fact, she may be even better than Tatsuya and Shigeki. Suddenly, there are a bunch of great players on Team Josui. Now all they need is a coach!

Available March 2005!

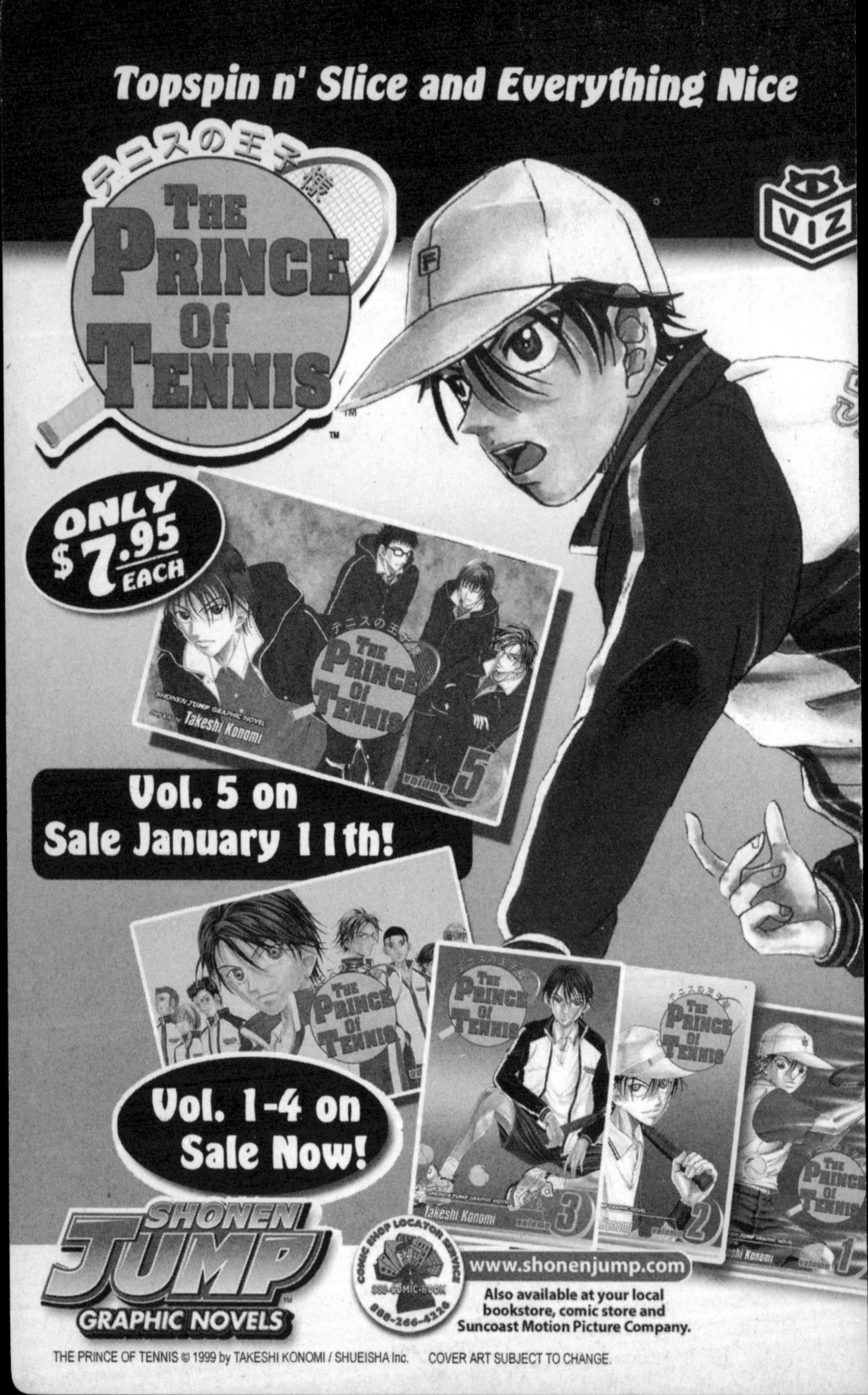
Topspin n' Slice and Everything Nice
テニスの王子様
THE PRINCE OF TENNIS™
VIZ
ONLY $7.95 EACH
SHONEN JUMP GRAPHIC NOVEL
Takeshi Konomi
volume 5
Vol. 5 on Sale January 11th!
Vol. 1-4 on Sale Now!
SHONEN JUMP™ GRAPHIC NOVELS
COMIC SHOP LOCATOR SERVICE
888-COMIC-BOOK
888-266-4226
www.shonenjump.com
Also available at your local bookstore, comic store and Suncoast Motion Picture Company.
THE PRINCE OF TENNIS © 1999 by TAKESHI KONOMI / SHUEISHA Inc. COVER ART SUBJECT TO CHANGE.

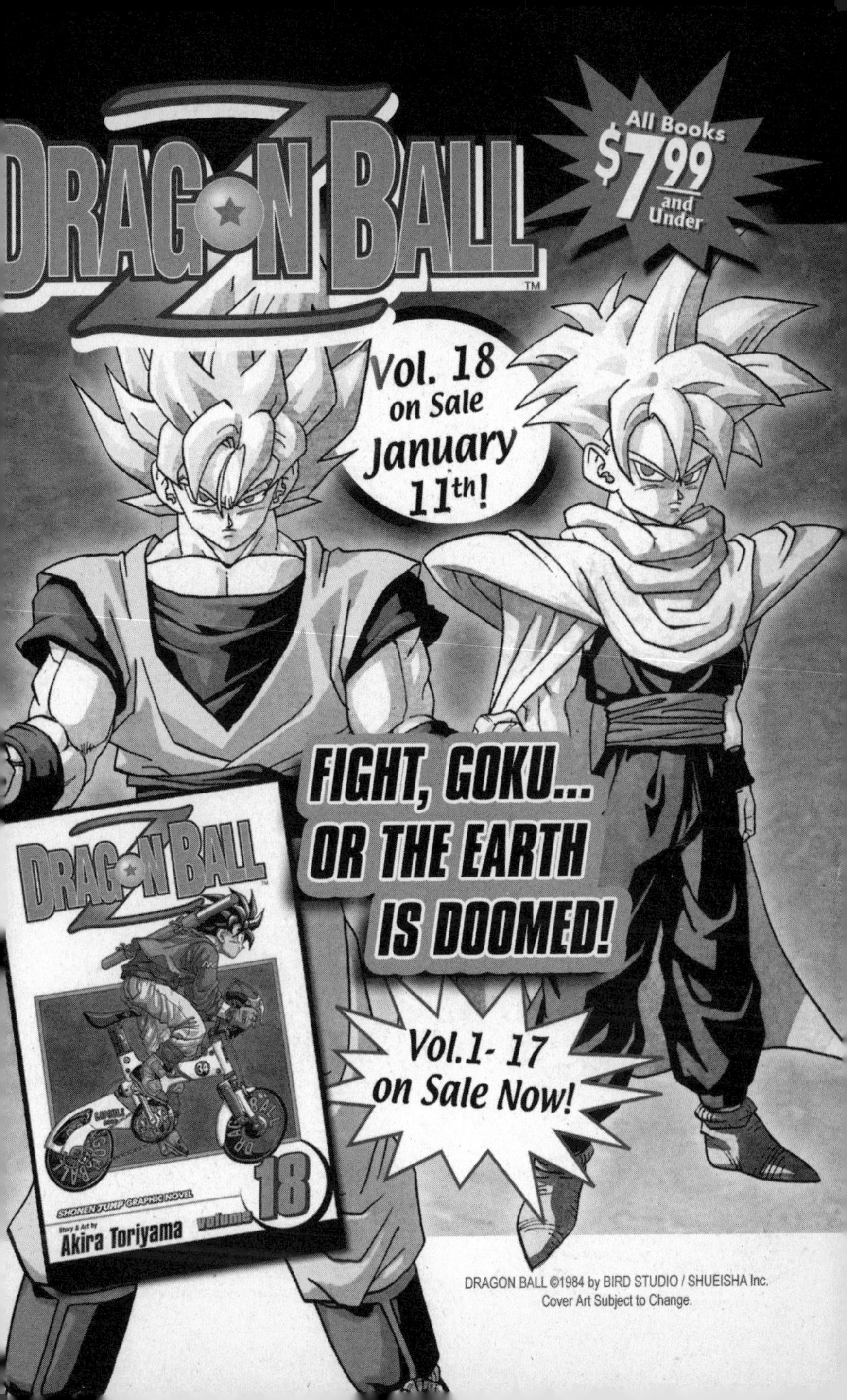

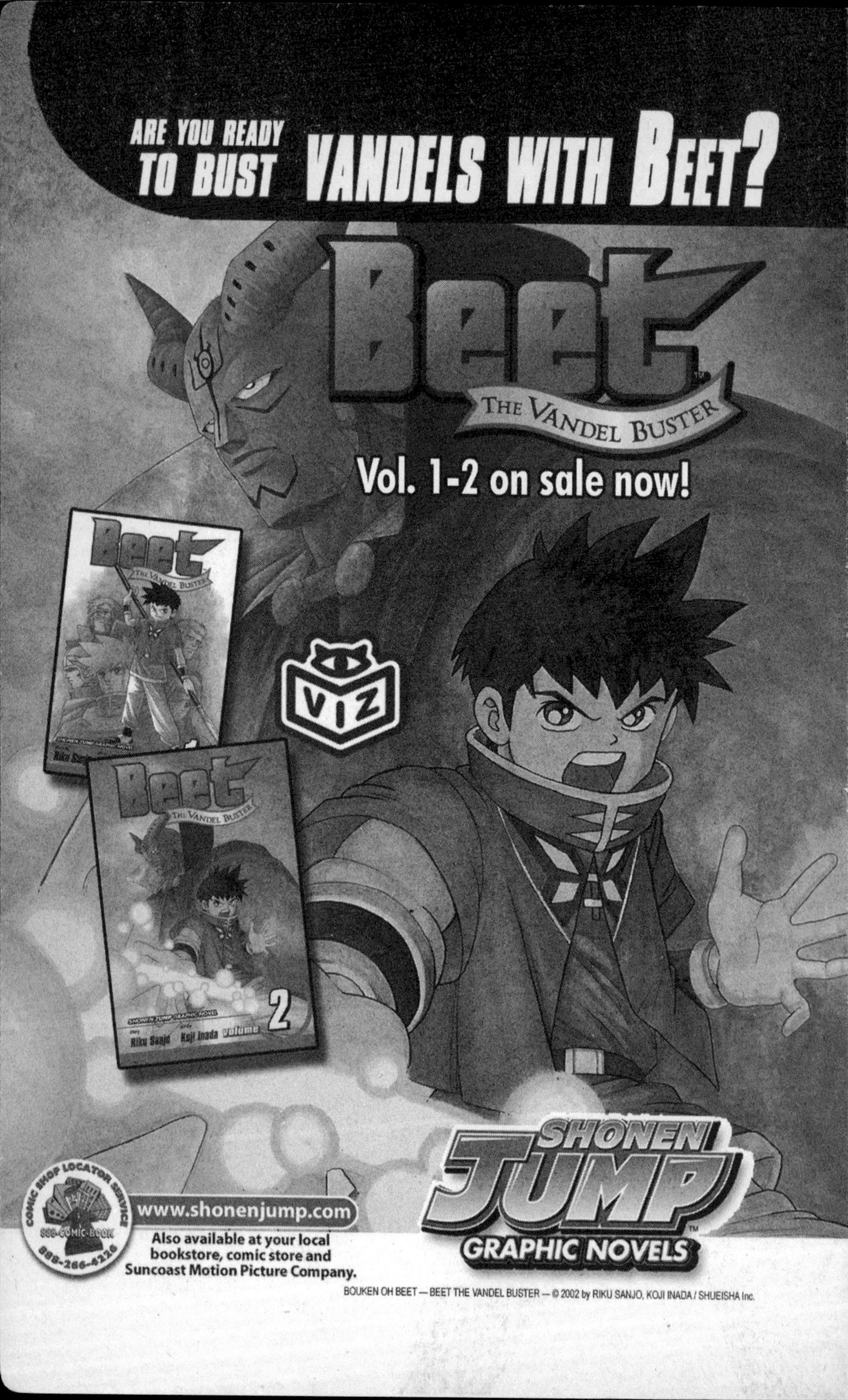

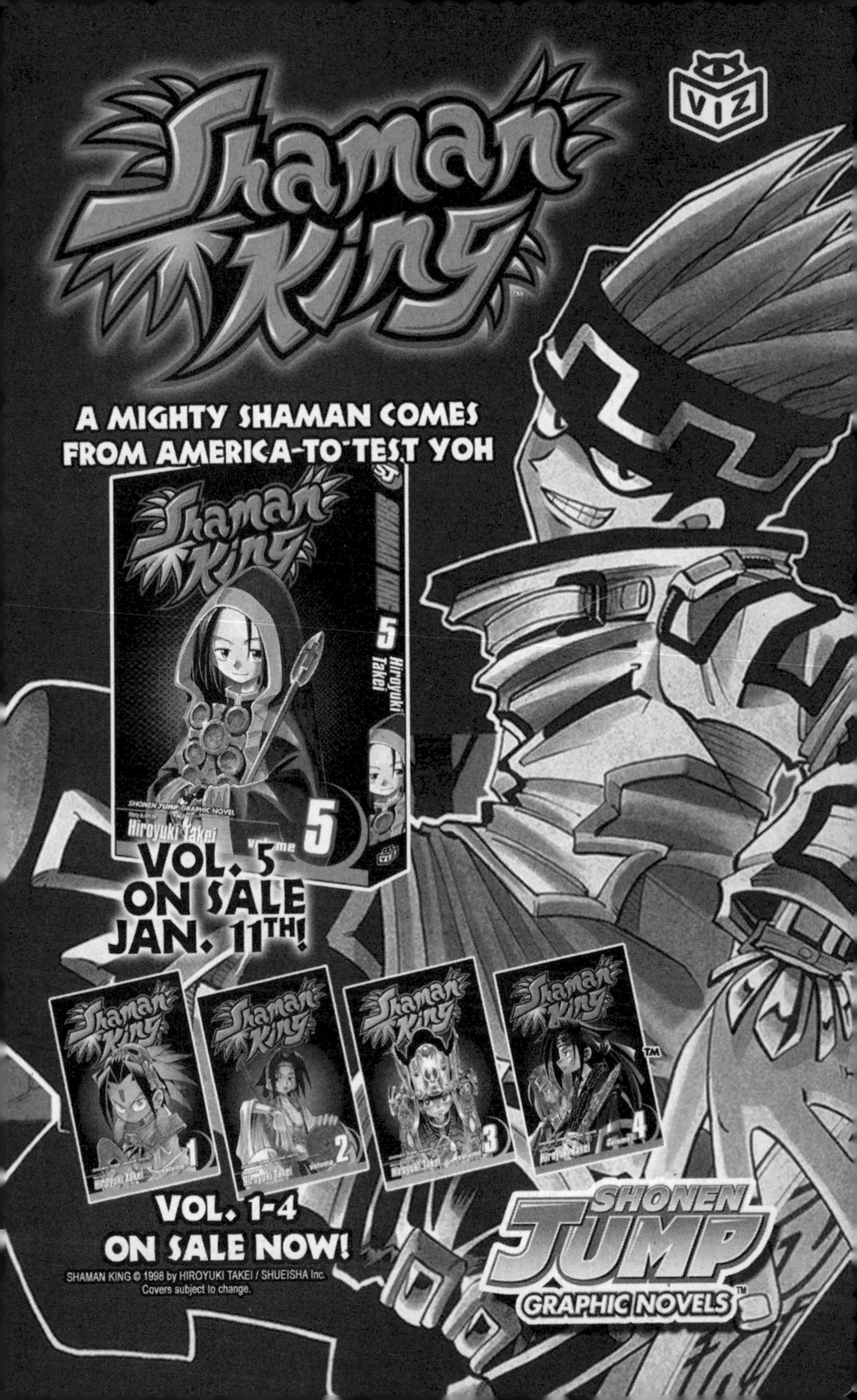
VIZ
Shaman King
A MIGHTY SHAMAN COMES FROM AMERICA TO TEST YOH
Shaman King
5
Hiroyuki Takei
SHONEN JUMP GRAPHIC NOVEL
volume 5
VOL. 5 ON SALE JAN. 11TH!
VOL. 1-4 ON SALE NOW!
SHAMAN KING © 1998 by HIROYUKI TAKEI / SHUEISHA Inc.
Covers subject to change.
SHONEN JUMP
GRAPHIC NOVELS

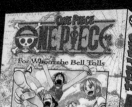

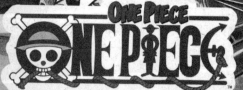

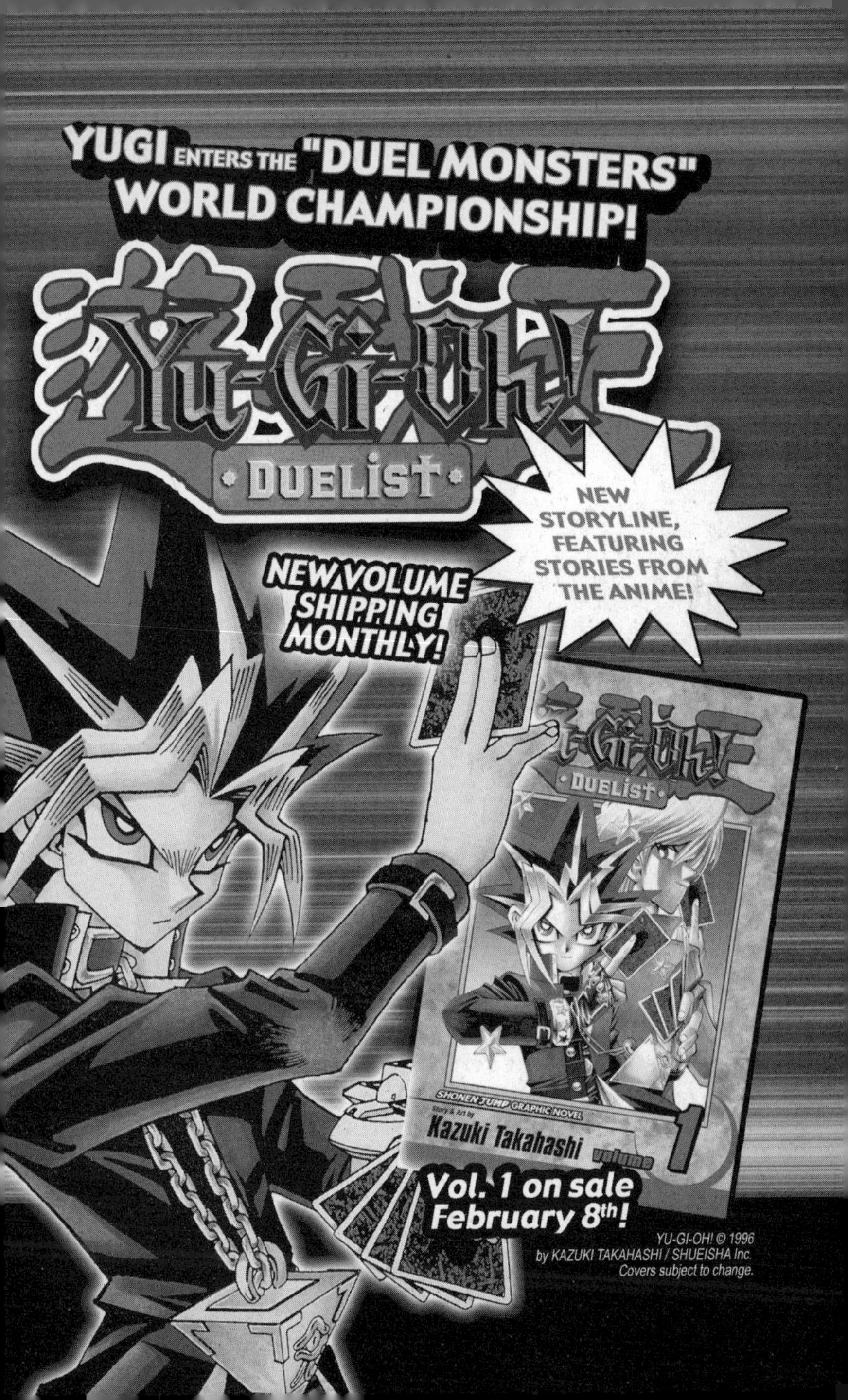
YUGI ENTERS THE "DUEL MONSTERS" WORLD CHAMPIONSHIP!
YU-GI-OH!
DUELIST
NEW STORYLINE, FEATURING STORIES FROM THE ANIME!
NEW VOLUME SHIPPING MONTHLY!
YU-GI-OH!
DUELIST
SHONEN JUMP GRAPHIC NOVEL
Story & Art by
Kazuki Takahashi
volume 1
Vol. 1 on sale February 8th!

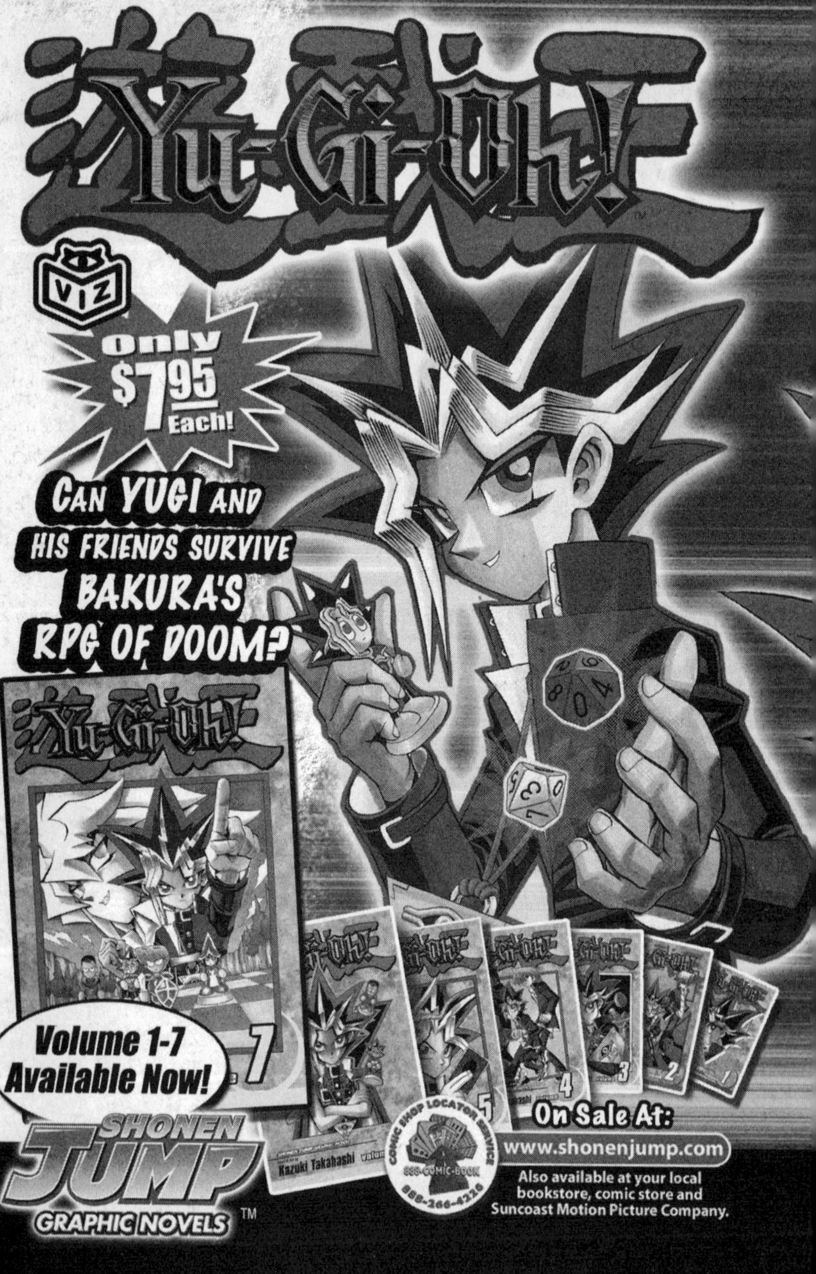

Yu-Gi-Oh!
VIZ
Only $7.95 Each!
Can Yugi and his friends survive Bakura's RPG of doom?
Yu-Gi-Oh!
7
Volume 1-7 Available Now!
Kazuki Takahashi
SHONEN JUMP GRAPHIC NOVELS™
Comic Shop Locator Service
888-COMIC-BOOK
888-266-4226
On Sale At:
www.shonenjump.com
Also available at your local bookstore, comic store and Suncoast Motion Picture Company.

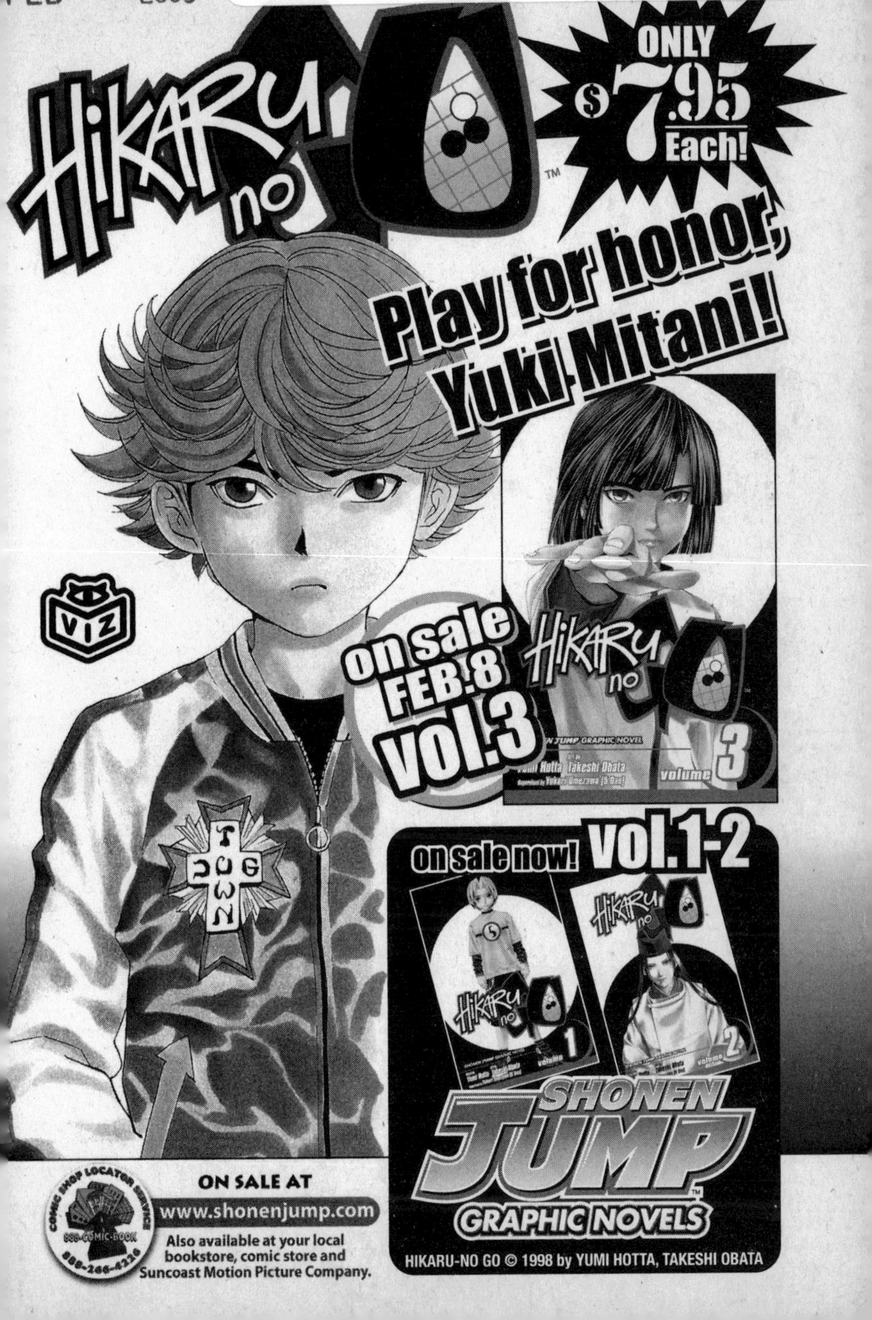

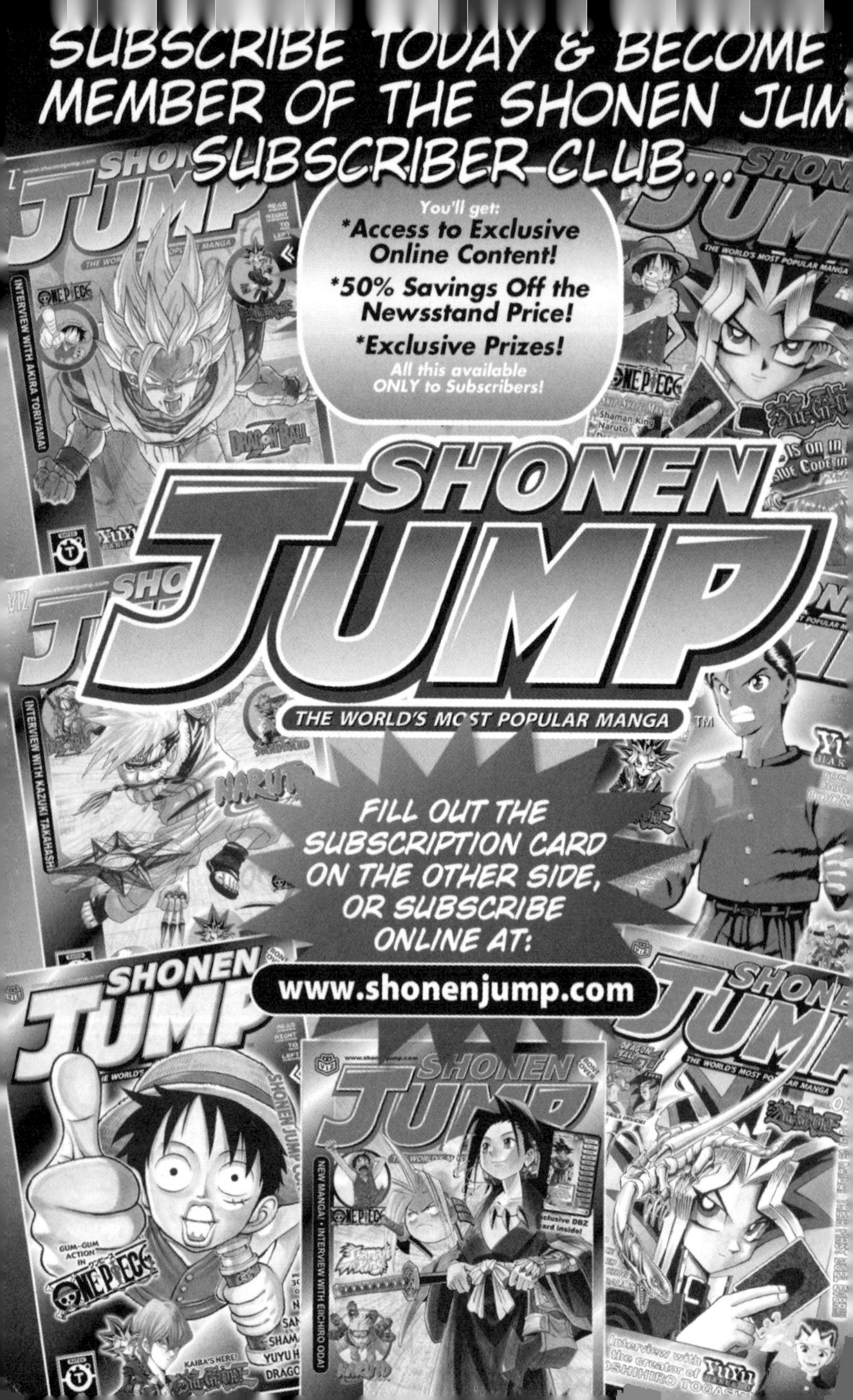
SUBSCRIBE TODAY & BECOME A MEMBER OF THE SHONEN JUMP SUBSCRIBER CLUB...
You'll get:
*Access to Exclusive Online Content!
*50% Savings Off the Newsstand Price!
*Exclusive Prizes!
All this available ONLY to Subscribers!
SHONEN JUMP
THE WORLD'S MOST POPULAR MANGA
TM
FILL OUT THE SUBSCRIPTION CARD ON THE OTHER SIDE, OR SUBSCRIBE ONLINE AT:
www.shonenjump.com

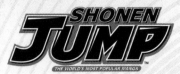

COMPLETE OUR SURVEY AND LET US KNOW WHAT YOU THINK!

☐ Please do NOT send me information about VIZ and SHONEN JUMP products, news and events, special offers, or other information.

☐ Please do NOT send me information from VIZ's trusted business partners.

Name: _____

Address: _____

City: _____ State: _____ Zip: _____

E-mail: _____

☐ Male ☐ Female   Date of Birth (mm/dd/yyyy): ___/___/___   (Under 13? Parental consent required)

1 Do you purchase SHONEN JUMP Magazine?

☐ Yes   ☐ No (if no, skip the next two questions)

If **YES**, do you subscribe?

☐ Yes   ☐ No

If **NO**, how often do you purchase SHONEN JUMP Magazine?

☐ 1-3 issues a year

☐ 4-6 issues a year

☐ more than 7 issues a year

2 Which SHONEN JUMP Graphic Novel did you purchase? (please check one)

☐ Beet the Vandel Buster   ☐ Bleach   ☐ Dragon Ball

☐ Dragon Ball Z   ☐ Hikaru no Go   ☐ Knights of the Zodiac

☐ Naruto   ☐ One Piece   ☐ Rurouni Kenshin

☐ Shaman King   ☐ The Prince of Tennis   ☐ Ultimate Muscle

☐ Whistle!   ☐ Yu-Gi-Oh!   ☐ YuYu Hakusho

☐ Other _____

Will you purchase subsequent volumes?

☐ Yes   ☐ No

3 How did you learn about this title? (check all that apply)

☐ Favorite title   ☐ Advertisement   ☐ Article

☐ Gift   ☐ Read excerpt in SHONEN JUMP Magazine

☐ Recommendation   ☐ Special offer   ☐ Through TV animation

☐ Website   ☐ Other _____

4 Of the titles that are serialized in SHONEN JUMP Magazine, have you purchased the Graphic Novels?

- [ ] Yes
- [ ] No

If **YES**, which ones have you purchased? **(check all that apply)**

- [ ] Dragon Ball Z
- [ ] Hikaru no Go
- [ ] Narut
- [ ] Piece
- [ ] Shaman King
- [ ] Yu-

D1622526

If **YES**, what were your reasons for pu

- [ ] A favorite title
- [ ] A fa
- one go
- [ ] I want to read it over and over ag
- agazine
- [ ] The quality of printing is better t
- [ ] Special offer
- [ ] Other

If **NO**, why did/would you not purchase it?

- [ ] I'm happy just reading it in the magazine
- [ ] It's not worth buying the graphic novel
- [ ] All the manga pages are in black and white unlike the magazine
- [ ] There are other graphic novels that I prefer
- [ ] There are too many to collect for each title
- [ ] It's too small
- [ ] Other ______

5 Of the titles NOT serialized in the Magazine, which ones have you purchased?
(check all that apply)

- [ ] Beet the Vandel Buster
- [ ] Bleach
- [ ] Dragon Ball
- [ ] Knights of the Zodiac
- [ ] The Prince of Tennis
- [ ] Rurouni Kenshin
- [ ] Whistle!
- [ ] Other ______
- [ ] None

If you did purchase any of the above, what were your reasons for purchase?

- [ ] A favorite title
- [ ] A favorite creator/artist
- [ ] Read a preview in SHONEN JUMP Magazine and wanted to read the rest of the story
- [ ] Recommendation
- [ ] Other

Will you purchase subsequent volumes?

- [ ] Yes
- [ ] No

6 What race/ethnicity do you consider yourself? (please check one)

- [ ] Asian/Pacific Islander
- [ ] Black/African American
- [ ] Hispanic/Latino
- [ ] Native American/Alaskan Native
- [ ] White/Caucasian
- [ ] Other

THANK YOU! Please send the completed form to:

VIZ Survey
42 Catharine St.
Poughkeepsie, NY 12601

All information provided will be used for internal purposes only. We promise not to sell or otherwise divulge your information.